BRINGING DOWN GADDAFI

ACKNOWLEDGMENTS

I would like to thank Lucia Müzell, M.T. Leal de Moraes, and Vinicius M. Netto for their support, Iran Garcia and Amal Daredi for their personal commitment to securing my release, and my management team Fuad Allen Lloyd and Kojo Bentil for their friendship and help in sharing this project.

CONTENTS

BRINGING DOWN GADDAFI
Copyright © Andrei Netto, 2014.

First published as *Silencio Contra Muamar Kadafi* in Portugese in 2012
by Companhia das Letras in Brazil.

First published in English in 2014 by
PALGRAVE MACMILLAN®
in the US–a division of St. Martin's Press LLC,
175 Fifth Avenue, New York, NY 10010.

Where this book is distributed in the UK, Europe and the rest of the world,
this is by Palgrave Macmillan, a division of Macmillan Publishers Limited,
registered in England, company number 785998, of Houndmills,
Basingstoke, Hampshire RG21 6XS.

Palgrave Macmillan is the global academic imprint of the above companies
and has companies and representatives throughout the world.

Palgrave® and Macmillan® are registered trademarks in the United States,
the United Kingdom, Europe and other countries.

ISBN: 978–1–137–27912–5

Library of Congress Cataloging-in-Publication Data

Netto, Andrei, author.
[Silêncio contra Muamar Kadafi. English]
    Bringing down Gaddafi : on the ground with the Libyan rebels / Andrei
Netto.
        pages cm
    Translation of: O silencio contra Muamar Kadafi.
    Includes bibliographical references.
    ISBN 978–1–137–27912–5 (alk. paper)
    1. Libya—History—Civil War, 2011—Personal narratives, Brazilian.
  2. Qaddafi, Muammar. 3. Libya—Politics and government—1969– I. Title.

DT236.N4713 2014
961.2042—dc23   2013041771

A catalogue record of the book is available from the British Library.

Design by Newgen Knowledge Works (P) Ltd., Chennai, India.

First edition: June 2014

10 9 8 7 6 5 4 3 2 1

Printed in the United States of America.

BRINGING DOWN GADDAFI

ON THE GROUND WITH THE LIBYAN REBELS

ANDREI NETTO

TRANSLATED BY MICHAEL MARSDEN

palgrave
macmillan

CHAPTER 1

THE END

Siraj was carrying an AK-47 when he grabbed hold of the Colonel. He was out of control; saturated with the violence of that morning's bloody fighting. In those few seconds he thought of his friend Mohamed Jamal, gunned down just moments before—now a *shahid*, a martyr—and of the many other rebel fighters he'd seen die on the battlefield. He remembered his family: one uncle dead, one injured, and one arrested since the start of the revolution. Now he could stick his weapon in the face of the "Guide," blow his head to pieces, and send him to hell. Instead of being arrested as a cold-blooded killer and facing justice, he'd be covered in glory and greeted with cries of "Allahu Akbar!" by the others in the brigade. Not only would it put an end to months of suffering, but he'd be able to beat his chest with pride and say, "I killed Muammar Gaddafi!"

But Siraj, a slender, brown-skinned young man, circumspect and determined, had received an order to take Gaddafi alive. Reason conflicted with instinct. There in front of him was the man he had learned to hate, and yet he could choose to reject the savagery the tyrant represented. With the help of his friends Mohamed Alwaib and Umran Ben Shaaban, Siraj dragged Gaddafi out from the culvert where the Colonel had been hiding and stumbled toward the other rebels who had come running in their direction and were now gathering around. Siraj handed the Colonel over to the commander, Umram Alwaib, and let others take hold of the captive.

Gaddafi was not only defeated, but also injured and in a state of shock. It was exactly 250 days since the outbreak of the first protests in

Benghazi; 245 days since Siraj, a 21-year-old student, had taken to the streets of Tripoli to join other angry Libyans in Green Square, one of the places most closely associated with the regime. Since then, some 20,000 people had died—most of them young men barely out of their teens, suddenly transformed into warriors. Countless others had suffered the pains of war—the loss of friends and family members, the mutilations, the amputations, the traumas.

Filled with rage but also with a sense of duty to his commanders, Siraj didn't step away as Gaddafi was engulfed by his would-be executioners. After all, he was part of the *katiba*—brigade—that had captured Gaddafi; he was proud of himself and could barely contain his euphoria. Gripping his weapon, the cries of "Allahu Akbar!," or "God is great!," reverberating around him, he followed the group of rebels who were now dragging their most hated enemy away. Some, like Umram, made a vain attempt to establish a cordon around the man who had ruled Libya for 42 years, as if now he should be taken prisoner and brought to trial. But the others, thirsty for revenge, pressed in close, straining to kick, punch, or pull the hair of the executioner now surrounded by his victims. It was a scene of absolute chaos, with everyone shouting at the same time:

"Allahu Akbar! Allahu Akbar! Allahu Akbar! We've captured him! Grab him and take a picture! Allahu Akbar! Allahu Akbar! Allahu Akbar! Muammar taghut, we've got him! We've taken him alive! Please, I want to take a picture! Allahu Akbar!"

Siraj himself was shouting as he took up position close to Gaddafi. He knew he should try to protect him but couldn't resist landing whatever blows he could. It gave him pleasure. To humiliate Gaddafi, he took off a shoe and struck him with the sole—the greatest expression of contempt in the Arab world.

One rebel, Ali Algadi, was filming on his mobile; within hours the pictures would be seen around the world, shocking the more sensitive viewers and in some quarters reinforcing the idea that Arabs are savages. Siraj can be seen in the first few seconds of the footage, wearing a camouflaged jacket and a military helmet. Gaddafi is surrounded by a forest of firearms as he slumps exhausted on the desert sand, bleeding profusely. He had lost all strength in his legs, having earlier been knifed repeatedly—and sadistically—in the anus.

While Gaddafi's life was ebbing away like that of an animal in an abattoir, Siraj again had the opportunity to finish him off. But he wasn't willing to go that far. He wanted him dead, but not quite yet. He didn't want to join the lynching that seemed about to take place. He put down his gun and moved back a little, keeping the scene fully in view. He pulled out his mobile, taking pictures and filming. The rebels around him revealed a range of feelings: disbelief, anger, the ecstasy of revenge—all expressed in excited cries that mingled with bursts of gunfire: "I want to film, please! Allahu Akbar! Allahu Akbar! We've captured him! Misrata! Allahu Akbar! Misrata! Allahu Akbar! Misrata! We've got him! Misrata! Misrata! Misrata! Misrata! Misrata! Allahu Akbar! Allahu Akbar! There is no god but Allah! Allah is great!"

At that moment there was still fighting going on around the electricity substation. But among the rebels who knew of Gaddafi's capture, it seemed no one was paying any attention to the exchanges of gunfire. In their delirium some of the rebels hadn't noticed that some other high-ranking officials had also been captured: Abu Bakr Yunis Jaber, the defense minister; Mansour Dhao, Gaddafi's personal security chief; Ahmed Ibrahim, a cousin of the dictator and, as head of the Revolutionary Committees Movement, a kind of unofficial prime minister; and also Mutassim Gaddafi—one of the Colonel's sons.

Swarming around Gaddafi, the rebels dragged him from the bottom of a dry canal up a short, dusty incline to the road, where a pickup truck had come to a halt. Siraj didn't know what the plan was, but the continuing screams of "Misrata! Misrata!" suggested the destination would be the city from which the majority of rebels had arrived to join the siege of Sirte. And in Misrata they didn't just hate Gaddafi: they wanted him dead.

Increasingly bloodied and disorientated, the Colonel stumbled forward, pushed by the crowd. Then, suddenly, he fell again. He was exhausted, humiliated, and now prostrate. Maybe he'd already been shot; Siraj wasn't sure. He knew that when he'd taken Gaddafi out from the culvert, he didn't have any bullet wounds. In the ensuing tumult, however, a major injury had been inflicted; his condition was deteriorating quickly. Now, with rebels crowding in front of him, he was being pushed backward toward the hood of the truck.

Still filming, Siraj captured the moment when Gaddafi was lifted into the back of the pickup. At no point did he show any sign of resistance; he merely wiped his bloodied face and eyes, as if trying to see more clearly. His face was etched with profound pain—an expression that, in these final moments at least, lent some humanity to a tyrant known for his cruelty. The rebels, meanwhile, were about to lose a certain amount of their legitimacy—but in such circumstances, what rational argument could possibly have prevented what was about to happen?

Siraj looked closely at Gaddafi and realized he was indeed severely injured. It was a little more than fifteen minutes since he had been snatched from the sewer pipe. His shirt had been ripped off and he was begging for help in a weakening voice. An ambulance had arrived from the Sirte battlefront to take him to Misrata, and he was dragged toward it. Trousers pulled down below his knees, he was bundled into the vehicle. Siraj also fought his way into the ambulance and saw seven of his fellow rebels inside—four he recognized from Misrata, and three from Tripoli. Now that he had another close-up view of Gaddafi, Siraj suddenly saw he had a bullet wound to his left temple and another to his abdomen, slightly above the navel. Taken aback, Siraj shouted: "Somebody shot him! Somebody shot him!"

Immediately he felt anxious about having failed to protect Gaddafi from the crowd, as he'd been ordered to do by the brigade commander. Having so often seen death up close during the months of fighting, Siraj knew the shot to the head would prove fatal. Seeing the Colonel slip into unconsciousness inside the stationary ambulance, surrounded by rebels who continued to shout and fire shots into the air, Siraj addressed the doctor who was now trying to provide first aid: "Does he still have a pulse, doctor?"

He did, but blood was pouring from different parts of his broken body: the head, the abdomen, between the legs. Only seconds passed before Siraj asked again, "Doctor, does he still have a pulse?" He got the same answer. The doctor was trying to stem the flow of blood, asking for help from the other *thowars*—revolutionaries—in the vehicle. Siraj was anxious to help and also intensely curious. Before the ambulance moved off he repeated the question: "Has Gaddafi still got a pulse, doctor?"

"No, he doesn't have a pulse anymore," the doctor replied.

Although his orders were to get Gaddafi to the hospital, at that moment Siraj was overcome by a surge of emotion. His first thought was *Libya can be proud that Gaddafi is dead.*

The fact that Gaddafi's heart had stopped only made the situation more urgent, but because of the crowds around the ambulance it was impossible to drive off quickly. Siraj was aware that the vehicle was moving, however, and as it gradually gathered speed the shouting began to fade away. He was sitting right next to Gaddafi, his attention focused on the doctor's efforts to resuscitate him. Suddenly there was a sharp jolt, a crash, and Siraj was thrown forward—the driver had run into another vehicle. None of the passengers were injured, so they carried Gaddafi's body as quickly as they could to another ambulance that was part of the convoy. Not long afterward, however, on the edge of Misrata, the second ambulance also ground to a halt, this time because of a burst tire, so the rebels took out the blood-soaked body and put it in the back of a white Land Cruiser. At the wheel was Ibrahim Abu Finas, a middle-aged small businessman and car importer who had volunteered to join the insurgents and now found himself driving Gaddafi's makeshift ambulance.

In fact, Gaddafi had been dead since the convoy left Sirte, his hometown—the place where he'd promised to fight to the bitter end. Siraj thought back and tried to work out at what precise moment—surely not far from where he'd been looking or from where his camera had been pointing—one or more rebels had disobeyed the orders from the high command of the National Transitional Council (NTC) in Tripoli and shot the Colonel, carrying out what was effectively a summary execution.

Siraj wasn't sorry the tyrant was dead. It was something he'd ardently wished for. Yet he knew many rebels would feel this wasn't the ideal ending. Siraj himself would have preferred a proper trial, as long as the outcome was eventually the same: a few feet of earth on top of Gaddafi's corpse.

It was lunchtime when Abu Finas drove into Misrata, proud to be transporting what was left of the country's most wanted man. The people had risen up against Gaddafi on February 17, 2011—and now here was a crowd celebrating his death, just as there would be throughout Libya soon. Abu Finas had been told to drive not to the hospital but to a military base, where there were ex-army officers who had deserted at the beginning of the conflict. Among the officers was the military commander of the NTC in Misrata, Ramadan Zarmouh, a man of diminutive stature and few words. He had led the rebels in their resistance to the regime in Misrata, then liberated and destroyed Sirte. He was therefore indirectly responsible for Gaddafi's capture, and was now one of the most important men in Libya.

Waiting with the political and military leaders were doctors who would confirm that Gaddafi was dead through DNA samples from his pubic hair. One of them, Abu Bakr Traina, carried out a brief examination, identifying the bullet holes in the slim, sexagenarian body and noting the other wounds, but finding neither fractures nor any sources of significant internal hemorrhaging. Afterward they set off again in the pickup driven by Abu Finas, this time in the direction of Misrata's Tunisian Market, about fifteen minutes from the city center. Siraj could feel now that his enthusiasm was waning; he was very tired after a night spent on guard followed by a morning of intense fighting. There was also the fact that the corpse was beginning to stink. Although Siraj had become used to the stench of corpses, he was taken aback by the odor, which all too easily penetrated the medical mask the doctors had given him to cover his nose and mouth.

When they arrived at the market, he helped carry the body into what appeared to be a cold-storage room. When he left the room there were lots of other people approaching, having apparently already heard about the arrival of the corpse. At the first opportunity he washed his face and hands vigorously, but the smell of Gaddafi was still on him. It was much worse than merely unpleasant; the smell of the blood sent shivers running through him and he thought he was going to vomit. Siraj watched the crowd of rebels arrive, celebrating. He joined in for a few minutes, but already felt his day was coming to an end. Gaddafi was dead; Siraj was free. Now he could go home.

IT WAS JUST PAST ELEVEN IN THE MORNING IN TRIPOLI WHEN RASHED TOLD ME there were strong rumors that Sirte had fallen. From his serious and emphatic tone I realized that this time the end of the military stalemate was near. I said goodbye and walked down the fifteen floors of Al Fateh Tower as fast as I could. Upon reaching the street I could tell the information was beginning to spread like a virus. Shots were fired into the air in celebration—something I'd hardly heard at all since my arrival the previous afternoon. Some cars were sounding their horns frenetically, although it seemed the majority of people still weren't quite sure what was happening. I asked the driver to take me back to the Asshajara hotel, where I would pack my equipment into my rucksack and decide what to do.

The scene on the streets in the Libyan capital was changing before my eyes. The number of vehicles was increasing quickly; many of the people inside them were celebrating loudly, some shouting revolutionary slogans, others the habitual "Allahu Akbar!" When I arrived at the hotel, there was a group of elderly people in the lobby who I'd never seen before. I greeted them in passing as I went to pick up my key. The man at the desk was an Algerian, whom I spoke to in French. There was a TV on, and some of the old men were watching the news. I asked them what was going on and the first reply, in French, was from a man with a calm, friendly demeanor. His name was Abib Fac al-Fagui. Sirte had fallen, he said. I asked if it had been confirmed. Abib assured me that yes, it had happened that very morning. And then he added, "They also got Gaddafi."

I froze. I asked for details but he said there was nothing more; the NTC hadn't yet made a statement. My sense of urgency intensified. It was already just after midday; in one hour's time I had an interview arranged with a diplomat, Jamel Abuguila, at the Rixos hotel, one of the main buildings used by the NTC. I ran to my room to call Abuguila and arrange to meet earlier, or at least get some information from him about what was going on. But there was no answer. I immediately tried calling other contacts, but the only ones I managed to reach all gave me the same answer: they weren't sure of anything. Rumors indicated that the Colonel had been arrested or killed. I went to the concierge desk to ask for a taxi as soon as possible, because my fixer—a driver, translator, and guide all rolled into one—was not available that day. When I got to the bottom of the stairs I got a call on my mobile from a number in Turkey. It was Amal Daredi, a good friend and an executive of the oil company Petrobras. Laughing, her voice full of happiness, she said, "They've got Gaddafi!" I pressed her for more details, surprised that the information had already reached Ankara.

I returned to the concierge desk and reiterated that I needed a taxi to the Rixos hotel as soon as possible. The young man at the desk seemed unable to reach any taxi drivers on his phone list. This left me stuck in the hotel, hoping for a driver to appear who might be able to take me around for the whole day. I asked the concierge to keep trying and returned to the lobby, where I spoke again to the group of old men. Some of them were complaining angrily of the bursts of gunfire that were becoming more frequent outside; they thought it was a stupid way to celebrate. I agreed, but that was the way it was. I went back up to my room, and while I was putting my equipment and a bundle of clothes in my rucksack, I got a call from my wife, Lúcia Müzell. She was in Paris, at work in the newsroom of Radio France Internationale, fascinated by the rumors that were coming out of Libya. "Andrei, you get to Tripoli and Gaddafi dies?! I can't believe it!"

I couldn't believe it either. Seven and a half months after my release from prison in Tripoli, only now was I beginning to think seriously about writing a book to describe everything that had happened. I asked Lúcia what information was arriving in Paris from the major international news agencies. She said nothing had been confirmed, it was still just rumors—some saying Gaddafi had been captured, others that he was dead. My first challenge, I decided, would be to establish exactly what had happened.

Back to the concierge I went, now with my gear on my back, ready to leave for the Rixos and then for Sirte, 450 kilometers away—a six-hour journey if I was lucky. As no driver had yet arrived, I went into the street to try to flag down any taxi I could. But I had no chance—not at that time, in that part of town, with the crowds pouring onto the streets to celebrate even though there was no official confirmation of what had taken place. I went back to the lobby and asked the old man who spoke French if he could translate the TV news for me. But Al Jazeera didn't seem to have any new information—or if they did, they weren't yet broadcasting it.

It was now 12:57 p.m., and Abib Fac al-Fagui observed my agitated state while calmly sipping his coffee. "I don't like this gunfire, and yet the people have been waiting for this for a long time," he said.

Abib was 68 years old, short, with a gentle manner. He was now witnessing the climax of the second Libyan revolution in his lifetime. The first had taken place 42 years earlier, when a group of young army officers led a coup to overthrow King Idris. He himself had helped the rebels achieve military victory. In those early days in 1969, when he participated in the siege of Tripoli and was later involved in imprisoning military officers and policemen loyal to the monarchy, Abib didn't know who would end up as leader; no one knew. Then a charming, charismatic figure emerged: a young man of 27 imbued with a compelling nationalist verve. He began to attract support after arriving from Benghazi. It was Muammar Gaddafi.

But, for Abib, the allure of Gaddafi didn't last long. He soon started looking less favorably on the new regime, and in 1972 decided to leave the army. Eight years later, with repression intensifying in Libya, Abib left for Egypt with political-refugee status. In the space of eleven years he'd gone from being an ally of the revolution to an opponent in exile. For a further eleven years he built a life outside his home country, until being allowed to come back in 1991 when Gaddafi authorized the return of certain dissidents. And now, another twenty years on, having always maintained his opposition to Gaddafi, Abib had answered the appeal of the revolutionaries on February 17 and decided to work toward the downfall of the dictatorship he had helped put in power.

It was the moment he'd been waiting for, he told me. He left for Tunisia, came back into Libya through Dehiba, went into the Nefusa mountains and then to Zawiyah, aiming to assist the efforts to capture Gaddafi's Bab al-Azizia compound in Tripoli, which served as the headquarters of the regime. I asked him how he felt now, with Sirte having fallen and Gaddafi either captive or dead. His reaction, which itself suggested he felt free to convey his feelings, showed how much Libya had already changed since the beginning of the revolution. "I can't describe the emotion and happiness I'm feeling. What's happening is huge. I hate guns, but I felt obliged to take up arms again. It was Gaddafi who led us to this violence. For 42 years we were oppressed. We all hoped for this moment."

As we talked, the taxi finally arrived. I jotted down Abib's phone number, said goodbye, and headed off to the Rixos hotel. By now the main streets were clogged with thousands of cars waving the green, red, and black tricolor that had been adopted by the revolution—the flag of the 1951–69 monarchy, an emblem of the pre-Gaddafi era. Although there were countless heavy weapons in the hands of civilians, many now being fired recklessly into the air, the tone of the celebrations, so far at least, was friendly and without any hint of violence.

On reaching the hotel entrance, which was guarded by rebel brigades, I felt a surge of happiness and expectancy. The rumors were still being investigated, and the NTC authorities had not confirmed Gaddafi's death, let alone the circumstances of it. I asked for Abuguila, the diplomat, and was told he was on his way. I waited for him in the hallway, chatting with some rebels. Until now only a few of them had been willing to fraternize with a journalist. One of them told me that shortly after 1:15 p.m. Abdel Majid Mlegta, one of the NTC's most senior military commanders, had said Gaddafi had died from his wounds. It was an important piece of information, albeit secondhand and impossible to verify.

Then Abuguila arrived. I introduced myself and immediately asked whether the rumors about Gaddafi were true. He said they were, and pointed to the TV; apparently there was about to be an official statement. Abdelhakim Belhadj, a radical Islamist who had become the military leader of the NTC in Tripoli, was live on Al Jazeera. At 1:47 p.m. on October 20, 2011, Belhadj announced Gaddafi was dead.

There was an explosion of shouts and screams as if a goal had been scored in a football stadium; the voices rose to fever pitch as the first images of the Colonel, semi-naked and blood-soaked, appeared on the screen.

I immediately called Brazil and asked to go live on air on the Grupo Estado radio station, Estadão ESPN. I passed along the news, ended the call, asked Abuguila if we could delay our conversation until a later date—which, as it turned out, would never arrive—and headed off for the Radisson Blu Al Mehary hotel, another NTC meeting point, where I intended to meet Mlegta. I was torn between leaving for Sirte immediately or hanging on in the capital for an official declaration by the NTC, which in the next few hours might announce the "liberation" of Libya and the end of the war. I was very conscious that the location of Gaddafi's body was still unknown.

I couldn't find Mlegta so I headed off toward Martyrs' Square—previously Green Square, the place where Gaddafi used to address his people. On the way I saw a familiar-looking young man wearing a military uniform and carrying an iPad. His appearance had changed somewhat—his head had been shaved when he joined up with the rebels for the battle at Bani Walid—but it was unmistakably Khaled Medhat, the fixer who'd helped me and some other journalists back in August. He'd earned quite a lot of money from the work, hence the iPad and the fact that he now drove a new 4×4.

I remembered Khaled as a staunch critic of Gaddafi who expressed a great deal of anguish about the future—both his own and that of Libya as a whole. We greeted each other effusively and yet I noticed he seemed tired, even annoyed. I was curious about his demeanor, particularly at a moment when Tripoli was celebrating all around us. He explained that he was disappointed: he'd wanted to see Gaddafi brought to trial rather than killed. In the minds of many Libyans, he said, the Colonel would be seen as having died on his home territory, fighting to the end, just as promised. He feared that from that day forward the dictator might be seen as a martyr.

As I was leaving the hotel I came across another young rebel I'd met in August, during the fall of Tripoli. Adam Ahmed, 22, was an American, the son of Libyan parents. He'd been studying for a sociology degree in Washington when, in March, he decided to set off for his parents' homeland to join the rebellion in Benghazi. A likeable extrovert, his slightly rounded physique and Rambo-style clothing were instantly recognizable. In the midst of the crowds of people and the hundreds of vehicles blowing their horns, I asked him what he thought about the death of Gaddafi.

"I can't tell you, Andrei," he said. "A Libyan can't describe a day like today. It's impossible to put into words. But look, it's not over, it's just beginning. The work's just beginning—reconstruction and everything else. Reconstruction's the hardest part. We need infrastructure. We need to reform the economy, the political system, and the education system. And we have to start now. The revolution's not over yet. The fighting part of the revolution's over. But the real revolution is in the education system, in politics…Now it's time to make a peaceful revolution, to change things in Libya."

Adam was interrupted many times, obliged to respond to the cries of "Allahu Akbar!" from the rebels who passed by and from the residents of

Tripoli who were greeting the armed men in festive spirit. By now, streams of vehicles driven by euphoric young people had taken over the main roads and Martyrs' Square. Adam helped me flag down a vehicle so we could hitch a ride toward the city center. When we got there, it was the strangest scene of celebration I had ever experienced. Weapons—including anti-aircraft guns—were being fired, fireworks were being let off, some people were banging drums and others were singing hymns—and amid it all, groups of young people were chatting quite calmly, as if oblivious to the surrounding mayhem. One of them was Mohamed Egwatn, a 29-year-old geologist from Benghazi. He had been arrested in early March after taking part in an antiregime demonstration in Tripoli. He had every reason to desire revenge, but he wanted it to be within the limits of the law. He too would have preferred to see the Colonel in prison rather than dead. He wanted him behind bars, suffering like so many of his compatriots had suffered. It was a shame, Mohamed said, that Gaddafi would never know the anguish of being thrown into prison and having no idea what fate awaited him.

In the same group was Mohamed Shawsh, a 26-year-old accountant, who told me no one could quite believe what was happening. Libyans had never previously experienced such a sensation, he explained. I asked what sensation he meant. "Of freedom!" he exclaimed, as if he were stating the obvious. "You don't feel freedom until the day when you can speak your mind and not be afraid of the consequences. It's something we've never experienced in our lives."

MISRATA WAS INCREDIBLY QUIET IN THE EARLY MORNING OF FRIDAY, OCTOBER 21. I'd just arrived from Tripoli in a pickup truck belonging to Nouri Glera, a fixer for the photographer Marcel Mettelsiefen, who was working for the German magazine *Der Spiegel*. We'd left the capital at sunrise; the 210-kilometer journey took a little under three hours. We stopped on the main street in the center of Misrata—"Tripoli Street" as it was known to foreign journalists—just in front of a museum that was being put together in memory of the victims of the city's recent siege. From there Mettelsiefen went off with another fixer in their car, while I stayed with Nouri for a few hours.

In bloody and nebulous fashion, Libya had brought an end to Gaddafi's 42 years as protagonist in the country's political affairs. Back in Misrata, which I had visited a few weeks previously, my aim was to find out what happened in the dictator's last hours and, if possible, to shed light on how the siege of Sirte had become a manhunt.

Tripoli Street was almost deserted. There was very little traffic and far fewer people than usual. One of the locals took an interest in me when he saw I was a journalist. He exchanged a few words with Nouri, conveying the message that he had something to show me. Then he took out a mobile phone and began to play a video he said he had filmed himself. The images were shaky and out of focus; at first it was clear only that the scenes had been filmed in the middle of a crowd of people who were shouting in Arabic. Whoever had filmed the images was trying to make way through the melee. Suddenly a small clearing appeared in the forest of bodies. On the floor was the body of a man; the trembling image showed there was a lot of blood on his abdomen and chest. Around him, young men—some in military uniform, some in civilian clothes—were doing their best to maintain a cordon and prevent the furious crowd from getting any closer. Then the image stopped shaking for a second—and the corpse of Gaddafi came into focus.

The following images revealed that the crowd was inside a closed room and were gathered around not one but two corpses. The other was that of Mutassim, Gaddafi's son. It was clear now that the film had captured part of a celebration for thowars and the local civilian population. Throughout the night, the man told me, the revolutionaries had streamed into and out of the room, the father and son having been put on display as trophies of war. The Colonel still had on the same khaki trousers he'd been wearing in the ambulance; his other clothes—jacket, scarf, socks, shoes—had disappeared on the outskirts of Sirte, taken away as souvenirs by those who'd managed to get close enough to the lynching.

There was also a second video, filmed by another combatant in Misrata, that showed Mutassim in two different situations. First, he was being held captive; he was injured, but not seriously, and seemed reasonably relaxed and was smoking a cigarette. Next, he was dead, a gaping hole in his chest, his corpse surrounded by insurgents. Hours later I learned that these images were in fact already being seen around the world, indicating that the dictator and Mutassim had indeed been summarily executed. They hadn't been given the right to stand trial, either in Libya or in the International Criminal Court in The Hague.

I got permission from the owner of the mobile to transfer the videos to my laptop and then asked him when and where they'd been filmed. He said it was the previous night and the early hours of that very morning, inside one of the pavilions in the Tunisian Market situated some way from Misrata city center. I would head there next.

Nouri, however, was about to lose me some time. First he asked to pick up a friend and take him with us. Then he wanted to have a coffee. He disappeared and only came back 40 minutes later. I explained that we were dealing with an important issue in international law, a revolution that had come to an end with the execution of an important political figure, an act that might come to be considered a war crime and did not augur well for a country aspiring to freedom. Nouri seemed to get the message. He said his friend, G.H.,* should still come with us as he lived in Misrata and could be useful. I agreed.

We went to the Tunisian Market, then to the city's main hospital. I wanted to investigate the rumors that Gaddafi's body had been put into some kind of cold storage, and also to find rebels who had taken part in the battles that had resulted in the capture of the Colonel. The market entrance was blocked by a katiba with orders not to let anyone enter. We left for the hospital minutes later. The corpse wasn't there, which was obvious by the absence of a patrol or any other security personnel. The evidence pointed to the body still being in the market. Nevertheless, I went into the hospital to talk to the wounded, and it wasn't difficult to find someone to point me in the direction of those who had been involved in the battle a few hours earlier. Wounded in the ankle by a sniper's bullet the previous day, Jalal Ali Gmati, a 34-year-old musician and a rebel from Nalut who spent three months fighting in the Nefusa mountains before leaving for Tripoli and then on to Sirte, spoke openly about the brutal nature of the final battles. He hadn't actually been in the very last battle, in Jarf, a little village beside Gaddafi's home city, but he still provided plenty of details. The previous day alone, he said, the total number of dead on both sides had been more than 300. The dead were Libyans, of course, but also mercenaries from Niger, Chad, Mali, and Mauritania. "Gaddafi was with a small group that ran away from the city after losing the battle that had taken place behind the mosque in Sirte. We found his car and chased him down," he said, adding that a group of young fighters from the Wazan katiba had been responsible for Gaddafi's capture.

This was important information. We left the hospital and headed for a rebel "headquarters" located on the Jazira road, on the edge of the city, where I hoped the commanders would give me a permit to enter the Tunisian Market. When we got there Nouri brokered a dialogue with the military commanders and leaders of the local NTC. At first the conversation seemed to suggest Gaddafi's body was in a secret location somewhere in Misrata, hidden from the civilian population and the international media. I argued

---

* Pseudonym

that the videos recorded in the Tunisian Market hours earlier showed the body was in Misrata and had been seen by a crowd the day before.

We negotiated a few more minutes, until suddenly, to my surprise, there was a positive response. We were told we would leave in a convoy to a location where I would be allowed to photograph the bodies of the Colonel and his son.

We took to the road. We'd been driving a few minutes when the car in front of us came to a halt; a man got out and came over to our driver's window. He said a few words in Arabic, which led into a brief discussion, then returned to his vehicle. As the two cars in front went off farther ahead, I asked what was going on. Nouri said the meeting would be delayed by two hours. I insisted on knowing the reason and didn't give up until he told me the truth: we'd been excluded because there was also a black man—G.H.—in the vehicle with the two of us.

I didn't understand, so Nouri explained: blacks, whether or not they were Libyan-born, had become collateral victims of the revolution. Due to the presence of particularly violent mercenaries from sub-Saharan Africa in the forces deployed by Gaddafi's deposed regime, blacks had ended up being the victims of overt discrimination and physical assaults. That was why we hadn't been permitted to follow in the NTC convoy. I could only be taken to the secret location on the condition that no black person was in the vehicle—not even G.H., who had been raised in Misrata and had fought for the liberation of the city during the siege.

Seen as bloodthirsty figures, the mercenaries had become a particular target for the rebels. I had been warned about Libyans' racial prejudices, which had increased during the conflict under the pretext that any black might be a mercenary. At the beginning of the revolution, economic migrants from sub-Saharan Africa who were trying to reach the north of the continent and then cross the Mediterranean to reach Europe had been mistaken for mercenaries; there had been unconfirmed reports of summary executions.

I asked G.H. what the man from the car in front had said to him. He refused to translate the insults and also asked me not to include his name in anything I wrote later. Then, suddenly, he crumpled in front of me, breaking into sobs, a picture of humiliation.

"The one who came over didn't say good things," G.H. explained. "I've lived in Misrata for 40 years. I have a wife and kids who were born here. This is just too hard for me."

Returning to the city center, I imagined any opportunity to find the body had gone for good. We went to the home of one of Nouri's friends and awaited the call. And then, finally, my fixer revealed just how useful he could be. Through a friend of his, a new contact had agreed to meet us. It was Ahmed Salam, a retailer in the city whose brother had become one of the leaders of the rebel resistance during the siege by Gaddafi's forces. We had lunch together and ate off the same shared plate in accordance with local tradition. Then, two hours after arriving, Nouri, Ahmed, and I left again for the rebel HQ on the Jazira road. There I met Khaled, my previous fixer, who was with reporters from the *Financial Times* and *Wall Street Journal*. I heard that a reporter from the *New York Times* was also in the area, with the same goal, of course. With this kind of pressure, I thought, the rebels were bound to lead us to the "secret" location. And that was indeed what happened a few minutes later, when Ahmed got the go-ahead from the local NTC commanders. We left in two cars: Nouri's in front with Ahmed and I as passengers, followed by Khaled's. We drove for about twenty minutes along dusty roads until we reached a hill on the edge of Misrata. Here, Ahmed said, we would see the body of Mutassim Gaddafi, which had been separated from that of his father earlier in the morning.

We were called over toward a large refrigerated container. The outer door opened for us, revealing a metal grill through which we could see the interior of a metal chamber. A couple of meters from the door lay the body of a man on yellow and red blankets on top of a mattress. His arms were by his side and the lower part of his legs, extending beyond the end of the mattress, rested on the floor. The corpse had several abrasions on the legs and scratches to the chest, shoulder, and face. But more significantly, there was a deep, gaping wound below the trachea, between the neck and chest, and a circle of blood on the upper abdomen. The former was clearly an incision, caused either by a bullet or a blade; the latter perhaps wasn't a hole but some other kind of injury. The face, beard, and hair left no possible doubt that it was Mutassim, who a day earlier had been sitting on a mattress, perhaps the same one, talking and smoking after being taken prisoner by the insurgents. Obviously, Gaddafi's son had been killed while in rebel hands.

In addition to the journalists a few other people, including Nouri, had been allowed to enter. They were taking photos and filming videos, similar to those that had been shown to me that morning on Tripoli Street. Then we left and the door closed behind us. For the time being I would hear no further comment about the circumstances of Mutassim's death, but I already knew I'd be hearing "explanations" the following morning in a meeting with Ramadan Zarmouh, the military commander of the NTC in Misrata, a hard man of few words who would tell me he'd never previously given an interview to a non-Libyan.

I set off for the Tunisian Market in Nouri's car, with Khaled's behind us. This time, Ahmed assured me, we had permission to go inside. About half an hour later the barrier set up by the katiba at the entrance to the market was lifted, allowing us to enter a huge enclosed area that would normally be throbbing with commercial activity but today was almost deserted. Inside, armored vehicles guaranteed security. We drove about five minutes before seeing a group of buildings that, it seemed, vehicles were not permitted to approach. I guessed this was where Gaddafi's body was. The reporter from the *New York Times* was already photographing a group of around 40 people who were forming a queue to enter what seemed to be another large refrigerated chamber—in which, I would discover, the cooling system was turned off. Ahmed led us past the queue and we entered a windowless room, illuminated only by the natural light coming through the open door. The smell of blood was strong and unpleasant, but the corpse laid out in the center of the room wasn't yet exuding the odor of putrefaction. Seeing him, I felt nothing—neither pity nor contempt.

The video I'd transferred to my laptop showed Gaddafi covered in blood, but now his body had been cleaned. There were cuts, scratches, and grazes along with the two wounds that would have proved fatal—a bullet hole in the stomach and another on the left side of the face. I was surprised he didn't have more wounds, given what he'd been through. I couldn't help thinking that yesterday's torture victims had become today's executioners, with the same arbitrary justice and the same violent principles—wholly incongruent with a revolution that preached democracy and freedom after 42 years of oppression and terror. I recorded the moment with a few swiftly taken photos and then left the chamber.

Outside, there were already dozens of people eager to see the trophy that lay in this new chamber of horrors. Ahmed said their curiosity was justifiable given what Misrata had been through during the war. It was a valid argument. One of those in the queue, Gerged Hamed, a 37-year-old engineer, thought the same way: "We've been ruled by the gun for eight months. I'm happy Gaddafi's dead. We can turn the page and think about a democratic Libya now."

Moments later the prime minister of the NTC, Mahmoud Jibril, would arrive at the Tunisian Market and be escorted to the place where the body of the dictator was being "preserved." Upon leaving he insisted to foreign journalists that after Gaddafi's capture there had been further fighting between rebels and loyalist forces, during which Gaddafi had been accidentally shot by his own side. A few hours later Jibril returned to Tripoli while the body of the ex-dictator remained unburied because of a disagreement between the Misrata and Tripoli branches of the NTC leadership. The rebels in Misrata said they could not allow the burial to take place there: the presence of Gaddafi's body in their soil would insult the memory of the local people massacred by the regime. As a result of this impasse the refrigeration chamber, supposedly a secret location, would become a kind of pilgrimage destination for Libyans from all over the country; they would come in the thousands to jostle for position inside, desperate to photograph and film the body.

As the hours passed, meanwhile, the NTC was coming under increasing pressure from the international community to produce a convincing explanation for the deaths of the Colonel and his son. Concerns were being expressed by the UN and by NGOs such as Human Rights Watch and Amnesty International. In response, the NTC leadership in Misrata offered a more detailed description of the events that supposedly led up to Gaddafi's death. They said he had been injured during the fighting, and that he had been carrying an AK-47 and one or two pistols.

THE NEXT MORNING, NOURI RETURNED TO TRIPOLI. AHMED ARRANGED FOR SAMI Daili, a 29-year-old engineer, to take over as my interpreter and fixer. I recognized Sami because he'd appeared for a few seconds in the videos that had been filmed around the corpses. He had done a postgraduate course in Scotland and prior to the revolution had been working at an industrial plant in southern Italy. He went with me to the NTC building where we met Ramadan Zarmouh, the military commander in Misrata responsible for the operations that had culminated in the fall of Sirte.

For a half hour I talked with Zarmouh about the isolated pockets of fighting that were still going on, the hunt for Saif al-Islam Gaddafi, another of Gaddafi's sons, and the need to disarm the population. But what I most wanted to hear was his version of how the dictator and Mutassim had been killed, and his efforts, or lack of them, to investigate the crime and put those responsible on trial. A man of dour, somewhat hostile demeanor, he rejected all the evidence that suggested the pair had been executed. He said both had died from wounds sustained during combat. It was an absurd story, already contradicted by the revolutionaries' own videos. "When we captured him, Gaddafi already had two bullet wounds, one to the head and the other to the abdomen," Zarmouh claimed. "We got medical help, took him away, but it was too late. As for

Mutassim, he'd been shot once. He survived but he was injured, and died afterwards." Then he assured me, "We would like to have taken the two of them alive."

I persisted, trying to extract further details even though Ahmed and Sami seemed uncomfortable with the way I addressed the commander. At the end of the conversation, in an ironic tone, Zarmouh said, "I don't understand why you [foreign journalists] forget the crimes committed by Gaddafi and Mutassim, and ask only about how they died."

But this was precisely the point. Zarmouh didn't understand—nor did many Libyans—that the way the leader and his son had died, and the attitude of the NTC toward the executions, was the problem. Even though the deaths had happened in the context of a war, the message the rebels were sending by having allowed the executions to take place, and then protecting whoever had carried them out, did not bode well for a country that aspired to rebuild itself on democratic foundations. And it was also embarrassing, to say the least, for the Western powers that backed the revolutionaries right to the end and could have demanded that the international conventions regarding prisoners of war be respected. Despite the mood of freedom in the air, Libya in the first few days after the end of the regime was not much different, in terms of justice, from the country Gaddafi had controlled for so long.

By denying the executions, the National Transitional Council undermined its own legitimacy as the entity responsible for bringing about a handover of power. In fact, some of the more moderate members of the NTC in Tripoli had long been aware of the potential international repercussions if Gaddafi were to be killed, and had therefore tried to convince the rebels in Misrata that he shouldn't be executed if captured alive. But those rebels in Misrata, who had suffered under the violent regime for 42 years, could not forgive the Colonel for the siege they had recently endured or for the mercenaries he had deployed, some of whom were given specific orders to rape women in any area recaptured from rebel forces. According to Muslim and Libyan traditions, the rape of a family member is the worst humiliation anyone can suffer, a crime for which death is the only possible punishment.

Faced with increasing pressure over the following days, the NTC promised that those among the rebel forces who had perpetrated acts classifiable as war crimes would face justice. Abdel Hafiz Ghoga, the NTC vice-chairman, guaranteed the deaths of Gaddafi and Mutassim would be investigated. The rebels had a "code of ethics," he said, for the "capture of prisoners of war." Gaddafi's death had been "an act carried out by an individual," not a revolutionary action. We would find out soon enough if Ghoga meant what he said, because the evidence of war crimes, torture, arbitrary detentions, and acts of revenge on the part of the rebels mounted by the day.

THE DAY AFTER THE MEETING WITH ZARMOUH, I LEFT FOR SIRTE WITH AHMED AND Sami. Before leaving I had to spend hours negotiating with the NTC in Misrata, who demanded that journalists wanting to go to Sirte present a written request for accreditation signed by the editors of whatever newspaper or media organization they worked for—a worrying sign that the habits of the previous regime, in this case restrictions on information and on freedom of movement, were still present in Misrata.

Although I had already seen videos and photos from the battlefront, it was only when I arrived on Gaddafi's home soil that I really appreciated the full force of the rebel assault. In 2009 I had visited some parts of Sirte; now, a little more than two years on, under a piercing sun that penetrated strangely gray skies, I returned to a scene of utter destruction. It was a ghost town. The physical damage to the city center was even greater than that in Misrata during the siege. Walking along the main street, I knew for certain: in this part of Libya, scores were being brutally settled.

Separated by 250 kilometers, Misrata and Sirte would both experience continued bitterness in the aftermath of the war. Partly destroyed by a three-month siege and bombarded throughout by the regime, Misrata was now celebrating the rebels' victory over Gaddafi's troops. Loyal to the dictator, or held hostage by him until the very end, Sirte had been demolished by the rebel onslaught. Most of the buildings had been shelled and burned; they were far beyond repair. The main street had clearly been an urban battlefield. But nowhere was the destruction greater than in District 2, northeast of the city alongside the turquoise waters of the Mediterranean. This was where Gaddafi had held out during the last hours of his life. Only ruins remained.

Residents who fled the two cities during the conflict returned to find not only, in most cases, that they had lost everything, but also that they were regarded with disdain by the rebels. Before the NTC attack on Sirte, the rebels tried for weeks to negotiate its surrender and the handover of the regime's officials in the region—including Gaddafi and Mutassim. The city was then encircled for a month, to apply pressure on the local population and the loyalist forces. During this period the majority of the 100,000 inhabitants evacuated. Now, with the fighting finished, those who dared to return—most of them of Bedouin origin—found homes and commercial premises destroyed by bombardment and widespread looting. Of the houses that remained standing, almost all had their doors forced open.

"This war was more than just a hunt for Gaddafi. They were taking revenge for what happened in Misrata, and for the fact that many people here supported the regime," one resident told me. He was afraid there might be further punishment for the city's previous loyalty to Gaddafi, and also nervous that his criticism of the rebel assault might have repercussions for him personally.

Shortly afterward I met a Muslim cleric, Amarah Othman, who had lived in Sirte for 25 years—half his life. On September 12 he had left with his family and many other residents for a village 90 kilometers away. We spoke for a few minutes and he seemed to feel he had nothing to fear, perhaps because he had not been one of the supporters of the regime.

"When the fighting broke out, on 12 September, I left. It was impossible to stay, because the attack was merciless, both from NATO and from the…revolution," he recalled, lingering over that last word. "For at least five years there had been many people here, myself included, wanting a movement to open things up. But in Sirte it was impossible. It was Gaddafi's home region—any protest would be punished by death."

At the end of the fighting Sirte was punished indiscriminately, with no distinction between locals loyal to the regime who might have contributed to its crimes, and those who for decades had adopted silence as the only viable means of indicating their opposition. Salam Ibrahim, an electrician, was 42, though he looked 15 years older. Despite the rubble all around him, he expressed a strong desire for reconciliation. It was a hope sustained by the backgrounds of his own family: his wife was originally from Misrata and he had an uncle from Benghazi, both revolutionary cities. He lived in District 2, the place chosen by Gaddafi's forces for their fight to the death. "We thank God for the revolution," he told me. "But we didn't want this destruction. It should have been possible to have a peaceful revolution."

If division and then war characterized the past, what were the prospects for the future? The question had hung over me for a few days, though I hadn't actually put it to anyone directly. But Ibrahim was about to answer it spontaneously. "It's difficult to imagine a future for the city," he admitted, looking around him with an obvious sadness in his voice. "But still, my family and I will come back and rebuild our home and our city. If the revolution helps us do that, good. Otherwise we'll have to do it house by house, one by one. It'll take time. It would have been more appropriate to live in peace, without destroying Sirte. One day, sooner or later, we'll have to learn to live in peace."

We left the city center and headed toward the village of Jarf, where Gaddafi, Mutassim, and other members of the regime had been captured 72 hours before. Ahmed, Sami, and I went along the same road where the fighting had taken place on October 20. We'd gone a few kilometers when we saw on the horizon a group of vehicles by the side of the road. It was the place where the final confrontation had taken place. When we got out another terrifying sight greeted me. Most of the bystanders seemed interested only in the culverts where Gaddafi had been captured by the young Siraj, but around them, largely ignored, were the dead bodies of dozens of loyalist fighters. They had been lying there, in the open air, for three days. Most of the corpses had been put into three rows, covered with white sheets or bags to stop them from becoming infested with insects. The smell of rotting flesh was sickening, its intensity fluctuating with the strength and direction of the wind. The bodies were a sad testament to the vengefulness of the war. Scattered around the charred wreckage of at least seven vehicles, destroyed either by NATO air strikes or in the rebel offensive, were decomposing body parts or whole corpses, apparently deemed not worthy of a sheet or plastic bag. The scene offered a grimly articulate summary of the conflict—as well as irrefutable proof of human stupidity. I hoped it would prove to be the last chapter in a story that had now ended, rather than the preface to a violent and pathetic narrative still to unfold.

Sirte was deserted, sinister. I wanted to get away from there as soon as possible, so we headed back toward Misrata. That same day, Human Rights Watch found the bodies of 53 loyalist soldiers; all appeared to have been executed during the final battles for Sirte, on or around October 22. Some had been dumped in a mass grave in the garden of the Radisson Blu Al Mehary hotel; others had been left in the hotel lobby, a particularly macabre choice of morgue. The evidence that war crimes had been committed in Sirte was blatant: there were dead soldiers with their hands tied behind their backs, their similar states of decomposition suggesting they had died on the same day, perhaps at the same moment.

That night, in Misrata, I met Tirana Hassan, an investigator from the Emergencies Division at Human Rights Watch. She told me it still wasn't clear who had been responsible for the crimes, and we agreed it was important that a proper investigation be carried out as quickly as possible. "If there's no investigation, the NTC will be sending Libyans the message that killing isn't a crime," Tirana said. "The majority of the victims, clearly, are Gaddafi's soldiers. They were shot after capture, many with their hands tied."

The circumstances surrounding the deaths wouldn't become clear until the middle of 2012. In Misrata, when I attempted to piece together what had happened in the battle for Sirte, more than one commander of rebel katibas told me that, in the days that followed the order to attack the regime forces that were making their last stand in District 2, military victory for the rebels also entailed "cleaning up the area" to "make sure there was no one left." But the commanders assured me that, in the minds of the young rebels who took part in the operation, this cleanup operation meant pursuing those enemy soldiers who were still holding out, with the objective of capturing them or obliging them to surrender. It didn't mean "extermination," they said.

The course of events suggested that revenge had become an increasingly powerful driving force as the war neared its conclusion. The losses on both sides had increased as the rebel brigades closed in on the last area still controlled by forces loyal to the regime. As the fighting for Sirte intensified, so too did the spiral of revenge, the settling of scores, just as in Misrata a few months earlier. And the situation steadily worsened, until finally District 2 was taken. The evidence pointing to war crimes added to the impression that NTC leaders and their military commanders had been incapable of enforcing discipline on the battlefield. It was, in fact, an impression some of us among the foreign journalists in Libya had already had for some weeks.

The rebels had become, in effect, a mass of fighters armed to the teeth, enjoying military superiority, moving around a country whose institutions had been destroyed and where accumulated hatreds were viscerally expressed. I was disturbed not only by what appeared to have taken place during the final battles, but also, again, by the possible implications for the country's postrevolutionary future. I feared that the rebel katibas, once freed from the shackles of dictatorship, would emerge from silent obedience not only to give voice to freedom but also to indulge in lawless revenge.

This fear was reinforced by the stories I had been told by some people in Misrata who were unhappy with the recent behavior of part of the local population. The city had been shelled more than any other and had suffered terribly. Misrata mourned not only over its dead but also the approximately 1,200 rapes committed by loyalist soldiers and mercenaries. Now liberated, Misrata was closing in on itself, adopting an attitude that was a mixture of perceived self-sufficiency—derived from its heroic resistance—and moral superiority over those who had not shared its nightmare. It was an attitude expressed in signs put up at various rebel checkpoints, which read, "If you left Misrata, you don't have the right to return." A few informal conversations with Misrata residents revealed that the aim of these messages was to convey a kind of "informal sentence" passed by political and religious leaders in the city, and which was being rigorously applied with the connivance of the local NTC.

In the districts of Gasser Ahmed, Gueran, and al-Jazira, for example, hundreds of homes belonging to families who had fled during the conflict had been expropriated or looted. Those who returned, if they were lucky enough to find their houses intact, lived in danger of being physically attacked and expelled from their homes. I first heard this from a young man whose friend had been forced out of his home soon after returning. Having been told I was a journalist, he came to talk to me. He requested that I didn't reveal his name, because his disagreement with the policy of expulsions put him in a difficult position; he, like many others, had already received threats. Throughout our long conversation he gave the impression of carefully weighing every word, and when he'd finished his story he again stressed that I mustn't use his name.

Although fearful, the young man clearly expressed an opinion that was already quite widespread in certain sections of society, particularly among more educated Libyans. It was the view that—after four decades of oppression and silence imposed by the regime, eight months of war, and more than 20,000 deaths—many rebels, particularly in Misrata, were filled not only with pride by their military victory but also with a sense of omnipotence and a desire for revenge against those who had opposed them during the final days of the conflict. "It's a very unfair situation, because people had the right to leave the city during the revolution," he said, adding that he had chosen to stay. "What's really serious is that we can't speak about this subject in public, at least not until we get to choose a free government, one that will guarantee freedom of expression."

One or two days later I met Mohamed Glewen, the coordinator of the 17 February Association, a kind of informal city council that had 8,000 volunteers at its disposal for rebuilding and organizing Misrata. I asked him about the ban on returning and about the expulsions some residents had described. Mohamed said quite openly that some restrictions on personal freedoms were in place; the local authorities might in the future ask anyone wanting to visit the city to provide ID and, if necessary, an additional document, a kind of visa for entry. He seemed indifferent to the symbolism of such measures in a country whose unity was still in doubt, justifying them by saying that Misrata was a potential "terrorist target." "If someone wants to come to Misrata and there are no problems, they'll be allowed," he said. "But no one close to Gaddafi can come here." It wasn't clear what he meant by "problems," or who might be considered "close to Gaddafi," and why.

There was a similar situation, though much more serious, in Tawergha, situated between Misrata and Sirte. Founded by immigrants from sub-Saharan Africa, it had become a ghost town. The majority of its residents were of Tuareg origin—in the Berber language *Tuareg* means "abandoned by the gods"—and most had sided with Gaddafi's forces during the conflict, many even fighting alongside them. In the minds of the people of Misrata, and according to their testimonies, the men from Tawergha had behaved more cruelly than any others during the siege of Misrata, participating in mass rapes. Following the rebel victory in August, the men of Tawergha had been obliged to abandon the city and head for other urban centers, such as Benghazi or Saba, or hide in remote areas. Months afterward, heavily armed Tawerghans would be found among the militias destabilizing parts of southern Algeria and fighting for the secession of northern Mali—where they had links with Islamist extremist groups that were implanting sharia law—from the rest of the country. In the dispute between Misrata and Sirte there was, according to residents of both cities, the hope of future reconciliation. For the banished Tawerghans, however, there was no chance of clemency.

BACK IN MISRATA, I PUT OFF MY PLANS TO RETURN TO TRIPOLI BECAUSE IT SEEMED I had a good chance of achieving two objectives: first, to find members of the Wazan katiba who had been responsible for seizing Gaddafi; and second, to get authorization from the NTC to interview members of the regime who had been captured alive with the Colonel, such as Mansour Dhao, Abu Bakr Yunis Jaber, and Ahmed Ibrahim.

In the early evening, Ahmed phoned with an update. "Get ready to interview Ibrahim," he said, explaining that a few minutes later Sami would be arriving at my hotel, the lobby of which had already been transformed into a makeshift newsroom by resident journalists.

Sami and I headed off to the base of a powerful rebel katiba at al-Jawara, on the darkened outskirts of the city. Upon arrival we had to spend the best part of two hours negotiating the terms on which I would be allowed to enter. When I did finally get in to the area where Ibrahim was being detained, which was guarded by dozens of armed rebels, I saw a large group of men of all ages gathering around a very small, rather ramshackle building and shouting toward the window. There were security guards at the door. Inside, there was Ibrahim—one of the most hated members of the regime, known as the man who had persuaded Gaddafi to close Libya to the outside world during the 1970s, a measure that contributed not only to the country's isolation but also to its radicalization and its involvement in terrorism.

With the deaths of Gaddafi and Mutassim, the hasty departure of other members of the family, and the disappearance of Saif al-Islam Gaddafi and of the head of the intelligence services, Abdullah al-Senussi, the rebels had destroyed the regime. Most of its highest-ranking members had either fled the country or changed sides during the conflict; the few who remained now found themselves in prison, including Ibrahim, a man no foreigner had interviewed since the beginning of the revolution. He had been one of the most infamous figures in the regime since 1984, when he ordered the hangings—in front of TV cameras—of eleven "counter-revolutionary students" in Benghazi. From that day onward he symbolized the oppression that the revolution had sought to bring to an end. Until his capture by rebels in Sirte, he commanded a huge apparatus of repression: 30,000 militiamen connected to the Revolutionary Committees Movement (RCM)—more than a third of all the personnel employed by the regime's internal security forces. Created in 1977, this "movement" had around 300,000 collaborators, including unarmed civilians, spread all over the country, including police officers, spies, and politicians in municipal and regional governments. Its different elements combined to form one of the main pillars of the omnipresent State and inflicted terror on the Libyan people. RCM militiamen had been responsible for my own imprisonment in Sabratha in February.

After waiting for another hour outside the small building I was allowed to go inside, accompanied by Sami and Ahmed. Both were nervous being in the presence of one of the most feared officials in the dictatorship. Ibrahim was sitting cross-legged on the floor. He was told to get up and sit on a mattress that was lying on one side of the room, against a wall. I was given a chair to sit on, which meant I would be looking down on him as we spoke. I said I wanted to talk about the revolution and the death of Gaddafi. Ibrahim replied that he had nothing to say—but then, changing his mind, as if he couldn't bear to remain silent, he told me that the so-called revolution didn't exist and that the Guide was still alive.

"Yes, there was a revolution. In February, in Benghazi, hundreds of young people were killed during peaceful protests, and that was what started the revolution," I said to him. "When was it that you and the Gaddafi government decided to use armed force against the rebels?"

"I never did anything against the rebels. I just stayed at home," he replied, before repeating, "I never did anything against the rebels."

"You'd been at home ever since 17 February? You weren't part of the government?"

"From that day on I just stayed at home. I didn't leave Sirte again, I never left my house. I saw what was happening on the television, twice."

"But you're the cousin of Muammar Gaddafi, and the person closest to him. You're the head of the Revolutionary Committees and certainly know that Gaddafi was facing a revolution which was developing in the principal cities in Libya."

"No, I didn't know anything. As far as I know there is no revolution in the cities of Libya. There are isolated battles, not a revolution. It's like a civil war, not a revolution. It's not the people against a government. And in the middle of this civil war there's NATO, interfering."

"And in your opinion the only solution was to respond to the protests with violence?"

"In a civil war there are various possible solutions. But because of NATO and the Western countries, which interfered in the conflict, we are increasingly divided. It's not clear to Libyans what's right and what's wrong. Once NATO interfered, it became difficult for the population to work out the best path to follow."

I argued that before the NATO intervention the Gaddafi regime was already cracking down on the protests, killing demonstrators in the streets of Benghazi and Tripoli. Ibrahim chose to fly in the face of the evidence.

"Until the NATO intervention, no one in the Gaddafi government killed people in the streets. Nobody killed anybody. Gaddafi hadn't ordered any protest to be put down before the NATO intervention. We have always been on the side of the Libyan people. Always."

I said again that this wasn't true and that in Benghazi there had been hundreds of deaths, weeks before the NATO intervention.

"They were invading military installations, barracks, arsenals, government buildings—everything—to attack the regime. They wanted to vandalize, loot, destroy, kill members of the government, eliminate the police and the security agents, so they could grab the weapons, taking control of Libya's arsenals. At that moment, we were on the side of the people. Because we defended ourselves. We believe this is a free country, with a free people, where any person can do as they wish. And we had to fight to keep things this way. We always held to the view that the people should have freedom. That's why we were on the side of the Libyan people, against these others—"

I wanted him to continue, but I sensed his argument was making the rebels around me increasingly agitated. So I interrupted:

"Aren't 'these others' the people of Libya?"

Ibrahim carried on regardless. "The situation became more complicated with the intervention of foreigners in Libyan affairs. When that happened, I shut myself at home and never went out again—"

Then a voice shouted out in Arabic. Ahmed came over and stopped the interview. I protested, as the interview was supposed to last 30 minutes and we'd only had 10. I complained to the commander, in English, but Sami didn't even bother to translate. As Ahmed led me to the door I could hear Ibrahim's voice in the background. I asked one of the rebels who was also going with me toward the door why I had been interrupted. He extended his right index finger, pressed it against his own temple, and then, moving his eyes in the direction of Ibrahim, pulled an imaginary trigger with his thumb. Shocked into silence, I let him escort me to the exit.

I returned to Misrata three more times over the following days, on each occasion asking the military authorities for another interview with Ibrahim. Each time the request was denied without any explanation. As an alternative I was promised an interview with Mansour Dhao, the security chief. He wasn't a priority for me but I accepted anyway. I was then told I would need to wait awhile, because Dhao was still recovering after having been tortured.

ON MY NEXT VISITS TO MISRATA I HAD A NEW FIXER, FAWZI TRESH, PREVIOUSLY A driver for Petrobras, the Brazilian state-owned oil company. He was serious, competent, and well-connected in the region of Suq al-Jum'ah, where he lived, and in the capital.

With Fawzi's help I tried to find the members of the Wazan katiba, the last pieces in the jigsaw that would hopefully reveal exactly what happened in the hunt for Gaddafi and in the final act of the revolution. I had a very useful contact in Ibrahim Ahmad Omar Ismail, one of the young insurgents in the katiba, whom the photographer Marcel Mettelsiefen had put me in touch with. Fawzi and I traveled to Misrata three times in an attempt to find a place to meet with the katiba, but on each occasion the promise of a meeting was followed by a late cancellation. In one of my phone conversations with Ibrahim, however, he revealed that he knew all the rebel fighters who had been in the battle at Jarf, including the one who had actually found Gaddafi in the culvert, his friend Siraj al-Abdallah al-Himali Zaede. Again we arranged a meeting, which Marcel and a reporter for *Der Spiegel* would also attend. Three days after the death of the dictator, it would be the first time I met Siraj face to face.

Siraj was one of four or five rebels from the Wazan katiba who drove up in a ZX Auto Grand Deluxe Hiland, a 4×4 vehicle that was a Chinese copy of the Japanese model. The front of the vehicle was badly damaged and had obviously been repainted by hand, in black, and adorned with the colors of the revolution. We were at a junction on one of the roads leading into Misrata. As soon as they arrived, Ibrahim pointed to Siraj and Mohamed Alwaib—the men who captured Muammar Gaddafi—with a certain reverence.

Although Siraj seemed shy, I immediately noticed he had an air of quiet determination. Eight months after joining the ranks of the rebels, the revolution was in his blood. Like the other young rebels who had participated in the final battles, he wore a green, beige, brown, and black camouflaged army uniform that looked quite new. Around his head was a black and white *kaffiyeh* similar to the one Yasser Arafat used to wear. His clothing struck me as a little strange and suggested something of a paradox: although its troops had been among the most loyal defenders of Gaddafi, the Libyan army had not lost its prestige. There seemed to be no particular animosity toward it among the Libyan opposition—perhaps because so many deserters from the army had fought on the side of the rebels.

Although Siraj greeted us politely, even a little deferentially, he was adamant that he couldn't give an interview. Nothing would change his mind—neither my indignation nor Fawzi's more conciliatory approach. I felt he was letting me down badly, until he explained that the commander of his katiba had ordered him not to speak to anyone. Despite the interest he might arouse among the international media, he was obliged to give his first interview to the local television station in Misrata. It was exasperating, but I understood that Siraj was a principled young man who loyally obeyed the orders he was given. He had grown up in the patriarchal culture of the Muslim world and had also internalized the hierarchy of the army, which was where he intended to pursue his career if he could combine it with studying at the university. "The most important thing for me is to continue studying. I don't need to join the army to help my country," he said. "We are all rebels, and at any moment when our country needs us, we'll be there."

This tall, slender post-adolescent, of somewhat fragile physical stature, wasn't a boy in search of celebrity; he would remain true to his word. He and his comrades would indeed grant me a long interview—the first he'd ever given, apart from the one with Misrata TV, of course. In fact, he would meet me not just once but on various occasions. The first time would be one month later.

"The whole of Libya can be proud that Gaddafi's dead. I feel proud to have participated in that moment, which was so important in the history of Libya," he later told me. "But I feel very, very sorry for my dead friends, and not just for them. I feel for all those who've died during this revolution."

CHAPTER 2

REBIRTH

Muammar Gaddafi's trademark eccentricity was on display as he took up position in one of the entrance halls of the Ouagadougou Conference Centre in Sirte. He was wearing large sunglasses and a flamboyant gold boubou—the wide-sleeved, flowing robe traditional in many black African countries. The occasion was the thirteenth summit of the African Union (AU), the date July 1, 2009. Tribal kings from the Ivory Coast, Senegal, Chad, Ghana, Burkina Faso, Uganda, Mali, and other countries came up to greet him one by one. Their deference was consistent with the newfound status of Libya's "Guide," who since August 2008 had boasted the additional title "King of Kings of Africa." It had been conferred upon him at a forum organized by his own regime in Benghazi, capital of Libya's eastern region of Cyrenaica, attended by more than 200 sultans, princes, sheikhs, and other leaders from throughout the African continent.

Gaddafi wanted to gather the tribal chiefs' support for his latest project: the unification of Africa. This grand ambition, seemingly reflected in his wardrobe choice, echoed the pan-African dream of the black activist Marcus Mosiah Garvey from a hundred years earlier, when the Organization of African Unity had been created. The idea of a federation of African nations—a United States of Africa with a single currency and passport, free of customs barriers—had been gaining traction since Gaddafi's election as president of the AU, a rotating position, at the Addis Ababa summit in February 2009. Controversially, the vote had taken place behind closed doors. And it wasn't just idealism pushing forward

Gaddafi's pan-African agenda: also playing a role were his "Samsonites," the suitcases full of cash that for many years he had been distributing to aspiring "revolutionaries" around the world, to tribal chiefs and heads of state, and to political candidates in Western countries who came to Tripoli in search of clandestine funding for their parties.

The tribal chiefs weren't the only visitors Gaddafi wanted to see at the Sirte summit in August 2009. He'd also invited political leaders from all around the world, but few of them turned up. The problem wasn't one of antipathy toward the Libyan colonel—indeed, his international standing had never been higher—but instead lay with one of the guests, Omar al-Bashir, the president of Sudan, who had been convicted in absentia by the International Criminal Court for his role in the Darfur conflict. Al-Bashir had been accused of ordering killings and rapes, of sponsoring ethnic cleansing, and of expelling around 1.5 million people of the Fur, Masalit, and Zaghawa ethnic groups. On top of that, he was also suspected of corruption. So the only leaders who accepted the invitation to Sirte were those who didn't particularly mind shaking hands and posing for photos with such an ignomious figure as al-Bashir. The biggest political name to attend was the president of Brazil, Luiz Inácio Lula da Silva, who a few months before had been warmly greeted as "my man" by US president Barack Obama at a G20 meeting in London. At the African Union summit, Lula celebrated the "advances" made in the previous six months in Brazil's trade relations with Africa and the Arab world.

Although it seemed likely he would be surrounded by dictators and other dubious figures—such as Iranian president Mahmoud Ahmadinejad, who in the end didn't turn up—Lula didn't seem concerned by the voices raised against his participation in the event: on the contrary, he said he was "grateful." I was waiting at the Corinthia hotel in Tripoli when he arrived there from the airport, informally dressed and in good humor. Later, when I asked him in an interview if he was uncomfortable about shaking the hands of so many dictators, he replied that he had accepted the invitation "without asking who else was coming," and added that every host had the right to invite whoever they wanted.

In reality, Lula's presence was a testament to Gaddafi's recently recovered international prestige. He was due to meet Gaddafi and his head of protocol, Nuri al-Mismari, a legendary figure who had been loyal to the regime for decades—but who would remain so only until October 2010—and was known to receive regular slaps to the face from

Gaddafi and to dish out the same treatment himself to government ministers. That day al-Mismari was wearing a 1960s-style navy blue suit with matching blue-tinted sunglasses, an outfit that certainly set him apart from the soberly dressed heads of state. As well as coordinating the arrivals of the foreign dignitaries, he dispensed orders to Gaddafi's famous "Amazons," women who, as later would become clear, were often recruited against their will and forced to become sex slaves for the tyrant and his accomplices—a fact that French journalist Annick Cojean deserves much of the credit for revealing. As the Brazilian journalists waited for Lula to arrive, al-Mismari approached some of us— including Marcelo Ninio of the *Folha de São Paulo* and myself—to offer an interview with Gaddafi, which would probably have taken place were it not for eventual logistical snags. Immediately after al-Mismari spoke to us, Lula appeared. He greeted Gaddafi and proceeded to the main hall where the AU summit would take place. The proof of his regard for Gaddafi came in the speech he delivered later, in which he referred to his host as "my friend, my brother, and leader." It was the first time I'd ever felt ashamed to be Brazilian.

The feeling was still with me a few hours later when we left the Sirte conference center for the airport. We waited for our plane in one of the Bedouin tents that Gaddafi was famously fond of. Lula's plane departed for Tripoli in the early afternoon; the journalists covering the trip would follow him in one of the other aircraft in the presidential fleet.

We had already taken our seats in the plane when the Brazilian pilot spotted among the passengers a man he didn't recognize. The Brazilian ambassador, Luciano Ozório Rosa, angrily demanded the unidentified man be expelled from the aircraft, suspecting, not unreasonably, that he was a Libyan secret service agent who had infiltrated the Brazilian delegation and was thereby disrespecting a space—the interior of the aircraft—in which Brazil's sovereignty should be guaranteed. Indeed, Libya was a country where the omnipresence of Gaddafi's security apparatus was noticeable almost all the time, from the identity checks and searches at Tripoli's international airport to the agents who kept an eye on the foreign journalists as we left our hotel for a stroll around the historic center of the capital. Ninio, Alexandre Malmegrin Rocha, the editor of the Brazil-Arab news agency, and I thought we had been able to escape the surveillance for a few hours during a trip to the city of Khoms to see the archaeological site of Leptis Magna, but even there we couldn't be sure. Evade, escape, or rise up: those were the only ways to taste freedom in Gaddafi's country.

Nevertheless, this was a time when words of praise for the dictator were emanating from various parts of the world. His reemergence into the international community, after almost two decades of Libyan isolation, had got underway in the late 1990s. Throughout that decade the Colonel had been building a close relationship with a towering figure among world leaders and a human rights icon: South African president Nelson Mandela. They were photographed together hand in hand, a clear symbol of friendship, during an official visit by Mandela to Libya in 1998. At the time Mandela was helping negotiate an agreement with the British government, headed by Tony Blair of the Labour Party, through which Tripoli would hand over two men suspected of having planted the bomb that brought down a Pan Am Boeing 747 over the Scottish town of Lockerbie on December 21, 1988, killing 270 people. The negotiations were aimed at ending the United Nations sanctions that had been imposed on Libya as punishment for supposed acts of state terrorism.

In 2001 the two suspects, Lamin Khalifa Fhimah and Abdelbaset Ali Mohmed al-Megrahi, were tried at Camp Zeist in the Netherlands under the jurisdiction of three Scottish magistrates. With various controversies still hanging over the case, Fhimah was set free and returned to Libya, but al-Megrahi was found guilty and sentenced to life imprisonment. He would complete his sentence on August 20, 2009, however, when the Scottish government released him on grounds of clemency; he was said to be suffering from advanced-stage prostate cancer.

Libya's atonement continued in 2003, when the Gaddafi regime agreed to pay US$2.7 billion in compensation to the families of the victims of the Lockerbie bombing, even though it continued to deny any involvement in the crime. Libya also took a clear step toward the United States in aligning itself with the "War on Terror" in the period following September 11. This actually fitted Gaddafi quite well, as he had been facing resistance from the Libyan Islamic Fighting Group since the mid-'90s, and in 1998 had himself called for an international arrest warrant for Osama bin Laden.

Over the years the cooperation between Libya's intelligence services and their US and British counterparts—the CIA and MI6, respectively— became increasingly close, as would be shown by diplomatic and intelligence documents that came to light during the Libyan revolution. After 9/11, Gaddafi's "collaboration"—which didn't preclude the occasional verbal attack on Washington—consisted partly of dirty work, such as providing a landing base for CIA rendition flights carrying terrorism suspects wanted in the United States, who were tortured with the connivance of Western governments. In 2004, Libyan secret service participation in the War on Terror received Western recognition when the US government of George W. Bush took Libya off its list of terrorist nations. Also, during the 2000s the Libyan regime would release more than 700 detainees accused of being involved with radical Islamic groups—a common technique employed by Gaddafi's regime to keep their enemies behind bars—a step seen as a significant indication of greater political openness.

In December 2003, after four years of disarmament proposals that ended up never being carried out, Gaddafi finally put an end to Libya's development of weapons of mass destruction, vowing to comply with the Nuclear Non-Proliferation Treaty. Inspections later conducted under the Chemical Weapons Convention revealed that Libya possessed stocks of lethal weapons such as mustard gas.

Gaddafi's words when he allowed inspectors to enter the country were that "Libya, from now on, will be at the forefront of the group of countries working to rid the world of weapons of mass destruction." It was a strategic move that would reopen the doors of the West to Libya, while setting Gaddafi apart from another dictator, Saddam Hussein, who had been deposed and would ultimately be killed during the American invasion of Iraq.

The cooperation bore fruit in 2004 when Gaddafi was allowed to travel to Brussels in his first official visit outside Africa or the Middle East since 1989. That same year, British prime minister Tony Blair became the first major Western leader to make an official trip to Tripoli. He went there on two further occasions after leaving office, in 2008 and 2009, both times traveling on a private plane provided by Gaddafi. French president Nicolas Sarkozy traveled to Tripoli in 2007 following the release of five Bulgarian nurses and a doctor of Palestinian origin who had been detained in the country since 1999 on suspicion of carrying out transfusions with HIV-infected blood, and thereby infecting 393 children at the al-Fateh hospital in Benghazi.

In December 2007 Paris rolled out the red carpet for Gaddafi as Sarkozy welcomed him on an official state visit. It lasted five days, three of which were filled with official commitments; I covered it in my capacity as Paris correspondent. The French government struggled to explain to the public why the dictator was allowed to erect his humble Bedouin tent in the gardens of the Hôtel de Marigny, a residence belonging to the French government, while crisscrossing the capital in an ostentatious white limousine. A further cause for consternation was the number of French corporate giants—including Areva, Suez, Thales, Total, Gaz de France, Dassault, Vinci, and EADS—queuing up to do business with him. All became clear, however, with the news of the contracts Sarkozy and Gaddafi had signed—including the sale of 21 Airbuses and 14 Rafale jet fighters, along with 2 billion euros worth of nuclear cooperation agreements whereby Libya would be provided with reactors to desalinate sea water.

It was ironic that while French government spokesperson David Martinon was declaring that Gaddafi's visit marked "a significant step in Libya's return to the bosom of the international community," some French politicians, such as Foreign Minister Bernard Kouchner, were doing all they could to avoid meeting him.

Gaddafi also had meetings with Russian president Vladimir Putin; Italian prime minister Silvio Berlusconi, whose hand he kissed in March 2010 during an Arab League summit; Spanish prime minister José Luis Rodríguez Zapatero; and US secretary of state Condoleezza Rice. The apex of his international trajectory was in 2009 when he was invited to the G8 summit in L'Aquila, Italy, where he was photographed next to world leaders including president Barack Obama. In September that year, a month after receiving Lula in Sirte, Gaddafi addressed the UN General Assembly in New York for the first time during his 40-year rule. He spoke for an hour and 40 minutes.

Around the same time, a new face was emerging as a representative of the regime, both inside Libya and abroad: Saif al-Islam Gaddafi, the dictator's son, reputed to be the driving force behind the opening up of Libya's economy to foreign companies, especially in the petroleum sector, and behind the supposed reduction in clientism. A graduate in architecture from al-Fateh University in Tripoli, and in economics and administration from Vienna International Business School, he would become known in Libya as "the engineer." Abroad, Saif became very close to the extreme right-wing Austrian politician Jörg Haider, whose campaigns Saif financed. In 2008 he completed a doctorate at the London School of Economics, but not before coming into conflict with certain members of staff and submitting a dissertation that raised doubts as to how much of it was his own work. Nevertheless, he represented Libya's aspirations toward modernization and the potential for gradual liberalization on the part of the regime. He cut a different figure from his brother Mutassim, also a potential successor to the Colonel, who was known in Libya as a hard-edged military commander and less identified with reform.

THE INTENSE EUROPEAN INTEREST IN LIBYA IN THE FIRST DECADE OF THE TWENTY-first century was not unprecedented, although it wasn't until the end of the nineteenth century that the areas known today as Tripolitania, Cyrenaica, and Fezzan—the three provinces that make up modern Libya—began to be coveted by a modern European nation, despite the rich ancient history crystallized in the Greek, Roman, and Byzantine ruins of Leptis, Magna, Sabratha, Cyrene, and Apollonia. The previous lack of interest on the part of imperial powers can be explained partly by the fact that only 1 percent of the territory was arable land. This inhospitable region had a population of only a few hundred thousand; the majority were Arabs and Berbers, but there were also Jews, Christians, blacks, Tuaregs, and other minorities.

In the nineteenth century, as today, European interest in the region derived partly from the opportunity to sell weapons. It was a connection first established between Italy and the Sanusiyya brotherhood, a religious movement founded in 1837 by Sayyid Muhammad ibn Ali al-Sanusi and which based itself in Kufra in the region of Cyrene, not far from the border with Egypt. The brotherhood did much to create the first governmental structure in the region, levying taxes, creating the basis of a system of justice for the resolution of intertribal disputes, and organizing the first army, which was equipped by Italy. From 1881 onward, however, Italy displayed greater ambitions, particularly after France took control of Tunisia. The result was Italy's military invasion of Libya and its occupation of cities such as Tripoli, Benghazi, Darna, Homs, and Tobruk.

It was in Cyrenaica, which had attained a certain degree of autonomy before the Italian invasion, that the first organized resistance to foreign domination would develop—a nonviolent cultural and religious movement that gained in size and strength when Italy entered the First World War and reduced its presence in the region. In 1918 Tripolitania, which after three and a half centuries of Ottoman domination passed into Italian hands at the end of the Italo-Turkish war, declared independence and established a republican constitution that, although short-lived, was the first in the history of the Arab world. Cyrenaica meanwhile regained some of its autonomy through a guerrilla movement led by the resistance hero Omar al-Mukhtar, a member of the Sanusiyya brotherhood who launched a holy war—jihad—against the Italian occupiers. When Mussolini came to power in 1922, Italy forcibly retook control over all three Libyan territories, pursuing and capturing al-Mukhtar. He was hanged in a square in Suluq on September 16, 1931, in front of a crowd of 20,000.

Italy's domination lasted until 1943, when its forces were pushed out by the British during the Second World War. Mussolini had introduced modern infrastructure, including roads and public services, but otherwise he left a bleak legacy: the complete social exclusion of all indigenous peoples and a death toll of between 250,000 and 300,000—around a third of the population of the three territories.

Under British protection the Emirate of Cyrenaica was formed, combining the territories of Tripolitania and Cyrenaica. The legitimacy of the country was recognized by the United Nations in a resolution dated November 21, 1949, and came into force on December 24, 1951, when Libya gained independence from Britain. Libya has been described by the political scientist Dirk Vandewalle, author of the excellent *A History of Modern Libya*, as "an accidental state," partly because it did not come into being as a result of genuinely nationalist sentiment. In Benghazi, Sayyid Idris al-Senusi, grandson of the founder of the Sanusiyya brotherhood and the first leader of the Emirate of Cyrenaica, was proclaimed King Idris of the United Kingdom of Libya, a parliamentary monarchy presiding over a population that was 94 percent illiterate, had an annual per capita income of about US$25, and above all possessed no real spirit of national unity.

Idris set up a federal state consisting of three regions—Tripolitania, Cyrenaica, and Fezzan—that were so autonomous a visa was needed in order to travel from one to another. He exercised power with discretion, without a cult of personality or any great inclination to get involved in political disputes. But he also lacked the ability to deal with parliamentary insubordination and corruption or to get any of his prime ministers—there were eleven in eighteen years—to build an organized state structure.

It was during Idris's reign that the American company Esso confirmed the existence of oil on Libyan territory. There was feverish interest from multinational companies, and no fewer than 84 exploration concessions were granted. By 1968, 2.6 million barrels per day were being produced. But the backdrop to the oil frenzy remained one of extreme poverty, and the Arab nationalist message proclaimed by Gamal Abdel Nasser in Egypt began to stir Libyan spirits.

In 1963 the monarchy did away with the federal structure, took the word "United" out of the country's name, and created the Kingdom of Libya, which immediately provoked dissatisfaction in Cyrenaica. Four years later there were anti-American demonstrations in Tripoli and Benghazi; among the protesters were workers in the petroleum industry, responsible for 99 percent of the country's export earnings.

King Idris was weakened by the suspicions of corruption that swirled around his government, cases of nepotism, and mismanagement of the country's natural resources. In 1969 he was deposed in a bloodless coup d'état, having been abandoned by the units of the armed forces based in Tripoli and Benghazi. As if the domestic problems weren't enough, the monarchy had also been undermined by the upsurge in Pan-Arabism across North Africa and the Middle East in the wake of the Six Day War, two years earlier, which had pitted Egypt, Jordan, and Syria against Israel.

A group of young army captains and majors took power, forming the Revolutionary Command Council (RCC). Among them was a 27-year-old captain nobody had heard of: Muammar Gaddafi. A man of few words, he came across as a slightly mysterious figure; as he gained in popularity he became known as "The Handsome One." A military leader of populist, nationalist, and revolutionary verve, he came from a Bedouin family and had been born in a small village, Qasar Abu Hadi, on the outskirts of Sirte. He took his name from that of his tribe, the Gaddafa, which was part of the Ghous clan. His arrival in power signified the ascension of a tribe not traditionally seen as prestigious, and thereby symbolized a break with the old elite. It also aligned Libya with Nasser's Arab nationalist discourse, which had made a major impact in Tripoli but was less readily received in Benghazi. Gaddafi was well aware of this as he took position alongside Nasser and other regional leaders, raising the pressure on the US and British militaries to abandon their bases in Libya. When Nasser died in 1970, the "Colonel," as Gaddafi came to be known, saw himself as his political heir and took over the role of champion of Pan-Arabism.

While for purposes of foreign policy Gaddafi became the most recognizable face of post-monarchy Libya, internally the first years of rule would be marked by a degree of power-sharing with his military colleagues. Among the members of the military junta, figures such as Abu Bakr Yunis Jaber—who would remain loyal to the very end—and the other members of the RCC were given posts in the ministries of the "revolutionary government." Together, they took control of the country.

From 1971, a section of Libyan civil society and of the nonmilitary bureaucracy joined together to form a political party, the Arab Socialist Union, which represented a counterweight to the RCC. But it didn't last long. On April 16, 1973, Gaddafi took an important step to remove the doubts raised by the antagonism between the two bodies. In the city of Zuwara he made a speech in which he launched a "popular revolution," declaring that parties and institutions operating as "intermediaries" should be suppressed. What this meant in practice was increased repression of opposition groups and the beginning of a "cultural revolution" that suspended the Libyan constitution and promoted the arming of civilians. These measures made it possible to imprison opponents and ban organizations considered hostile to the regime and the revolution.

In his second wave of *zahf*, or reforms, Gaddafi announced the creation of 2,400 Popular Committees, subject to approval by the RCC. These local bodies functioned as tentacles of the regime to facilitate the oppression of dissident voices while also accelerating the breakdown of institutions; the country plunged into administrative chaos. Oblivious to the negative impact of the changes, the Colonel strove to demonstrate to the population and to the international community that his rise to power was not a *inqilab*, or coup, but a *thawra*, or revolution. He announced significant economic measures, such as land confiscation and redistribution, and also wider cultural changes, such as the prohibition of alcohol, closure of nightclubs, conversion of Catholic churches into mosques, and application of Islamic principles to the penal code.

Although economically Libya remained almost entirely dependent on exports from the oil sector, which employed a mere 1 percent of the country's workforce, the changes introduced by Gaddafi had a profound impact. Drastic measures were implemented, including the abolition of private property. The regime benefited from increased royalties and taxes on oil production, not to mention the fourfold increase in the price of oil during the 1970s due to measures taken by the Organization of the Petroleum Exporting Countries (OPEC) in 1973 and 1978, in response to the Yom Kippur War fought by Egypt and Syria against Israel.

In this period, helped by the favorable economic context, Gaddafi set about consolidating his political project, launching the first part of the "Green Book," his equivalent of Mao Tse-tung's infamous Little Red Book. An extraordinary mixture of dubious political science, retrograde morality, and messianism, the Green Book included the "solution to the problem of democracy" and a "political basis for the Third Universal Theory," whatever that was supposed to mean. The core political message was that power should be given directly to the people through the elimination of political representatives. Parliamentary assemblies, Gaddafi said, usurped the power of the people, while political parties were "the machinery of government used by contemporary dictatorship." He purported to offer "the definitive solution to the problem of the machinery of government," and to "show the peoples the way to pass from the era of dictatorship to one of true democracy."

More than an exercise in pseudo-intellectualism, however, the book laid the foundations for the tyrannical rule that would continue for decades. It spoke of "Popular Congresses" and "Popular Committees" while providing a basis for the abolition of the constitution, the adoption of tradition and religion as the country's laws, and the censorship of any attempt at independent journalism.

The second part of the book, "The Solution to the Economic Problem," preached the adoption of a form of socialism and the prohibition of terms such as "wages," "workers," and "employees," without detailing any accompanying changes that might take place in the real world. "The Green Book not only solves the problem of material production but also prescribes a complete solution for all problems in human society," Gaddafi claimed.

In its third and final part, devoted to the "social basis of the Third Universal Theory," the book offered moral guidance to the family, the tribe, and the nation. It observed that "both the man and the woman are human beings" and expressed the conviction that menstruation was an innate trait that conferred different existential functions on the two genders. "The woman is the homemaker, because this is an appropriate and necessary role for the woman who menstruates and takes care of the children," opined the Colonel, who also insisted on monogamy and prohibited forced marriages. By dictating the norms of social behavior without regard for established Islamic customs, Gaddafi opened a gap between Libyans' public and private behavior. In the latter realm, regardless of the wishes of dictator, many traditional principles continued to apply.

THE SO-CALLED CONCEPTS CONTAINED IN THE GREEN BOOK WOULD BE PUT INTO practice after the speech at Zuwara. However, even before most of them came into force in everyday life, political and social dissatisfaction with the regime revealed the existence of an active opposition. Looking back, it is not difficult to identify when the spell was broken and the split between Gaddafi and his people began to form.

The moment arrived as early as 1973, just four years after the coup that overthrew King Idris. It was in Libya's universities that the first signs of popular resistance emerged. The catalyst was an arbitrary yet, at first sight, hardly earth-shattering decision taken by the regime: the introduction of compulsory military service for students, due to start the following year. Some students in Tripoli and Benghazi demonstrated against the measure, and were promptly arrested. Gaddafi then banned the National Union of Students. In 1975, however, the organization resurfaced, voicing students' continuing anger. In Benghazi a young man named Mustafa Mohamed Ben Nasser was elected president of the regional section of the union. In response to the protests the government modified the law, reducing the number of hours of compulsory service, but refused a request from the student commission to be granted an audience in Tripoli.

Ben Nasser recalled what happened when I met him in Misrata, 36 years on. "So we decided to protest against the law on 22 February 1975. We went out into the streets to hold a silent demonstration. After that, we didn't protest only about the law [introducing military service]. We also started to ask for greater freedom of expression."

In March 1976, when a new intake of students was supposed to begin military service, many of them didn't show up. The regime labeled them "military deserters" and set up two special courts to try members of the student union. Ben Nasser was arrested in Misrata and taken to Tripoli. There he had his first encounter with Gaddafi, who demanded he obey the law. Ben Nasser said no.

The Colonel's next words, as far as Ben Nasser could remember, were: "I can deal with you like [General] Francisco Franco did—he killed students and no one said a thing. My pistol's in my belt, I'm still a revolutionary, and I can get rid of the lot of you."

The student uprising, and the threats made by the regime in response, caused a fracture in Libyan society. Segments of the armed forces supported the students, as did many Libyans overseas, who quickly began to protest against Gaddafi in their countries of residence. Three and a half weeks later, Gaddafi responded to the pressure by freeing all the students who had been imprisoned in Tripoli and Benghazi, hoping he could smooth over the whole episode. The seeds of instability, however, had already been sown.

In July 1976, exchanges of gunfire around the capital led to rumors of a coup against the RCC. In August, Bashir Hauadi and Umar al-Muhayshi, two members of the original military junta, made the first significant attempt to depose Gaddafi—and failed. Gaddafi expelled all the individuals he suspected of turning against him, leaving the RCC with only five members. The regime cracked down further on dissidents and "traitors," increasing the powers of military loyalists over civil society. Simultaneously, however, it made overtures toward the students, calling them to a meeting at the Bab al-Azizia military compound in Tripoli. The strategy didn't work out as the regime expected. The winners of the next elections for seats on the student union, held in November, were won by opponents of the regime. Among them was Ben Nasser, now just one step away from becoming head of the union. Gaddafi refused to recognize the results and called for a new election. The voting took place in December 1975 and in January 1976; soldiers took the ballot boxes to the polling stations and were confronted by angry students. On January 4, pro-Gaddafi students, who had infiltrated the student movement and been provided with weapons, entered the scene; on the Benghazi University campus opposing groups exchanged gunfire. One of the Gaddafi loyalists who fired shots that day was a young humanities student, Ahmed Ibrahim, whom I would interview 35 years later when he was in prison.

The tumult quickly spread beyond the university campus. Opposition students who had fled from the shooting congregated in the center of Benghazi, where they received support from the local population. There was similar unrest in Tripoli, and soon the events also had repercussions overseas as Libya's embassies in the United States, United Kingdom, West Germany, and Egypt were invaded by Libyan students determined to express their opposition to the regime.

Demonstrations were held on three consecutive days, and on each occasion soldiers used live ammunition against the protesters, leaving a significant number of dead and wounded. The crisis continued until January 13, when the government, faced with a gathering wave of opposition, decided to recognize the results of the student elections and, again, freed the students who had been imprisoned. The student movement quickly grew in size and influence, took advantage of Gaddafi's momentary weakness—to maintain his absolute power Gaddafi had to arrest more than 300 military personnel who had joined the opposition—and released a list of social and political grievances, demanding greater openness and freedom. The uprising lasted for three months. On April 6 the

regime used force to regain the ground it had lost to the protesters: soldiers invaded the university campuses in Tripoli and Benghazi, shooting
as they went. The next day, Gaddafi visited Benghazi University, but the
students there left the campus in protest. It was then that the regime
started to use terror tactics, arresting the relatives of the principal student activists. Two of Ben Nasser's brothers were detained; to get them
released he had to give himself up.

"And then I suffered the worst torture sessions I've ever experienced,"
he told me, without going into details.

The regime began to carry out torture and executions of student
activists on a large scale, under the pretext that the universities provided
bases for outlawed political parties. The government wanted to depict
student leaders as part of an alleged plot against the regime, a crime
that would obviously carry severe penalties. On April 7, eight students
were killed: it was a day that plunged the country into a state of shock
and passed into history as a significant date both for the regime and the
opposition.

Deaf to the growing opposition, Gaddafi gave the order for all university campuses to be retaken by force and for dissidents to be imprisoned. New student leaders were to be chosen. As for the previous leaders,
Gaddafi wanted them hanged. When Ben Nasser had been in prison for
two weeks and tortured on a daily basis, he received a visit from Ahmed
Ibrahim, who tried to persuade him to abandon his cause given that the
government intended to present the student uprisings as a new coup
attempt, which implied that the main figures involved would be sentenced to death.

The 300 military personnel who had sided with the students were
tried a year later, on April 2, 1977; 21 were sentenced to death by firing
squad. On April 7, five civilians, including three students, were also convicted: two of the students were hanged on their university campus. That
same day Ben Nasser received a five-year prison sentence, to be served in
Tripoli Central Prison.

Gaddafi decreed that henceforth April 7 would be "Student Liberation
Day." It would be marked by public celebrations—and also by more executions on university campuses, as in 1984 and 1985.

That same year, 1977, Gaddafi renamed his country for the third
time since the coup. There had already been the Libyan Arab Republic
(1969–1973) and the Union of Arab Republics (1973–1977); now he
launched the al-Jamahiriyya al-Arabiyya al-Libiyya al-Cha'biyya al-
Ichtirakiyya, or Great Socialist People's Libyan Arab Jamahiriya.

While the term *Jamahiriya*—state of the masses—paid lip service to people's power, in reality the regime moved in the opposite direction. New institutions supposedly created to convey the wishes of the population served instead to consolidate the absolute power exercised by the Colonel. He finally extinguished the junta, replacing it with *sha'biyat* (local revolutionary committees) and the People's Congress, a kind of parliament that would appoint a secretariat composed of executives with roles equivalent to those of ministers and a prime minister. Gaddafi would supposedly withdraw from public office and become the "guide of the revolution," a role transcending any notion of hierarchy or indeed of term of office. He therefore extended and consolidated his autocratic powers, sharing them with his five remaining military allies from the 1969 coup.

In 1978, alongside the repression and the political changes, the dictator launched a series of populist economic reforms bearing slogans such as *al-beiti li sakinihi* (the home belongs to whoever lives there), which entailed the expropriation of real estate and a new law that made home loans available to the population on generous terms. The expropriations continued with the confiscation of factories and land, while agriculture was boosted by subsidies and an ambitious irrigation scheme, the Great Man-Made River (total cost US$27 billion, according to Dirk Vandewalle), which succeeded in expanding the area of arable land, an achievement that would have been impossible without the oil money flowing into the regime's coffers.

Although by now the regime had managed to suffocate the student rebellion, the loss of support from certain sections of civil society would have permanent repercussions. Discontent was exacerbated by rampant repression, with the rule of law entirely discarded. Ben Nasser, for example, was not released at the end of his five-year sentence in 1984, but was instead transferred to the infamous Abu Salim prison. "The leader has ordered that you should stay here," they told him. "You're like a blanket—we'll keep you as long as we want, then we'll throw you out."

The former student leader would stay behind bars indefinitely, without the right to receive visits. Outside the prison walls the instruments of oppression were ubiquitous. Foremost among them were the local revolutionary committees—led mostly by "students" loyal to the regime, such as Ahmed Ibrahim—which acted as paramilitaries and paid informers, constituting a nationwide spy network. Also playing important roles were the Central Coordinating Office for Revolutionary Committees, directly subordinate to Gaddafi and based at his Bab al-Azizia stronghold; the *Mahkama Thawaria* (revolutionary courts), which operated according to "revolutionary laws"; the state media, whose mission was to defend the revolution and help eliminate its enemies; and the intelligence agencies, responsible for pursuing and assassinating opponents of the regime, and their relatives, both inside Libya and abroad. In 1988 the apparatus of state repression employed no fewer than 85,000 people, in a country whose population at the time was 4.1 million.

The intelligence services included the Maktab Ma'lumat al'qa'id (intelligence office of the leader), set up with the assistance of the *Stasi*, the state security ministry in the former East Germany; and the al-Mathaba al-Alamia (World Centre for the Struggle against Imperialism, Racism and Fascism), whose function was to hunt down "traitors" at home and abroad. Among the numerous other security agencies were the cabinet of Abdullah al-Senussi, the revolutionary guard, the popular guard, the purification committees, and all sorts of paramilitary groups that infiltrated tribes, clans, and families. And then there were the armed forces, which existed not to defend the state, as they did for example in Egypt, but to protect Gaddafi's regime. These multiple strands formed a web of repression that imposed the law of the land: that of silence.

The terrorism practiced by the regime would become visible to the outside world in the late 1970s and early '80s in the context of the Cold War, which placed Libya in opposition to the United States, kept it in a permanent state of tension with Israel, and also caused friction with neighboring Chad, a country protected by France. In each case the Libyan regime's message of Pan-Arabism was one of the factors stoking up animosity.

Upon entering the White House in 1981, Ronald Reagan labeled Gaddafi a "mad dog," accusing him of developing chemical weapons and of supplying arms and explosives to terrorist movements in Europe such as the Irish Republican Army, ETA in Spain, and the Red Brigades in Italy. Reagan also accused Gaddafi of interfering in the peace process in the Middle East by giving political support, money, and arms to jihadi groups and to the Marxist-Leninist-inspired Popular Front for the Liberation of Palestine. The regime didn't wholly deny that it was subsidizing "revolutionary" movements abroad; indeed, Gaddafi made use of his dubious status to depict himself as a leader of the "resistance" to the United States, a posture that in turn made it easier for the West to demonize Libya.

The following years saw not only mounting conflict in the diplomatic sphere, including the closure of Libyan embassies, but also US
planes shooting down Libyan fighter jets over the Gulf of Sirte, suspected
Libyan involvement in terrorist attacks at airports in Italy and Austria,
and then a bomb explosion at the La Belle nightclub in West Berlin on
April 5, 1986, which left three people dead and 229 wounded, including US soldiers. On April 15, 1986, after seeing diplomatic dispatches
from the Libyan embassy in East Berlin that indicated Gaddafi's direct
involvement in the attack—although the Colonel denied it—the Reagan
administration launched Operation El Dorado Canyon, a bombing raid
by US aircraft on Tripoli and Benghazi. Some commentators were critical of the US response, arguing that it took place without UN authorization and that there wasn't enough evidence to consider the nightclub
bombing an act of aggression by Libya.

I was 9 years old at the time of Operation El Dorado Canyon and can
remember it vividly. I was sitting next to my mother on a brown leather
sofa in front of the TV in our apartment in Porto Alegre when suddenly
there was a newsflash with a deep, serious voice announcing what sounded
like a US declaration of war. I had no idea where the conflict might lead,
or if it might endanger our lives in southern Brazil. Only one thing was
clear to me: Gaddafi, the leader of a distant land, was public enemy number one—the Osama bin Laden of the 1980s.

The consequences of the US bombing raid—in which, according to
the regime, the dead included Gaddafi's adopted baby daughter, Hana—
proved to be far-reaching. In December 1988 a bomb brought down Pan
Am Flight 103, a Boeing 747 flying from London to New York, over
the Scottish town of Lockerbie. In September 1989 another explosion
destroyed a DC-10 belonging to the French airline UTA, en route to Paris
from Brazzaville, Congo, over the Ténéré desert in Niger; the crash killed
170. International investigations suggested Gaddafi had given the order
for both bombings and that his secret services had carried them out.

The US attacks on Tripoli and Benghazi—and Libya's defeat in a
conflict in Chad, where French and US forces were involved—left cracks
in the regime. Gaddafi responded with a policy of greater openness and
released some political prisoners. Ben Nasser was one of the beneficiaries:
he finally left prison in 1988, seven years after the end of his sentence.
Gaddafi also ordered the destruction of thousands of intelligence files on
alleged dissidents and the demolition of the Ras Jdir border post on the
Tunisian border. The latter gesture was meant to indicate Libya's people
were free to come and go as they pleased.

The Colonel reached out to the Libyan diaspora, in whose ranks a new opposition leadership had emerged, through a program of "forgiveness" that offered them amnesty and jobs back home. In May 1988 he made a speech calling for an end to injustices such as arbitrary laws and imprisonments, as if he weren't actually the person responsible for them in the first place. A month later he published a new text, *The Great Green Charter of Human Rights of the Jamahiriyan Era*, in which he revoked previous policies, including the abolition of private property, and introduced new principles such as—supposedly—the independence of the judiciary.

The overall picture, however, was still one of ferocious repression. Although the military, the diplomatic service, and the massed ranks of government employees were loyal for reasons of self-interest, a new opposition movement began to emerge out of the shadows in Tripoli and Benghazi, and in smaller cities where there were tribes hostile to the government. Voices of dissent broke the silence. Graffiti appeared on walls in Tripoli, challenging Gaddafi's authority. In Cyrenaica the 1990s saw Islamic uprisings, some of them led by the Libyan Islamic Fighting Group (al-Jama'a al-Islamiah Muqatilah bi-Libya). One of its leaders was a graduate in civil engineering from al-Fateh University, Abdelhakim Belhadj, a veteran of the war in Afghanistan against the Soviets during the previous decade. Members of the group would be among 1,200 prisoners killed in a massacre at Abu Salim prison in Tripoli in 1996—an atrocity that showed the regime had lost none of its sadism.

By the end of the 1990s, economic instability and incessant state violence, added to the fact that the discourse of Pan-Arabism had run out of steam, meant there was no longer any semblance of mass support for Gaddafi. And yet according to the Colonel's continuing rhetoric, the masses were supposed to be at the heart of his revolution. Fearful of the Islamist presence in Libya, the West now tended to turn a blind eye to Gaddafi's regime, whose terrorist activities abroad had in any case diminished.

In its 42 years of existence the government of Muammar Gaddafi played a geopolitical role far more important than the small population and desert landscape of Libya might suggest. But in the domestic sphere, dissatisfaction spread inexorably after the beginning of the student revolts, taking root among the middle class. The first to aspire to greater freedom and to resist the omnipresence of the dictatorship, the students of the 1970s became Libya's intellectuals over the course of the decades.

The opposition in exile—represented initially by Abdalhamid al-Bakush, who had been prime minister under King Idris, and by the army officers who fled after the failed 1975 coup—more or less succeeded in retaining its legitimacy in the eyes of the Libyan people and the international community and continued to give hope to opponents of the regime within the country. In 1985 Hassan Ichkal, from the same tribe as Gaddafi, led a brief uprising before he was assassinated. In October 1993 there was a clash in Bani Walid; the regime said it was the result of a plot involving various figures in the armed forces, which resulted in many suspects being imprisoned in the cities of Gharian, Kufra, and Zawara. From 1992 onward, however, the opposition grew both inside Libya and abroad. Among its different political forces were the monarchists of the Libyan Constitutional Union, led by Mohamed al-Hassan al-Ridha as Sanoussi, which proposed a return to Libya's 1951 constitution.

The most important opposition movements, however, were republican and committed to the ideal of democracy. This was the case with the Libyan National Alliance (LNA), led by the nationalist Mansour al-Kikhiya, who had been part of the regime until 1980 but became a dissident after objecting to Gaddafi's continuous executions of opponents. Al-Kikhiya disappeared in December 1993 in Cairo, during a conference on human rights. Two other dissidents, Jaballah Matar and Izzat Youssef al-Maqrif, had vanished in the same city in March 1990. Al-Maqrif had been general secretary of another prodemocracy group based abroad, the National Front for the Salvation of Libya, which proposed the creation of a provisional government in exile ready to take power, and whose spokesperson was Mahmoud Jibril, who would later switch sides and work with the regime. The Front believed that when Gaddafi was ousted, Libya should be governed for a maximum of one year by a transitional council whose basic role would be to guarantee basic liberties and organize elections for a constituent assembly, followed by presidential elections. The Front liaised with secret opposition movements inside Libya, such as the Democratic Constitutional Alternative, and with other groups abroad, such as the Libyan League for Human Rights and the Libyan Amazigh Congress. These three movements merged in 2005, forming the National Conference of the Libyan Opposition.

When the revolutions took place in Tunisia and Egypt in early 2011, Gaddafi's regime backed the neighboring dictatorships. On January 15, 2011, the Arab News Agency revealed the content of a telephone conversation between Gaddafi and deposed Tunisian leader Zine al-Abidine Ben Ali, in which the Colonel took it upon himself to address the people of Tunisia: "Tunisia has been plunged into bloody chaos because its inhabitants hastily deposed their president. You have suffered a great loss. There is nobody better than him to govern."

Meanwhile Gaddafi was taking economic measures he hoped would help prevent a similar uprising in his own country, such as lowering customs duties on basic foodstuffs including milk. On January 24 the video-sharing website YouTube was blocked in Libya to prevent the dissemination of images of any protests that might take place, as had happened in Egypt and Tunisia. Three days later, US$27 billion was released for economic development and housing. On February 9, Gaddafi again questioned the legitimacy of the Arab revolutions, accusing the TV network Al Jazeera and the Israeli secret services of destabilizing the Arab world, although ironically the Israeli stance at the time was just the opposite.

It was inevitable that there would also be protests in Libya. They broke out on February 15, 2011, when veterans of the 1970s student protests, including Mustafa Mohamed Ben Nasser, took to the streets alongside the younger generation—first in cities in Cyrenaica such as Benghazi, El Beida, and Darna, and then all over the country. As in Tunisia, where the revolt began in the city of Sidi Bouzid after the self-immolation of a street vendor, Mohamed Bouazizi, whose goods had been confiscated, the revolution in Libya would also be triggered by one arbitrary act. The tipping point was the arrest in Benghazi of lawyer and human rights activist Fathi Terbil, 41, who represented the families of the victims of the 1996 Abu Salim prison massacre, in which Terbil had lost a brother and a cousin.

Terbil was well known to the security services, having been detained on seven previous occasions. Young people and adults who supported his cause went onto the streets to protest his arrest, precipitating the demonstrations that had already begun to be organized in opposition circles and through forums and social networks on the Internet. Terbil was released the next day, February 16, but the wheels had already been set in motion. Thousands of people clashed in the first night with security forces, which used water cannons and rubber bullets against protesters and were assisted by proregime militias. Rather than retreat, however, the Libyan people were determined to make a stand. Gaddafi responded with a declaration that merely confirmed he was deaf to their demands.

"Down with the enemies, down with them everywhere! Down with the puppets!" he said, reprising some of the old nationalist, anti-American, and anti-Zionist terminology. "The puppets are falling like autumn leaves."

But Gaddafi was mistaken. It wasn't autumn: it was the Arab Spring.

CHAPTER 3

SPRING

It was just after 3 p.m. on Tuesday, February 22, and I'd lost all hope of getting a visa to enter Libya. I'd already tried in Paris, with the assistance of the Brazilian embassy, but the Libyan embassy was closed and I didn't even receive a reply. Next I traveled to Tunis, where I arranged a meeting with the Brazilian ambassador; I asked him if he could use the diplomatic channels to request a fast-track visa from the Libyan embassy on my behalf.

That strategy had served me well in the past when covering presidential trips—for example my first visit to Tripoli, when the Brazilian embassy in Paris got me a Libyan visa in two hours rather than the usual two weeks. But this time luck wasn't on my side. I was told Libya's embassy in Tunis had been taken over by Libyan and Tunisian protesters. Although it was a positive indication of the scale of the uprising, it didn't do much for my travel plans. Nevertheless I took a taxi to the embassy, on Rue du 1er Juin in the city center, and saw as we approached that the rebel tricolor was flying from the flagpole outside, having already replaced the plain green flag of the Gaddafi era. Outside the building was a crowd in celebratory mood, shouting slogans calling for a "free Libya" and denouncing Gaddafi along with the recently deposed dictators in Tunisia and Egypt, Zine al-Abidine Ben Ali and Hosni Mubarak: "Gaddafi, coward, the Libyan people will not be humiliated!"

I realized I would be wasting my time in Tunis and needed to get to the border as quickly as possible, even without a visa. I asked some Tunisians who were watching the demonstration about the fastest way to Ben Gardane, the last town before the border post of Ras Jdir, where I knew foreign journalists were beginning to gather. They advised me to get a minibus taxi from Moncef Bey bus station. This, I discovered, was a huge place, choked with vehicles and people; there were droves of street hawkers, mostly selling contraband goods, and an extraordinary amount of rubbish, either packed into barrels awaiting collection or just strewn on the ground. There was a strong, unpleasant smell: a mixture of urine, rubbish, oil and exhaust fumes. As I went inside dozens of drivers pounced on me—many of whom, I was told, were specialists in unexpected detours and petty extortion, taking advantage of an absence of regulation and supervision. They shouted out their destinations as they rushed around in pursuit of passengers—Sousse, Monastir, Ksar Hellal, and finally the one that interested me: Ben Gardane.

"Come, we're leaving in a few minutes!" the driver said.

I bought a ticket for the equivalent of about 20 euros and waited beside the old minibus that would apparently make the seven-hour, 530-kilometer journey. An hour went by with no sign of imminent departure. The infernal jostling of motor vehicles continued on all sides; they seemed to be leaving for every corner of Tunisia except Ben Gardane. Then, suddenly, a paler face appeared: a tall young man wearing a cream Burberry jacket, Levi's jeans, and a Tag Heuer watch and carrying an expensive-looking leather bag—all in all an amusing contrast with the filthy surroundings. He asked me if I knew how to get to the resort of Djerba on the Tunisian coast.

"You're a journalist," I said, ignoring his question.

He nodded. "And you are too," he said.

I took down his contact details, which I noticed included a British phone number, although I didn't yet know his name, nationality, or whom he worked for. We both intended to enter Libya but had different border crossings in mind; we discussed the relative merits of Djerba and Ben Gardane, based on what we'd been told, and made a few calls to try to find the latest information. At 3:31 p.m. I received a text message confirming that Ben Gardane was the better option.

Such were the circumstances in which I got to know the Iraqi journalist Ghaith Abdul-Ahad, 35, the Beirut correspondent for British newspaper the *Guardian*, who had been sent to cover the developing situation in Tunisia and Libya. Our chance meeting led quickly to an instinctive mutual trust. I didn't yet know he was a rising star in British journalism, but his abilities would become obvious during the three weeks that followed, part of which would be spent together in western Libya. Seventeen days later I would be phoning various contacts and speaking with CNN, the BBC, *Le Monde*, and France 24 on behalf of a campaign running on the social networks, "#free4ghaith"—Freedom for Ghaith.

Born in 1975 in Baghdad, the son of an Iraqi father and a British Indian mother, Ghaith would strike me as a modern version of Pip, the main character in Charles Dickens' *Great Expectations*—not because he had received a fortune from a benefactor, but because in the space of a decade he had escaped the wreckage of his country and used his talents to achieve recognition in one of the world's great cities. An architecture student at the University of Baghdad, Ghaith had deserted from the army of Saddam Hussein. For six years he was obliged to live an underground existence in the Iraqi capital, moving from one residence to another whenever he suspected the authorities were closing in and he might be arrested. In 2001, with Saddam still in power, he started taking photographs on the streets of the city, documenting events such as the arrival of foreign tanks during the 2003 invasion. His discovery of photography came at the price of three separate prison sentences, however.

Only much later would I discover that in 2005 his work—published by the *New York Times*, *Washington Post*, *Los Angeles Times*, *Guardian*, and *Times* (London)—had won various prizes for human rights photography. In the 2008 British Press Awards he was voted foreign correspondent of the year for his work in dangerous parts of North Africa, the Middle East, and Asia—notably Afghanistan, where he was twice taken captive by the Taliban. In this period Ghaith began to concentrate on covering the insurgencies in Iraq, especially in battle-torn cities such as Fallujah and Najaf. For six years he had written articles for the *Guardian*, typically using a pen and paper before transferring his work to a computer. Although he was 29 before he left Iraq for the first time, or saw the sea with his own eyes, in the following few years his passport steadily filled up with visa stamps as he grew into a role that was a mixture of reporter and special correspondent. The problem with his latest visa, however, was that it was for Tunisia—not Libya. As we didn't have authorization from the Gaddafi regime, which didn't want media entering the country, he and I were both looking for a way to enter Libya illegally. Before we went our separate ways that afternoon, we exchanged the information our respective contacts had sent us about our possible next steps.

THE MINIBUS FINALLY COMMENCED THE EIGHT-HOUR JOURNEY THROUGH THE NIGHT to Ben Gardane, a small town of some 2,500 inhabitants founded by the

French in the nineteenth century. It wasn't on any tourist itinerary, but with its handful of basic hotels it did offer accommodation quite close to the Libyan border. It was an arid place with very few trees; the dusty streets were lined with old buildings whose residents gazed at Western visitors as if we had arrived from another planet. But the town had a vibrant economic life based around money-changing—either legal or black market—and the sale of "imported" goods including electronic products, new and secondhand clothing, car parts, cattle, sunglasses, and Senegalese sardines. The abundance of foreign products was explained by the proximity of the Ras Jdir border post, just 33 kilometers away.

Before that night was over I made my first visit to the border post to assess the prospects for crossing into Libya the next day. It obviously wasn't going to be easy: there were a lot of soldiers and border agents, and an empty space more than 100 meters wide separated the immigration officials from the border crossing itself. I went back again in the morning, hoping to talk to the Libyan refugees crossing the border and to find people who could help me make the crossing in the opposite direction. I felt confident that somehow, sooner or later, I would get across.

Journalists of many different nationalities had begun to arrive in the area. Our shared thinking was that if the revolution progressed quickly, as it had done in Tunisia and Egypt, the Gaddafi regime would soon lose control over the country's borders—then, surely, it would only take a few hours before we could enter the country and make the 200-kilometer journey to Tripoli. In fact, however, a greater number of journalists were heading for Libya's border with Egypt, in response to sketchy reports that the uprising was confined to the east of the country while the west remained under Gaddafi's control, as the regime itself was claiming. This alternative, eastern route went via Cairo and offered the possibility of traveling into parts of Libya that had already been liberated, as far as Benghazi. It offered journalists the prospect of talking to the Libyans who had initiated the uprising—a fantastic story—but the route came to an abrupt end after the town of Ajdabiya, still 860 kilometers from the capital, where troops loyal to Gaddafi had been strengthened by reinforcements.

It soon became obvious that crossing the border at Ras Jdir without a visa—and none of the journalists had one—would be impossible. That Wednesday night, already frustrated at being unable to cover the story, I also had to contend with the unexpected cold. The hotel room didn't have any heating and the one blanket provided was pitifully inadequate, so

I went to bed wearing every item of warm clothing I'd brought with me. I lay awake for hours, turning the possible options over in my mind.

As I left the hotel on Thursday I was determined that somehow I would get across the border that day. During the sleepless early hours of the morning I had pored over a road map of Libya. In southern Tunisia there was another border post at Dehiba, in the province of Tataouine, which was smaller and less likely to attract journalists. Nearby, on the Libyan side of the border, was the Berber town of Nalut, from where there was a road to the Mediterranean coast, near Zuwara, 120 kilometers from Tripoli. Heading for Dehiba would mean a 500-kilometer U-turn, though obviously it would be worth it if there was much less border security than at Ras Jdir. But what if security were just as tight at Dehiba? Another option, perhaps, was to try to cross the border through the desert. I drew a rudimentary map of the region in my notebook and decided there were three things I needed to do as quickly as possible: find out which roads in Tunisia—and, if possible, Libya—were the safest for a Western journalist to travel on; discover what the Dehiba border post consisted of, and whether there might be smugglers crossing the border illegally in the region; and finally, get hold of a fixer with a pickup truck who would be willing to drive me into Libya through the Sahara if necessary.

I started to get some answers shortly after leaving the hotel. To get to Dehiba I was told to use the P19 and C112 through the interior of Tunisia rather than the slightly shorter C203 that ran close to the Libyan border. As for the border post, the initial information was promising: it was closed, but apparently there were very few journalists in the region—and lots of smugglers. It seemed it might be possible to cross the border at Dehiba without a visa, counting on the tacit cooperation of both the Tunisian and Libyan authorities, and on permission from the rebels in Nalut, 60 kilometers inside Libya.

The third problem remained unsolved: the fixer and the pickup. At the hotel I bumped into two journalist friends, Marcelo Torres, a reporter with *SBT*, and Azul Serra, a camera operator, who had a translator with them. Both agreed with the idea of heading toward Dehiba and seeing what conditions on the road were like; what we lacked, however, was an appropriate vehicle. I sent a text message to Ghaith. "Do you want to check out the border post at Dehiba? Looks like there's a road to Zuwara from there. Zuwara, as you probably know, is in rebel hands."

Ghaith replied quickly: "Yes, very interested. Been looking into that option since yesterday but I don't know any smugglers. Would be great to try it."

We met a few minutes later. Ghaith was ready to go but hadn't managed to find the kind of vehicle we needed. In fact, all the "professional" fixers with pickup trucks had already been hired by the major TV networks that had journalists in the region. I talked to the reporter and camera operator from the French TV network France 24, who were sitting in the hotel lobby watching TV. At first they showed interest in the Dehiba idea, but not for long. "The truth is, we're at the wrong border. We should have gone in from Egypt," was the reporter's defeatist conclusion.

Marcelo and Azul negotiated with various drivers until they found one who was willing to make the trip for a reasonable price. But his vehicle was a van in a similar state to the one that had brought me from Tunis two days earlier. I hesitated, thinking we needed to find something better, but the other two were keen to leave as soon as possible. I found Ghaith on the street corner outside the hotel, talking to a man who was about 50 and looked, I thought, like another journalist. I told him we were about to head off, and he said he would also be leaving soon. We agreed to keep in touch.

THE 220-KILOMETER JOURNEY FROM BEN GARDANE AND DEHIBA PASSED WITHOUT incident. On the way we passed through the oasis of Tataouine—"water springs," in Berber—a historic city with a population of about 60,000. In the popular French saying, *aller à Tataouine* means to go somewhere very distant and remote; indeed, traveling through that region, referred to as the "gateway to the desert," we did feel we were getting ever closer to the Sahara, in all its immensity and raw beauty. Visible from the left of the vehicle were the Nefusa mountains in Libya; on the right were sandy plains punctuated by olive groves, an important resource for Tunisia. The view was completed by a vivid blue sky that became tinged with other colors as the sun began to sink toward the horizon. On all sides there was a fresh, dry wind, typical of the desert in winter; I guessed it was the Harmattan trade wind, but I wasn't sure. I was sure, however, that very soon I'd be bringing my time in Tunisia to a close.

When we arrived in Dehiba, in the late afternoon, we were greeted by the sight of long, chaotic queues of people and vehicles arriving from Libya. Representatives from humanitarian organizations were there too, trying to help the refugees.

The border post was surrounded by hills, which would obviously make a clandestine crossing more difficult, and yet Libya was tantalizingly close. Its green flag was easily visible; so too was a large portrait of Gaddafi, his gaze fixed on Tunisia. Looking at that image, I had two different feelings: the first was of déjà vu, of my first visit to Libya in 2009; the second was that now, unlike at Ras Jdir, Gaddafi's territory was within touching distance.

Within moments of our arrival local people surrounded us, curious about the Western journalists who had made the trip to this remote town. Many locals were also gathered around the border post, attracted by the presence of the first Libyan refugees. One man who came up to us was particularly keen to talk and very interested in the fact that we were Brazilians—very rare creatures in this part of the world. His name was Imed Meliene. In French peppered with errors but easy to understand, he told me he was married, with no children as yet, and worked for the municipal government as a civil engineering technician. His job gave him an elevated status in a region characterized by poverty and a lack of employment opportunities, where the illegal trafficking of fuel, food, and consumer goods from Libya was profitable and widespread. With his brown skin wrinkled and worn by the Saharan sun, he seemed older than his 31 years. He asked what had brought me to the region: my initial reply was that I'd come to interview Libyans who had left their country because of the conflict. Friendly and eager to help, he immediately offered his services as an interpreter and enabled me to talk to various refugees within the space of a few minutes. What I heard from them was surprising. Not only, they said, was there an armed uprising in the west of Libya—the richest, most densely populated, and most influential area of the country—but much of the region was already in the hands of the rebels, who had achieved victories against the loyalist forces.

In between conversations with the refugees, Imed told me he was in touch with people in various countries in Latin America through Facebook and other social networks. There seemed to be no signal for my mobile phone, so I was surprised Dehiba had Internet access. Imed said I could use his Internet connection if I wanted. Already sensing he was acting out of generosity rather than an expectation of being paid, I accepted the offer; it was a good opportunity to send an article to my newspaper. But before that, I said, I needed to know if he could help me get across the border. Imed recoiled in surprise; he pushed his finger to his lips, took me gently by the shoulder, and suggested we walk away from the crowd so that we wouldn't be overheard.

"Why do you want to get into Libya?"

I explained I'd come to Dehiba in the hope of covering the Libyan revolution. I told him I'd been at Ras Jdir and that there seemed to be no chance of getting across the border there because of the large number of journalists and the strong security presence. Here in Dehiba, I said, it seemed different; there was less security at the border post and it was an area with a lot of smuggling going on.

"I'm sure you can help us," I added, imagining this was the moment he might ask for money.

Imed nodded, and said in a low voice, "Yes, I can help. But you mustn't speak out loud about this."

I asked him whether it was feasible to cross the border through the desert. He replied that it was, and that he had friends who could make the trip. But then he said that in fact it wouldn't be necessary; he was friendly with the authorities so he could arrange for us to get across at the border post itself, perhaps even with the right stamps in our passports.

This was music to my ears, but there was still a problem: I explained that I hadn't managed to speak to any of my Libyan contacts who might have been able to come to Dehiba to collect me, so now I needed to find someone in Dehiba to take me into Libya. Imed frowned and said that unfortunately the Tunisians had stopped making their "business" trips into Libya because Nalut, the main town on the other side of the border, had fallen to the rebels. Gunmen opposed to Gaddafi controlled all the roads, he said. What we needed, therefore, was to find a Libyan he trusted and who might be interested in helping us. Imed wandered off; when he came back into view a few minutes later he was walking beside a pickup truck that came trundling toward us. He introduced me to the driver, a Libyan whom he said I could interview. I understood that he was a rebel who had come across the border on some kind of mission; he said his name was Ali, though I assumed that wasn't his real name.

Ali was reticent at first. He didn't actually say he was with the rebels, and when he spoke about the conflict—the deaths in Benghazi, the uprisings in other cities—he did so only in the most general terms. He seemed inhibited by not knowing who I was or what I was doing there, and by the curious bystanders listening in on our conversation. So we moved away from the crowd and I asked Imed to translate what I was about to say to Ali: "I imagine you're one of the rebels and I want you to know that I have nothing, absolutely nothing, against your cause. Quite the opposite: I admire your people's determination to seek freedom. I know that much of the country is under rebel control but that Gaddafi is saying otherwise and will do everything he can to regain control. The world needs to know that the Libyan people no longer want this regime. And I need your help to enter the country."

Ali seemed touched by this, and his demeanor changed. He began to speak in much more specific terms. He said he was from Nalut, that the town had risen up against the regime, and that the rebels now controlled much of the surrounding area. The same thing had happened in Zintan, not far from Nalut, and in other, smaller towns. He said he had crossed the border only for a few hours, to go to Tataouine to pick up food supplies. On his way back from there he could give me a CD containing photos taken during the first few days of the uprising in western Libya. "And you can come with me into Libya if you want. I can guarantee your safety for 60 kilometers, as far as Nalut. Beyond that, I can't."

I accepted the offer immediately. Ali suggested we meet again in the same place two and a half hours later, and then drove off. The countdown had begun. I went to see Marcelo and Azul, who were filming the refugees, and told them about Ali's offer. I could tell Marcelo wasn't very keen; he thought, reasonably enough, that remote parts of Libya probably wouldn't have the communications infrastructure necessary for him to send his video footage. In truth it was the response I was hoping for. I suggested it was best if I crossed the border alone but that we should stay in touch; if it did seem possible to send images from that part of Libya, I would tell them. With that, we said our goodbyes. I asked to use Imed's Internet while waiting for Ali to come back; he agreed without hesitation and invited me to have dinner with his friends.

I WENT WITH IMED TO HIS FAMILY'S HOME, WHERE I SENT A REPORT TO BRAZIL ON the refugees who were leaving Libya at the various border crossings and seeking safety in the interior of Tunisia, far from the armed conflict that was breaking out in their homeland. I wrote that at least two cities in western Libya, a region supposedly controlled by Gaddafi, had fallen to the rebels in the previous 36 hours. The news agencies were beginning to give the same information, and it was also corroborated by Libyans in the interior of the country that I spoke to on the phone—contacts I'd picked up through the Libyan community in Paris. According to the reports, the uprisings had begun in the cities of Zuwara, about 120 kilometers from Tripoli, and Zawiyah, only about 30 kilometers from Gaddafi's Bab al-Azizia compound. Both places, my contacts said, were of strategic importance to the dictatorship: Zuwara because it was close to Tunisia and the Ras Jdir border crossing; Zawiyah, of course, because it was on the outskirts of the capital itself. Although there were discrepancies between the different accounts I was hearing from Libyans in Dehiba or over the phone, it did seem that the regime's grip on power was already loosening. This, I thought, meant that within a few hours the international media would have access to reliable witnesses who could describe the acts being committed by Gaddafi's security apparatus—the police, the army, the mercenaries, and militiamen—and also give an idea of the regime's durability.

What we already knew for sure was that in the wake of the popular movements that had deposed Ben Ali in Tunisia a month earlier, and then Hosni Mubarak in Egypt, there had been an explosion of street demonstrations in Libya against the 42-year rule of Muammar Gaddafi. Beyond that, the accounts coming out of Libya were conflicting. According to foreigners who had fled the country, more than 2,000 people had been killed in Benghazi during the first three days of protests, starting on February 15. On the Internet there was already video footage from Benghazi showing demonstrations being put down by the security forces; in the streets and squares, protesters were being pursued by the so-called forces of law and order, which didn't hesitate to shoot indiscriminately into crowds—hence the extremely high number of casualties in the first week of the uprisings.

The previous day had been chaotic, with rumors circulating both inside and outside Libya that Gaddafi had ordered his air force to bomb the crowd gathered in and around Green Square in Tripoli, possibly killing many thousands of people. I spoke on the phone with two Libyan exiles in Paris, Mohamed Rifaat and Ismail Sakal, who told me they'd heard from family members in Libya that such a massacre had indeed taken place, but they acknowledged they couldn't be sure what was going on. No one could. There were nongovernmental organizations (NGOs) saying about 300 people had died, a number that was still impossible to verify. What was certain, however, was that a government minister had resigned, some Libyan ambassadors abroad had given up their posts, and two air force pilots had deserted by flying their Mirage fighters to Malta, where they promptly denounced the violence of a regime determined to stay in power at all costs.

Then there were the rumors about the rebels' supposed capture of the cities of Zuwara and Zawiyah. A few of the people leaving Libya for Tunisia and Egypt spoke of bloody repression in the west of the country, not just the east. In Zawiyah, 90 demonstrators were said to have been killed. In both cities there had apparently been attacks on the "popular committees," the local representatives of the regime, in which their buildings had been destroyed. Reports suggested that commanders in both the police and the armed forces had abandoned their posts, but also that mercenaries paid by Gaddafi had joined the fight against the rebels.

"The west of the country is becoming free," one of the refugees assured me. "Soon, only Tripoli will be left" was his audacious prediction.

The rebels' advance in the west was sapping the strength of the regime, which had already lost eastern cities such as Ajdabiya, Tobruk, and Benghazi, a thousand kilometers from Tripoli. Loyalist forces were fighting with rebels for control of the oil terminals at Ras Lanuf and Marsa el Brega on the Gulf of Sirte. Together the two terminals pumped out 1.5 million barrels of oil per day, accounting for most of the country's total production. Since oil and gas were Libya's two most valuable resources, it appeared the regime's ability to keep hold of the oil and gas installations would be vital for its survival.

Despite the rebels' successes on both sides of the country, there was as yet no sign of a coordinated movement to take control of the capital. Agence France Presse reported that members of the Revolutionary Committees had gone into hospitals in Tripoli to kill demonstrators who were receiving medical attention. It struck me as a highly unlikely scenario, even bearing in mind the regime's grisly record. The Libyan League for Human Rights had managed to convey its version of events to the press; they said people had indeed been murdered in hospitals and their bodies taken away to an unknown destination.

Meanwhile, the regime was urging its opponents to put down their weapons and offering financial rewards for information about the individuals leading the rebellion. The Libyan People's Committee for General Security declared that there would be amnesty for anyone who put down their weapons and "repented." Without mentioning money—even though the government was paying rewards to informers—the committee also called on citizens to provide information "about those who manipulate the young people, or corrupt them with money, goods or hallucinogenic pills." In fact, like al-Qaeda's supposed participation in the uprisings, drugs were a recurring theme in the regime's propaganda during the early stages of the conflict. For Gaddafi to depict the revolutionaries as drug-crazed youths at the service of foreign terrorists was pathetic—just like his brief appearance in front of the TV cameras carrying a superfluous umbrella. "These young people are going to buy drugs in Tripoli" and "Bin Laden is obviously behind this" were two of his pronouncements.

At the same time it was denouncing the popular movement and unleashing extreme violence, the regime also offered the prospect of change. Saadi Gaddafi, one of the dictator's sons, announced that reforms were on the way but would be enacted with his father still in power. He also told a bare-faced lie: that the regime was still in control of 85 percent of the country.

Although the accounts I heard from Libyans at the Ras Jdir and Dehiba border crossings were far from consistent, they all contradicted Saadi Gaddafi's claim. In three days, 15,000 people had already left the country, most of them carrying whatever possessions they could. My first sight of the refugees had been at Ras Jdir, where they arrived looking ragged, exhausted, and dirty; many of them were also hungry. It was obvious that a humanitarian emergency was developing—one that would duly explode in Tunisia, where another revolution was shaking the foundations of the already weakened state structure.

These refugees—men, women, and children—chose to leave the country on foot because, according to reports, there were already some 10,000 people gathered outside the terminal building of Tripoli airport in the forlorn hope of boarding nonexistent international flights. Nongovernmental organizations were responding to the exodus—especially the Red Crescent, which was setting up the first field hospitals in case the regime caused a bloodbath over the following days.

At each checkpoint they passed through on their way to the Tunisian border, the refugees were robbed by Gaddafi's soldiers or proregime militiamen. Money, cameras, laptops, mobile phones: all were taken. Even the SIM cards in the refugees' mobiles were being taken out and destroyed, such was the regime's determination to prevent images of demonstrations or state violence from appearing on the Internet. Among the refugees who sympathized with the revolutionaries but had nevertheless opted to leave the country was Omar Mohamed Chebli, 42, from Tripoli, who had come to the border by car carrying all the belongings he could. "In Tripoli and various other cities there are fires everywhere," he told me. "Lots of people have been killed. There are no longer any police on the streets and in lots of places the situation's changing really quickly. More and more people are going into the streets to protest."

Other Tripolitans who had left the country said the situation was much calmer and that there were no major street demonstrations, or at least not compared with the first few days of the uprising when gunshots—including those of the police firing at protesters—were heard regularly. The alleged bombing by the air force had not taken place, said one of the last refugees I spoke to at the border, Mohamed Trizou, a Tunisian who worked at an oil terminal and had decided to leave the country with his wife and son. But it did seem to be true that in Tripoli and in nearby cities such as Sabratha, 70 kilometers west of the capital, soldiers had been sent to disperse demonstrators who were threatening police headquarters and government buildings.

I learned that on the main road from Ras Jdir to Tripoli—a 207-kilometer journey that journalists from all around the world wanted to make—the regime had set up around twenty separate checkpoints to control the arrival and departure of foreigners. It was also said that government troops were guarding all the approaches to Tripoli because rebel groups from other cities had already made attempts to penetrate the capital.

This poured cold water on my plans. It seemed I didn't have much chance of making it to Tripoli to cover the protests that, I imagined, would erupt all over the country in the next few days. Everything I'd heard suggested that the regime still had control of Tripoli and that an uprising in the capital, as in Tunis and Cairo, might not take place, or at least not for the time being. On the other hand it was increasingly obvious that Gaddafi's declarations about the west of the country still being loyal to him were nothing more than empty rhetoric.

It wasn't impossible to find supporters of the regime among the refugees arriving at the border, and their accounts tended to cloud the picture. At Ras Jdir I spoke to Bashir Lilioush, a 78-year-old retiree who had come to Tunisia to seek medical help after suffering a fracture to his left leg, which had now become severely swollen. Crossing the border for medical treatment was actually common among Libyans even in peacetime, given the generally precarious state of the public health system in their country. The main hospitals in Tripoli, capable of providing specialized care, were merely an exception to the rule. Lilioush was pale-skinned by Libyan standards, with white hair and a trembling voice that made him seem even older than his years. Sitting in the backseat of his car, anxious to get treatment as soon as possible, he showed a flash of anger when I stopped inquiring about his injury and instead asked about the popular revolt. He insisted the police were in control, denied that there had been any aerial bombing in the capital, and attributed the disturbances to "some drunk people wanting to make trouble" and "the Americans and British, who are against Gaddafi." "Gaddafi is good for the people. I, for example, get 700 dinars," he said emphatically, staring me in the face. "What can I say against this government?" His monthly pension was equivalent to 350 euros, a reasonable sum given the low cost of living in Libya, where the government subsidized all sorts of goods.

Later, after leaving Ras Jdir and Dehiba, I learned that the stream of refugees turned into a flood, with tens of thousands of people leaving every day. Apart from Tunisians returning home there were also Lebanese, Syrians, and Egyptians, fleeing to the west because the routes to Libya's eastern border, especially near Misrata and Benghazi, were either closed or extremely problematic. Once inside Tunisia, the poorest refugees would stay in camps hastily set up by international and local NGOs. Initially, however, they would sleep in the open air, tormented by nighttime temperatures that fell to below 50 degrees Fahrenheit and by gusts of wind that seemed to penetrate all kinds of clothing. They received blankets and hot food, but in the few days I spent close to the border there were hardly enough supplies to go around and disorder was breaking out at the distribution points—not a good sign given the imminent surge in the number of arrivals. The refugees also received medical care and counseling at two field hospitals set up by the Red Crescent, the larger of which was about five kilometers from the border. One of the doctors there, Mouldi Hajji, told me the camps would soon be overcrowded. "Yesterday alone we had 8,700 refugees arrive. We think any day now will be D-Day, and then we'll certainly receive a lot of injured," he said.

Hajji explained the Red Crescent was setting up the same facilities as it would in the aftermath of a natural disaster. I imagined the field hospital becoming surrounded by an enormous tent city within a matter of days, which indeed turned out to be the case. There would be no piped water, no sewage treatment, and not much hope for those obliged to stay there indefinitely. Some months later I would return to the camp Hajji told me about: there were still thousands of tents. On many of them there were flags of countries in sub-Saharan Africa; their occupants had fled from Libya where, before the revolution, they had found jobs and some temporary stability.

IMED WASN'T A SMUGGLER, BUT HE HAD CONTACTS WHO WOULD HELP ME GET across the border illegally, which at that time no one else was able to do. He asked for nothing in return. I presumed he was a revolutionary, involved in some way in overthrowing the 23-year-old dictatorship of Zine al-Abidine Ben Ali a few weeks before. But in fact he turned out to have an utterly different perspective on the political situation in North Africa: he was a reactionary.

We'd been chatting for a couple of hours when his views on the insurgency in the Arab world began to emerge. He said the protests that toppled Ben Ali had not spread to Dehiba. I never actually got the opportunity to ask any other local people whether this was true. From the way our conversation was heading, I could tell that this warm and obliging man actually took a lenient view of dictatorships. And it wasn't just Ben Ali; he also admired the other "leaders" in the region, saying they possessed the "firm hand" needed in order to "control" their populations. He viewed the Arabs as a restless and dissatisfied people, unable to cope with freedom. His sentiments made me uncomfortable, especially when he began to express admiration for Saddam Hussein, saying the ex-dictator had "maintained order" in Iraq in the face of external threats. I guessed his convictions mirrored the thinking of a minority of people across the Arab world who for different reasons felt protected by the despots at the helms of their countries.

Interested though I was in Imed's worldview, I was more curious about the social and economic conditions in the border region. He insisted that life had not improved—and definitely wouldn't improve—with the winds of democratic change. Even in the small, poor town of Dehiba in the largely Berber province of Tataouine, 600 kilometers from Tunis, he said his monthly salary of 650 Tunisian dinars (about 370 euros) gave his family a reasonable standard of living. His house, built from concrete blocks, was spacious; it had a tiled floor and was decorated with a modest yet elegant simplicity, displaying a mixture of Western and Arab influences. It seemed to reflect greater affluence than most of the neighboring houses, or indeed most of the other homes I'd visited in Tunisia.

Imed also explained that, given the low prices of many essential goods, his salary went a long way. The bread his family bought, for example, cost only 25 cents. Food in general, fuel, water, and electricity were all easily affordable for him. His house had air-conditioning, and as we sat talking in his living room he pointed out his various electronic goods, including an LCD TV and a stereo as well as the computer with high-speed Wi-Fi Internet. Many such goods, he explained, were "imported" from Libya, where everything was cheaper and where the average person's purchasing power, with oil money ploughed into subsidies and social benefits, was much greater than in Tunisia. This explained, in part, his admiration for Gaddafi: "a man who gives everything to his people."

"They understand the mentality of the people. They know that when they give the Arabs freedom, they don't know what to do with it," he said. "The same goes for Gaddafi. He doesn't give the people freedom but he gives them cars. Like the Toyota Camry, for example—in Europe it costs 40,000 euros. How much is it in Libya? The equivalent of 7,000 euros. So he's giving the people 33,000 euros. And he gives them houses as well—interest-free loans of 60,000 to 100,000 euros."

I wasn't there to discuss the merits of the uprising in North Africa, as our respective opinions weren't going to change anything, but I did suggest that providing cheap cars wasn't the be-all and end-all. Imed talked about the older generations in his family; his father and grandfather, he said, believed Gaddafi had "liberated" Libya from Sidi Mohamed Idris al-Mahdi al-Senussi. They thought King Idris "worked with the Italians" against his own people. He also signed agreements with the United States to install military bases in Benghazi, which changed the regional balance of power to the detriment of Egypt and in favor of Israel. So all in all, he continued, Idris was "much worse than Gaddafi," the latter being a man who actually brought wealth to Tunisia's neighbor. "My grandfather told me that when the king was in power, all the Libyans were over here working in Tunisia because there were no jobs for them at home."

Imed tried to dissuade me from going to Libya. The only safe countries in the whole Maghreb, he said, were Tunisia—either with or without Ben Ali—Morocco, and, with certain caveats, Egypt. Algeria and Libya, certainly not. And he thought there was no sense in my wanting to hear what Libyans had to say about Gaddafi's regime.

"What is freedom? What are its limits? Most people don't even care about that!" he said, raising his voice, apparently not satisfied with my neutral "uh-huhs." "You don't understand! We need ten Gaddafis, ten Ben Alis, ten Mubaraks! C'est la vérité!"

I asked him why he thought I shouldn't go to Nalut, 60 kilometers inside Libya, if my safety had already been guaranteed and the town was in rebel hands. "It's because I don't trust Libyans," he replied, with the air of someone making a reluctant admission. "It's dangerous for you. They're not open, they're not transparent. We're related to them, so we understand their mentality. You never know what they're thinking. You could meet ten of them and nine will be against Gaddafi, only one in favor. But if circumstances change it could suddenly be nine for Gaddafi and one against. You won't really know which side they're on."

Imed's argument seemed full of clichés, generalizations, and preconceptions, but some of what he said was worth bearing in mind. First, his view added to my perception that the years of isolation under Gaddafi had made Libya a kind of bogeyman in the popular imagination of the other peoples of the Maghreb—a land of terrorists and all sorts of other bad people. Imed's words seemed to betray a fear of Libyans, perhaps a fear of the unknown. There is no natural barrier along the border between

Tunisia and the Libyan region of Tripolitania, nor are there any major differences of language, ethnicity, traditions, or values between the peoples on either side. There should be a close bond between those peoples, I thought; if it had been broken, the decades of isolation and disinformation must be to blame.

Still, Imed's warning was valid. I had no reason to be complacent. It was true I needed to be wary; to trust everyone would be to invite trouble. As a journalist in a war zone I would need to act in a calculated and rational manner, plan my every move. Sure, I wasn't prepared to believe Libyans were treacherous barbarians by nature, but Libya was undergoing a revolution; it was a lawless country with a corrupt government that didn't hesitate to use its economic muscle to employ mercenaries and militias against its enemies.

And one of those enemies was the press.

IT WAS ABOUT 8 P.M. ON THURSDAY, FEBRUARY 24, AND THE CONVERSATION WITH Imed was going on too long. In the midst of so many unconfirmed reports about the developing situation, and the signs of an imminent humanitarian emergency, I hoped the moment was approaching when I would finally cross the border. I was anxious to meet Ali, my *passeur*, the revolutionary who would get me into Libya. I needed to finish the article I was writing and send it as soon as possible to the newspaper in São Paulo. I was also waiting for my editors on the foreign desk to give me the go-ahead to enter Libya. I'd told them in an email: "I'm in the town of Dehiba, on the border between Tunisia and Libya, more than 200 kilometers south of Ras Jdir. I've got a chance of getting into Libya illegally in 2 or 3 hours' time."

According to my plan, that night I would reach the Libyan town of Nalut in the Nefusa mountains, 60 kilometers from my current location and 140 kilometers from Zuwara, which had apparently been the first city in western Libya to fall into rebel hands. Once there, I'd said in my email to Roberto and Rodrigo, it was quite possible I'd lose contact with them for some time. The mobile phone network had been disabled, as had the Internet, because the regime wanted to prevent its opponents from spreading their message on the social networks. I could only guess what kind of working conditions I was going to find in a barren, mountainous region that was theoretically still under Gaddafi's control.

There were risks, obviously: this was Libya, after all. I had no intention of going ahead without the newspaper's consent, but the email I was hoping for arrived soon afterward from São Paulo: I had the green light to go. I started my final preparations while Imed still tried to convince me it was better to stay in Tunisia at his house. There was one other person I needed to contact. Ghaith had texted me at 4:47 p.m., asking if I had any news. I replied at 6:18 p.m., when my mobile finally got a signal: "I've met someone who agreed to cross the border with me. He's a Libyan who lives in Nalut. Says he can guarantee my safety for 60km, after that he can't. Do you have a contact who could give us a safe place to stay?"

In fact I already knew that Ghaith had a contact in the Nalut area. His reply arrived: "Don't cross the border alone. I'm on my way. My contact can come and pick us up if we can get in touch with him." Then another message: "Where are you? I'll be there in 1 hour."

I began to hesitate. With Ali it seemed I already had my opportunity to cross the border: I didn't want to let it slip. And yet there were two big advantages in waiting for Ghaith: first and foremost, with him I wouldn't need a translator; and second, also very important, he was someone with whom I'd be able to swap ideas, make plans and then change them if necessary, and come to quick decisions in a hostile environment. We would be putting our minds to the same problems. He could be prudent if I got carried away, or bold if I hesitated unnecessarily. My gut feeling was that I had a lot to gain from being with Ghaith, and the next few days would prove me right. On the other side of the border Ghaith would display a rare gift for communicating and for establishing valuable contacts. In covering stories of conflict, oppression, and hope in the Arab world, it was as if he was telling his own life story.

But waiting for him meant abandoning the idea of crossing the border right away—a situation I accepted with a twinge of regret. Ghaith arrived on time, when Imed and I were having dinner in a small, basic, but friendly restaurant a few hundred meters from his home. Imed had already offered to put both of us up for the night and we gratefully accepted, there being no hotels or any other place to stay in the area. I wondered if Imed was going to reprise his discourse in defense of the Arab dictators; it was amusing to imagine the response he might get from Ghaith, who had personal experience in Saddam Hussein's prison cells. In fact they spoke together for a long time that night, in Arabic, translating for my benefit whenever they were discussing important details of the Libyan conflict. While they talked I studied some road maps of the region and sent emails to a few people I thought might prove useful when we were in Libya.

After Imed went to bed, Ghaith and I chatted for an hour or so about his coverage of Afghanistan, my first visit to Libya, and our respective thoughts on the Libyan revolution and how the media was covering it. We also shared in a certain pleasure that we knew was egocentric, a little stupid, and utterly typical of journalists: the knowledge that if we got across the border we would be the first reporters to arrive unauthorized in the Libyan region of Tripolitania, the most powerful, populous, and affluent area of the country. We would be able to find out if Gaddafi really did have the support of the local population, or if, as we suspected, the insurgency that had started in Benghazi had spread to the rest of the country.

We slept in beds that were warm and comfortable, even though they were just mattresses Imed had put on the floor. In the early morning we were eager to arrange our transport across the border. I tried to reestablish contact with Ali and to get hold of another contact I believed might be able to open doors for us once we were in Libya. Ghaith, meanwhile, tried to contact Saleh Khalifa, the Libyan who was apparently willing to assist us in traveling through the interior of the country. Imed went to speak to the border agents, trying to convince them to not only let us through the border post but to also stamp our passports, which would allow us to claim, if we were caught without visas in the interior of Libya, that we had entered the country with the permission of the authorities.

Despite our best efforts we ended up waiting another 26 hours for our next chance to cross the border. There was another day of strenuous negotiations with border agents and Libyan rebels, with Imed or local smugglers as go-betweens. The cutting of telephone lines by the regime made it very difficult to get hold of our contacts; we tried dozens of times before getting through to anyone. Ghaith, fortunately, had a satellite phone, which was bound to prove useful in the interior of Libya, yet neither Ali nor Saleh answered our calls. A further problem that Friday morning was a temporary decrease in the number of Libyans crossing the border into Tunisia. My confidence that we would soon enter Libya was based partly on the assumption that rebels would continue to arrive at the border; we could talk to them face-to-face rather than by phone and persuade them to take us with them back into Libya—that was how it had worked with Ali. But now the biggest group of refugees coming across wasn't even Arab: they were Koreans, employees of a petrochemical company, whose departure had been organized by the South Korean embassy.

Despite Imed's attempts to be discreet, as the hours went by we could only assume that everyone around the border post, including the Tunisian and Libyan soldiers, could guess what we were trying to do. But no one had told us to leave; that was a good sign. Ghaith and I persevered with our phone calls and continued to make plans. Twice he asked me whether I really wanted to enter Libya, as if he doubted my commitment. The second time I felt obliged to remind him it had been my idea, the previous day, to come to Dehiba in the first place—so he really shouldn't be asking me that question. In a tone of mock exasperation he let out a cry: "Crazy Brazilian!"

Eventually Ghaith managed to reach Saleh, his contact, who confirmed the reports we'd been hearing about the situation on the other side of the border. The people of Nalut had risen up against the regime, deposed the local Revolutionary Committee, seized weapons from army and police premises, and launched an armed offensive throughout the surrounding region. They now had control of the roads and various other towns. Sooner or later the army would probably try to retake the whole region, but the rebels were confident they could hold out.

Thanks to their firepower the Nalut rebels had overcome loyalist forces in Wazen, the town closest to the border. Saleh said on the phone he'd meet us in Dehiba—in the late morning or early afternoon, he couldn't be sure—when he arrived there with a group of rebels. When they turned up it was clear Saleh was the leader, although he didn't match my mental image of a rebel commander: short and chubby, he was wearing glasses, a turban, and a cream kaftan. There were four or five other men—including, to my surprise, Ali, who greeted me with a smile and a wave as if I were an old friend.

I felt at that moment we were well on our way to crossing the border. I was wrong. A three-way conversation in Arabic ensued between Ghaith, Saleh, and Imed; Ghaith translated the main points for me. Saleh revealed that his group had been watching Ghaith and me for a few hours, analyzing our movements. I was neither surprised nor worried by this; I was far more bothered about finally crossing the border. I understood that Ghaith was explaining our situation to Saleh, whose demeanor was friendly but serious. Saleh had bad news: his group was willing to take us across, but the soldiers at the border post didn't want to let us through. It was an impasse that reflected the wider situation: the rebels were keen to have media coverage of the uprising, but the regime was grimly determined to hide what was going on from the outside world. A few minutes later Saleh, Ali, and the other rebels got into their vehicles and drove away. Nothing seemed to be resolved, although they did say they expected to be meeting us in Nalut by the end of the day.

As the hours went by it seemed we were faced with a brick wall. Whether out of genuine optimism or a desire to say what we wanted to hear, Imed insisted it would be possible to make it across the border, though he also continued to advise us to stay in Tunisia. His ambiguity wasn't encouraging; we couldn't help wondering if coming to Dehiba had actually been a waste of time.

My frustration peaked at about 4 p.m., when we next saw Imed and the group of rebels. They had set up a table outside a café and were preparing to have a leisurely game of cards. I knew Africans and Arabs were said to have a different perception of time, but I couldn't help being furious. While Ghaith tried to establish new contacts over the phone, I stormed over to the table. I told Imed that as a journalist trying to report on a war I couldn't hang around any longer: I needed an answer, yes or no.

For a moment I feared I'd been too rude, but Imed didn't seem offended. He abandoned the card game and promptly contacted two other friends whom he said would be able to help. Not long afterward, Ghaith and I went with them by car to have a look at a stretch of the border that was at the top of a hill, a long way from the checkpoint; we were thinking again about crossing through the desert and bypassing the border post. The trip ended up being fruitless, but at least it felt like we were on the move. We drove back to the border post and waited for another 40 minutes. The sun was setting, and even in my agitated state I could enjoy the beautiful colors shifting across the rocky hills and the Saharan sky. Then the sunset gave way to an array of stars, and the temperature plummeted.

After a few more minutes speaking on his mobile, Imed seemed to recover his optimism. Standing by the side of the road about 200 meters from the border post, he explained the relations between Gaddafi and the various tribes in Libya; it sounded like a final briefing before we said goodbye. He said the people of Nalut, a Berber town with a population of 26,000, had opposed Gaddafi for more than a quarter of a century. The animosity dated back to 1984 when one of the local tribal leaders, Sassi Zekri, was executed by the regime. Zekri had led a rebellion against the regime because—so the story went—Gaddafi was contracting mercenaries to reinforce his army. A figure known even in Tunisia for his bravery and fondness for alcohol, Zekri was arrested and hanged. His widow, profoundly traumatized, later committed suicide. Imed said the continuing ill feeling toward Gaddafi ensured that Nalut would be a safe place for Ghaith and me. But we should still be very careful, he added, because other towns nearby, such as Wazen and Tiji, were not opposed to Gaddafi and could serve as launching pads for military counterattacks against the rebels.

We walked up to the border post. Imed went inside while we waited in the night air. When he reappeared he told us he'd be able to sort out the passport stamps from the Tunisian officials, proving we'd left the country via the border crossing, but not from the Libyan side. Well, we thought, that would have to do. Imed said the Tunisian border agents wanted to have a word with us. In French with a strong Arabic accent, one of them asked what we intended to do in Libya. I replied that we wanted to cover the conflict. This didn't provoke a response; he simply led us inside the border post where there was a young Tunisian soldier sitting at a desk. The soldier requested our documents, flicked through them, asked a few questions, and took some notes. Then, after looking me up and down from his chair, his face broke into a smile—and suddenly, much to my surprise, he started speaking Portuguese. He was very pleased Ben Ali had been deposed, he told me. He found blank pages in our passports and stamped them firmly. As he handed them back he spoke again in Portuguese: "Have a good revolution."

CHAPTER 4

REVOLUTION

Ghaith and I passed through the Tunisian border post and found ourselves walking across a kind of diplomatic no-man's land, a narrow
strip of land about 100 meters wide that belonged neither to Tunisia or
Libya but was brightly illuminated by floodlights from both sides. The
night air was cold as we headed for the Libyan border post with its green
flag and giant picture of Muammar Gaddafi, his hands clasped in a victory sign. It was the kind of visual welcome only a dictatorship would
offer, but it also meant, finally, that we were in Libya.

As we approached the Jamahiriya's immigration authorities a white
pickup truck came toward us. It accelerated and then turned and braked
sharply, coming to a halt with its passenger door open in front of us. It
was Saleh and the other rebels; they told us to get in and we did so without hesitation. A young man of about 25 was at the wheel. Ghaith got in
first, sitting in the middle of the front seat beside the driver. Then, as
I got in, at least two other men jumped up on the back of the truck and
banged on the roof of the cab to tell the driver to pull away.

The truck accelerated and left the road, going straight up a hill
of sand and stones that served as a natural barrier beside the border
post. Behind us there was a convoy of other rebel vehicles. It was obvious we weren't going to be showing the Libyan officials our passports;
this would be very much a clandestine crossing. The vehicle bumped
and lurched as it climbed up the hill, but the passengers in the back
didn't seem to mind. Ghaith, swaying from side to side, clung to his
equipment. We remained silent as the driver concentrated on avoiding

the boulders and bushes in his path. A few minutes later we turned
to the left and went downhill. By now we had left the Libyan border
post behind; it had been a symbolic gesture of contempt from the rebels toward the soldiers and border agents, who were powerless to stop
two foreign journalists entering the country in defiance of Gaddafi's
orders. This show of strength reassured me we were indeed entering
a rebel-controlled area, contrary to the information the regime was
feeding to the media. At that very moment, in fact, foreign news organizations were beginning to arrive in Tripoli at the invitation of the
regime, which was sure to exercise strict control over what the journalists covered.

We had been driving for about twenty minutes when in the distance I saw the lights of cars traveling on the Dehiba-Nalut road,
which featured prominently in the rudimentary map I'd drawn in my
notebook 36 hours earlier. When he got on the road the young driver
accelerated—"for security reasons," he said—and the rest of the convoy
followed. On the other side of the road my attention was caught by some
vehicles coming in the opposite direction, traveling conspicuously slow.
Breaking the silence that had indicated our tension when crossing the
border, Ghaith and I commented on the rebels' attitude toward the border agents. Ghaith then turned to the driver and asked him a question
in Arabic. The driver replied, "We're not afraid, we're not hungry, we're
not tired. Gaddafi's had a gun aimed at our heads for many years. Now
it's time for freedom."

Seemingly at ease in our company, he launched into a description
of the political situation in the west of Libya. Nalut, the biggest town
in the region and now our destination, had been under rebel control
since the first night of the uprising. For decades the city had suffered
various privations at the hands of the regime, not least the banning of
the Berber language in favor of Arabic. Given the Berbers' predicament
it seemed ironic that the origin of the word for "Berber" in their own
language, *amazigh*, is taken by many linguists to mean "free people."
The Berbers opposed Gaddafi for historical, cultural, and religious reasons, the driver said, and as a consequence lived under close surveillance
from the military and the intelligence services. To counter the power
of the central government, the people of Nalut had a tradition of bearing arms that went back to the 1980s, when the first uprisings against
Gaddafi took place. With their weapons and their willingness to use
them, their message to the regime had been: "Leave our families alone

and we'll leave you alone." This tacit agreement had ended only a few days before when a few dozen residents of Nalut had sparked the uprising that deposed the local Revolutionary Committee. It was Nalut's way of "showing solidarity" with Zintan, a town in the mountains of western Libya where there had been a revolt in the wake of the protests in Benghazi.

Keen to tell us about the insurgents' security operation in the region, the driver explained that they had managed to persuade many police officers and soldiers of Berber origin to abandon their posts. They succeeded in driving out the remaining police and soldiers, more or less taking control of proregime towns such as Wazen and Tiji. They set up checkpoints on roads throughout the district surrounding Nalut, searching vehicles and seizing weapons from any civilians not involved in the rebel movement. They also had surveillance teams whose role was to drive along the roads looking out for suspicious vehicles and to monitor the movements of troops loyal to the regime.

We'd been driving for more than 30 minutes, passing two small checkpoints, when the truck left the road again; it was impossible to tell where we were heading as there was no sign of even a small village nearby. Suddenly a clutch of figures showed up in the headlights—and then dozens, perhaps hundreds, of men emerged from the darkness. They were wearing kaftans and some of them had turbans wrapped around their faces. Many of them were carrying AK-47s, some had pistols or hunting rifles, others were holding walkie-talkies. One of them came toward us with the rebel tricolor flag—red, black, and green with a white crescent and star. In other circumstances it would have been a frightening sight; here before us was a civilian population suddenly armed to the teeth, in a situation where they could dispense their own justice. We got out of the truck as the rebels, shouting enthusiastically, gathered in the glare of the headlights so we could photograph them.

Given the nature of Gaddafi's regime, I found it surprising that so many of them were prepared to have their pictures taken with their faces clearly visible. It suggested they knew the regime was in jeopardy, for there was no going back for them now: either the revolution would prevail or any of them whose photos appeared in the international media would end up with a price on their heads. They were exultant at our arrival, as if the presence of Western journalists in this part of Libya was a victory in itself, showing that the regime was losing control and, more importantly, that the outside world cared about the Libyan uprising after

42 years of dictatorship. Before we could interview anyone, however, we were shown toward another pickup, which I imagined might take us to see a similar gathering.

We drove back to the road and followed it for a few minutes before arriving at what looked like a major checkpoint. Fires burned in oil drums and huge piles of sand had been dumped on the tarmac. It turned out to be a road junction where the rebels had occupied a kind of large shed. There was no electric light in the building, only lanterns. Led inside, I saw on my right four black men with their backs to the wall. Surrounded by armed insurgents, they had obviously been taken prisoner. The light from nearby lanterns was in their eyes, apparently causing them discomfort. Their expressions conveyed fear and shame.

"They're mercenaries," one of the rebels declared, in a tone of absolute certainty.

"We found knives on them," said someone else.

Ghaith and I looked at each other, unconvinced. The four men weren't dressed like mercenaries; they were wearing the trainers, jeans, and sweatshirts typical of young people almost anywhere in the world. One rebel showed us the rucksacks the prisoners had been carrying; they contained clothing and an album of family photos, but no object that gave much of a clue as to what they were actually doing in Libya. Ghaith came over to me and said under his breath, "Look at their clothes. They can't be mercenaries. They must be immigrants who've turned up here at the worst possible moment."

It was exactly what I was thinking. A year and a half earlier I had taken a long trip from the north of Italy to the south, writing a piece about illegal immigrants from sub-Saharan Africa who tried to get to Europe in rickety fishing boats. Among the places I visited were the island of Lampedusa and a detention center in the southern city of Foggia. In both places I saw hundreds of young people who looked just like the four in the warehouse: trapped by poverty and a lack of opportunities in Africa, they had scraped together the money for a place on the boats that crossed the Mediterranean, departing for Europe from ports in Tunisia and Libya. Among the most common points of departure was Zuwara, north of Nalut. It was quite plausible the alleged "mercenaries" were nothing more than economic migrants.

But this was a sensitive issue. The possible existence of mercenaries hired by Gaddafi in the early days of the conflict was a major concern for the revolutionaries. They feared an influx of men from Mali, Chad, Somalia, and other countries in the region, attracted by the rewards the

Colonel would be willing to pay in order to reinforce his troops. Months later, during the siege of Misrata, the presence of mercenaries would be confirmed.

Feeling uncomfortable, I left the warehouse as soon as I could. The sight of the captives disturbed me; here in the midst of a revolution they faced accusations that put their lives at risk, and there was no public authority or NGO to defend them. I thought the best thing I could do was appear uninterested in such an unnecessary spectacle. But I decided that as soon as I got the chance I would question the rebel leaders about the fate of the prisoners. Ghaith had also left the building and was walking toward me; he seemed as uneasy as I was.

The rebels we had traveled with were ready to set off for another meeting point. We drove for a few more minutes, off-road, again climbing rocky hills. At the top of one of them we came to an encampment with a panoramic view of the whole region. Presumably it was a good spot from which to observe the movements of any loyalist troops, prepare to fend off an attack, and organize a response.

Opening the door of the truck I felt an icy gust of wind and could see my breath in the night air. Around me were dozens of men with turbans and layers of outer clothing I assumed offered greater protection against the cold than my jeans and leather jacket. We were greeted once again by Saleh Khalifa, who introduced us to his brother, also a rebel leader. There were many men standing close to us, interested to hear our conversation. Saleh was obviously prepared to talk openly to us, and we started by asking about how the uprising in Nalut began. He explained that the local people had been encouraged by the rebellions in the Maghreb and started to defy the regime on February 14, though the real uprising exploded some days later.

"In every village," he said, "the men in the regime's security forces are our relations, even if they're not close relations. They're our uncles, our cousins. At first they tried to prevent the rebellion. But we put pressure on them and they abandoned their posts, joining the demonstrations and the armed movements."

During the first days of the revolution, Saleh explained, those who worked for the government faced a dilemma: should they be faithful to their communities and tribes, or to their employer? Significantly, Libyan moral codes give precedence to tribal bonds over political structures. We already knew about the desertions and the consequent expansion of the rebel movement, but I was curious what motivated those who had initiated the uprising.

"We're tired of this regime," Saleh said. "We don't have health, we don't have education, we don't have anything. But wherever we look—in Tunisia, in Egypt—we see revolutionary movements. We broke through the barrier of fear."

I was struck by the simple rationality of Saleh's response, which didn't contain moral or religious concepts. Articulate and convincing, he was a military leader who seemed to have a high level of education. Ghaith asked him what the movement intended to do next. Looking toward the horizon as if to indicate other towns nearby, Saleh replied that the Nalut rebels had a hundred pickup trucks and therefore could monitor the whole region. Moreover, they had men, guns, and anti-aircraft cannons. "We've split into two groups. The first will stay in the region to defend it in case of attack. The other will head to Tripoli to organize our offensive."

It was the first time I heard about an offensive. According to Saleh, the Libyan rebels were not counting on an uprising taking place in Tripoli—unlike the international media, which anticipated the same scenes in the Libyan capital as in Tunis and Cairo, with crowds taking to the streets. Tripoli, he explained, was suffocated by a very strong military presence quite apart from the security and intelligence apparatus. There would be no "Tahrir Square" there. From the very beginning of the uprising, at least in the west, the rebels anticipated that it would be necessary to attack Tripoli from the outside. Therefore, said Saleh, their group had made it a priority to increase their firepower. To get hold of more weapons they had successfully attacked an army camp in the first days of the uprising. They had also tried to overrun another military base, but the resistance there was stronger, preventing them from getting their hands on the arsenal.

Saleh spoke to us without fear. He wanted to convey a message to the international community, to assure the West there was no risk of Libya fragmenting. This touched on a topic of particular interest to us: I asked Ghaith to ask Saleh if, given the scale of the challenge facing the rebels, connections had been established between the movement in Nalut and those in other cities such as Benghazi, 1,300 kilometers away. This particular question, however, seemed to make Saleh slightly more circumspect.

"The movements arose spontaneously and are growing spontaneously," he replied, rather vaguely.

We repeated the question, wanting to hear more.

"Obviously there's coordination between the movements, because we need to become stronger and confront the regime. There have been two instances of coordination: the first in the initial spark, when we all began to act almost at the same moment, in solidarity with each other. The second is now, as we're getting organized to take Tripoli."

"Do you really intend to attack Tripoli?" we asked, surprised.

"Yes, we're expecting the [rebel] forces coming from the east. They have tanks and more men. When they reach Tarhuna we'll set off from our region."

Tarhuna is on the outskirts of Tripoli. I wondered whether Saleh's idea about allies arriving from the east was a little optimistic. There was indeed a major revolt in the east, but also a huge number of obstacles in the path of the insurgents if they tried to advance westward along the coast. For a start, there was the loyalist stronghold of Sirte, a city I already knew. It was home to a tribe whose name gave a clue to their allegiance: the Gaddafa. But I didn't think it was a good moment to argue against Saleh, so instead I asked him about the movement's main objective. Was it to seize power and establish a democracy, or to get rid of Gaddafi and replace him with another leader? Saleh replied that the rebellion was aimed at overthrowing the regime and beginning a "constitutional process." "Because of Gaddafi, Libya doesn't have a constitution," he said.

I asked Ghaith to try to get Saleh to be more precise: did he want a constitution with democratic elections, or one with a leader to substitute Gaddafi?

"With elections, of course! We Libyans need elections. The West has nothing to fear. We understand Libya's society, its culture. We know how the country is organized. We know about the minorities, their cultural differences. That's why we can fight for a constitutional process." Saleh explained that the rebel movement in Libya was political in character, not religious; what it wanted was a constitution and the rule of law. The prime motive was not religion but the desire to have rights and to build a better future for the country. He gave the country's oil resources as an example: they should be used for the good of the population as a whole, he said, which under Gaddafi seemed a distant prospect. "Yes, we have a religion. But our motivation is political."

I asked what kind of state the rebels wanted to build: secular, as in the West, or theocratic, as in Iran or in Afghanistan under the Taliban?

Anxious to convince us that the insurgency was not sectarian, as the Western powers feared, Saleh said it would be difficult to establish a theocratic state in Libya. He didn't explain why, but I knew most of the population followed moderate rather than fundamentalist variants of Islam. Saleh believed that after the rebels took control there would be freedom of belief; it would be possible to follow other religions, such as Christianity, just like "in other democratic states."

This brought to an end a somewhat tense part of the conversation. Standing there on the hilltop, Saleh, Ghaith, and I were exposed to the biting cold; so too were the many rebels who had gathered around to listen, watching us with interest and making comments among themselves whenever our conversation turned to military strategy and the rebels' chances of victory. I asked Saleh and his brother, who was standing close by, why the rebels let themselves be photographed with their faces uncovered, and apparently gave us their real names, when the political situation was so volatile and could turn in Gaddafi's favor.

"The reason we're not afraid is because we think Gaddafi's regime is finished, *inshallah* [God willing]."

It was an incisive reply that sounded convincing. But I figured there was something more Saleh could tell me. I wondered if the Nalut rebels had another leader in the background, someone we hadn't yet had contact with. Yes, Saleh said, there was such a figure. He was responsible for orientating the group—taking decisions on matters ranging from military strategy to food distribution—and he had political ambitions, but for the time being he would stay behind the scenes. "It would be very stupid of us to expose our leader at this point, when we still don't know how the rebellion will turn out," said Saleh, momentarily revealing less self-confidence than he probably wished to convey.

Our open-air interview came to an end with smiles and friendly words all round. Saleh seemed more relaxed, commenting on the cold—even though he must have been used to the desert in winter—and expressing surprise at the determination Ghaith and I had shown to enter the country with a revolution going on. "No one's going to believe you've come here. Nobody else has come," he said, lamenting the absence of journalists from TV networks, particularly the BBC and Al Jazeera. He attached importance to the former because of its huge audience in the West, and to the latter because it had come to be regarded by the rebels as a kind of mouthpiece for activists across North Africa and the Middle East.

Ghaith and I were wondering where we were going to spend the next few nights, but before we could ask the question Saleh told us to return to the truck because we were about to leave. We drove off again in convoy, returning to the main road. A few minutes later we entered Nalut—population 26,000, situated in the arid Nefusa mountains on the fringes of the Sahara. Its streets, lit by orange lamps, were deserted. It was already late, around midnight, but the absence of people was due more to the cold and, of course, the dangers arising from the political situation. As we entered the city the convoy slowed down, then it dispersed. Our driver stopped the truck and indicated we should get into an old car that was waiting nearby. Inside was Saleh's brother, sitting in the passenger seat with a Kalashnikov between his knees.

We drove to a district where tarmac gave way to dirt roads. The car slowed to a walking pace and the driver turned off the headlights; he was checking the surroundings were safe before leaving the vehicle. Sitting on the back seat next to Ghaith, I could see no one nearby. The driver stopped, got out, looked around again, and walked up to a nearby house. He knocked gently on the metal door and then beckoned for us to go inside; we soon realized it was Saleh's home. It was a simple but solid-looking building, protected by high walls; we were led to a room with two sofas joined together in an L-shape, a low table and an armchair. Ghaith and I were happy to have a little comfort, a shelter from the cold, and to be in what appeared to be a safe place. Above all, we were pleased with the way our journalistic coverage had begun.

We were very conscious, however, that after more than six hours of total silence we had editors and family members to contact. We reached for our mobiles, only to find there was no signal whatsoever. Ghaith's satellite phone wouldn't work either. I searched for a Wi-Fi signal, hoping for a miracle like the one at Imed's house in Dehiba, but it wasn't to be. In fact, I wouldn't find a Wi-Fi signal anywhere in Libya.

When Saleh arrived he explained that the house didn't have an Internet connection—and added that the nearby houses that did have one had since been cut off. But to our surprise his mobile was working; he said it just needed charging and then we could use it. Whenever he left the room he closed the door behind him, preventing us from seeing his family in the adjacent room.

Saleh then came to sit on the floor by the low table, bringing a file containing photos, newspaper cuttings, and various handwritten and typed texts. In an obvious gesture of kindness toward me he tried to communicate in the smattering of Italian he'd picked up when he spent a few months in Italy, but it was too limiting so he soon reverted to Arabic, with Ghaith again in the role of patient translator. We talked for more than an hour, covering various subjects but starting with Saleh's life story.

He was born on August 31, 1967, in Nalut, where his tribe lived. He was, as I'd already guessed, a cultured man, writing poetry in the Nafusi dialect of his native language, Berber. There were about 180,000 Nafusi speakers in Libya, he said. Berber and Nafusi had both been banned for many years, a draconian measure that had stirred local resentment toward the regime. For his activism on behalf of his people and language, Saleh had spent one year, 1997, in prison. Pulling his trousers down to his knees he showed us the scars he bore from that time: three circular marks on the inside of one leg, a large gash in the other. His torturers tried to instill loyalty to the regime using a drill, a machete, and a pair of pliers, with which they pulled out some of his teeth. He told the story without any loss of composure or even any change in his tone of voice.

Leafing through the papers in the file, he mentioned other instances of violence or repression he'd either witnessed or suffered personally. His writing had clearly been an outlet for some of his pain and anger. He was particularly keen to show us one piece, a "poetic manifesto" that no doubt lost some of its beauty in translation. He read some of it out loud: "What would you do on the day you looked in the mirror and the reflection was not yours? / What would you do if they called you a name that was not yours? / What would you do if you slept and then woke / But even in your dreams you were imprisoned?"

The conversation led fairly naturally to the political situation in Libya. I asked Saleh about the historical origins of the clashes between the people of Nalut and the Gaddafi regime. Saleh explained that the Libyan Berbers had been a persecuted minority for a long time. Since the 1980s there had been various clashes between the people of Nalut and the regime, some more significant than others. The same, indeed, was true of many parts of Libya—but the isolated outbreaks of resistance never cohered into a nationwide protest movement. This made it easier for Gaddafi to depict Libya not as a nation but as an agglomeration of backward and volatile Arab peoples who needed the smack of firm government to prevent civil war. "For decades the regime has made it necessary for us to resist in order to defend our interests, and for that we had to fight alone, in different parts of the country. For a long time the regime has used the argument that we were just isolated tribes in conflict with each other. As a small minority, we [Berbers] tried to defend our rights against the Gaddafi regime."

Ghaith and I knew that Libya comprised countless different tribes, with different cultures; in essence they were their own small, separate societies, in some cases even having their own languages. So how did the rebels intend to pull these different strands together to form a genuine nation? Saleh replied that the latest in Gaddafi's long line of mendacious arguments was that the uprising was the work of drug addicts and traffickers, along with al-Qaeda. The drugs theme was bound to have some resonance in a conservative Muslim community such as Nalut. In fact, Saleh said, the local communities had for many years been confiscating small amounts of drugs and handing them over to the government, which incinerated them. Since the previous September, however, the regime had been refusing to receive the drugs, so the local communities had to store them in warehouses—Saleh's own group had involuntarily accumulated 36 kilos of various substances. Saleh thought it was all a devious ploy: Gaddafi was ensuring communities had narcotics in their possession to incriminate them or to back up his argument that the revolution was the work of drug addicts.

Another of Gaddafi's rhetorical strategies was to create the image, both within Libya and abroad, that the country was riven with incessant internal conflicts. But the existence of different tribes and cultures, according to Saleh, didn't mean there was an adversarial relationship between them. "That's simply not true. Just look at the way everyone is getting behind a single movement to depose the regime. There's nothing stopping us from working together and seeking something in common. Look at us: we are together in the struggle against the regime. And all the tribes, together, will depose Gaddafi."

Now, it seemed, Saleh had recovered his absolute confidence that the rebels would prevail. When we expressed doubts, this poet-turned-militant expressed amusement at the fact that so many observers of events in Libya did not share his optimism. He said even the Tunisians were skeptical—despite having just deposed their own leader. An obvious question was how they could ensure the Colonel wouldn't return to power at a later date if the rebels did manage to depose him. But we already knew the answer to that one: there was simply no way of guaranteeing he wouldn't come back. Ghaith asked if Saleh was aware of the anti-Gaddafi protests that had taken place that Friday in various capital cities across the Arab world; Saleh replied that he was, but that in some respects Libya differed from those other countries. "It's no longer a revolution along the lines of Tunisia and Egypt," he argued. "It's a popular uprising that's being met with very violent repression. People have been brutally killed, and that's why we've decided to revolt, even though we don't have the protection of a strong army like the Tunisians and the Egyptians did."

The popular movements in Egypt and Tunisia were essentially peaceful in character, even though they had suffered a violent reaction from the authorities. Why, then, did the movement in Libya need to be armed? Saleh pointed out that the first protests in Benghazi and other cities had also been nonviolent—but the regime responded with heavy weaponry, even anti-aircraft guns, against its own people. In his opinion the simple truth was that Libyans needed to take up arms to protect themselves, their families, their tribes, and their interests. Libya, he said, had to "defend itself" because there were mercenaries in the country and the regime was brutal. And the armed forces weren't there to defend the population.

Again I was again struck by the measured way Saleh spoke and by the calmness of his demeanor. He never became agitated, even though at times our questions might have sounded impertinent. There was a striking self-confidence about him, expressed in a succession of affirmative sentences that were curiously moderate in tone. All in all, he had credibility.

Our discussion was interrupted by various calls to Saleh's mobile; short conversations would ensue, generally about organizational issues. At one point he again offered us the use of the phone, explaining it was possible to make international calls but difficult to receive them. Ghaith promptly accepted, calling one of his editors in England to report that we had managed to enter Libya, then giving an outline of the situation in the west of the country. His conversation went on much longer than Saleh and I expected and there were a couple of moments when the two of us exchanged looks: embarrassment on my part, anxiety on Ghaith's.

When Ghaith finished his call, Saleh passed the phone to me. I too spoke to a journalist: Lúcia Müzell, my wife. I told her where we were and that I was alright, but also that we wouldn't be able to communicate regularly until I could get hold of a Libyan SIM card and find a way to access the Internet. I also asked her to be in regular contact with the editors at my newspaper, the *Estado de São Paulo*, on my behalf.

Ghaith and I chatted a little while longer with Saleh about the situation in Libya until Saleh left the room and then came back with the news that we had to leave for another house. It crossed my mind that it might be a precaution and that Saleh could be aware of some kind of threat, but he seemed relaxed. When we'd gathered up our equipment and notebooks we followed Saleh outside to discover we were only going as far as the house next door, which belonged to his brother. It was more spacious than Saleh's house, with a carpeted floor and large cushions lining three of the four walls. Close to the other wall there was a heater and also a television, tuned to Al Jazeera.

It was very cold inside the house, so Ghaith and I took turns in front of the heater while we watched the news. A few minutes later Saleh's brother turned up with a big plate of spicy noodles and various meats. And so we all sat around, each with a spoon in hand, enjoying a shared Arab meal and a long, friendly discussion. I felt very much at ease in that room but couldn't help thinking that with their dark skin, long beards, and Berber clothing, my hosts might appear vaguely threatening to many in the West—or indeed to some Tunisians just across the border, such as Imed. After the meal, blankets were brought out; this, obviously, was where we were going to spend our first night in Libya.

Before the lights went out, I received a gift. With a look of immense satisfaction on his face, Saleh's brother came over to me with a rebel flag made of paper. I thanked him and put it by the side of my rucksack, knowing I couldn't risk carrying it around with me if there was the slightest chance of an encounter with Gaddafi's forces.

GHAITH, CRASHED OUT ON THE CUSHIONS ON THE OTHER SIDE OF THE ROOM, seemed to fall asleep as soon as the lights went out. Maybe I dozed for a short while, but I was wide-awake for the rest of the night, my mind whirling with ideas for my next article and with the imagined events of the next day. Ghaith and I had spoken about our intention to get to Tripoli and monitor the uprising from there. Saleh couldn't take us to the capital for security reasons, but he'd promised to help us with one of two possible alternatives: a 230-kilometer journey to the port city Zuwara, along the coast from Tripoli; or southward to Zintan, the biggest of the rebel-held cities in the west of Libya.

This journey to Zuwara would include two and a half hours—180 kilometers—on a road that runs roughly parallel to the coast and that, according to rebel groups in the area, would be safe as long as we took certain precautions. Zintan, situated high in the Nefusa mountains in the district of al-Jabal al-Gharbi, seemed at first to be a less attractive proposition because it meant heading away from Tripoli, but Saleh convinced us it would in fact be a good place to spend the Saturday, if necessary, as it was still only 160 kilometers from the capital and would allow us to find out more about the situation in the west.

Around 6 a.m. I gave up the fight against insomnia and started to write an article. I later discovered it was one of the first pieces—possibly the very first—to be sent by a foreign journalist from a supposedly Gaddafi-controlled region outside Tripoli. In the capital itself, journalists were not so thin on the ground; indeed, agencies such as Associated Press and Agence France Presse already had reporters there when the conflict began. The first line of the article came to me almost automatically: "We're not afraid, we're not hungry, we're not tired." I was still a long way from finishing, however, when Saleh's brother came in to wake Ghaith up; after that it was impossible to concentrate and in any case it wasn't long before we were gathering our gear and leaving the house. We set off on a tour of Nalut in the same car we'd arrived in the night before.

It was a mild day, with a brilliant blue sky. As we left the district where Saleh and his brother lived, I saw a woman in the street for the first time; she was wearing a *niqab*, the full black veil that leaves only the eyes showing. We drove along a few different streets, slowing down in places when we saw graffiti against the regime. One of the messages was "Gaddafi, get out. We are growing old." There was also more dramatic evidence of the uprising in the form of destroyed buildings, including the headquarters of the local Revolutionary Committee. We were taken to see the remains of an obelisk in the center of a roundabout at the edge of the town—a monument to Gaddafi that had been blown up at the beginning of the uprising. We were also shown video footage of the monument's destruction: a large crowd celebrated the successful start to the revolt but also mourned the deaths that had already occurred.

We then drove up into the mountains to a lookout point that offered a superb view of the surrounding area. The cloudless sky above us was deep blue, fading to a lighter shade where it met the light brown of the sandy, rocky landscape. The horizon was almost a straight line, composed of a string of plateaus that seemed to be of identical altitude. It was obvious the Nefusa mountains gave the rebels a significant advantage over the loyalist forces they had expelled from the local cities: they offered vantage points from which to monitor the roads below, particularly the one linking the city of Ghadames with Tripoli. The rebels could anticipate their enemies' next moves and take measures to minimize the losses they would incur in any attack. The Nefusa mountains had served this military purpose for many centuries, or at least that's what I gathered when Saleh and his men led us to one of the oldest ruins in the region, the Ksar Nalut, a fortified granary dating from the eleventh century. Berber peoples built it on a hilltop 640 meters above sea level to protect the ancient city of Bnalot, the forerunner to Nalut. The original buildings, some of them six stories high, were made of stone, wood, and clay, and the remains were perforated with openings to chambers where grain, cereals, and olive oil used to be stored. As a historical site it is less well known and less beautiful than Leptis Magna, which I'd visited in 2009, but it was equally fascinating. I'd never heard of it and I would have been happy—on any other day—to spend hours learning about its history.

But as a journalist in the midst of a revolution, to be stuck in the role of tourist was sheer torture. Ghaith and I did our best to grin and bear it, chatting with the rebels about the ruins and dutifully taking photos. To appear impolite would be to run the risk of having doors closed in our faces. This was something I think Ghaith had long understood, whereas I was learning the hard way. From the first moment in Libya it was obvious that portions of our time would need to be sacrificed: to interminable lunches, conversations which yielded very little, photo sessions with people we knew would never see the images because they didn't have computers or email addresses. But still I found it hard to suppress my impatience. As for Ghaith, I was beginning to discover his ability to face such setbacks with an ironic sense of humor.

"What were you doing when Muammar Gaddafi fell?" he joked as we wandered down yet another of Ksar Nalut's alleyways.

In addition to losing time, another source of frustration was Ghaith's Iridium satellite phone. We'd hoped it would allow us to overcome any barrier to communication, but even on a hilltop under a cloudless sky it still refused to work.

There was also a bit of bad news that was not unexpected but came sooner than I'd hoped. As we were driving back into Nalut, Saleh suggested we stop for a coffee in one of the few grocery stores that was still open for business, saying he intended to talk to a couple of people regarding our journey toward Tripoli. Ghaith and I were also thinking about Tripoli and our options once we arrived there. The first possibility, we thought, was to carry on in our clandestine role, embedded with the rebels in one of the districts of the capital that had already risen up against Gaddafi. It would be risky but would obviously also give us a high degree of journalistic independence. The second, less attractive option would be to use diplomatic channels to let the regime know we were there, and then to offer to present ourselves to the authorities in exchange for a guarantee that we would be able to work in Tripoli. By this time, unknown to us, Gaddafi had invited some foreign journalists into the country, where they would work alongside the news agency correspondents who were already there. As we drank our coffee Ghaith and I discussed the pros and cons of both options, along with other questions such as where we might be able to stay in the capital. We were interrupted by the arrival of three men we had not seen before. One of them greeted all the rebels and then sat down next to Ghaith on the other side of the table from me; he started talking to Saleh while Ghaith and I resumed our own conversation.

A few minutes later the three strangers got up and left. When they were out of earshot Saleh pointed to one of them, who was wearing a long leather jacket, and said "Those guys are with the regime. One of them is a spy. But this isn't the time for revenge. We're not doing anything to increase the tension between the two sides in the conflict. Later, when we have laws, we we'll take action."

Saleh said spying was part and parcel of the regime; in 41 and a half years it had built up an extensive network of agents in public institutions such as the Revolutionary Committees, in addition to the militias also in the pay of the dictatorship. This helped explain the anger that had been unleashed against such institutions, whose headquarters were always among the first buildings to be attacked wherever uprisings broke out. Ghaith and I were pretty sure we had just been identified as foreigners and would now be monitored. We weren't pleased to have come to the attention of the regime so early on, but we weren't going to let it change our plans. Saleh didn't say anything more about possible risks, appearing confident in the rebels' ability to ensure our safety. Of course he also knew full well that we were bound to be identified as foreigners—and also, sooner or later, as journalists. We paid the bill and left the café, this time being driven away not in the old car but in another pickup. Inside the vehicle Ghaith received a SIM card from a local mobile phone operator Libyana, and the equivalent of US$500 in phone cards—more than he could possibly spend. I would finally get my Libyan SIM card the following day. Now that we had a functioning mobile we lost no time in contacting editors and relatives, warning them we would be moving farther into Libyan territory in the hours to follow.

But our journey toward Tripoli was about to be put on hold again. Since the previous day we'd known the rebels were planning to capture the border post at Dehiba to open a channel of communication between the rebel-held cities and the outside world—as had already been achieved in the east of Libya—and now we were told the operation was going to be carried out early that afternoon. Although it certainly wasn't our original aim, we decided to accompany the rebels, thereby retracing our steps back to our point of entry into the country. As had happened the night before, we were taken to one of the three places in the desert where the rebel forces had congregated. The *fedayeen*—the same name used to refer to Palestinian guerrillas—were monitoring the local roads and awaited the order to advance on Dehiba.

Some of the fighters were carrying old rifles but the majority had Kalashnikovs. Some of the better-armed groups had adapted their pickups to carry heavy weapons—mostly Russian-made 23 mm ZU-23 anti-aircraft guns, but also 25 mm MK38s and Swedish-made 40 mm Bofors guns. There was no doubting the destructive power of such weapons, but I was beginning to realize that only a minority of the rebels I'd met had any kind of military training. The majority had never had any contact with the armed forces and no instruction in using the kind of weapons they now had in their possession. I wondered, therefore, if they had much chance of firing them with any precision, though as yet I had no notion of the human cost that might ensue from such a lack of preparation.

Alongside these men we waited for the commanders in Nalut to give the order to advance toward Dehiba. It came about an hour and a half later. We moved off in the pickup at the back of the convoy of vehicles that stretched along the road. There were rumors the army was moving its own heavy weapons toward Dehiba and that Tunisian soldiers would also resist a rebel attempt to take over the border post. Even so, not all the insurgent groups were heading toward Dehiba; one of them would stay behind to protect Nalut from any attack by pro-Gaddafi forces from the neighboring town of Tiji, believed still to be loyal to the regime.

On the way we learned that the first attempt to take control of the border post would be peaceful and negotiated, although some of the men were carrying Kalashnikovs, hunting rifles, and clubs. The aim was to persuade the soldiers at the customs and immigration barriers to lay down their arms or join the revolution. We could feel tension in the air as we arrived. We got out of our truck but the vehicle didn't move away. In the distance we could hear shouting; I couldn't understand what was being said but it sounded like an angry discussion. Amid the war of words I saw an armed soldier break into a run. Bursts of machine-gun fire were let off into the air, but no shots were fired in anger. As the discussions continued we could see the symbols of the regime being taken down, including the green flag and the picture of Gaddafi with his hands clasped in a victory sign. Without further resistance the officials let the rebels raise the border gates, thereby opening Libya to the outside world after 25 years of progressive closure that had culminated in total isolation. Not only was the revolution a reality in western Libya, it was also making significant progress. Three days earlier there had merely been rumors of uprisings, but Ghaith and I had just witnessed the seizure of a border post that would open a vital supply and evacuation route for the rebels of Nalut and the whole western region throughout the conflict. We had also seen proof that, at least in certain circumstances, the rebel movement was capable of advancing by means of persuasion, without violence.

Amid the euphoria that erupted when it became obvious the border post would be captured successfully, a young man who seemed particularly enthusiastic approached Ghaith and me. When we asked for his name he said we could call him Naji Sassi—*naji* means "survivor" in Arabic. Not long into the conversation he told us the uprising against Gaddafi had a special, personal significance for him. At the age of 10, he said, he had seen his father murdered by agents of the regime—and now he was seeing that regime fall. "I remember the day they attacked as if it were yesterday. They broke into my house, took my father away, and executed him. They arrested my brother. They took everything we had—car, house, money. They ruined us. After all that my mother killed herself," he said, with anger in his voice.

Ghaith and I suddenly realized we were talking to none other than the son of Zekri Sassi, the rebel leader in Nalut in the 1980s who was hanged for defying the regime. I listened carefully to what Naji was saying; I observed his posture, facial expressions, and nervous tics. He was short and slightly built, and looked young despite the wrinkles on his face. He had the excited demeanor of someone who was seeing a dream come true, but it also struck me that this "survivor" of Gaddafi's crimes bore signs of emotional instability; something about him suggested he was strangely detached from the events taking place around him. It also seemed that, unlike his father, he didn't have a leadership role among the rebels, although he obviously had more than enough motivation to be right in the front line. I found one of the expressions he used particularly memorable: he said that ever since the crime against his family, he had "brought fear inside his chest." But now, he added, he was beginning to believe that the time for revenge had arrived.

SALEH SAID IT WAS TIME TO LEAVE, SO WE SAID GOODBYE TO NAJI AND DROVE AWAY, leaving the rebel-held border post behind. I imagined the operation had been useful not only for the rebel movement but also for Ghaith and me: from now on, if necessary, we could probably escape the country without having to deal with pro-Gaddafi border officials. Needless to say, I had no interest in fleeing: I wanted to move on to Zuwara as soon as possible. And after several hours' delay, we were finally on the way.

Saleh called over one of the drivers and we set off in another pickup. I looked at my notes and saw that we were now traveling on the road in the map I'd drawn in my notebook two days before. Our progress had been slower than expected, but it felt like my earlier plan was coming together. The main thing was that we'd gotten valuable information about the regime's lack of control in the west, thereby disproving Gaddafi's assertions and doing something to break the silence to which Libyan dissidents had been subjected for decades. As we drove I made some further notes while also admiring the view: for about fifteen minutes we descended from the Nefusa mountains along a sharply curving road carved out of rock and sand. It was almost like a lunar landscape, extremely arid yet strangely beautiful. In certain places we could see across into Tunisia; in others we could see nothing but the sheer rock faces rising on both sides of the road.

But the journey to Zuwara was no sightseeing trip. Only a few minutes after leaving the border post, we went through a rebel checkpoint where we were told army vehicles had been spotted farther ahead. This sparked a frenetic series of phone calls as Saleh and the driver made contact with the rebels responsible for protecting the road. The gap between conversations was never more than a minute; the driver's mobile seemed never to stop ringing. After a few more kilometers there was another checkpoint. Saleh had to explain who he was, and who we were, before being allowed to proceed. As the tension rose again inside the vehicle, I realized we were leaving the region controlled by the Nalut rebels. Twice we had to stop, turn around, and drive back the way we had come. When we stopped for a third time we were told there were probably pro-Gaddafi soldiers on the road—so at that point we abandoned the idea of going to Zuwara and instead went all the way back to the road connecting the border post with Nalut. Saleh and the driver made more phone calls and discussed possible alternative routes. A change of plan was announced: we would head for Zintan, two hours and 147 kilometers away. We stopped for about half an hour at a petrol station to talk to another group of rebels; the sun was sinking behind the mountains and the cold wind began to bite. After so many delays it was obvious we wouldn't be getting anywhere near Tripoli that Saturday, so we'd have to content ourselves with Zintan, one of the biggest population centers in the region and the epicenter of the revolution in western Libya.

Another car arrived, this time an old sedan, which we understood would be taking us to Zintan. Saleh wouldn't be coming with us; instead his brother accompanied us and sat in the passenger seat with a rifle between his legs. The tension of the earlier attempt to reach Zuwara had dissipated; now it was a calm journey with very little conversation and no further phone calls. The road was in good condition and there was no other traffic, just the silent desert. We passed police and army checkpoints that had been abandoned by the regime and torched by the insurgents. We also saw the metal hulks of a few destroyed armored vehicles, glowing red in the sunset. Ghaith was yielding to exhaustion, sitting in a twisted position on the back seat and dozing off occasionally. Our serene progress through this part of western Libya was interrupted only by improvised rebel checkpoints consisting of destroyed vehicles and large piles of sand. Here was proof that the Nefusa region was under the complete control of the rebels, at least temporarily, even though Gaddafi was still declaring—to the international community as well as his domestic audience—that the area was still loyal to him. As the light faded outside, it struck me as a great pity that the dissatisfaction with the regime had been suffocated for so many years.

We'd been driving for about an hour and twenty minutes when the car slowed to a halt by the roadside. Waiting for us was a middle-aged man of medium height with graying hair and an austere expression. Ghaith and I understood we were about to change hands again; now, according to the unwritten moral codes that govern life in the interior of Libya, our "protection" would be the responsibility of another tribe. Before going to Zintan, however, we decided to visit two other small towns in the region where we had an opportunity to talk to the local leaders of the rebel movement and get some more insights into the conflict in the west of the country.

When we arrived in the first town we were taken to a government building that had been taken over by the insurgents in the early stages of the uprising. In a large, cold room without furniture Khalid Sukri, one of the coordinators of the insurgency, greeted us. He was surrounded by local political leaders who spoke to us about the military situation in the surrounding area, and also about the ideals of the revolution. Sukri explained that the uprising in the town had been very difficult for the first two days, but then the population went over to the side of the rebels, the protests increased dramatically in size, and it became possible to seize power without any deaths or even any major violence. Now, he said, we were inside the former headquarters of the Revolutionary Committee in Jadou, which the rebels were using as a base from which to organize security and distribute food. They needed to be vigilant because the region around the Nefusa mountains was still unstable, despite the rebel advance into urban centers such as Nalut, Zintan, and Yefren. His analysis was not excessively enthusiastic, but it seemed to me a realistic appraisal of the strength of the Gaddafist state at that time.

"If we're speaking about government in the traditional sense, then the regime has already collapsed: the police, the security personnel, the Revolutionary Committees—none of them exist anymore," he explained. "But if we think of the government as the presence of militias throughout the country, then we have to conclude it's still strong and will defend its positions around Tripoli."

As we talked, a group of tribal elders gathered around us in a circle. Sukri explained that the patchwork of different ethnic groups and tribes in western Libya were seeking to achieve the greatest possible degree of coordination, thereby not only bolstering the uprising but also making it impossible for Gaddafi to raise the specter of intertribal civil war to justify his hold on power, as he had done so often in the past. Berbers and Arabs fought side by side, Sukri said, to topple the regime and liberate the country.

I asked what kind of state he envisaged in Libya in future. In his reply he demonstrated a clear notion of what a modern state entailed, speaking articulately about democracy, the rule of law, respect for human rights, and political and cultural pluralism. With his calm, considered way of expressing his ideas, this middle-aged man in his Berber robes came across more as an intellectual than a fighter. When Ghaith asked Sukri what role Islam should play in the future society, the answer came in a tone that suggested a profound conviction. "Personally I would advocate a secular state for Libya," he said, looking us both in the eye. "We are all Muslims here. But for many years our religion has been used as an excuse to do away with our country's constitution, our laws, and our rights. We no longer support these arguments."

As Sukri spoke I noticed that the others standing around were nodding in agreement. One of them, Abdallah, joined the conversation. "The form of Islam we practice here is very tolerant," he said.

I wanted to see what reaction I'd get if I introduced Gaddafi's argument that in reality the Libyan rebels were Muslim fundamentalists linked to al-Qaeda. Everyone in the room immediately burst out laughing.

"Perhaps it's the first time Gaddafi has come up with that argument for a foreign audience," Sukri said. "But we're tired of hearing it, year after year, the same old fantasy."

We suggested it should at least be acknowledged that Libya's revolution was the first in North Africa to take the form of an armed uprising, with the consequent risk of civil war. This was partly due to the fact that the regime itself had destroyed the country's public institutions, reducing the Libyan state to the figure of Gaddafi and his clan. Someone in the room pointed out that the student revolts had been put down by force in the 1970s, with a high death toll, and that opposition within the armed forces in the '80s and '90s had also been crushed. "Gaddafi has always attacked us in our homes. He's always attacked our culture. Inside Libya the dissatisfaction has been building for a long time, but only now has it become visible to the West."

Sukri, nodding in agreement, emphasized that the political situation in Libya was different from in Tunisia and Egypt. The regime's violent suppression of opposition, he said, explained the rebels' quick decision to take up arms. He mixed a couple of scientific metaphors to illustrate his argument that Libya was now at the point of no return. "When you heat water there comes a moment when its physical state changes. We've had to suffer all sorts of violence for a long time. Now we're at saturation point." What I heard in that room, and indeed ever since we'd entered Libya, left me with a sense of relief. Declarations can be empty and insincere, occasionally nothing more than devices for manipulating opinion and gaining support, but with the rebel leaders I'd met so far in Libya I really didn't feel that was the case. Their proposals were impeccable. They were fighting not in the name of sectarianism—although elsewhere there might be small groups who were—but for freedom and justice. Ghaith and I knew that our instincts about the rebels had been well founded. We entered Libya in the dark, in every sense, not knowing what we would find. We had heard obscurantist arguments based on stereotypes but were not deterred. And now, it seemed, we had our reward in discovering the noble, almost poetic aspirations of men pursuing a just cause.

CHAPTER 5

SECRET

Sukri confirmed that the Libyan armed forces, supported by militias and mercenaries, had taken up positions on all the approaches to Tripoli to protect the city from attack. This was a wall Ghaith and I would obviously need to break through if we wanted to reach the capital—and to do so we would need the rebels' help.

We left Jadou in the same car that had taken us there. The driver, disconcertingly, was silent and made no effort to appear friendly. We got back on the road toward Zintan, a 35-kilometer journey through rebel-held territory. As the minutes passed, the peaks of the Nefusa mountains came into view in the distance; it struck me that for the rebels in Zintan, as in Nalut, the mountains could present either an advantage or a disadvantage in the case of a counterattack by the army.

We entered the center of Zintan under a clear night sky and sensed immediately that the atmosphere was different from in Nalut. The city seemed more agitated, more belligerent. Barriers had been set up using burned-out cars and piles of rubble, suggesting the inhabitants feared an invasion. Whereas the streets of the other towns we'd seen had largely been empty, here the local population was out in force—many of them were armed. Under the glare of the streetlights, hawkers sold jerry cans of petrol while long queues formed outside shops selling basic foodstuffs such as rice and sugar. Shots were constantly being fired into the air, not just from machine guns but also from anti-aircraft cannons.

We were driven to the hospital, where the situation also seemed somewhat chaotic. And even here, as the wounded received treatment, bullets were flying into the night sky. On entering the building we were greeted by a doctor, Mohamed Othman. But before we could talk to him a figure came striding toward us, shouting and gesticulating with an automatic pistol in his hand. Wearing military fatigues and with a kaffiyeh wrapped around his head, there was an air of Rambo about him. Some other men gathered around, trying to calm him down. It was a strange scene; I had no idea what he was saying but my first thought was that he didn't want Ghaith and me to be there. His name, we would discover, was Abdul Satar. What in fact he wanted, Ghaith explained, was to be the first in the queue to speak to us, ahead of any political or religious leader. When we assured him we would listen to him, his hysteria subsided. He lowered his voice and told us we were safe in Zintan.

"Don't worry about the shooting. We're just trying to stop the mercenaries from coming near," he explained.

With Abdul under control, Dr. Othman was able to introduce himself in perfect English. This was a relief; I could have a conversation without Ghaith as interpreter. In a professorial tone the doctor explained that we had been brought to the hospital because it was considered the safest place in the city, not yet having come under mortar fire. The intensive-care unit was full, he said, and medicines were already being rationed. He told us this as we walked with him toward a room nurses, doctors, and armed guards were using as temporary living quarters. There, he said, we would find food and water, and a group of tribal elders would come to speak to us later that night.

The room had at least ten people inside, most of them watching Al Jazeera on a small TV. There was a constant coming and going through the open door. Abdul was there, keen once again to monopolize our attention, but Dr. Othman stopped him in his tracks. The doctor sat down on a sofa that had been placed against the wall, adjusted his long, light-colored woolen garments, and gave us a brief overview of the situation in Zintan.

He was keen to emphasize that the city had provided the initial spark for the uprising in Tripolitania, Libya's western region. Peaceful protests had given way to armed confrontations with the security services. As in other cities, the headquarters of the Revolutionary Committee had been attacked and destroyed. After that, the city center became the scene of urban guerrilla warfare. Several buildings housing government agencies were invaded, destroyed, and covered in anti-Gaddafi graffiti. The uprising came about, Dr. Othman said, because the local people, inspired by events in the neighboring countries and in Benghazi, decided they weren't going to suffer political and cultural oppression any longer. "In the space of a few days, everything changed dramatically in Libya. The people broke through the barrier of fear," he said.

Ghaith and I explained that very little was known in the West about the uprising in Zintan, or indeed about the situation in Tripolitania as a whole. When we asked how many people had been killed, the doctor replied that there had been only "two or three" deaths on either side, despite the intensity of the fighting, but that sixteen rebels were counted as missing. He told us the people of Zintan were historical enemies of Gaddafi and that the regime wanted to retaliate against the city, to crush the uprising, before turning its attention to Benghazi and the east. In order to do so, he said, Gaddafi would use mercenaries who were arriving from Niger, Chad, and Mali. Also, the regime was offering every Libyan citizen a payment of 20,000 dinars—about US$150—if they took no part in the revolution.

In short, the regime was trying to buy foreign reinforcements as well as popular support. Over the next few days we would see queues at banks: some people were taking Gaddafi's money even though they remained sympathetic to the rebels. Others, including some of the poorest Libyans, simply said no to the tyrant's bribe.

"There was a big battle and we held out against a fierce offensive from the regime's security forces," said Dr. Othman proudly. "There were dead and wounded on our side. But in that first period of fighting, this place tilted the balance of the revolution—it's moved from the east of the country to the west."

Although during the previous 24 hours Ghaith and I had discovered a revolution in full swing, it wasn't clear to what extent the different cities and tribes were coordinating their actions. Dr. Othman acknowledged that this was the biggest challenge facing the uprising: to organize the kind of collective effort that would be necessary to sap the strength of the regime. "It's not yet an organized movement. Things have happened spontaneously and it's only now that we're thinking about coordinating our struggle," he said, with reference to recent meetings between Zintan's tribal leaders and those in other towns. "We're trying to organize the sharing of weapons and ammunition with Zuwara, for the big battle for Tripoli."

Up until that point the international media had not considered the possibility of a war of national liberation culminating in an invasion of the capital, where Gaddafi's Bab al-Azizia compound was situated. Although clearly an armed insurrection was spreading through Libya, this was the

first time Ghaith and I had been led to envisage a truly large-scale conflict. The rebels discounted the possibility that isolated local uprisings
could bring down the regime: what they wanted was to join forces with
other cities such as Zawiyah. Indeed, efforts had already been made to
send ammunition there, but proregime forces had captured it.

The doctor explained that one of the most urgent challenges for the
insurgents was to organize committees to restore a minimum level of
public services. Health care, public safety, and social welfare were quickly
becoming urgent problems. And in addition to the pressing needs of the
local civilian population, the rebels needed to forge some kind of political organization that could represent the uprising in the west of Libya,
along the lines of the nascent National Transitional Council in Benghazi
in the east.

"We want to start coordinating with them," said the doctor, before
leaving to attend a meeting at which, apparently, the movement's next
steps would be discussed.

Ghaith and I noticed that although the rebels acknowledged their
lack of coordination, their plans of attack seemed focused very much on
the short term, almost as if they believed the assault on Tripoli was imminent. Indeed, one of the men responsible for protecting Zintan said to us
that the "march to Tripoli" should have started the day before but had
been "postponed" due to various problems, primarily that of coordination. He insisted it was necessary to "send armed men" to the capital
because defenseless protesters were being "massacred" there. We made
no comment but were both thinking the rebels couldn't possibly capture
the biggest city in Libya without extensive preparations. Perhaps they
had commanders already hard at work behind the front lines, plotting a
combined operation capable of taking the capital's defenders by surprise.
Either that or they were wildly overconfident.

After Dr. Othman left we were taken to a part of the hospital where
local political leaders were waiting to speak to us. When we arrived we
found a large number of elderly men seated together in a row, obviously
curious about the presence of journalists. As in Nalut, we were the first
Western faces to appear since the beginning of the uprising. In front of
each man was an empty chair, as if they were all expecting to have their
very own foreign journalist to talk to. On the far left was one of the tribal
elders, a white-haired man who looked at least 80, his hunched posture
accentuated by the thick layers of his woolen cloak. His name was Amin
Milad, and he made it clear he wanted to talk to me. Our interpreter was
Ali Taher Saleh, a Libyan who had been living in exile in Canada until

he returned to help organize the movement. Milad explained that he'd come to see Ghaith and me at the hospital because, in his opinion, the Libyan people needed the media, keen as they were to explain the nature of their uprising to the outside world. "You're the first to reach Zintan. All the other journalists we've heard about are in the liberated part of the country," he said.

To my right, Ghaith was doing his best to speak to various men at the same time. The beginning of my conversation with Milad had already been revealing. He had the calm, careful, patient manner of someone who had lived a long time and was no longer in a hurry. He explained that in Zintan the catalyst for the rebellion had been an attempt by Gaddafi's forces, on February 16, to recruit 2,000 young men to combat the protesters in Benghazi. But the young men, since referred to as "the Zintan two thousand," had refused to fight against their compatriots—an act of bravery and defiance that sparked the local revolutionary movement.

From the first night, Milad told me, it was clear the dictatorship was incapable of responding peacefully to peaceful demonstrations. Sensing the threat they faced, young people burned cars and buses, challenging the authority of the local police and soldiers, who numbered about 500 in total. Two police officers were almost lynched, being saved only by the intervention of older local people. When the protesters took over the main government buildings, the armed forces, assisted by mercenaries from sub-Saharan countries, tried to surround the city—an attempt that was still ongoing and was giving rise to armed clashes on a daily basis.

There was a price to pay for the rebellion: for four days Zintan had suffered shortages of food and other basic supplies, as well as power outages. But Milad, who said he was speaking on behalf of other leaders in the city, showed no sign of regret. In his croaky voice he explained that adversity had made the local people more determined to face up to the inevitable siege from the pro-Gaddafi forces and then, when the opportunity arose, to break out and expand the rebellion.

"Libya's been ready for this for at least twelve years, because of the injustice and tyranny of the Gaddafi regime," he said, adding that the uprisings in Tunisia and Egypt had had a decisive influence. "Gaddafi's using Libyan money to hire mercenaries from elsewhere in Africa to kill Libyans. He's a psychopath. We always knew he was a scoundrel, but we didn't know quite how bad he was."

It was obvious Milad was proud of the popular reaction against the regime—especially as it took place quite close to Tripoli, where most of the army was concentrated, and was therefore likely to face a counterattack. The courage of the "two thousand" had transformed the uprising in Benghazi from an isolated event into a national movement capable of overcoming separatist tendencies and showing the international community that Libyans were indeed united. Libya, Milad said, was one nation, and now it wanted to be rid of Gaddafi. "We sent a clear message to Benghazi, saying that we're a unified country. Just like them, the people here are fighting for a cause and aren't afraid anymore," he said, with a look in his eyes that suggested profound conviction.

Ali, sitting close by, interjected: "As well as resisting we want to send the message that we're not a bunch of barbarian tribes but a strong and unified country. And together we will liberate Libya."

Just as Dr. Othman had done, Milad explained that the movement in Zintan, Nalut, and the neighboring towns was seeking to coordinate with the other major population centers in the west of Libya, such as Zuwara and Misrata. The goal was to organize the struggle and make the best possible use of manpower, arms, and ammunition. After all, he said, everyone in Libya knew Gaddafi wasn't going to step down like the leaders in Tunisia and Egypt had done.

Because he was one of the religious leaders in Zintan, I asked Milad what kind of nation he wanted to help build after the revolution. As in Nalut and Jadou, I received an answer rooted in a sincere belief in democracy and the rule of law. "We want to turn a dictatorship into a free democracy, with a president elected by men and women, under a constitution," he said, breaking into easily understandable English. "It won't be a religious regime. We will have a secular state."

Libyans, he said, would take their own path toward democracy, but perhaps Turkey was a good model in the region. I told him I'd heard similar opinions in favor of democracy, a constitution, and human rights in the other places we'd passed through. But I was curious to know how people in a country like Libya, which had suffered for so long under a bloody dictatorship and been isolated from the outside world, had apparently incorporated so many Western values into their conception of the ideal political culture. Milad explained that Libya had a foreign-educated intellectual elite along with access to international TV channels and the Internet, which had made possible the emergence of a new political consciousness infused with Western ideas. "You know very little about the Libyan people, because the country has been closed for many years. But we know a lot about you."

Ghaith seemed to be getting impatient, so I thanked Milad for his time and we followed Ali out of the room. He had convinced us we should visit the hospital morgue to see the bodies of alleged mercenaries killed in the early stages of the fighting. As in Nalut, we sensed a neurosis about the possible involvement of large numbers of sub-Saharan African mercenaries in the conflict. Ghaith was increasingly uncomfortable about the lack of concrete evidence linking black Africans to the regime. Inside the morgue, Ali opened one of the drawers to display the body of a black man who had been killed by a shot to the face. Immediately I wondered if he was executed rather than killed in battle. At that very moment, in fact, rebels were searching for supposed mercenaries in the outskirts of Zintan; we had heard there were some sub-Saharan African mercenaries under guard in the hospital, receiving medical treatment, but we were told it wasn't possible to see them. Instead we were shown confiscated Malian identity cards and passports—proof, supposedly, of the presence of foreign fighters who were in the pay of Gaddafi. Later, still in Zintan, Ghaith saw a black man being taken somewhere in a car by four rebels; they were pushing his head into the back of the seat in front of him. As far as Ghaith was concerned, the rebels were adopting some of the old vices of the regime they opposed.

We'd heard upon arrival in Zintan that close to the hospital the rebels had set up some kind of office that had Internet access, where they were able to give interviews about the uprising in Tripolitania to international TV networks such as Al Jazeera and CNN. We asked Ali to take us there, eager at the prospect of having Internet access and getting some updates on the situation elsewhere in Libya. When we got to the room, we discovered it was indeed a full-fledged communications center, created by an engineer named Adel el-Zenteni. Aged about 40, Adel was intelligent, articulate, and talkative, and like Ali he had been living in exile in Canada before coming home to join the revolution. Not wanting to carry a weapon, however, he decided his role could be to help reestablish communications between Zintan and the outside world, which had been cut off by Gaddafi's forces at the start of the uprising. His efforts so far had been hugely successful. There was a computer with Internet access, including Skype, along with a radio set, telephone lines, and a TV with access to international channels such as Al Jazeera. In the adjacent room was a large table with Ethernet cables snaking across it, and a couple of Internet access points that were used by young rebels to upload video footage from their mobile phones to YouTube and other websites. It was also from here that the local insurgents were able to bombard social networking sites with messages. In Zintan, as in Tunisia and Egypt, Facebook was a weapon deployed for purposes of mobilization and propaganda—one of the most efficient tools for smashing through the regime's wall of silence.

Adel greeted us enthusiastically; he was anxious for journalists from as many countries as possible to come to western Libya, believing their presence could have a dampening effect on the expected counterattack by Gaddafi's forces. Foreign journalists were arriving in Tripoli, he said, but had been invited by the regime and were therefore kept on a tight leash. Obliged to spend most of their time inside the Rixos hotel, close to Gaddafi's Bab al-Azizia compound, they couldn't expect much contact with the opposition; their journeys outside the hotel were to places chosen by the regime and were always made in the company of minders. That day, Ali said, the journalists' destination was Sabratha, a historic city on the Mediterranean coast that was thought to be largely pro-Gaddafi despite its location between two hotbeds of rebel activity: Zuwara and Zawiyah.

Adel spoke excitedly about the support for the rebels from the United States, the United Kingdom, and France, all of which were permanent members of the United Nations Security Council. He clearly believed political pressure from abroad could deter Gaddafi from intensifying the counterattack—although in the last few hours, he said, there had been worrying signs that the armed forces were regrouping in the region. In relation to the rebels' chances of victory, this was the first piece of bad news we had heard since entering the country.

"We're facing problems around Nalut," Adel said, thereby explaining why we hadn't been able to get to Zuwara a few hours before. "Gaddafi's sent reinforcements toward the Dehiba border post and now they're putting pressure on Nalut. Right now the city's under attack."

Adel went on to say that another twelve or thirteen armed "Africans" had been captured. In North Africa, the word "Africans" is in some circumstances a discriminatory term for "black people." Even though many Arabs live in Africa they don't view themselves as African. The way he referred to blacks suggested a prejudice that seemed quite widespread among Libyan Arabs. Uncomfortable at what I was hearing, I excused myself and went into the other room to use one of the Internet access points, leaving Ghaith with Adel, Ali, and others. I looked on the websites of the news agencies for information about what had been happening elsewhere in Libya over the previous 48 hours. The situation was changing all the time, especially in the west. According to unconfirmed reports from Misrata, Libya's third-largest city, a crowd gathering for the funerals of local people killed the previous day had been fired on by "mercenaries" in helicopters.

This was a significant piece of news; it put another city on the revolutionary map. In Tripoli, on the other hand, the reports spoke of largely empty streets patrolled by soldiers in pickup trucks who prevented demonstrations from taking place. There was speculation about rebel movements around the outskirts of the capital, but very little was known for sure. Equally unclear was the situation in Zuwara, where an uprising was taking place against loyalist troops and militias. The regime's spokespeople insisted the country was under control. Saif al-Islam, one of Gaddafi's sons, had given an interview to Al Arabiya in which he declared the security situation was "excellent" throughout the country. What really stood out in his interview were the hints of a more conciliatory approach. He recognized that there was "a desire for change" even though he attributed the demonstrations to "foreign manipulation."

"Tripoli is secure," he said, though his tone was markedly different from the belligerence of his father, who had appeared the previous evening in Green Square, in the center of Tripoli, to declare that the government "would fight and win."

I was struck by what appeared to be the increasing international repercussions of the conflict. From the TV I learned that US president Barack Obama had ordered the assets of the dictator and his family frozen. Following the example of the White House, France announced an investigation into suspected money laundering by the Gaddafi family, and also froze their assets. Also, more importantly, the French foreign ministry had withdrawn its diplomatic representatives from Libya "because of the deterioration of the security situation." The French ambassador and his staff had left the country—as, indeed, had a total of 654 foreign workers, 498 of them French. The United Kingdom had also withdrawn its diplomatic staff, along with another 150 British people who had been working at locations in the desert.

An anti-Gaddafi bloc began to emerge, including the United States and European countries led by France and the United Kingdom. In fact, unknown to me at the time, that very night there would be eleven hours of diplomatic deliberations by the UN Security Council in New York, culminating in the unanimous approval of Resolution 1970, which banned arms sales to Libya, froze the assets of Gaddafi and his family, and prohibited them from leaving the country. Also, the Security Council decided to go ahead with the idea—proposed by Canadian prime minister Stephen Harper—of instructing the International Criminal Court to investigate the possibility that war crimes had taken place in Libya.

An important factor in the decision taken in New York was the defection of the Libyan ambassador to the UN, Mohamed Abdel Rahman Shalgham—a close friend of the Colonel—on the very first day of the discussions, which left Libya increasingly isolated and reinforced the arguments in favor of the sanctions. Among the few voices raised in support of Gaddafi were those of Venezuelan president Hugo Chavez and his Nicaraguan counterpart, Daniel Ortega, who were staying faithful despite the violent crackdown. Ortega denounced a "ferocious campaign" to take control of Libya's oil reserves, suggesting that events in Libya were being orchestrated by the West and choosing to ignore the spontaneous rebellion spreading across the country. From two other countries, however, came seemingly more significant support. First, the prime minister of Turkey, Recep Tayyip Erdogan, disapproved of the actions of Gaddafi's regime but did not believe the UN sanctions were an appropriate response. And then Brazil, which remained silent, refused to make any diplomatic overtures toward the Libyan rebels.

Based on the information available on the Internet, it didn't occur to me that the United States, France, and the United Kingdom might intervene militarily. What I read suggested the West was trying to deter Gaddafi from using force against the civilian population and to make it possible for the protesters to repeat in Tripoli the kind of demonstrations that had taken place in Tunis and Cairo. What I was seeing on the ground, however, proved the rebellion had already become an armed movement that left no further scope for a peaceful transition.

Meanwhile, the number of people leaving Libya through the various border posts continued to increase. A rapid international mobilization occurred, aimed at getting foreign citizens out of the country. Around 38,000 people had already departed via the Ras Jdir border post—18,000 Tunisians, 15,000 Egyptians, 2,500 Libyans, and 2,500 Chinese. Within the space of 48 hours two Turkish ships evacuated 1,200 Turks and 500 other foreigners, of 25 different nationalities, from Benghazi to the port of Marmaris in Turkey. India was also beginning to organize the evacuation of its nationals; already, 300 had flown out on an Air India plane. There were about 18,000 Indians in Libya, most working in civil construction, transport, and public health. China was preparing a huge operation to provide fifteen aircraft per day for two weeks in order to evacuate its 33,000 nationals; 16,000 were already on their way to Tunisia, Greece, Egypt, and Malta. Indeed, the Maltese port of Valletta would be the destination for large numbers of people fleeing the conflict.

Brazil had sent a ship to Benghazi to pick up foreign nationals, among them 148 Brazilians. Brazil's diplomatic representatives in Libya, led by Ambassador George Ney Fernandes, and the employees of a few major Brazilian companies, such as Odebrecht, had the task of trying to round up their remaining compatriots. I had been trying to contact the ambassador every day, even before my departure from Paris for Tunisia, but hadn't yet managed to speak to him, despite leaving numerous messages.

THAT SAME NIGHT I SENT MY FIRST ARTICLES TO THE NEWSPAPER. THE FIRST WAS A short piece, written with my deadline already looming. I wrote that although the Colonel was still in place at the apex of the regime, he was progressively losing control. I explained that after our clandestine entry into Libya and a 400-kilometer journey incorporating three of the most important cities in Tripolitania, a region Gaddafi said was loyal to him, we witnessed an unprecedented situation: in much of Libya, power was effectively in the hands of the people. It seemed to be a genuine grass-roots movement, without any high-profile leaders. Furthermore, contrary to the Colonel's claims, the rebellion had already spread far beyond Benghazi into all corners of the country. A new national flag was flying above public buildings, replacing pictures of the dictator; it was the banner Libyans were carrying forward in a battle against dictatorial power, a sense of national unity in their hearts. The movement brought together tribes, villages, towns, and cities—and was getting much closer to Tripoli than previously thought. Although the population did not want a bloodbath, they would not give up on the armed struggle, their leaders having decided it was necessary to completely liberate the country. I wrote that guerrilla actions were multiplying in the west, making possible the seizure and occupation of symbols of power such as police stations and military buildings. In place of the Revolutionary Committees created by Gaddafi after 1969, there were now popular committees using the state structure to distribute food and fuel and attempting to coordinate the actions of the rebel groups.

The prospect of the end of the regime, I reported, was a source both of euphoria and concern, but above all it was swelling the ranks of the opposition. Even people who had long been on Gaddafi's side—members of the Revolutionary Committees, police officers, soldiers—were now joining the uprising. Others were simply deserting. The overall picture was that tribes were uniting against the terror tactics Gaddafi had used so often over the years to stay in power.

My second piece, published on February 21, focused solely on the prospect of a battle for the capital. I wrote: "They already dominate much of the interior of Libya, and now they are preparing to take Tripoli. Gathered in their hundreds in every village, armed with AK-47 rifles and communicating via radios and mobile phones, the rebels are getting ready for what they refer to as 'the Battle of Tripoli,' the simultaneous attacks on the capital." I added that the word of the moment was "revolution"; any hope that the regime would relinquish power peacefully was fading. "The rebels are taking up arms," I said, "because they no longer believe Gaddafi will be brought down by peaceful demonstrations, as in Tunisia and Egypt."

We left Adel's communications room and returned to the hospital by car; it was a very short journey, but according to the rebels, security issues made it inadvisable to walk. Abdul, who had earlier greeted us at the hospital with a 9 mm pistol in his hand, was waiting for us. He sat down to talk, this time holding between his legs a Kalashnikov with a bayonet attached. His words gushed forth without a single pause for Ghaith or me to ask a question. He started by telling us that his group of rebels was attacking checkpoints around Zintan, which Gaddafi's forces had set up to control the movement of civilians. He had just returned from one of these attacks; he had killed one soldier and brought back three prisoners, all of them wounded. With their guerrilla tactics the rebels had successfully gained access to military camps in the desert where weapons for Gaddafi's soldiers were stored. "We've captured all the weapons in those arsenals," he said.

As the monologue carried on, my attention began to drift, but Ghaith continued to translate the parts he considered most important. After a few more minutes Abdul stood up, shook my hand, then put his hand to his heart and said, "Salaam alaikum" ("Peace be with you"). He did the same with Ghaith and then he left, promising he would help us get to Tripoli the next day, just as Adel and Ali had promised earlier.

We went to a part of the hospital used as accommodation by nurses and doctors. A bedroom had been prepared for us in a flat used by a nurse whose complexion, eyes, hair color, and accent immediately made it obvious she was from Eastern Europe. She lived there with her husband; neither of them had any intention of leaving, despite the danger and hardship the conflict had brought. The bedroom had a worn brown carpet, a TV tuned to Al Jazeera, and two single beds along opposite walls. A third mattress had been placed on the floor, perpendicular to the end of one of the beds. Various people had come with us into the flat, and I suddenly realized one of them was the uncommunicative driver who had brought us to Zintan from Jadou. I wondered why he was still in Zintan, thinking that perhaps he didn't want to return home at night. A couple of minutes later, however, when Ghaith managed to get a few words out of him, we discovered the actual reason for his presence was quite different, and more than a little surprising.

Due to tribal moral codes, he felt responsible for our safety and had decided to stay in Zintan and accompany us, because now we were the responsibility of a different tribe and he wanted to make sure we were being treated correctly. The third mattress, therefore, was for him. I felt a mixture of admiration and discomfort: I was impressed by the notions of responsibility, solidarity, and loyalty in the behavior of the Arab and Berber tribes toward people they consider their friends, but I also had the disconcerting feeling of being in custody. And, like Ghaith, I wanted to avoid putting anyone else at risk as a result of our choice to cover an armed conflict. Anyway, I was grateful for his assistance and insisted he take one of the beds while I slept on the mattress on the floor. Exhausted, I fell asleep almost as soon as I lay down, despite the intermittent firing of Kalashnikovs, occasional bursts from anti-aircraft guns, and the sporadic shouts in support of the revolution.

WHEN WE WOKE UP ON SUNDAY MORNING THERE WAS LESS SHOOTING GOING ON outside. Ghaith and I said goodbye to the driver, who now seemed satisfied we were in good hands. Ali turned up with an improvised breakfast of biscuits, water, soft drinks, and *laban*, a kind of curdled milk drink. I had tried it before and found it horrible, but Ghaith greeted its appearance with unrestrained glee, saying it had been his favorite drink when he was a child in Iraq. Here, I thought, was evidence that Ghaith wasn't the image of a hard-bitten war reporter. As a journalist he was smooth and soft-spoken, an expert in the gentle art of persuading people to talk to him, and even in the midst of an armed conflict he also found time to delight in these gifts—and his mobile phone. The constant target for his sugary words was Safa, the journalist he lived with in Beirut. Ghaith, I discovered, was a courageous, focused, and determined reporter—and, when it came to the opposite sex, a sweet talker.

After those few moments of relaxation over breakfast, Ali told us the challenge of getting to Tripoli looked even more difficult than previously thought. He would carry on searching for a way through, as would Ghaith and I, but a Plan B was also emerging: the idea of heading initially for Zawiyah rather than Tripoli. The city was in rebel hands and Ali assured us he had contacts there; he would try to persuade two of them to come to Zintan to pick us up and then take us back to Zawiyah with them. The idea had a certain appeal. Zawiyah isn't very far from Tripoli, but obviously it wasn't what we really wanted. Ali left, looking somewhat worried, and instructed us not to leave the room until he came back with news from his contacts.

So there we were, left in a room measuring about three by four meters, with not much to do except watch the news on TV. Abdul paid us a brief visit, saying he was also talking to his contacts and trying to arrange for us to travel in the direction of Tripoli. Soon after he left, another man turned up outside the bedroom. He looked somewhere between 30 and 40 years old. He asked for our permission to come in and then sat on the edge of one of the beds, holding his Kalashnikov by the barrel, the butt resting on the floor. He told us he'd come because he was a deserter from the army and wanted to tell us his story. His commanding officers were still members of the regime. His account of the violence in Tripoli was horrifying, coming as it did from someone who had been part of the apparatus of repression.

"When the demonstrators arrived to protest peacefully," he said, "we received orders to shoot. We refused, and we were treated as traitors." He and the other soldiers who had refused to fire on the protesters were sent to a military installation in the desert. Their guns were taken away, as were their mobile phones, and they were accused of "collaboration." They were then locked up, six to a cell, and were informed of their sentence by one of the commanders: "'You're going to be executed.'"

Among the others in his cell were men who, as he put it, were "Africans, not Libyans." Armed soldiers appeared and put the prisoners in a vehicle to take them to a place in the desert where, they imagined, they would be shot. But he and three other prisoners attacked the driver, killed him, and were able to overcome the other five soldiers in the vehicle.

Having escaped from almost certain execution, he decided to head for Zintan, arriving late the previous night—and that was the end of the story. He stood up, thanked us, and left. His testimony had lasted ten minutes at most. He sought us to share his harrowing story, as if in doing so he could rid himself of the psychological torture he had suffered and at the same time, perhaps, shed some light on the methods of Muammar Gaddafi's regime. His arrival had certainly taken us by surprise, as indeed did his sudden departure. Ghaith was as affected as I was by the rawness of what we had just heard.

Ali came back a little while later and took us out into the center of Zintan, allowing us to see it in daylight for the first time. A week after the beginning of the uprising, the local people were trying to re-create a semblance of normality despite the dangers brought about by the conflict and the increasing disruptions to transport and to the provision of basic goods. On the busy pavements hawkers did a brisk trade in jerry cans of petrol, which was already in short supply and therefore rising quickly in price. But people were blaming these hardships on the regime's determination to stay to power rather than on the insurgency. We left the city center and drove around the outskirts, passing through checkpoints at regular intervals. At one of them, most of the road was blocked off using tanker trucks, leaving only a narrow passage for vehicles to pass through in single file under the watchful gaze of half a dozen men carrying AK-47s. Patches of the road surface were blackened by fire.

Back in the city center we visited the former headquarters of the Revolutionary Committee, which provided the most glaring evidence of the violence that had taken place. In the road outside were more than a dozen burned-out cars. The building itself—modern in style, and not unattractive architecturally—had charred, gaping holes where its windows used to be. The main door had been smashed off its hinges. Inside, nothing remained: all furniture, electronic equipment, and documents had been taken away. The word "Traitors" had been painted on the fire-damaged back wall of the entrance hall. Ali explained that in the week since the attack on the building, every day àt 5 p.m. there had been a protest march through the center of the city, the purpose being to mobilize the community against the counterattack that was bound to come sooner or later.

WE RETURNED TO THE IMPROVISED COMMUNICATIONS CENTER WHERE GHAITH AND I were able to work for a while in the company of Adel, Ali, and various young rebels who came in to spread the anti-Gaddafi message on social networking sites. I connected my mobile to the computer, hoping to discover why it still wasn't working even though it now had a Libyan SIM card. I'd already recorded a large number of interviews on my smartphone because the batteries on my voice recorder were running low. I hoped the mobile and the computer would synchronize their data—which they did, giving me a precious backup of dozens of interviews. When the process was complete I inserted a new SIM the rebels had given me from Libya's second-biggest mobile phone operator, Almadar. Fortunately, it worked.

In the meantime I borrowed Ghaith's phone to try again to contact George Ney Fernandes, the Brazilian ambassador in Tripoli. My previous attempts, all unsuccessful, had been from outside Libya. Now that I was in the country making the call from one Libyan number to another, I got straight through. He told me he'd been extremely busy organizing the evacuation of thousands of Brazilians, most of who had been working for big companies such as Petrobras and Odebrecht, which had contracts with the Libyan government. "A ship has just sailed from Tripoli," he said, clearly very pleased to be nearing his goal of getting every Brazilian national out of the country.

I had many things to discuss with the ambassador, but suddenly we got cut off. I'd hoped to hear more details about the revolution in the capital and about the political and diplomatic situation in which the regime now found itself. I didn't even have time to tell him I was now inside Libya, covering the conflict.

Ghaith and I had drawn up three different plans in some detail, each of them containing alternative courses of action if something didn't work out. In the first plan the objective was to go straight to Tripoli; in the second we would go to Zawiyah instead and bide our time there until it became possible to move on to the capital; in the third, if neither of the first two proved viable, we would use diplomatic channels to inform the Libyan foreign ministry that we were in the country covering the revolution without the regime's permission, and that we were willing to present ourselves to the authorities if they would guarantee our safety and give us formal authorization to work in Tripoli. The third course of action was definitely the least appealing; it meant losing our autonomy and being watched over by the regime, but it still needed detailed planning. I'd intended to ask the ambassador to inform the Libyan foreign ministry that we were in the country; if the ministry replied that it was prepared to give us the guarantees we wanted, we could proceed with discussions. But, despite trying a few more times, I couldn't get through to the ambassador again.

In my last attempt to call the ambassador, I brought up his number on Ghaith's mobile via the list of recent outgoing calls and happened to notice one of the other names in the list was Jon Lee Anderson: a journalist I regard as one of the best in his field, and whose writing—for example on Che Guevara, and on the fall of Baghdad—I had read avidly. With a smile on my lips I went back into the room where Ghaith was working and asked him, "Are you friends with Jon Lee Anderson?"

"Yes, we're friends," Ghaith replied, looking puzzled by my question.

"That guy's one of the greats! You should have told me!"

Ghaith smiled, stopped what he was doing, and reminded me of the moment we'd met on the street in front of the hotel in Ben Gardane, when I interrupted a conversation between him and another man to tell him about my decision to leave for Dehiba. That man, Ghaith now informed me, was none other than Jon Lee, who had decided to leave Tunisia and instead go to Cairo, then on through eastern Libya to Benghazi. "He said that entering via the western border would be very dangerous." Ghaith laughed, a little nervously. We were now in a war-torn country in which two sides were fighting for control over territory—and a country whose government had promised that any journalists entering clandestinely would be treated as "agents of al-Qaeda."

Both of us, therefore, were very concerned about our safety; indeed, so far our every move had been based on security considerations. Hearing about a warning issued by a reporter of Jon Lee's stature would only intensify my focus on safety—but it also increased my satisfaction at having already done something to reveal the extent of the uprising in western Libya.

While we were getting our things together in preparation to leave Adel's office, a middle-aged man, Hakim, came in. He introduced himself in a friendly manner, saying he was one of the men responsible for "security" in Zintan. He told us the rebels had taken control of major pipelines through which gas was exported to Italy—a significant development given the importance of gas for the national finances. As we left, Hakim smiled broadly, wished us good luck, and made a request: "Please, don't believe we belong to al-Qaeda."

GHAITH AND I WERE STILL WAITING FOR REPLIES FROM OUR CONTACTS AND FROM the rebels in other cities that Ali, Adel, and others in Zintan had spoken to. Time was passing by and we weren't making progress toward Tripoli, or at least not as quickly as we wanted. Some of our hosts were also getting impatient on our behalf, but they said all we could do was wait for the discussions to come to a conclusion. We were taken back to the bedroom in the hospital where we'd spent the night and were asked to stay there until it was time to leave.

Ali finally returned two hours later, around 3 p.m. He told us the prospects for reaching Tripoli now looked quite good; his contacts in Zawiyah would come to pick us up some time that day, or perhaps the following morning. In the meantime he invited us to join the daily protest march he'd mentioned to us before; he said people would begin to gather for it at 4:30 p.m. at a major crossroads in the city center, near the destroyed Revolutionary Committee building. It seemed to me there was no longer any point in having protests in Zintan—unless they were a means of bringing people together and keeping them alert to the threat of a counterattack, as Ali had said earlier, or simply an outpouring of pride at finally having freedom of expression. When we arrived at the meeting point a few hundred people were already there, and we chatted with some of them as we waited for the march to begin.

The march set off around the scheduled time, accompanied by vehicles used during the uprising; some were equipped with anti-aircraft cannons, others were full of armed men. As I walked I chatted with Ali, finding out that although he was originally from Zintan he now lived in Tripoli with his wife. He said Ghaith and I were welcome to use his house if we reached the capital and needed a place to lie low. As we talked, I realized my phone was finally working with its new Libyan number: this would enable me to talk to many more people, although the downside, which neither Ghaith nor I had taken properly into consideration, was that there might be a risk involved in having a Libyan number because the mobile phone operators were in the hands of the Gaddafi family and we might be tracked.

It was only when we returned to Adel's office that I found out the UN Security Council had approved the first resolution, imposing sanctions on Libya and, perhaps most importantly, placing an embargo on sales of weapons to the regime. Although everyone knew a government seeking to buy arms abroad didn't always need to go through the proper channels, it was nevertheless a change in posture by the international community. Gaddafi was being backed into a corner. Barack Obama had issued an ultimatum demanding Gaddafi step down, and the International Criminal Court in The Hague had opened an investigation into possible crimes against humanity committed not only by the Colonel but also by his sons and the highest-ranking officers in the armed forces. As a consequence of the investigation it was possible that, in a few weeks, the number of countries in which Gaddafi could seek exile would be drastically reduced. Meanwhile, the revolutionaries were getting organized. With Benghazi liberated, at least for the time being, the former justice minister in the regime, Mustafa Abdel Jalil, announced the creation of a provisional government—the embryo of what would become known nationwide as the National Transitional Council.

Gaddafi was not only ruling out any possibility of stepping down but also insisting to the international media that Libya was "completely calm": there were no disturbances in the interior of the country, he said, and those responsible for the trouble in the east were "terrorist groups" linked to al-Qaeda. His disconnection from reality would cost him dearly. The regime had invited a group of foreign journalists to visit Zawiyah, the idea being to show them that the west of the country was under control. What the reporters witnessed, however, was a demonstration, with people yelling "Down with the regime! We want freedom!" During this protest, the armed rebels in western Libya appeared on TV screens for the first time, providing the outside world with a snapshot of the situation Ghaith and I witnessed wherever we went.

Leaving Adel's office late on Sunday night, we walked out into a sandstorm mixed with light rain. I tried to cover my nose and mouth as we got in Ali's Japanese sedan. It quickly became impossible to see more than a few meters ahead. What looked like a swirling yellow fog surrounded us, the color of the sand accentuated by the streetlights. Whipped up by the wind and moistened by the rain, the grains of sand stuck to walls, pavements, our clothing, car windscreens—pretty much everything. For three days Ghaith and I had been unable to have a shower or bath; our skin and hair, regularly exposed to sand blowing in from the desert, was accumulating an opaque layer of dust that we'd tried to diminish with occasional splashes of water from taps and wash basins. But even so, I couldn't help but marvel at the sandstorm, a phenomenon that obliges the inhabitants of the desert to adapt their lives to the rhythms of hostile nature.

Back at our bedroom in the hospital, we went to bed without receiving any further news about our departure for Tripoli. We were both aware that the pressure we were putting on our contacts, and on Ali and Adel, was beginning to cause some displeasure. Ali in particular seemed to be getting annoyed, although he hadn't actually said anything to us.

On Monday, hours passed before Ali appeared. Again we found ourselves confined to the hospital building, having been told we shouldn't risk going out into the streets of Zintan unaccompanied. We realized our chances of getting to Zawiyah, where the idea had been to stay with Ali's contacts, were fading. We obviously had to think about alternatives, but I was making no progress at all through my contacts in Tripoli.

What I did manage to do, after more failed attempts, was to speak to Fernandes, the Brazilian ambassador. I finally told him we were inside Libya and looking for a way of getting to Tripoli. His reaction, however, could hardly have been worse. First he told me his phone had been bugged by Gaddafi's secret services, as was the case with the diplomatic representatives of other countries. Then, raising his voice, he said, "Don't try to get to Tripoli. The military have control over all the roads in, and there's no way around that. Get out by the same way you came in!"

To my surprise, he then insisted I tell him where we were and also to give him my wife's phone number. I found his attitude exasperating. I replied that I was a professional doing my job, reporting on an armed conflict that was having a serious impact on the civilian population. I made it clear I wasn't going to reveal our location or tell him anything about my family—and added I was surprised, given that his calls were being intercepted, that he had even asked for such information in the first place. On that sour note, our conversation ended.

Ghaith and I realized we needed to adapt our plans in order to reach Zawiyah or Tripoli. We decided that if Ali's contacts didn't prove fruitful we would try to find a fixer ourselves. We could ask Abdul if he knew anyone. When Ali turned up he took us to see Adel again, and we talked to him about the options. He told us regime troops were advancing out of Tripoli; they were guarding all the routes into and out of the capital and were surrounding Zawiyah, poised to try to recapture the city. Gaddafi was preparing a counteroffensive; we would realize later it was part of a large-scale attack launched in both western and eastern Libya. Zintan, Nalut, and the Dehiba border post were all under threat. It looked like Gaddafi wanted to take back control of Tripolitania, which he considered crucial for the stability of the regime.

Contemplating this situation, Adel said something we'd not heard from him before. "We don't want to prevent you from moving on, but we'll only help you in the safest possible conditions. And right now, it's not safe enough."

Despite the warning, Ghaith and I felt more keenly than ever that we needed to head for Zawiyah. If there were public protests, a violent crackdown, and the possibility of a major military offensive against the city, we needed to be there covering the story. Our sense of urgency increased a few hours later when we learned that on the outskirts of Zawiyah an army convoy with heavy weapons was trying to enter an area under rebel control. The offensive Adel spoke about seemed to have materialized sooner than expected.

We managed to get in one of the vehicles heading for the combat zone outside Zintan. To get there we took a road that snaked down all the way through the mountains; on the way was a lookout point from which it was almost possible to see the battle unfold in the distance. Hundreds of rebels had gathered at the lookout, tension etched into their faces.

The army convoy consisted of about twenty vehicles carrying troops and heavy weapons, and it was traveling on one of the roads supposedly under rebel control. But from that distance it was impossible to know exactly what was going on. We continued down the winding road until we came out on the plain where the battle was taking place, although at this stage we were still quite a few kilometers away from it. To approach the battlefront we drove at high speed between the various defensive positions the rebels had set up, changing vehicles with frenetic regularity. At some of these positions we stopped for a short while to take pictures of the rebels gathered around the anti-aircraft guns they had captured from the regime and were using to exchange fire with the forces loyal to the regime.

What we were witnessing there, outside Zintan, was very much a battle scene. A few minutes before sunset, on a desert road, we watched the rebels reloading their guns, which were spitting fire in the direction of the loyalist forces, although the distance to the enemy was such that they didn't seem to have much chance of shooting accurately. We didn't want to get too close to the guns; they were bound to be a target for the loyalists' artillery, though again we didn't know how accurate that might be.

We proceeded in another pickup, traveling alongside rebels carrying machine guns and belts of ammunition. Amid their discussions in Arabic about combat strategy, they never failed to greet us and express satisfaction at our presence. In the distance we could actually see anti-aircraft shells streaking through the air, not far above the ground. We were still on a stretch of road that was considered safe, however, and the rebels were still willing to take us farther forward. At one point, when our vehicle stopped for us to get out, another waited right there to pick us up; it was an impressive and unanticipated show of organization. I opened the back door of the pickup waiting for us; Ghaith jumped in and sat in the middle of the back seat, then I got in—repeating the "salaam alaikum" with which I was greeted—and sat to his left, taking the last empty place. I looked around at each of the other men in the vehicle. To Ghaith's right was a man in traditional Libyan clothing, looking as grimy as Ghaith and I were. He had a long black beard and had a belt of ammunition draped around his neck, which fell down across his chest all the way to the floor. He looked like an archetypical radical Muslim fighter—an arresting and, at first glance, quite a frightening sight. As I looked around out of the window, Ghaith struck up a conversation with him. Aware that I couldn't understand what they were saying, Ghaith explained that the man was, in fact, a university professor with a PhD in history who had left behind his wife and children in Tripoli to come and fight in the rebellion. It was impossible to take notes as the pickup was now bumping along off-road toward one of the rebels' forward positions, so I got out my mobile and used its audio recorder to capture what the professor was saying. Two days later the recording would be lost forever. But the presence of that man in the vehicle, with his surprising backstory, made me realize the Libyan uprising was a complex affair involving different social groups, including the middle class, and certainly not a movement of sectarian Islamic radicals at the margins of society.

We got out of the vehicle with the professor and continued on foot, accompanied by dozens of rebels. It was cold, but the effort of carrying a rucksack full of equipment soon warmed me up; the rebels were carrying very little apart from their AK-47s. We went over a few hills of sand and stone, with patches of dry scrub here and there; we heard the crack of gunfire and saw projectiles flashing through the sky but hadn't yet glimpsed the frontline. Then, suddenly, we were given a signal to turn around and go back; we didn't know what had happened, but we returned to the vehicles as fast as we could. Back in the truck, driving off at high speed, we heard that the army convoy had been forced to withdraw from the area—thanks, apparently, to the courage and tactical skills of a group of only five rebels. Furthermore, we were told the rebels had found a store of food and ammunition in the desert nearby; we headed in that direction and arrived, as darkness was falling, to find dozens of insurgents running into and out of a small warehouse carrying sacks of grain. We stayed there for ten minutes, in which time the store was stripped bare. The rebels celebrated the successful operation with cries of "Allahu Akbar" and shots into the air, then got in their vehicles and headed back to Zintan.

A battle had been won, but for Zintan there was still a very long way to go. The victory over the convoy wasn't due to organizational skills or firepower but to the efforts of a handful of men we had valiantly defended their positions, unseen by the majority of the rebel forces. Some rebels had been wounded but, at least that night, none killed. Twelve prisoners had been captured, supposedly all Malian mercenaries; none of them were injured and they were all taken back to the city. When the rebels arrived in Zintan they were greeted as returning heroes; the locals screamed words of praise and blasted their car horns. A large traffic jam formed as people spilled into the road. Right behind our vehicle was a pickup with an anti-aircraft gun on the back; a rebel was firing it into the night sky, shouting joyfully.

Although Zintan had something to celebrate, the fate of the neighboring towns hung in the balance. Gaddafi's forces now surrounded Zawiyah, a city of strategic importance taken by the rebels a few days before. But the rebels weren't sure of their enemy's intentions: some thought the troops were simply consolidating their defense of Tripoli, but the majority imagined they were planning an offensive against Zawiyah itself. The army had mounted an offensive against Benghazi when the uprising was only a few days old: the resulting death toll was thought to have been around 2,000. Further south, the situation was also tense. The army was reinforcing its positions around the Dehiba border post, which the rebels had taken control of during the previous weekend. And an attack on Nalut was being prepared, apparently with the assistance of forces from neighboring Wazen.

By the time I sat down to write a piece about Gaddafi's counteroffensive later that night, the army had already recaptured the Dehiba border post. But, I wrote, Gaddafi's forces had not yet been successful in their offensives against Zawiyah, Zintan, Nalut, and other towns and villages around Tripoli that were still in rebel hands. The army used heavy artillery in the battles taking place around the outskirts of Zawiyah; although the soldiers were repulsed after hours of fighting, they still had the city surrounded and controlled all the access roads. The death toll was unknown.

Loyalist forces were also besieging Misrata, although so far they had failed to regain control of the city's airport. But, I wrote, various cities across the region celebrated the rebels' resistance and hoped an uprising might take place in Tripoli, piercing the ring of steel around the capital and opening the way to an invasion.

For safety reasons I didn't state our location in the article. Apart from the looming threat of the counteroffensive in Tripolitania, there was also the constant worry that we might be betrayed and handed over to the regime. This wasn't just a concern for Ghaith and me but also for the men who'd been helping us. Late that night, for example, after we'd gone back to Adel's office to work, we experienced some extremely tense moments when an unidentified man turned up outside in a car without number plates and banged on the door. We immediately fell silent, turned off all the lights, and strained to hear what was going on outside. Then Ali came over to me and said quietly, "Take the SIM card out of your mobile. We don't know who's out there."

We turned off all our equipment and left the building as soon as we were sure the man had left and that there were no other suspicious people in the street outside.

That night I had a long phone conversation with my wife. In tears, she complained about the distance between us, the lack of regular contact, and the fact that I couldn't tell her exactly where I was. "The way things are, you could disappear forever in Libya and no one would ever know what had happened to you," she said.

CHAPTER 6

RISK

When we left the bedroom in the hospital for the last time, our rucksacks on our backs, we saw the Eastern European nurse in the corridor outside. She smiled and wished us good luck. As we walked away Ghaith turned to me and said, without the slightest hint of irony, "I'll miss this place."

It was just after 10 a.m. on Tuesday morning, March 1, 2011, and we were leaving Zintan for Yefren, a nearby town with a majority Berber population, from where we would hopefully continue to Zawiyah and Tripoli. In the two days we'd been waiting for Ali and Adel to give us the go-ahead to leave, we'd explored alternatives. Yefren had come up when Ghaith spoke to a prominent Zintan rebel who had contacts there. The capital of the district of al-Jabal al-Gharbi, Yefren is a town of around 70,000 inhabitants situated in the Nefusa mountains 120 kilometers southwest of Tripoli. It had risen up against the regime on February 18 but would only come fully under rebel control much later, on April 6. Abdul told us leaders of the Berber community, from the Banu Ifran tribe, would secretly be waiting for us. They would help us organize our journey to Zawiyah, which had been cut off by the army and where there was the risk of a massacre taking place. But the route to Zawiyah would have to be via Sabratha, a city still loyal to Gaddafi. We therefore had every reason to be cautious and to make plans that minimized the chances of contact with the military.

We set off for Yefren by car, accompanied by Abdul and a driver. As we were going through the outskirts of Zintan, I called Ali to thank him for his hospitality and for all his efforts to ensure our safety. I also reiterated that we had to leave and continue on our way to Tripoli, since our aim was to give a true description of the revolution as opposed to Gaddafi's version, according to which the Libyan people not only supported his regime but also loved him personally. Ali wished us good luck, assured us we would be welcome to visit Zintan again in future, and told us to be careful. His tone was serious, his words punctuated by long pauses, as if he were silently contemplating the risks ahead of us. A year and a half would go by before I spoke to him again.

Minutes later, we changed vehicles at a rebel checkpoint. Abdul wouldn't be going any farther with us but left us in the hands of the driver, whom he trusted. As we said our goodbyes I noticed Abdul's demeanor had changed; he seemed to have lost some of the enthusiasm we'd seen when he greeted us, pistol in hand, upon our arrival at the hospital. He seemed deflated by the fact that Gaddafi's forces had regrouped, and even more so by the rebels' inability to mount an attack on the capital. The stark reality was that the Libyan conflict would not be over quickly, nor would the death toll be low.

"Give me ten men and we'll defend the city," he declared. "Give me a hundred men, armed and well trained, and we'll smash through the roadblocks and get to Tripoli," he added, gesturing aggressively as if to reaffirm his own bravery. But Abdul knew the rebels were incapable of defeating Gaddafi without outside assistance. As if he wanted to send a message to the international community through Ghaith and me, he then said, "All we need is an American bomb dropped on Bab al-Azizia. We'll do the rest."

This was the first time I'd heard a rebel say they would be in favor of Western military intervention. To hear an armed Libyan Muslim call for the United States to bring its military might to bear on the Arab world was surprising, to say the least. Over the decades, people in other countries had come to believe that the Libyan people not only supported Gaddafi but approved of his acts of terrorism against the West—but what I was seeing now suggested not only that the Colonel was hated by many of his compatriots but also that the Americans might be seen, by some, as saviors rather than demons.

We carried on toward Yefren, a one-hour journey on a road that curved around the mountainsides. The driver listened to Arabic music on a battered old cassette tape; Ghaith and I were silent for most of the way. We knew we were taking a much bigger risk now that we had left Zintan and were in the company of a single guide rather than under the protection of the rebels. The possibility of betrayal, or of walking into a trap set by militias, mercenaries, or the police, loomed large in my imagination.

As we arrived in the outskirts of Yefren, our driver stopped by the side of the road to wait for the contact who was due to take us to the local Berber leaders. All three of us got out of the car. The hillside plunged steeply away from the far side of the road; laid out below was the vastness of the desert, partially obscured by a fine winter mist. The region is home to the Berbers of Yefren, also known as the Ifranids or Banu Ifran, an influential tribe with a very long history. They are regarded in Tripolitania as descendants of the Zenetas, a Berber nation that had occupied the Maghreb and, in the eighth century, invaded the Iberian Peninsula. Later I learned the Ifranids had a long tradition of resistance against foreign occupiers, including uprisings against the Roman and Byzantine empires. Such was their importance in the northern Sahara that, according to some linguists and historians, the word "Africa" actually derives from the Roman word for the Ifranids. Standing there on the approach to the city, it was satisfying to think that in my foray into this corner of Libya I was crossing paths with the history of the African continent itself.

I was still gazing over the landscape when Ghaith called out to me. Our contact had arrived. Greeting him, I immediately felt more comfortable with him than with our previous driver. We got into his car and headed for the place where we were due to meet the tribal leaders and have lunch with them before continuing on toward Zawiyah. In less than fifteen minutes we were in Yefren, driving along dirt roads toward our destination, which turned out to be a house some way from the city center. The atmosphere in the town was the opposite of Zintan: the streets were very quiet, with no weapons in view and no checkpoints. The presence of foreigners wasn't likely to go unnoticed, however, so Ghaith and I tried to be inconspicuous, sitting back in our seats rather than peering out of the window. From what I could see the city hadn't suffered any significant damage; it was almost possible to believe there wasn't an uprising going on there at all. A few days later, however, Yefren came under siege and suffered bombardment by Gaddafi's troops until early June, when the rebels would finally prevail.

When we arrived at the house a man with graying hair and a moustache greeted us at the door; he wore slacks, a shirt, and smart shoes, which gave him a slightly austere air of respectability. He introduced himself as Issa Sijuk, a member of the Libyan Amazigh Congress. We removed our shoes and went inside, entering a room that had cushions against the walls and a carpet on the floor. A friendly conversation began, starting with a few comments about the history of the Berbers and their role in the formation of Libya. Quick to realize the many gaps in our knowledge, Sijuk patiently explained the historical importance of his tribe and then moved on to its more recent history, at which point the subject of Gaddafi was unavoidable.

"Everyone has suffered greatly under the regime, but the situation of the amazigh is somewhat different," he said. "Within Libyan culture we are a specific case. We are part of the Libyan nation but we have different habits, different clothing. Our cities have different names from the others."

Sijuk calmly explained that the Gaddafi regime saw his people as traitors. Many of them had been imprisoned, tortured, and killed during the 42 years of the dictatorship; others' homes had been confiscated as punishment for expressing opposition.

Ghaith interrupted and asked whether the frictions of the past explained the current uprising. "What's happening now is an uprising against more than 40 years of oppression," Sijuk replied. "Every country has a certain amount of patience. Ours has run out. When we saw the popular movements in the neighboring countries, we felt that this was our moment. We wanted to demonstrate peacefully, and that's how it all started. There was another wave of violent repression."

Sijuk said the first protest in the city was a relatively minor one on the evening of February 18, when sixteen people took to the streets to express their discontent. The next day, however, a much larger crowd gathered. Some young people were arrested, but Sijuk believed the security forces were taken by surprise and feared the consequences of a major confrontation. "One of the problems in our country is precisely the fact that, over the years, the government has armed the population. This has always been used to create tensions. But it's also opened the way to what is happening now," he said, noting the irony of the situation.

"The movement started in Benghazi," I said. "So what made Yefren and the other cities in Tripolitania join in?"

"Benghazi was the spark for a national uprising because they were expressing the ideas of the whole country, not just of their own city. The proof of this is that they began to attack the symbols of the power of the regime, such as the Revolutionary Committees, police stations, military installations. We, in the west, did the same. The uprising against Gaddafi is new, but our experience of confronting the regime goes back a long way."

According to Sijuk, some tribes and cities had been preparing for a major confrontation with Gaddafi for decades and had already clashed with the dictatorship. But the difficulty, he said, lay in the ambiguous relationship between Gaddafi and the rest of the world—or more specifically, the fact that Gaddafi received a lot of arms from the West. And not just weapons: foreign powers had also provided military training. "I'd like you to know that the British, for example, eat food that was paid for using money obtained from bloodshed."

Sijuk was keen to clarify the differences between his tribe and the many others in Libya, and to explain how the Ifranids fit into the overall political picture. It was a subject Ghaith and I wanted to hear more about, as we had been wondering about the significance of tribal differences. The underlying question in both our minds was whether Gaddafi told the truth when he depicted the relations between Libya's tribes as unstable and hostile.

"So there are no divergences between the cities of eastern and western Libya?" asked Ghaith, perhaps a little provocatively.

Sijuk insisted there weren't. "The regime would like to create tensions, to cause a split between the movement in the east and the cities in the west. They say there's a power struggle between different tribes, that there'll be a civil war. But there's no power struggle whatsoever. We all support the National Transitional Council in Benghazi. They're the people who are best placed to provide political leadership when the time comes for a new government. Tribalism isn't a political issue in Libya, it's a cultural and social issue. What the regime says isn't true."

"So can we assume that if Gaddafi's regime falls, your tribe will want it to be replaced by a democratic government, as Benghazi does?" I asked.

"I can assure you there's a consensus in the country, even though the international media is preoccupied with the tribal question. That's Gaddafi's agenda. The tribes really don't have different feelings about this. We have confidence in the way the process is being carried out," he said, before returning to answer my earlier question. "As for what kind of democratic government we want, the best kind of democracy is one that's created when people have been deprived of democracy. Libya isn't as shut off as it looks. We have contact with the outside world through TV, the Internet, through various other channels. We understand what human rights are. We hope for a national unity government which will give us a constitution. But until Tripoli falls, we can't have it."

Other tribal and political leaders had come into the room while we were talking. Abderezag Madi, another member of the amazigh organization, continued where Sijuk had left off. "We suffer under the dictatorship in two ways: by being Libyans and by being amazigh. What we need, as Libyans, is democracy and freedom. And the most important thing in this time of transition is to draw up a constitution, which is something we've been deprived of for over 40 years."

"You said you suffer as a Libyan and as an amazigh. But what are your aspirations as an amazigh?" I asked.

"We want cultural freedoms, such as the right to speak our language, express our values, and enjoy religious freedoms," Abderezag replied.

I remembered that Salah, one of the Berbers we'd spent time with in Nalut, had told us that although his people had embraced the Muslim faith they were in favor of religious tolerance, and that their Berber ancestors had been pagans, Jews, and Christians before the spread of Islam. Even today, Salah had said, there were Jews among the Berber tribes, and their faith was respected.

By this time there were different conversations going on in the room, and we started discussing the extent of the rebel movement in Yefren and around the interior of Libya. A third amazigh, Sefao Madi, Abderezag's brother, joined the conversation, addressing me in English. "What we're doing in Libya is a revolution, not just isolated protests in different cities. Our country needs freedom. We've had the regime for 42 years, and that's too long. Our neighbors in Tunisia, in Egypt, are fighting. Why can't we fight for our freedom? It's our chance to be free. Why shouldn't we also be free? I'm sure a lot of people are afraid. But it's been 42 years of frustrations. Now we have to face the guns. Our movement isn't afraid of guns."

I asked how it was that silent discontent had suddenly exploded into protests. Before replying Sefao hesitated for a few moments, then let out a sigh. "I don't know how that came about," he said. "You don't think about it, you just make the decision to go ahead and fight for your freedom. It's instinctive. We're all in the same position: we, as protesters, are afraid of getting shot, but the army also has the same fear. And now, neither side can back down." Abderezag added some words of regret: "The civilians have done their bit, up to this point. This would be the moment when the armed forces take the initiative. But you can't expect the Libyan army to act like, for example, the army in Tunisia, which wanted to preserve the state. In general they're very poor people, very badly paid, who don't have the ideal kind of training, and they don't have sufficient understanding of what's going on."

Abderezag said that Gaddafi encouraged his armed forces to be prejudiced against the Berbers. "The way the regime depicts the amazigh is racist. But we're not interested in our origins, in where we came from. Right now it doesn't make any difference. All we want to able to do with our culture is preserve it. Our children are prevented from studying our language. They don't learn to write in it. The dictatorship does all it can to suffocate our culture, even though we don't have any kind of ideology and have no wish to spread our culture elsewhere. We just want an end to the oppression."

At this stage in the discussion it was increasingly clear that the revolution in Yefren, as in other places, was being led by a group of intellectuals. But these were intellectuals with armed men alongside them. Shortly afterward, at the request of Sijuk, Abderezag, and Sefao, these armed men would head off on the route that led to Zawiyah to look for army checkpoints and any sign of troop movements.

To get to Zawiyah, the last rebel-held city before Tripoli, we would have to pass through a city loyal to the regime, Sabratha. In fact we needed to cross an area entirely under Gaddafi's control; it was impossible to predict how long it would take to be back in rebel-held territory. Sijuk, Abderezag, and Sefao knew this would be a challenge but believed that with the support of the rebels it was a viable plan.

While we waited for the men to report back we had a Libyan-style lunch, sitting on the floor around a large plate of bazeen, a local variation on couscous, served with a spicy stew of meat and vegetables. At about 2 p.m. the information came through that there were two checkpoints, the first not far outside Yefren, the second on the approach to Sabratha. But after Sabratha, things looked much more difficult: all the routes to Zawiyah had checkpoints. The immediate imperative was to plot a route that would allow us to bypass the first two checkpoints. The first probably wasn't a problem; it seemed to be unmanned, at least for that day. But the second, at the junction of two roads, was manned by soldiers who were stopping vehicles to check they weren't carrying arms or any suspicious-looking passengers—a category we certainly fell into. Looking at the maps, it seemed to Ghaith and me that in order to avoid that checkpoint, the only viable option was to cut across an area of desert. The rebels' first idea was that the two of us should go on foot, unaccompanied, across a stretch of desert about 600 meters wide. Once we were back on the road, beyond the checkpoint, another car would pick us up.

When we said it sounded too risky, they suggested we cut across the desert by car instead. Sefao agreed that the most important thing was to avoid going near the checkpoint, so he proposed a longer route, about three kilometers in total. This already sounded better. But, referring to a rudimentary hand-drawn map, Ghaith and I saw there was another possibility: a route of about six kilometers that, although much longer than the alternatives, also seemed the safest.

Sefao agreed to the idea and made arrangements for our departure. We ended up waiting for another hour, however, which was much longer than we expected. It was already mid-afternoon, and I began to doubt we had much chance of actually reaching Zawiyah that day. I didn't have time to share my concerns with Ghaith before someone suggested we should spend the night in Sabratha. Although the suggestion wasn't greeted with any particular enthusiasm, it immediately felt like a significant moment: I sensed things were beginning to slip from our control in a way that might compromise our safety.

When our pickup truck arrived we greeted the driver and his "navigator," and took our places on the back seat. Sefao would go ahead of us in another vehicle to check that everything was alright on the route. We passed the unmanned checkpoint without incident: one down, one to go. Suddenly we veered off the road and into the desert. The air in the cab became thick with tension; we were all afraid we might be intercepted by the army, militiamen, or mercenaries. I couldn't take my eyes off the point on the horizon where the checkpoint was just visible.

We knew hostile eyes might be drawn to our vehicle by the sun glinting on the metal and glass. Our driver—a friendly man, aged about 40—asked us what weapons we were carrying. I could tell from his expression, visible in the rearview mirror, that it was a serious question. Ghaith replied that as journalists we didn't carry weapons. For my part, I held up my pen and indulged in a terrible cliché: "Here is my gun."

"You're mad," said the driver, shaking his head and smiling.

We seemed to be making good progress across the desert and began to feel more confident we weren't being followed. It was clear, however, that it would have been stupid to try to cross that stretch of desert on foot, especially unaccompanied. Not even the driver and navigator, who both knew the region very well, were entirely sure where they were going; the track ahead was never clearly defined and was studded with various forks where it would have been possible to set off in the wrong direction. There were also some unexpected hazards, such as a pack of jackals that chose to follow us for a few minutes. It struck me that only with the help of the nomadic Bedouins would we have a chance of making the desert crossing exactly as planned.

Eventually we did see the Yefren-Sabratha road again and drove parallel to it for about ten minutes, looking at the traffic and trying to spot the driver who was due to meet us. When we saw him we left the sand and rocks behind and, thanks to the power of our 4×4, climbed back on to the tarmac. As the driver came clearly into view, Ghaith and I had a shock: we would now be in the hands of someone who looked no more than 20 years old. His name was Hussein al-Azzabi. Quiet and unassuming, he was chosen by the Yefren rebels to help us on the basis of his driving skills and his knowledge of the roads in and around Sabratha, including the routes to Zawiyah. We said goodbye to the two men who'd brought us across the desert and got in Hussein's car, a battered old sedan that quickly proved surprisingly fast and nimble. By now it was late afternoon, and again I found myself contemplating the unattractive prospect of spending the night in Sabratha, a pro-Gaddafi city bound to have people who would inform on us if they discovered our presence.

We drove for about an hour without going through a single town or village. Then, up ahead, we saw a car parked on the edge of the road and a man standing by it. As Hussein slowed down, Ghaith saw that the man—much to our surprise—was Sefao. He told Ghaith he'd been waiting for us for a while and just wanted to check that everything was alright, to wish us good luck, and to tell us we could count on his tribe in the future if we ever needed anything. And with that, we parted again. As we drove away Ghaith turned to me and said, "That's an amazing show of commitments toward us."

I was thinking the same thing. Sefao, who went on to become one of the principal rebel leaders in the region, would certainly have been known to the secret services and had risked his life by going through military checkpoints to make sure we were alright. His actions increased our confidence in Hussein, who despite his age had the trust of the Berber rebels. We were no longer under the direct protection of the Libyan tribes, but we could still count on them.

THE SUN WAS DISAPPEARING OVER THE HORIZON, WHICH WASN'T A GOOD THING AS far as we were concerned. We were in Sabratha but weren't yet on a road that led to Zawiyah. Hussein suggested we stop at a rural property belonging to one of his friends. We could rest there, he said, while he could get information about the latest movements of Gaddafi's troops, and on that basis choose the safest route to Zawiyah. Already anxious about time slipping away, I didn't think it was a good idea. But I kept quiet, hoping we could still continue on toward Zawiyah later that evening. After driving more than an hour, Hussein pulled off the road and went a couple of hundred meters down a dirt track and stopped next to a house and a large concrete shed. As we got out, Hussein said Ghaith and I would indeed spend the night there, as it was going to take quite a while to work out the next stage of our journey.

I received the news with resignation, but I was pleased to see there were no other houses nearby. The immediate surroundings consisted of a field of green grass—a rare sight in Libya—with goats, sheep, and chickens. Although it seemed a safe location, I felt cornered; we were now in the hands of Hussein and his friend, cut off from the rebels who could have come up with new ideas about how we should continue with our journey. Ghaith was similarly uncomfortable, but there seemed to be nothing we could do. It would be too risky to push ahead when we still lacked reliable information about the obstacles ahead. I attempted to disguise my mood as I was introduced to Hussein's friend, Mohamed, who would be putting us up for the night. He was a very thin, fragile-looking man, aged about 50. My first impressions weren't good. He didn't seem enthusiastic about our arrival, and unlike the people who'd welcomed us to the other places we'd stayed, there wasn't the slightest sign that he valued the presence of journalists. On the contrary he seemed inconvenienced by us; he avoided eye contact and spoke very little, at least initially.

Mohamed led us to the shed where we would spend the night. I had the impression he was arguing about us with Hussein, but of course I wasn't sure and couldn't understand what they were saying. Although Hussein had assured us we were in a safe place, our host's discomfort suggested otherwise.

On one side of our improvised bedroom was a filthy-looking sofa and a table with some pieces of old bread on it; on the floor was a ragged old carpet, also with a scattering of breadcrumbs. On the other side Mohamed put three mattresses. He also brought a small electric heater, which he attached to a socket that was almost falling out of the wall—a fire risk if ever there was one. Then he left and came back with some coffee and fresh bread. It was starkly different from the family dinners we'd been invited to share elsewhere, but I guessed that as well as wanting to keep us hidden away, Mohamed was also poorer than our previous hosts.

Without much else to do, Ghaith, Hussein, and I settled back on the mattresses. As neither Hussein nor Mohamed understood English, Ghaith and I at least had a language in which we could talk confidentially. Indeed, Ghaith made immediate use of the language barrier when I asked him what he thought about our situation.

"I don't trust this kid," he said. "We shouldn't be in the hands of someone his age."

I told him I'd been about to say the same thing. Ghaith decided to call Sefao to discuss our options, and also to ask him if he really trusted Hussein and Mohamed. The reply was positive; Sefao said we could rest easy. We still weren't entirely convinced, but there seemed to be nothing more to say so we dropped the subject and talked about other things while Hussein went off with Mohamed to try to get the information we needed about the route to Zawiyah.

A few minutes later we heard a vehicle approaching. Ghaith was sitting on his mattress, his back to the wall, while I was lying on mine a couple of meters away. We both jumped at the sound of voices coming toward the building, assuming something was wrong. My first thought was to pretend to be asleep and to pull the covers over most of my face: that way I could keep silent and make my Western features less conspicuous. As for Ghaith, as a native Arabic speaker he'd be able to hide the fact he was a journalist who worked for a British newspaper—but he wouldn't be able to convince anyone he was Libyan.

The door opened and four or five men came in, all speaking Arabic. I half opened one eye and watched them for a few moments. They weren't looking in our direction but at Mohamed, who was talking. One of them, wearing a black jacket and talking more than the others, had the look of a leader. Mohamed came over and gently placed more covers on me: it seemed my act was convincing. Then I heard the visitors asking Ghaith questions; I couldn't understand the conversation, but Ghaith was obviously trying to keep his voice down and make his answers short. He later told me they had been asking where we were from: his answer on my behalf was that I was an employee of Ente Nazionale Idrocarburi, a big Italian oil company. The company was involved in the Western Libyan Gas Project, extracting natural gas for export to Europe via the Greenstream pipeline, which ran under the Mediterranean for 520 kilometers. Ghaith's answer had been suggested to us in Yefren; it was plausible because there were reports of dozens of employees of multinational companies still traveling around the interior of Libya trying to get to points on the border from which they could leave, having for whatever reason missed the evacuations organized by their employers or governments.

I wasn't in a position to tell whether the men found the cover story convincing, but the mood in the room was calm—so much so that I really did drop off to sleep for a few moments. About half an hour later, all the men left. When they'd gone, Ghaith was amused to inform me that "at least one" mouse had come under my blankets while I'd been pretending to be asleep. I laughed, even though I was already starting to feel anxious again: the unexpected visit was ominous for two people trying to be as inconspicuous as possible. I started to feel like a net was closing in and it was just a question of time before we were discovered. Ghaith spoke first. "I didn't like that visit. And I don't like the idea that we're in the hands of a 23-year-old," he said, repeating his earlier comment.

"We're exposed to too many risks here," I said.

Ghaith's expression changed when he heard my words, as if what I'd said had awoken a similar feeling in him. We both reached for our phones and tried to call Sefao, anxious to check with him—again—about the trustworthiness of the people around us. When Sefao finally picked up, Ghaith, speaking in English so that Hussein wouldn't understand, gave him a full update: we were in Sabratha, not Zawiyah, in the care of a man we didn't like the look of, with a young man as our driver—and now we'd been visited by a bunch of strangers. On the other hand, a factor in favor of our hosts was that if we were discovered by Gaddafi's security services, they were sure to suffer serious consequences as well. Sefao was taken aback by our anxiety and reiterated that some of the tribal leaders in Yefren had a good relationship with Hussein. But, he added, if we really wanted to get away from Sabratha before the night was over, he would try to sort out an evacuation plan.

Ghaith put down his phone and told me what Sefao had said. We were both pleased, again, with his positive assessment of Hussein, and we agreed to stay put for the night; after all, leaving Sabratha immediately would be no less risky than doing so the next day. My intuition was still telling me we were nearing the end of the line, but I tried to be rational and to concentrate on the concrete facts. We hadn't yet got into trouble. So, I told myself, we were safe. End of story.

GHAITH CHATTED WITH HUSSEIN WHILE I WENT BACK TO WORK, TRYING TO SET UP an access point to the Internet. The farm had no Internet, obviously, and neither of us had a BGAN, a modem used to connect to the Internet by satellite. Ghaith's satellite phone, through which we would have been able to connect, wasn't working. My mobile didn't have an Internet signal, but Ghaith's Libyan mobile did have a faint 2G signal. I set about trying to create a Bluetooth hotspot, an improvised network for my laptop and Ghaith's tablet. I tried connecting cables, swapping SIM cards, doing all sorts of tests—all to no avail. Ghaith watched me with a mixture of curiosity and incomprehension.

"I feel like MacGyver, looking for solutions," I joked, but the reference seemed to be lost on Ghaith. "MacGyver, the guy who stopped a leak of sulfuric acid using chocolate. You're not going to tell me you've never heard of him?"

But Ghaith had indeed missed out on that particular 1980s American TV series—which, to be honest, was probably no great loss for him. Failed jokes aside, Ghaith and I were getting on really well, despite our very different backgrounds in Iraq and Brazil. We were the same age and shared many interests, and he wasn't a practicing Muslim, so there was no religious barrier between us. But the main reason for our good relationship seemed to be mutual respect. Ghaith seemed to pay attention to whatever thoughts I expressed, even the most banal ones, and I certainly listened to him—not so much because he spoke Arabic and therefore had more contact with our interlocutors than I did, but because he showed every sign of already having had a life full of difficult and character-forming experiences. One mark from his past was constantly visible—a large scar on his right cheek, the origin of which I wasn't inclined to ask about.

Eventually I gave up on the Internet connection and decided to write my article on a smartphone. I wrote that the regime had retaken control of some roads and cities in western Libya as part of a wider counter-offensive. That very day the rebels had said that Brega, in eastern Libya, was now back in the hands of Gaddafi's forces. A municipality comprising seven small towns, Brega was important because it included the second biggest oil terminal in the country, which had fallen into rebel hands a week previously. Fighting also raged in Ajdabiya, another strategic town, where the rebels had earlier taken control of a military base and an arms depot. The mounting death toll was a testament to Gaddafi's determination to cling to power. Although the figures were difficult to verify, the Libyan League for Human Rights claimed 6,000 people had already been killed, including 3,000 in the capital.

To respond to the counterattack and at the same time achieve a degree of political organization that would give them a voice both inside Libya and abroad, the rebels had named the former justice minister, Mustafa Abdel Jalil, as chairman of the National Transitional Council. I found this decision difficult to understand as Abdel Jalil had only just abandoned the regime in protest "against the bloody events and the excessive use of force against the protesters." He was, therefore, a politician close to Gaddafi. Still, it had obviously been necessary to establish a leadership structure, and the rebels in the west of the country welcomed the move. To Abdel Jalil would fall the task of conveying to the international community the demand for foreign military intervention—at least in the form of an air embargo, or control over the entry of mercenaries into the country—which was beginning to be heard inside Libya. Meanwhile, the spokesman for the uprising, Abdel Hafiz Ghoga, called on the UN and all the countries that supported the revolution to "launch airstrikes against sites and positions occupied by mercenaries, which have been used against civilians and against the Libyan people."

This message to the international community was in tune with a rising sentiment inside Libya. There was outrage over the regime's deployment of mercenaries, even though there still wasn't much visible proof of this tactic. Furthermore, Gaddafi's counteroffensive made it clear that the overthrow of a violent dictatorship, which had been in place for 42 years and survived a succession of coup attempts, would be neither quick nor painless. But the prospect of outside intervention still seemed distant, and there was disagreement about it among Western political leaders. That same day, French foreign minister Alain Juppé spoke of the reticent mood he had witnessed at a meeting of NATO ambassadors in Brussels; they were concerned at the prospect of Arab discontent arising from the arrival of any Western troops on North African soil. On the other hand, Juppé said, it was possible "to continue to plan a no-fly zone," on the condition it was created by the UN Security Council. Whether deliberately or not, Juppé failed to clarify what this measure would actually entail.

As I wrote a piece about the growing support among Libyans for foreign intervention, I noticed Hussein had already fallen asleep. Ghaith, meanwhile, provided humorous commentary on the movements around the shed of an increasingly bold family of mice. I couldn't help noticing, however, that his voice was tinged with anxiety. This was a gratifying moment: it pleased me no end to realize that an award-winning war reporter, covering a violent revolution in a land controlled by a pitiless dictator, was afraid of mice.

"I'm not afraid of mice!" he exclaimed.

Such protestations notwithstanding, Ghaith settled down to sleep only after I assured him I would stay awake a little while longer to monitor the rodents' activities. A couple of hours later I woke Ghaith and myself up with an involuntary cry of "Fucking hell!,"* having sensed in my sleep that a mouse was moving around close to my ear. I'll never

---

* The actual expletive in Portuguese was "Puta que pariu!," which literally means "The whore that bore you!"

know whether it was real or just a dream. Either way, Ghaith was in fits of laughter and lost no time accusing me of sharing his fear.

WE AWOKE THE NEXT MORNING TO CLEAR SKIES, THE SURROUNDING COUNTRYSIDE bathed in sunshine. Apart from an occasional car, the only sound we heard inside the shed was that of the animals in the field. Mohamed came in to tell us he was going off with Hussein to work out the best way of getting across Sabratha without being stopped at checkpoints. While they were gone, Ghaith and I phoned some of our contacts, which in my case included Ambassador George Ney Fernandes again. To try to get a signal I went out and walked around the field, constantly checking to make sure there was no one else nearby.. In the end mine wouldn't work and I had to use Ghaith's number. When I got through to the ambassador, his demeanor was very different from our previous conversation. He was friendly and attentive from the very start of the conversation and immediately apologized for having pressed me to give him my wife's telephone number and for having told me to leave the country. He said he wasn't particularly familiar with the work of journalists, but that he understood we needed to report on the conflict. Next we spoke about the evacuation of Brazilian citizens from Libya, which had apparently been successful thanks to the efforts of his staff.

I decided I'd take advantage of the positive mood by returning to the subject that had led me to speak to the ambassador in the first place: the idea that he might be able to inform the Libyan foreign ministry of our presence in the country. If he could do that, I said, we might be able to get authorization to work in Tripoli. We'd already been with the rebels for several days, and one of our options now was to get Gaddafi's regime to accept our presence based on the fact that it would be better for them to keep us in the capital—where we would certainly be monitored by the secret services—than to leave us roaming freely around the interior of the country, where we had virtually unrestricted access to the leaders of the uprising in the west. The ambassador listened to me without raising any objections. He said the 70 foreign ambassadors who were still in Tripoli had been summoned to listen to a pronouncement by Gaddafi in a couple of hours; he would see representatives from the foreign ministry then and would raise the subject with them. He hoped to have a reply for me later that day.

I told Ghaith about the conversation, and we concluded that getting authorization from the foreign ministry should be our fallback plan, to be adopted only if we felt sure the regime was closing in on us and forced us to abandon our preferred option of reaching the capital independently and maintaining maximum journalistic autonomy.

Later that morning I heard what sounded like a protest march. I imagined it was some kind of anti-Gaddafi demonstration—which could only be good for us, I figured, because unrest in Sabratha would decrease our chances of being stopped on the way to Zawiyah. But as I watched from the door it soon became obvious that the march—a very small-scale affair, comprising just a couple of dozen women and children—was in support of Gaddafi. For obvious reasons I wanted to interview the participants, but for equally obvious reasons it was out of the question. Supporters of the regime were under instructions to inform the authorities if they discovered any Western journalists in the country. All I could do was discreetly observe the demonstrators as they passed by.

Mohamed and Hussein were quick to return but didn't bring good news. Soldiers manned checkpoints on all the main routes to Zawiyah; any attempt to get through would be very risky. They said they'd look for an alternative route via the back roads, but in the meantime we'd have to stay cooped up in the shed. The situation was becoming unbearable, but the subsequent calls we made to our contacts confirmed that pro-regime forces were closely monitoring the local area. As we waited, Ghaith made further calls, speaking to his editors and also giving a live report to the BBC.

To pass the time and reduce our anxiety, Ghaith and I chatted about various subjects that morning, including our career paths and our families. We talked about the personal motives that brought us to Libya, which ranged from the noble—such as a sincere wish to contribute to the safeguarding of human rights—to the foolish and egotistical, namely the desire to say we were the only journalists reporting from the west of Libya, the most important region in the country. We laughed as we told each other stories about funny incidents during past assignments. In a more somber tone, we discussed our thoughts about death. Ghaith had lived through the American invasion of Baghdad and knew all about the horrors of war. For my part, I had experienced Brazil's urban violence firsthand; I knew what it was like to have a gun pointed at my head by a teenager high on drugs, my fate depending on whatever his next impulse happened to be. We both had scars, physical and psychological, that the prospect of imminent death leaves forever.

"That day, I felt something strange, as if I had already died once already," I said. "Since then I have not being afraid of dying."

Ghaith, who'd been lying on his mattress, sat up and replied solemnly, "I know what you're saying. I feel the same thing."

STILL WAITING FOR THE GO-AHEAD TO LEAVE SABRATHA, I MADE ANOTHER CALL TO Ambassador Fernandes. He answered in a low voice, giving the impression there were people nearby he didn't want to inconvenience, but again he was warm and receptive. He also had some important news: Gaddafi had just invited Brazil to be one of three international observers of Libya's "political crisis." The Colonel made the proposal during his meeting with the foreign ambassadors, when he also made a speech that was more conciliatory in tone than his belligerent rhetoric about crushing the opposition. "The invitation is for Brazil, the African Union, and the Organization of Islamic Cooperation to be observers of the conflict," the ambassador explained.

Then I gathered that the ambassador was pointing his phone so that I could hear what was going on in the background. It sounded as if someone was making a speech. "Can you hear? Gaddafi's talking right now!" he said.

I expressed my appreciation for the unexpected opportunity to listen to the Colonel and then asked for more details about the proposal. The ambassador didn't have any, however, because he hadn't yet met with the regime's representatives. I asked again about the chances of the ambassador acting as an intermediary between us and the foreign ministry, but Fernandes said he hadn't had time to raise the issue. We planned to talk again in the early evening, although I knew that would be difficult due to the communications blackouts that tended to happen every day from late afternoon onward.

A couple of minutes later Mohamed and Hussein came back. Now, they said, it was finally time for us to leave. Ghaith and I already had our equipment and rucksacks ready. Strangely, although our hosts had been checking the back roads, they said that we'd be taking the main roads instead. We set off for the center of Sabratha, where the task would be to find ways around a series of checkpoints. It was the first time we'd traveled through an urban center that was under control of the regime; the mood in the car was very tense as we looked around to see how many people there were on the streets, how many shops were open, how much of a security presence there was. There were numerous burned-out buildings that, according to Mohamed and Hussein, had all housed either the police or the secret services. But there were also lots of buildings flying the green flag, a declaration of loyalty to the Colonel.

For the first time, the two Libyans helping us appeared very nervous. Hussein was sweating and wore a frightened expression; Mohamed reprimanded him, erupting into bursts of anger. During one of their altercations Hussein stopped the car and swapped places with Mohamed, letting him drive instead. Although Hussein had shown himself to be a good driver, I was relieved to have someone more experienced behind the wheel in such a tense situation. Then Ghaith received a call on his mobile from a man who introduced himself, in Arabic, as "a friend" who wanted to "help" us get through the checkpoints on the way to Zawiyah, and asked where we were. Ghaith spoke to him briefly, declined the offer of help, and hung up. The phone rang again. It was the same man, now insisting that Ghaith tell him our location or describe our vehicle. Ghaith again refused. It was obviously a trap. We realized that at least one of our mobiles was being tracked and that the police or the intelligence services knew we were driving around in Sabratha. From that moment onward Ghaith's mobile rung almost continuously, but he didn't answer it again. We tried our best to keep cool, but now we clearly risked being intercepted by the authorities at any moment.

Then my mobile also rang, immediately sending a shiver down my spine. I decided to answer, as it was worth knowing whether my phone was also being monitored. The voice on the end of the line was a familiar one: Roberto Simon, a reporter on the foreign desk at the *Estado de São Paulo*, who that day was covering for the foreign editor. I smiled as he asked whether I'd be able to send him a piece that evening about Brazil's role as observer in the Libyan conflict. Rather optimistically I said yes. I didn't want to stay on the line for very long for fear of the call being tracked, but before I hung up I did give him some information about our whereabouts—the first time in Libya that I'd told anyone my geographical location over the phone. I said I was in Sabratha, without mentioning our intended next moves.

It was already getting dark when we stopped by the side of the road that cut through Sabratha. We'd arranged for someone else to meet us in another vehicle, to help in our attempt to get through the checkpoints. When he turned up a few minutes later, Hussein got out of our vehicle and got into his. The two of them would go ahead to see how heavy the security presence was at the checkpoints and keep us informed by phone. We set off in the direction of Surman, a town on the route to Zawiyah, leaving the main road and driving slowly along the adjacent streets. The first of two checkpoints lay ahead. Inside the car there was absolute silence, the air thick with tension. But when we got to the barrier we were simply waved through; the soldiers didn't ask to see our documents. My throat was dry and my heart pounded as we continued on toward the next checkpoint, which we knew was more heavily manned. As we approached, Mohamed's phone rang with bad news from the car in front: they thought there was little chance we'd get through the second checkpoint without being arrested. By this stage Ghaith's phone, now on silent, had received literally dozens of calls from whoever was monitoring our movements. We drove off through the side streets and then came back round again, passing for a second time through the first checkpoint. If we could get past the other barrier we would be on our way back to rebel-held territory. But this would have to be our last attempt; we couldn't risk going around another time. Again we waited in silence for the call from the other car. I was desperate to receive the go-ahead, but again it didn't come.

Mohamed said something in Arabic to Ghaith, who looked at me with an expression that made it quite clear we weren't going to make it to Zawiyah. I had the feeling our fate had just been sealed there and then. I asked Ghaith what Mohamed thought we should do: return to the shed on the farm or stay there in the city? If the farm was the only viable option, it suggested the game was up and that we should get out of the country as quickly as possible by retracing our steps all the way back to the border.

Now that we were surrounded, however, leaving Libya clandestinely would be no less difficult than pushing ahead. Ghaith told me Mohamed's idea was that we should go to another property he owned, a house in the center of Sabratha. We didn't have a choice. We were entirely in Mohamed's hands and imagined that now, in these circumstances, he was risking his life by helping us.

Just over ten minutes after our last attempt to get through the checkpoints, Mohamed turned off the main road and took a dirt road that ran along the side of a square. He slowed down and asked us all to be silent. He stopped outside a house, got out, looked carefully all around, opened the front door and gestured for us to follow him. It struck me as a middle-class home, albeit one in which some of the rooms were completely empty. The furnished rooms were at the front, but we were to have no contact with the family living there. We were taken instead to a bare room at the back.

Mohamed, visibly tense, offered no explanation about where we were. He brought mattresses and blankets, so clearly we would be staying put for the night. He also showed us a bathroom we could use—with a shower.

Ghaith and I smiled as we commented on the prospect of having our first proper wash in a week; it was a moment of light-heartedness that temporarily reduced the stress level. Mohamed said we would have another go at getting through the barriers the next day, and requested that in the meantime we shouldn't make any phone calls or access the Internet. He told us specifically not to use Facebook, which struck me as odd because there was no chance of our doing that anyway.

It was about 8 p.m. as we settled into our room. We were desperately hungry after 30 hours without a proper meal; Mohamed provided some biscuits and I scrabbled around in my rucksack to find a few more. That evening Ghaith and I were more tired than usual and also less talkative, partly due to anxiety. We briefly discussed our options, but without talking directly with Mohamed there wasn't much point in trying to draw up a plan.

As our adrenaline subsided I got out a cotton sheet Adel had given me from the hospital in Zintan. I ripped it down the middle and threw one half over to Ghaith so he could use it as a bath towel. When he came back from the bathroom my Iraqi friend was wearing a broad grin; he was clean for the first time in a week, although he still had to put back on the same filthy clothes. The bathroom, I discovered, was in a deplorable state after his visit, but it didn't detract from my pleasure in removing the thick layer of desert dust that clung to my skin and hair. When I returned to the bedroom Ghaith was already falling asleep. I turned out the light, sat down on my mattress with my back to the wall, and typed out a few ideas on my laptop that I thought might serve as the basis of future articles. Peering at my notebook, dimly lit by the computer screen, I read some notes I'd written about references to the foreign media made by the Colonel and his political heir, Saif, in their recent speeches. The previous day Saif had said his country was the victim of a propaganda campaign on the part the foreign media and the UN Security Council, the latter having "for the first time in history" passed a resolution "based on false reports." In response, Saif said, the regime was inviting some foreign journalists to Tripoli: "You are welcome in Libya. Open your eyes, show me the bombs, and show me the wounded! Take a walk through Tripoli!"

Obviously this needed to be taken with a grain of salt. The journalists in question would stay at the Rixos hotel in the center of the capital, just a few hundred meters from Gaddafi's Bab al-Azizia compound and from other military and secret service bases; they would need permission to go anywhere, and when they did venture out they would generally be followed by agents of the regime "for security reasons." Well, I thought, at least Ghaith and I were still free. And although we were facing huge problems, perhaps Saif's speech about the press might count in our favor. Whereas a few days previously the regime had threatened to treat journalists in the same way as al-Qaeda terrorists—who were generally arrested, tortured, and murdered—the message now seemed to be one of respect for human rights and for the freedom of the press. I figured that while the regime indulged in this kind of propaganda, the execution of foreign journalists would cause a major diplomatic incident. That thought lifted my spirits slightly in the face of whatever ordeal lay ahead of us.

In the Nefusa mountains in western Libya, rebels from Nalut pose with their weapons and display the tricolour flag during their first encounter with foreign journalists.

Bombs hitting Tripoli during the offensive that ousted Muammar Gaddafi.

An insurgent fires into the air from inside the main building in Gaddafi's Bab al-Azizia compound.

Insurgents celebrate the capture of Bab al-Azizia. In the background is the monument erected by the regime following the US airstrike in 1986.

A defaced picture of Muammar Gaddafi in the center of Tripoli. Images of the Colonel were among the symbols of the regime that the rebels were keenest to destroy.

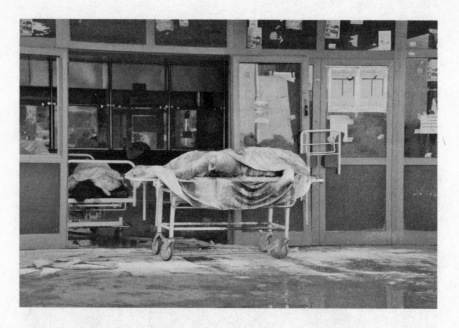

The dead bodies of patients at Abu Salim hospital on the outskirts of Tripoli, abandoned during the rebel offensive.

The ashes of rebel soldiers and regime opponents found in an improvised detention centre in the district of Khilit al-Ferjan on the outskirts of Tripoli soon after the fall of the regime.

Destroyed vehicles and abandoned equipment in the city center.

The last bastion of Gaddafi in Sirte, destroyed by rebel forces during the siege that resulted in the death of the dictator.

The drainage pipe where Gaddafi surrendered.

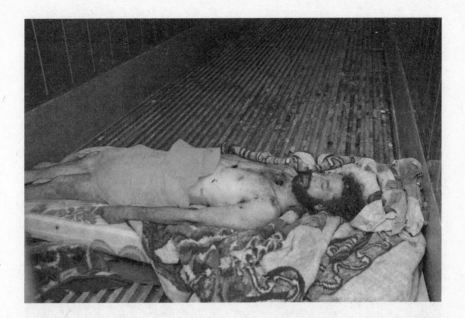

The body of Mutassim Gaddafi, one of the dictator's sons, put on display for journalists. The circumstances of his death—or execution—remain unclear.

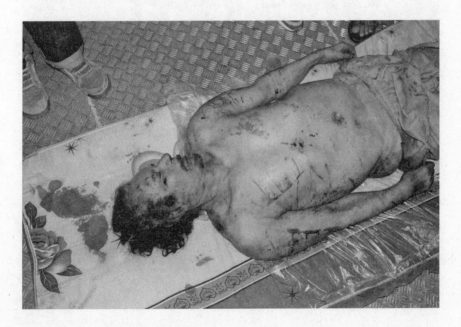

The body of Muammar Gaddafi.

In a museum in Misrata, after the end of the conflict, a boy holds a picture of a family member killed during the siege. The museum contains photos of hundreds of people who lost their lives during the regime's offensive against the city.

CHAPTER 7

BETRAYAL

In the dark, empty room, the only light came from my computer screen, whose brightness I'd turned down to minimum. I decided to turn on our mobiles to check them before I went to sleep. With mine nothing was out of the ordinary. I watched the screen of Ghaith's phone light up, the little symbol appearing in the top left corner to indicate there was a signal—and then immediately the phone rang. It was the same man as before. It was now around 11 p.m.; he'd probably been calling nonstop for four hours. I turned the phone off again. I picked up my notebooks and pen from my mattress and leaned across to grab one of the straps of my rucksack. As I did so I heard a loud, aggressive voice in one of the other rooms. A cold shiver ran through my body as I realized it was Mohamed, and that he was coming along the corridor in our direction. Shouting in Arabic, he burst into our room and switched on the light. "Get out of here! Get out of here now! Out!"

In a sequence of terrified movements I slammed shut my laptop and leaped off the mattress. Ghaith awoke in an instant and also jumped up, his face a picture of total confusion. Mohamed's shouting quickly took on a desperate tone and he kept raising his hands to his face, looking as if he might burst into tears. He gestured for us to gather up our things. I asked Ghaith what was going on but he had no idea. Mohamed said he'd warned us not to use Facebook, that our whereabouts had been discovered, and that we had to get out of his house immediately. Ghaith tried in vain to calm him down. I hoped we were simply being thrown out into the cold and darkness to fend for ourselves in a pro-Gaddafi city; the worst-case scenario was that we'd been betrayed and were about to be handed over to the regime, to face possible torture and death.

Ignoring Ghaith's pleas, Mohamed pushed us out into the street. My body recoiled from the chill night air but I was relieved, briefly, to see there was no one else around. All I could see were houses with no signs of life and a couple of dirt roads weakly illuminated by streetlights. But there could be no doubt: this was the end of the line for us. Mohamed, now speaking much more quietly, shepherded us across the road and onto the veranda of a half-built house on the other side. He opened the door and told us to go inside while he stayed in the open doorway. While Ghaith tried to get him to explain what was going on, and to understand that we hadn't connected to the Internet at all, never mind Facebook, I walked farther inside the house to see if there was another exit. There wasn't.

From inside the house I could hear cars on the main road, not far away. As the initial terror subsided and my mind began to clear, my first thought was that someone had definitely betrayed us.

A few minutes later we heard a diesel engine; a car came slowly along the road behind the house and then stopped outside. The car doors opened. Ghaith and Mohamed fell silent. Time stood still. Then, through the open doorway, I saw four men in black jackets coming toward us. One of them had a gun, the others carried pieces of metal tubing. Mohamed stepped aside and one of the men grabbed hold of Ghaith. Another came up to me and searched through my pockets until he came across my iPhone. I tried to keep hold of it, knowing it contained the recordings of dozens of interviews, but the man used both hands to pry it from my grasp.

Neither Ghaith nor I resisted as we were pushed out of the house and onto the dirt road. One of the men said in Arabic, "You sons of bitches, Zionist Jews, betrayers of the Arabs!"

I didn't want to be seen to react in any way. They forced us to walk toward the square we'd driven past four hours earlier. It seemed a lonely, secluded place, perfect for a summary execution. But I knew I needed to think rationally—and was surprised to realize I was in fact reasonably calm, my heart not beating any faster than usual. I tried to take in our surroundings in case I needed to describe them later, though in the semidarkness it wasn't easy. After we'd walked about 100 meters it became obvious they weren't about to kill us: instead there was a jeep waiting for us with a kind of large cage in the back. Ghaith was forced in first. As I followed him I realized I'd have to release one of the shoulder straps of my rucksack in order to fit through the door. As I began doing so, with an exaggeratedly slow and careful movement, I felt the brutal impact of metal against my head. I lost balance and felt all my strength flood away, but someone held me up so I didn't collapse. My ears filled with a high-pitched buzzing. I looked around me and everything was hazy; Ghaith's mouth was moving but I couldn't make out any words. Intense pain flashed across my forehead as I was shoved inside the vehicle. Then voices became discernible through the buzzing; one of them was Ghaith's, anxiously asking if I was OK. Someone grabbed my head and put a blindfold over my eyes. Behind me, also in the back of the jeep, a man was shouting in Arabic, "You want to overthrow Gaddafi?! We'll rape your mothers! We'll rape your mothers! Gaddafi's going to teach you a lesson!"

At that moment I actually felt relieved that my hearing was coming back. I started to prepare myself for what lay ahead. The training course for war reporters that I'd done with the Inter-American Press Association in Argentina came back to me; their advice for this situation was to stay calm, not to react or argue, and to cooperate until the moments of greatest tension passed. The insults, the shouts, the threats—they were all just attempts to intimidate us.

The jeep pulled away and Ghaith and I spent the next few minutes in complete silence. Then the vehicle stopped. I heard doors opening and could tell that the loudest and most aggressive-sounding men were getting out. One man entered the vehicle; I heard him give the order to drive on, then a few minutes later he told us to take off our blindfolds. My immediate impression was of an unremarkable-looking man with an apparently calm demeanor—and no weapon in his hand. "Don't worry, nothing will happen to you," he assured us, having asked Ghaith to translate for my benefit. "You're safe."

Without introducing himself or saying what part of Gaddafi's security apparatus he worked for, he asked us where we were from and what we were doing in Libya. When he found out I was Brazilian he made a curious assertion. "You're safer in Libya than in Brazil," he said, then paused as if waiting for a reaction. "You're safer in Libya than in Brazil," he repeated.

"You know what? I believe you," I replied, risking a touch of irony.

His apparent friendliness didn't convince me for a second. I had the feeling it was part of a good cop/bad cop routine and that both approaches spelled danger. I wondered what his motive was for allowing us to take off our blindfolds, and it very soon became clear. He announced that we were in the center of a town—I guessed it might be Surman, between Zawiyah and Sabratha—and he pointed things out to us as we drove along the darkened, almost deserted streets.

"You see that shop? Do you think it would be open if we were really in the middle of a revolution? See those buildings? Do they look like buildings in a war zone?"

The idea, obviously, was to persuade us the uprising didn't exist or was limited to certain areas dominated by tribes hostile to the government. It struck me as a rather simple-minded ploy: did he really think a few undamaged buildings would convince us the revolution wasn't happening? Indeed, over the following weeks and months the feeble arguments with which the regime tried to influence Western journalists often puzzled me. Anyway, Ghaith and I nodded obediently at all the man's observations, without offering any comment. We'd been driving around the town for a few minutes when he told us to put our blindfolds back on, then we arrived at what we later saw was an austere-looking building made of gray concrete—I subsequently found out it served as a police station and regional headquarters for the intelligence services. Various men in plain clothes waited for us at the entrance, none of whom we'd ever seen before. We were led, still blindfolded, to an upper floor of the building and then to a room I assumed belonged to one of the commanders. Other men came in behind us carrying our rucksacks, which they then began to empty. They paid attention to our notebooks—especially Ghaith's, in which some of the writing was in Arabic as well as English—but were especially interested in the electronic equipment. Ghaith's camera became the focus of attention when one of the men went through the photos on it and found those of the armed rebels, taken between Nalut and Yefren.

"Where were these photos taken?" asked one of them. Ghaith answered truthfully.

Among my possessions the item of greatest interest was a Sony voice recorder that contained some of the first interviews I'd conducted on Libyan soil. Seemingly unfamiliar with such devices, however, the men couldn't work out how to turn it on. When they asked me why it wasn't working, I said that maybe the batteries were dead. One of the men set about changing the batteries while his colleagues turned their attention to my MacBook laptop. They seemed unfamiliar with its commands—maybe they were all PC users—and made slow progress in looking through the files on it. I had no intention of helping them unless forced to—but then, much to my surprise and silent indignation, Ghaith piped up and explained to the man still struggling with my voice recorder that he merely needed to slide a switch on the side to turn it on. A huddle of security agents formed around the device to listen intently to my interviews with various rebels.

The men also took an interest in our documents. I remembered that my passport contained a Libyan visa from my visit to the country in 2009 to accompany the Brazilian delegation led by Luiz Inácio Lula da Silva; I hoped that page with its Arabic writing might count in our favor, but unfortunately they didn't ask about it. Indeed, as interrogations go it had started to feel distinctly informal: the questions were few and far between, and no one bothered to record anything Ghaith or I said. We weren't blindfolded, our hands and feet were untied, and we were even starting to feel safe, at least in comparison to the ordeal of our arrest in Sabratha.

Eventually they asked what newspapers we worked for, what we were doing in Libya, and how we had managed to enter the country. We said we'd come in via the border post at Dehiba; we'd gone through all the necessary procedures on the Tunisian side but hadn't received stamps in our passports when we crossed into Libya. We tried to convey the image of naïve journalists who'd tried their best to enter Libya legally. I chose this moment to mention my Libyan visa from 2009; not only was I friend of the Libyan people, I said, but I'd been in the company of Colonel Gaddafi two years previously, at the African Union summit in Sirte. And now, I continued, our objective wasn't just to cover the conflict from the point of view of the rebels but also to hear what the supporters of the regime had to say—which was absolutely true. But unfortunately, I said, supporters of the regime had been told to avoid talking to foreign journalists and instead to report them to the authorities. I realized I was being given time to talk, so I carried on. I said Brazil's ambassador in Tripoli knew we were in the country, as did the Libyan foreign ministry—indeed, the latter had been asked to grant us authorization to stay in the capital. All of this information could be checked simply by picking up the phone to call Ambassador George Ney Fernandes, whose numbers I duly provided. But the men showed no immediate inclination to do so.

"If that's true, you'll be released tomorrow morning, after we've spoken to the ambassador," said the agent who seemed to be in command. "We've got nothing against the press, even though you're against us," he continued, echoing what Gaddafi had said to the assembled foreign ambassadors just a few hours before. "We'll phone the ambassador tomorrow morning, and if your story's true you can leave. We can even take you around Sabratha so you can speak to the local people, who all love Gaddafi."

"Excellent!" I replied, though I doubted the sincerity of the offer.

The interrogation probably lasted somewhere between 90 minutes and two hours. I knew if we ended up facing some kind of investigation or even a trial, certain factors would count against us: the lack of visas and stamps in our passports; the hours of interviews we'd recorded with enemies of the regime; the photos of the rebels, and the articles we'd written that made clear our proximity to them. But I also figured that the turbulence of the political situation and the fragility of the regime might end up working in our favor. We were facing a few hours of captivity at the very least, but given the less hostile way we were now being treated, the prospect of being kept in the building didn't seem such a bad outcome.

Things started to look different, however, when the man who'd driven us around the town and later inspected my voice recorder came back into the room and gave us some alarming news, albeit in a friendly tone of voice. "You're going to be taken to another unit and handed over to the military until they can check your story with your country's ambassador," he said. "Don't be alarmed. You'll be blindfolded again, and handcuffed, but nothing bad will happen to you."

A question immediately came to me. "Where's the other unit? In Tripoli?"

The man hesitated, but then replied, "Yes, it's in Tripoli."

BY NOW IT WAS THE EARLY HOURS OF THE MORNING AND THE TEMPERATURE OUTSIDE had dropped significantly. Ironically, Ghaith and I were about to pass through the same checkpoints that had blocked our path the day before and to cross the city of Zawiyah on the way to the capital—exactly the journey we'd wanted to make before our arrest. It was obvious the reasonably friendly treatment we'd just received was merely a prelude to our being handed over to a different organ of the state security apparatus. Now blindfolded again, we were escorted into the back of a van where we sat facing each other. A guard wearing plain clothes—despite the blindfold I could see his shoes and jeans—told us to remain silent. He stood close to the vehicle for a couple of minutes but then walked off to talk to some of this colleagues; their conversation was just audible from inside the van.

Ghaith and I spent at least two hours just sitting there, becoming increasingly cold. The bigger problem, however, was that Ghaith started to have difficulty breathing. I thought he was having some kind of delayed reaction to the ordeal we'd been through, but he explained that in fact he suffered from claustrophobia. I was surprised and worried; clearly there was no immediate prospect of escaping the enclosed space in which we now found ourselves. I asked what I could do to help, and he said he would probably feel better if we talked rather than remained quiet. So we quietly chatted about the decisions that had led us into our current situation and the possible scenarios that awaited us. Then we discussed what we should say to the authorities if, as was likely, they split us up and questioned us separately. "Let's do the safest thing and just tell the truth," suggested Ghaith. "Making up stories will just cause us more problems."

"Sure," I replied. "So we're journalists with newspapers in Britain and Brazil, and in covering the revolution we entered the country without legal authorization. We'd tried to get that authorization in various places but it wasn't possible."

Anticipating the questioning we might face, I thought the most important things were to dissociate ourselves from the rebels, so that no one could accuse us of being foreign agents playing a supporting role in the uprising, and to avoid saying anything that might be prejudicial to them, for example by revealing anything about their military strategy. Ghaith and I went back over our journey through Libya so far to make sure we hadn't forgotten anything. We would say which towns we had traveled through and what kinds of scenes we'd witnessed, but we agreed we should be evasive when it came to the practical help the rebels had given us, and above all with regard to the names of the individuals we'd had contact with. Twice the guard outside the van told us to stop talking, but by lowering our voices to a whisper we were able to carry on our conversation. Eventually we were confident we had prepared matching accounts that didn't have any suspicious gaps in them but were also shorn of incriminating details.

Ghaith's claustrophobia had subsided. Still whispering, we reviewed the events of the previous evening and agreed we'd been lucky only to have spent a few minutes in the hands of the militiamen who'd arrested us: they were the kind of people who had already tortured and killed many rebels. But we were indignant at the thought that one of the contacts we'd met since leaving Zintan must have betrayed us. We analyzed the behavior of every one of them, wondering who it could have been. My suspicions focused on Mohamed. I said I thought his behavior when he threw us out of his house was very odd. Despite his show of anguish he'd justified our expulsion by saying we'd used Internet connections on our mobiles and computers that had allowed the regime to discover our location. But it was obvious we hadn't accessed the Internet: that's why a piece I'd written for my editors in São Paulo was still unsent. Also, Mohamed had acted as if the security forces were about to burst through his front door at any second—but then he took us to another house and basically kept us there until the men arrived.

"Did you notice that one of the militiamen who arrested us was the guy in the black leather jacket who came into the shed on the farm the night before?" asked Ghaith.

I hadn't been aware of that—and the shocking observation seemed to confirm my suspicions. Also, Ghaith had received dozens of calls to his mobile while I hadn't received any: surely it was significant that Ghaith had given Mohamed his mobile number but I hadn't given him mine. Months later, people from local tribes would suggest to me that Mohamed had indeed been complicit in our arrest, and yet it was also difficult to believe he acted alone.

Eventually the police van moved off toward our destination. Still blindfolded, we had the impression that for some of the time we were driving not on paved roads but across sandy, rocky terrain. There were various stops at checkpoints. For most of the way the security agents in the van chatted and listened to Arabic music, but occasionally the music was turned off and a tense silence briefly took hold—I imagined it might have been when we were going through rebel-controlled areas around Zawiyah, on the outskirts of Tripoli. Thinking of the road maps I'd studied, I tried to work out what route to Tripoli we might be taking—if that was where we were really going.

Unlike when we were in the jeep with the militiamen, there were no insults or questions; indeed, it now felt like we were being ignored. This seemed odd, as I was sure there was no way the regime would be satisfied with the little information it had got out of us so far. I imagined we wouldn't be freed until we'd been thoroughly questioned about our journey through Libya, the people we'd spoken to and photographed, the articles we'd written, and the emails and text messages we'd sent and received. That process could take days, even weeks. And if the regime wanted to make examples of us, the consequences could be very serious indeed.

I was aware that the sun was rising when the van slowed and came to a halt. I heard the doors of various vehicles open and close, and then a discussion among what sounded like quite a large number of men. Not recognizing any of the voices, I assumed they weren't the same people who'd been with us at the police station. Now, it seemed, we were going to be handed over to a different branch of the security forces.

The door of the van opened, letting in an icy desert wind. Someone grabbed me and pulled me outside, shouting as he did so: the friendly treatment was already over. I felt a push and stumbled away from the vehicle. There was a cacophony of different voices and I could no longer sense the presence of Ghaith close by. Then I was searched by at least a couple of men at the same time; they ran their hands around my belt and lower legs and emptied my pockets. Money, documents, notebooks, pens—everything was taken from me.

Next, without my showing any kind of reaction, they began taking off my clothes, starting with my kaffiyeh and leather jacket, then my other jacket, T-shirt, belt, shoes, and socks. I was left with only my jeans on, shivering with cold. I heard an order and was prodded in the back with what felt like a metal pipe. I walked forward, feeling cold sand under my feet. I called out to Ghaith and he shouted back from some distance away; there was trepidation in both our voices. As the other voices receded I understood I was now alone with the man who was taking me into the empty desert, prodding me in the back from time to time and saying things in Arabic that I couldn't understand.

I was overcome with the feeling that my fate was sealed and I was about to disappear forever, just like Lúcia had warned. The prospect of being executed filled me with immense sadness—exactly the same feeling I'd had in Brazil ten years earlier when staring down the barrel of a teenager's gun. Time seemed to slow to a halt and I felt utterly alone, my chest invaded by emptiness. There was none of the fear I'd experienced at other moments, however: if I was about to die I was sure it would be quick and without suffering. I regretted the suffering my death would bring to my loved ones. I thought of Lúcia and wanted to tell her I was sorry. But I regretted none of the decisions I'd taken. I knew I'd take all the same risks again, without hesitation, because they were an integral part of the life I'd chosen.

I heard another order and felt a push against my left arm: the man wanted me to turn around. Then he walked me back toward the vehicles, which were waiting with their engines running. Soon I was surrounded by other voices again; my clothes were returned to me and I was told to get dressed. Someone shoved me, apparently wanting me to hurry up. When I had all my clothes back on, my hands were tied behind my back using plastic handcuffs. Then I heard Ghaith's voice, shouting something I didn't completely understand; he seemed to be saying we were about to be separated. I was bundled into a pickup truck and pushed into a horizontal position on the back seat; a man got in through the door on the right side and thrust my head down toward the floor of the vehicle, sat on my legs so that I was immobilized, and then pressed a gun against my right temple. Again I thought I was about to die, although it also struck me that it didn't make sense to execute someone inside a vehicle unless the idea was to fabricate a crime scene.

Or maybe, I thought, I was about to undergo a mock execution, a common practice among sadists employed by authoritarian regimes in the region. Again I was aware of the absence of any sound that might indicate we were near a town or village; all I could hear were the men's voices and the sound of vehicle doors opening and closing, and the suspensions squeaking as men got in and out. The only language spoken was Arabic, until the man holding me down tried to communicate with me by asking simple questions.

"*Sahafa?*" he inquired.

"Yes," I replied. "I'm a journalist—sahafa."

"Country? America?" he asked, after a pause.

"No, I'm not American. I'm Brazilian."

The dialogue proceeded haltingly along those lines. He seemed to be trying either to confirm information I'd given earlier that morning or discover a contradiction in my story. He was translating my answers into Arabic for the men outside the vehicle, who I imagined might be his superiors. I sensed the situation was becoming calmer and that the men were waiting to receive an order to drive off.

The man with the gun took his weight off my legs, grabbed hold of my jacket and pulled me into a position in which he could search through my clothes. Through a gap at the lower edge of my blindfold I saw he was wearing camouflage fatigues, which confirmed what I had previously suspected: we were in the hands of soldiers. He brought a plastic bottle close to my mouth; I could see it contained a clear liquid but immediately assumed it wasn't water, so I didn't open my mouth. He persisted, pressing the bottle to my closed lips and tipping it up so the liquid poured out over my chin. Other men entered the vehicle, closing the doors behind them. The engine started up and we drove off at high speed, the wheels skimming across the sand. Finally I was pulled up into a seated position, although still with my head pushed down toward my thighs.

Soon I became aware of vehicles traveling in the opposite direction, which suggested we were entering an urban area. We passed through a barrier and came to a halt in front of a building. I was escorted inside, stumbling up a flight of stairs, and then I was left standing against a wall. I sensed that someone stood next to me.

"Ghaith?" I asked in a low voice.

"Yes," he replied.

Nearby, it sounded like a group of men were rummaging through various objects. Ghaith was taken to stand close to a table, then I was ordered to follow him. They removed my blindfold, but I avoided looking at any of the men apart from the one who sat at the table. In front of him were all my and Ghaith's possessions, mixed together alongside our empty rucksacks. Various pieces of equipment were held up in front of me; inferring that I was expected to say which of us they belonged to, I answered truthfully in every case. Again the electronic devices aroused the most interest, especially the satellite phone. The men looked closely at my passports—the old one, which contained the Libyan visa from 2009, and the current one. One of them opened my wallet and took out every document. In one of the pouches he found a small piece of paper with an image of Nossa Senhora Aparecida;* my grandmother, Julieta, had given it me but I'd forgotten it was there. "Oh, fuck," I thought, imagining the little keepsake might now cause me problems. The man looked carefully at the image and then placed it to one side, according it a respect that wasn't being shown to any of my other belongings. Among the jumble of objects on the table I spotted one of the pieces of paper on which I'd written the telephone numbers of the Brazilian embassy and Ambassador George Ney Fernandes. I said, "Excuse me," picked up the piece of paper, and pointed out the numbers, explaining they could be used to confirm that we had tried to contact the Libyan authorities. The paper was promptly taken from my hand and put back on the table; no one was interested. At this point I remembered Gaddafi's regime had never closely observed the international conventions regarding the imprisonment of foreigners—and it was unlikely to now, in the midst of a revolution. I repeated my request that a call be made to the ambassador, but again I was ignored.

A SOLDIER ESCORTED GHAITH OUT OF THE ROOM. MY BELT WAS TAKEN AWAY FOR "security reasons," despite my protests. I'd lost weight since arriving in Libya and my trousers slipped down around my waist. I was blindfolded again and escorted through the building until I arrived in another room some distance away, where the blindfold was taken off again. I found myself facing the thick metal bars of a cell, which I was promptly taken

---

* Our Lady of Aparecida, the patron saint of Brazil and an iconic image in Brazilian Catholicism.

inside. I heard the metallic clunk of the door shutting behind me, then a bolt sliding across it. The cell was about twelve meters square and occupied about half the room; the bars ran all the way from one side of the room to the other. I initially felt indifference toward this confined space; I refused to accept the possibility that I would be staying there for an unknown length of time. It could be a few hours, or given the madness the regime had exhibited in the past, it could be years—as had been the case of the Bulgarian nurses and the Palestinian doctor who were given life sentences and eventually released eight years later.

I looked around and was unhappy to see there were no windows; the only ventilation came from a small but very noisy extraction fan stuck in the wall, almost three meters off the ground. And yet ironically, accustomed as I was to writing articles criticizing Brazilian prisons for their overcrowding, violence, and outrageously poor sanitation, I didn't think this Libyan cell was too bad. It was brightly lit by fluorescent strip lights, and there were boards of about one meter in height separating the main part of the cell from the "bathroom," which contained a tap, about 30 centimeters off the floor, and a filthy toilet bowl encrusted with shit. There was a dirty carpet covered in crumbs, empty plastic bottles, and wrappers and packets for the kind of mass-produced foodstuffs that, I would soon discover, constituted breakfast. In one corner against the back wall was a broken wooden bed frame. I tested its strength and concluded that the wood might come in handy.

In another corner, diagonally opposite, were two thin mattresses, looking just as dirty as those we'd slept on in the rodent-infested shed in Sabratha. On top of them was a duvet and a pillow; neither had a cover, and yet they actually looked like the cleanest items in the cell. I found myself looking at the walls and assessing how strong they might be; I had some background knowledge from having studied architecture at the university in Porto Alegre in 1996 and '97—a course I ended up dropping because I couldn't stand the part in which we learned about concrete. I also checked out the thickness of the metal bars before concluding that the physical structure of the cell had only one weak point: a hole low down in the bathroom wall where the pipe came through to the tap. The cement around it was already cracked and could easily be pried off.

I WOKE UP WITH A GASP OF PANIC AND JUMPED OFF THE MATTRESS, FEELING LOST and afraid. I had no idea what time it was. I remembered that once I'd "explored" the cell, I'd sat down on one of the mattresses, fully clothed, expecting that soon someone would come and collect me, either for questioning or to let me go free—but now here I was, standing up, facing the bars. I felt an overwhelming surge of anguish and found myself struggling to breathe. However long I'd been in the cell, it was too soon to have lost track of time. I thought about my editors in São Paulo and Lúcia in Paris: they must have realized something was seriously wrong because I was supposed to be in regular contact. I imagined they were all very anxious, especially my wife. Soon, I supposed, there would be no further doubt in their minds that I'd disappeared.

So far, despite the surges of adrenaline I'd experienced since our arrest, I'd been doing my best to keep calm, to control my reactions and to think rationally. Indeed, I was quite surprised by the sangfroid I'd managed to maintain throughout the events of that early morning—but now I began to feel the overwhelming psychological pressure caused by the uncertainty of my predicament and by my lack of contact with the outside world. Although it seemed I was safer now behind bars than at any other point since our arrest in Sabratha, I still felt a torment, a fury, I'd not experienced at any other moment since I entered Libya.

Over the following days I discovered the psychological torture of isolation, lack of information, and above all the inability to communicate. My state of anguish was constant, though it fluctuated in intensity. It came upon me very soon after the cell door closed behind me and increased when I suddenly noticed some marks on the wall obviously left by a previous occupant. There were six of them, apparently signifying the passing of six days. A shiver ran through me. The prospect of spending 144 hours in silent isolation made me explode with rage for the first time.

My most urgent need was to find out what time it was, so I too could keep track of the hours passing by. I started hitting the bars of the cell with one of the wooden slats from the bed frame to attract the attention of the guards. I heard voices that seemed to be coming from other rooms or cells, but no one responded to the racket I was making. So I pulled myself up on the bars of the cell so I could look through the small gap around the extractor fan to try to gauge the strength of the sunlight outside. I concluded it might be late morning.

About one hour later, my cell door opened for the first time. A small, skinny man came in, his face covered by a kaffiyeh. His cowardice made me laugh—it was almost as if he was the prisoner, the one with reason to be afraid. As he came toward me he gestured for me to pick up the empty food packets and wrappers on the floor. I did so, just to gain his confidence. He handed me a pack of six bottles of mineral water and a shoe box containing a hard bread roll with sardine paste, a small carton of fruit juice, a carton of the sour milk drink that Ghaith adored and I detested, and a packet of chocolate biscuits. So that was my breakfast. I made a point of not showing much interest in the food, but I still thanked the man and asked him what time it was, pointing at my wrist. Looking intimidated, he seemed to have understood the question but his response was merely to wag his finger at me. He wasn't going to tell me the time.

As the cell door closed again, I consoled myself with the thought that it was probably still morning, and that the situation might be resolved before the news of my disappearance reached the people who would be most distressed by it. "Perhaps this will be sorted out quickly," I said to myself, imagining an intervention by the Brazilian or perhaps the Iraqi embassy.

There would be no quick solution. Some hours later I received a second visit. This time it was a different guard, tall and heavily built; he wore military clothing and his face was uncovered. He brought me my first prison lunch: spicy couscous, a piece of stringy beef, an apple, and a carton of fruit juice. I was surprised: the food wasn't as disgusting as I expected. Also, my brief interaction with the guard was friendly enough. I asked him the time in a mixture of English and hand gestures.

"Two," he promptly replied, raising two fingers.

Knowing the time gave me renewed hope, and yet the seconds and minutes still dragged by without the slightest sign of any change to my circumstances. I kept all my clothes on, as if I were about to receive the call to leave. Rather than try to adapt to the cell as best I could, I regarded it as a place to which I was only making the briefest of visits. Freud would probably have said I was showing symptoms of denial. I was behind bars, with no way of knowing what was going to happen to me, in a building belonging to an army facing a revolution, in a country that lacked a constitution and whose institutions operated at the whim of a tyrant who was now being backed into a corner by a popular insurrection. I was perfectly aware of all that, and yet still I believed a rapid exit was possible.

As time passed, the psychological burden of the waiting and the isolation increased, but I slowly became more aware of things going on elsewhere. Despite the thick walls I could hear some sounds coming from beyond the room, and I began to listen more carefully to try to identify them. The first was the *al-Athaan*, the call to prayer emitted by mosques before each of the salah, the five daily prayers that are obligatory for practicing Muslims. A mosque was obviously not far away, which suggested the prison was in or at least close to a populated area. Also, I thought

I could hear the sound of propellers. At first I couldn't distinguish it from the constant noise of the fan, but gradually I became aware of a separate sound that fluctuated in volume. And then I realized: it was an aircraft. This was the first clue to our location. If we were indeed in Tripoli, which is where the agent in Sabratha had said we were going, and if my memory of the maps of the region served me correctly, the aircraft noise had to be coming either from the international airport, about 30 kilometers south of the city center in the district of Qaser Ben Ghashir, or Mitiga airport, eight kilometers west of the city center; both were close to heavily populated areas. It struck me as odd that Ghaith and I might be held in a location close to either airport, given that neither was far from rebel-held territory. I imagined the international airport was probably more vulnerable to attack from the Zawiyah and Zintan rebels since it was outside the city perimeter, while the threat to Mitiga could come from nearby Suq al-Jum'ah, the first district of Tripoli to rise up against the regime and come under rebel control.

Anyway, I would now be able to shed some light on my location when—or if—I had contact with the outside world. But there was also the worry that the prison might be close to a potential target in the case of foreign military intervention. Mitiga, for example, was one of the main targets for American aircraft during Operation El Dorado Canyon in 1986, when it was a military airbase going by the name of Okba Ben Nafi. Before our arrest the UN Security Council was discussing the possible creation of a no-fly zone, which in practice would necessitate the bombing of Libya's airports and air defenses. And so another, darker thought crossed my mind: might we even be used as human shields? The idea might sound paranoid and absurd, but in the past the Gaddafi regime had indeed protected military installations by surrounding them with civilians—and would do so again in the near future.

As well as noticing the noise of the aircraft, I became aware as the day went on that interrogations were going on not far away. I could hear what sounded like different soldiers talking aggressively to a prisoner, asking him a series of questions. There were a few moments when the prisoner's voice sounded like Ghaith's; weeks later, when I spoke to him on the phone, he told me he had indeed been interrogated for four hours that first day. Hearing the interrogation made me think that I too should prepare myself for a grilling at some point in the next few hours. Actually, I was impatient for that moment to arrive, as at least I'd have the opportunity to demand some answers and insist I should be allowed to make a phone call.

When the moment did come, however, it was when I was no longer expecting it. At around 9 p.m., after I'd had dinner—spicy pasta with a small piece of chicken—two men entered the room, their faces uncovered. They opened the cell door and put a blindfold on me, without explaining why. I didn't resist, nor did I feel afraid; I merely hoped that now I was going to get the chance to speak to the outside world. I was led along corridors until I arrived in a room where I sensed the presence of others. I was ordered to sit down on a chair in the middle of the room, with what felt like a desk in front of me. Behind the desk sat the man who would lead the interrogation, with the assistance of other "investigators" and an Arabic-English interpreter, who would arrive a few minutes later. The session began with questions about my general state of health, my swollen forehead, and the theft of my mobile phone.

"We're sorry for the assault you suffered, and for the theft. You were arrested by men who are not part of our organization and are untrained, incompetent. We're in the midst of a dangerous conflict. I hope you understand that," said the commander. "Regarding your mobile, the Libyan state will compensate you for any loss you might have incurred."

"Thank you. But the best way to help wouldn't be to get me a new phone but to give me back the one that was stolen, which is a piece of equipment I use for my work," I replied, before taking the chance to raise the subject of the isolation to which I was being subjected. "And a phone call is more important to me than any phone."

The commander was evasive, merely saying that the subject would be discussed later. He moved on to the first questions, which were all fairly basic: my nationality, my profession, what I'd intended to do in Libya. I answered truthfully; there was no reason not to. They asked me about the *Estado de São Paulo*, Paris, what my work as a correspondent consisted of, and how I had come to be sent to Libya in 2009 and now, in 2011. They were simple questions, many of which I had already answered in Sabratha. The tone was brusque but there were no threats, either verbal or physical. I ended up sitting there for almost two hours, in which time I was asked to reconstruct our clandestine entry into the country, explain why I didn't have a visa, and describe the contact we'd had with rebel leaders in the places we'd traveled through.

When this latter subject arose I detected the first, surprisingly crude attempts at manipulation. The men were particularly interested in the conduct of the rebels in Zintan, an opposition city for which Gaddafi reserved special hatred. "The terrorists wore long garments and had long beards, no? Didn't you find their clothes and their appearance strange?"

To avoid falling into any traps I replied that yes, some of them did have long garments and beards, but there were others who didn't. I added that I'd traveled quite a lot in the Arab world and didn't pre-judge people based on their clothes or customs, but I didn't pursue the argument.

My answers didn't deter the interrogators from seeking to establish links between the rebels in Tripolitania and the terrorist organizations active in some parts of the Maghreb and in neighboring countries. Their crude strategy was to get me to agree that the rebels, because they were "bearded and armed," were followers of Osama bin Laden. Simple as that. Gaddafi himself repeated this argument ad nauseam, but the difference was that the Colonel possessed greater oratorical skills than my interro-gators. Although the men sounded completely serious, they were talking nonsense. It was true, of course, that Africa's recent history was marked by armed conflicts and by the further spread of Islam—but those phe-nomena are not necessarily linked with Islamist terrorism, even though the latter does undeniably exist on the African continent. But the men obviously weren't going to drop the subject, so I knew sooner or later I would hear the explicit allegation that the Libyan insurgents had links with terrorism.

"You know that the people who use those clothes and have long beards belong to al-Qaeda, don't you?" asked the commander, through the interpreter.

Gradually I realized that something was at stake, some kind of bar-gain. If I agreed there was indeed a connection between the rebels in western Libya and al-Qaeda, I might obtain some kind of reward, such as a shorter stay behind bars. I had no intention of playing the hero, nor did I want to make any concessions. I certainly didn't want to put myself in a position to be used as a tool by the regime, saying things that might be incorporated into its propaganda, either for a domestic or interna-tional audience, in order to justify the mass killing of civilians fighting for liberty.

Despite my attempts at evasion, the questioning carried on in this vein. When it was finally over, the inquisitors said they were satisfied with my "clarifications" and told me the blindfold was about to be taken off for a few moments. Instructing me not to look directly at anyone in the room, they put a document on the desk in front of me and asked me to sign. It looked like a page from an exercise book, without a letterhead, on which about twenty lines of text had been written by hand in blue ball-point pen. It was all in Arabic and there was no sign of an official stamp or of anyone else's signature. Before I had a chance to ask what the text said, I was informed that it was my statement.

"Is it all here?" I asked, with a touch of irony.

"The main parts are," replied the commander.

"In Arabic only," I noted.

"Don't you trust us?" asked the commander, leaning over the desk toward me, his expression a mixture of doubt, mockery, and menace.

I let out a sigh, again laced with irony. At the bottom of the text I put a scribble that vaguely resembled my signature. Then, as most of the men in the room were leaving, my blindfold was put back on. As far as I could tell there were now only two people in front of me: the commander and the translator. I asked when I would be set free, whether the Brazilian embassy had been contacted, and if I might be given permission to make a call to Paris.

"We can't guarantee you'll be able to make the call. We'll ask our superiors," said the interpreter.

The commander shook my hand and said something. Before I could ask what he'd said, the interpreter spoke again. "Don't worry. You'll be freed tonight or tomorrow morning. Tonight is less likely because it's already late."

I tried not to break into a smile. I was taken back to the cell and sat down and waited for someone to come and tell me it was time to leave. No one came. Halfway through the night I concluded that I'd be set free in the morning. But I stayed fully clothed, due to the cold. It was difficult to sleep because the strong lights in the room were never turned off; the best I could do was pull the hood of one of my jackets over my eyes. And when I did drop off to sleep, if I moved my head at all my eyes became uncovered again, which woke me up immediately. In the morning, therefore, I was very tired but also extremely excited at the prospect of being released. I climbed up on the bars to look through the gap in the fan. It was still very early. I sat down again, my back against the wall, close to the door of the cell. The call to leave, I thought, would surely come in the next few hours.

My next human contact came at around 8 a.m., when I received my breakfast. It was brought by a different guard—frail-looking, like the first one, but more extroverted. I asked him what time I'd be set free but he obviously didn't understand a word I was saying. I tried not to appear irritated, imagining the guy might later prove useful in some way. More hours went by, and the anguish of not being able to communicate became more acute again. By the end of the morning I was just as desperate as

I had been during my first hours in the cell. In the early afternoon the same guard came back with my lunch; it was exactly the same food as the previous day, which even then had been difficult to digest. Entirely in mime, I asked him the time again and asked when I was going to be released. He answered, also in gestures, that he didn't have a clue.

Although I hoped it wasn't the case, I began to think the promise of freedom might just have been a form of manipulation. The situation left me bewildered; I started going back over the whole interrogation in my head, wondering if there was a moment that made the men change their minds about releasing me and asking myself if I'd been too intransigent. But then the thought occurred to me that this could actually be one of their objectives: to wear me down through fatigue, confusion, depression, and psychological pressure. For a few minutes I felt stronger but then I gradually succumbed again, overcome with anxiety about the probable suffering of my family, friends, and colleagues.

But now that I thought I might be freed, I found myself paying more attention than ever to the sounds coming from outside the room. There were various moments when I heard voices in the adjacent rooms. Toward the end of the afternoon I heard male voices shouting; it wasn't the first time I'd heard them, but now suddenly I had a clearer mental picture of what was going on. One of the men seemed to be barking orders in Arabic; I had the impression he was the one in control of the situation. The sounds the other man was making were much more alarming: they were howls of pain. Although I couldn't hear any blows being landed, the cries of the victim left no doubt I was listening to torture. I wasn't shocked—I hardly expected anything else in a military installation belonging to a savage dictatorship. But those sounds filled me with anguish because at times the voice of the man whose suffering I could hear, and who at times seemed to be trying to remonstrate with his tormentor, was similar to Ghaith's. It was a horrible few hours, going from the promise of freedom to the fear that my colleague was being tortured—and that it could happen to me next.

THAT NIGHT, WHEN THE DINNER OF SPICY PASTA PREDICTABLY ARRIVED, I HAD NO appetite whatsoever. Psychologically, it was my lowest point so far. Around 9 p.m., or so I estimated, I was overcome by fatigue, or despondency, and fell asleep, hoping that unconsciousness would extend well into the following morning and allow me to escape reality for as long as possible. It didn't happen. A nightmare awoke me just a few hours later. It was the early hours of the morning of my third day in prison. I tried to get back to sleep but it was impossible, partly because of lights constantly shining in my eyes. Over the following nights I would suffer from insomnia.

As I had done the previous morning, I watched the tiny patch of sky lighten through the gap in the extractor fan and heard the call to *Fajr*, the first of five daily prayers. Again I was fully dressed in readiness for the soldiers to come and tell me to leave. I'd had a wash, of sorts, using the tap in the "bathroom," a small sponge, and a few slivers of soap left over from the cell's previous occupants. Although I no longer really believed I was about to be freed at any minute, I did find myself thinking that maybe the only reason I hadn't been released the previous day was because it was a Friday, the day of the week of greatest religious importance for Muslims—I suppose it was a way of controlling the negative feelings that were rising within me.

The little man who hid his face brought my breakfast about two hours after sunrise. I tried to get some information from him, which clearly wasn't going to happen. But by persisting in asking him questions in English, none of which he understood, I did at least get him to call one of his colleagues. The man who entered the room, on the other side of the bars, was one I'd seen before. Tall, brown-skinned, and dark-haired, he wore camouflaged military fatigues and his face was contorted into a frown. He gruffly demanded to know why I was making so much noise and bothering the other jailer. It was as if his weedy little colleague had called in his big brother to stand up for him.

"I didn't mean to scare him," I said, diplomatically. "I just want to know what's happening. The day before yesterday I was told I'd be leaving that night or the next day, which is to say yesterday. I need to know what's going on, because if there's some kind of impasse maybe I can help."

I could tell by the way the soldier was looking at me that he hadn't understood much of what I'd just said. So I reduced it to a shorter question: "I was told I'd be released yesterday. When will I get out?"

"Ah! Tomorrow after tomorrow!" he replied, without any conviction.

"Tomorrow or the day after, you mean? How do you know that?"

Both men turned their backs and left the room.

Anger rose up in me at the lack of information and proper communication. I took a thick pen from by rucksack and wrote in big letters on the fibers of the carpet, in English, "YOU PROMISED. LET US GO NOW," making sure it was legible from outside the cell.

Later I heard more screams from somewhere in the building. It was another reminder that we faced a regime that imprisoned, tortured, and killed without any regard for laws, either national or international. It wasn't a government that made promises. Or if it did, it certainly didn't feel any obligation to honor them.

When the door of the room opened and a different guard brought my lunch, I grabbed a can of soft drink but gestured that I didn't want any food—and that I wouldn't be eating anything more until I was released. The guard shrugged, looking irritated. He called in another soldier, one I'd not seen before, who came up to the bars of the cell. Looking at what I'd written on the floor, he said, "You want to get out? Maybe you'll get out, but it won't be by stopping eating. Don't make us force-feed you."

I hadn't really considered a hunger strike; it was just anger that made me refuse the food. But I took advantage of the officer's presence to argue that I should have been released already, in accordance with what the interpreter had said at the end of my interrogation. So something had gone wrong. I said I'd be willing to make another statement, and would start eating normally again, but reiterated that I needed to speak either to the Brazilian embassy or to a colleague or family member, to tell them I was alive and safe. The officer listened with an air of indifference, then replied, "Don't make me come back here."

During the next few hours no one else appeared. I heard more shouting but this time wasn't sure whether someone was being beaten. In any case I thought I should prepare myself for a similar ordeal now that the prospect of being released was becoming more distant. I wasn't really of value to the regime, but maybe the soldiers thought differently. I imagined, for example, that they might want the names of rebel leaders, or information about rebel positions and battle plans in Tripolitania. In that respect, I did have some knowledge. I got up from the corner of the cell where I'd been sitting, the can of drink in my hand. Outside I heard the call to the Maghrib, the prayer just after sunset. I emptied the can into the toilet, grabbed a piece of wood from the bed frame—one with long nails sticking out of it—and returned to the corner of the cell. I used the nails to tear the empty can, detached a strip of thin metal, and worked it into a small blade. My train of thought, that melancholy Saturday, was that I could hide the blade in my clothes or hair, ready to slash my wrists or my carotid if the moment came when I couldn't take any more. I looked at the sharp piece of metal and remembered the conversation with the driver who'd taken us across the desert on the way to Sabratha. Now, ironically, I did have a weapon, albeit one I only envisioned using against myself.

THAT NIGHT, THE JAILER WHO CAME TO THE CELL WAS THE ONE WHO'D BEEN MOST open, although he only spoke Arabic to me. Trying to get him to show me where the prison was located, I drew a map of the region on the carpet, including all the main cities in Tripolitania. He understood my intention and refused to help. Disappointed, I lay down and tried to get some sleep.

I woke up early the next morning, Sunday, March 6, trying to come to terms with the idea that I might be staying in that prison indefinitely. My first step was to count the days, scratching on one of the walls of the cell with a second blade I'd prepared. I wrote the day of the week followed by the date—not just to orientate myself but also to give the next occupant of the cell an idea of how long they might be staying. As I made my marks I felt certain that by now my family and my editors would know I had gone missing.

My anguish had started to give way to depression. I was sitting on the mattress, my back to the wall, waiting for the next visit from one of the guards, when I noticed the sound of gunfire in the distance. The shooting surprised me, even though I'd already suspected I was being held in an area of the city that might come under attack from the rebels. I hoped the attack might be directed against the military installation, but couldn't really believe it was the case. And yet the gunfire was becoming louder and more intense; it was getting closer and I could now distinguish the sound of heavier weapons being used—anti-aircraft cannons like those I'd seen being fired in Nalut and Zintan. Interspersed with the bursts of gunfire I heard anxious voices shouting: if the soldiers in the building were alarmed, it suggested the fighting really was nearby.

The pressure from the rebel attack increased to the point where the soldiers in the building began firing back from just on the other side of the concrete wall of my cell—just a few meters away from me. It was astonishing and frightening, particularly as a captive with no way of protecting myself. For days I'd wanted the rebels to turn up and storm the building, but now this desire seemed close to becoming reality, and I was acutely aware of how dangerous my predicament was. The prisoners could be the unintended victims of artillery fire aimed at the building. Or worse, if the soldiers faced defeat, they might attack us in revenge. All I could do was steel myself for an actual invasion of the prison.

The gunfire and the shouting carried on at the same volume and intensity for more than 45 minutes and then faded into an enigmatic silence broken only by helicopters flying overhead. In the hours following the battle, no one came to the cell. Nor could I hear anyone in the adjacent rooms. I wondered whether the building had been abandoned, but then, around 2 p.m., a soldier brought my first meal of the day, a lunch identical to all the others I'd had. He was a soldier I'd not seen, with an air of authority about him. Before I even had chance to ask him what had happened, he informed me that rebels had tried to invade the installation: "If those rats come back here and we're attacked, we'll fight until we die. And you'll be the first."

Weeks later, after our release, Ghaith and I talked about the gun battle, which was definitely one of the most harrowing episodes in all the time we spent as captives. Throughout that day, he said, the cells in the part of the building where he was being held filled with new prisoners. They included rebels from Zuwara and Zawiyah, as well as a man who seemed to be North American. In a piece for the *Guardian* he wrote that during the battle the prisoners all assumed the soldiers would attack them if the building were invaded. And that same Sunday, a man—certainly the same one who came to speak to me—told Ghaith, "We'll crush the dirty Europeans under the toes of our shoes. If those rebel dogs come here to attack, we'll all die together. The sons of Gaddafi will never run. A man lives once and dies once, so it's better to die fighting."

The battle only increased my anxiety to escape, so much so that I found myself hoping desperately for another rebel attack. If it happened, I preferred to believe it would result either in liberation or in the soldiers surrendering. But in all the time I spent in that prison, the second attack never came.

My breakfast the next morning was brought by one of the friendlier guards. When I asked him the time, he came toward to the bars of the cell with an old Nokia mobile phone in his hand, the screen of which had a digital clock. As he got closer I extended both my arms through the bars to touch the phone; my instinct was to grab it from the guard, which wouldn't be difficult, and then try to make a call immediately. But the consequences of that could be very serious, so I discarded the idea as quickly as it had come to me—although I still wondered whether I could overpower the same guard at some point in the future, if my circumstances didn't change at all. I realized that aggression was rising in me, a tendency toward increasingly violent thoughts. Instead of attacking the guard I asked him, in gestures, to call one of his superiors. The man who appeared was one I'd seen before. I only had one question for him, the same futile one as before: when was I going to be released?

"Tomorrow after tomorrow," he replied.

Hearing this, a cold shiver went down my spine. Those words—exactly as I'd heard before—were apparently just a standard response to the prisoners, and in no way could be taken to mean I would soon be let go. My last hopes of a quick solution to the impasse had just been dashed. From now on I would be left to drown in uncertainty. A person's morale can quickly be shattered by imprisonment in a country where the law has been suspended and the notion of justice is fluid—and the process of demoralization can happen even without our being completely aware of it.

Isolated in a cell and deprived of contact with the outside world, I discovered that liberty is not just a human condition, a rational desire for self-determination. It's also an elementary physical sensation, revealed in simple daily experiences such as interacting with other people, seeing things that are more than a few meters away, inhaling fresh air, or feeling the warmth of the sun. For example, now that I was forcibly exposed to artificial lighting 24 hours a day, natural light quickly came to have a new degree of significance for me. Sunlight was available only as a narrow strip that shone fleetingly through the extractor fan. As I followed this beam of light around my cell I had the sense that all the good things in my life were dissolving. The people who meant most to me seemed to be disappearing into the distance, becoming nothing more than memories. The realm of flavors and smells seemed to have been reduced to the stink of a filthy toilet and my own body, despite my attempts to maintain a minimum of hygiene. The richness of existence was being obliterated by the routine of silence and loneliness. The only way I could possibly keep my spirits up would be to adapt to the limits imposed on me. But doing so meant dying a little with every passing second, giving up life for a state of mere subsistence. It is a predicament familiar to so many people who have been unjustly imprisoned in Libya and elsewhere. The vast majority of them, of course, know it far better than I do.

At night the psychological suffering caused by my isolation became more intense, and the prospect of leaving the prison most distant. I had nightmares that became worse as time went by, to the point where I grew afraid of the images sleep might bring me. In the early hours of Wednesday morning, my seventh day, I dreamed I was being arrested in my bedroom in Paris, in front of Lúcia. We both knew I was about to disappear forever. Then I found myself captive in a brightly lit room, in a building that turned out to be a lunatic asylum. I woke up with a jolt, totally disorientated, struggling to distinguish reality from the nightmare. I sat up with my back to the wall, hugging my legs to my chest, telling myself that it had all been just a dream. But my real predicament was just as bad as in the nightmare. Terrified by the thought that I was going mad, I couldn't get back to sleep that night. I scratched words into the wall using one of the blades I'd made from the tin can:

The night
is the hardest part of the day
All the demons are free
But me

On that Wednesday afternoon, March 9, I again tried to exert a little pressure on the guard who brought me my lunch, asking him to go and fetch an officer for me to speak to. The request had never previously been granted, but this time, to my surprise, a Libyan colonel appeared shortly afterward. Standing behind the wall so I couldn't see him, he spoke to me in an irritated tone. "What do you want?"

"I want to know when I'll be leaving here," I replied.

"You want to know when you'll be leaving?" he asked disdainfully. "You can forget it. You'll be staying here until these problems with al-Qaeda finish. And then, we'll see."

It was obvious that his intention was to ratchet up the psychological pressure on an "enemy" of the Gaddafi regime, which was how foreign journalists were regarded. But, I thought, as well as trying to spread fear in that prison cell, the colonel also provided an accurate illustration of Gaddafi's 42-year rule. Libya was a land without laws or a constitution, in which state functionaries took it upon themselves to imprison people, practice physical and psychological torture, and carry out summary executions—as witnesses in a number of rebel towns and cities had already described to me.

Throughout the time I spent in captivity, what struck me most was the absence of the rule of law, of a judicial framework, of a constitution to constrain the whims of the regime. Without these things, anything was possible. They could keep you behind bars without having been formally accused of anything, with no right to see a lawyer, make a phone call, see the sky, or even have a proper wash. They could force you to sign documents written in a language you didn't understand. They could deprive you of any notion of how long you might stay trapped behind bars, constantly exposed to the tacit threat of torture and execution.

The profound realization that I was in a lawless country, with the prospect of not being released until the conflict was over, had a devastating effect on my morale—an effect exacerbated by the knowledge that although the rights violations Ghaith and I had suffered were serious, they were trifling compared to the things we'd heard about in so many of our interviews. I thought, for example, of Saleh in Nalut, tortured in the 1990s for being a "heretic," and of Naji Sassi, from the same city, who in the 1980s had seen his home invaded and his brother imprisoned, followed by the execution of his father and subsequent suicide of his mother. I concluded that Gaddafi and his regime, which had spent 42 years silencing its opponents and suffocating them in prisons, would not survive for much longer. It would soon fall.

I heard the call to Dhuhr, the noon prayer, and realized I had now spent eight days muttering "My God!" every time I imagined the torment of my family and friends outside Libya. I'd also realized that the only way to lessen my own torment was to pray, in just the same way as the local people were doing, five times a day in the mosque near the prison. I asked God to grant me serenity, trying to recall the Catholic prayers I'd known when I was younger. I was perfectly aware that resorting to prayer was irrational; there were many moments when I asked myself what on earth I was doing, given that I'd abandoned religious faith many years previously. The reason I tried to reconnect with God was that there seemed no longer any other source of hope—especially after the conversation with the colonel. This experience made me think that in countries whose populations were deprived of personal and political freedoms, such as the dictatorships of North Africa and the Middle East, it made sense that religion—and its sectarian derivative, extremism—was used as a last resort in confronting oppression, humiliation, and injustice. And wasn't faith, religion or God, the last alternative before insubordination? Did a desperate rebellion not signify the point of no return, the unstoppable urge, the destruction of the barrier of fear and silence?

Sprawled on the mattress and sinking into depression, I had all the time in the world to reflect on such pseudo transcendental questions. And then, unexpectedly, the door opened on the other side of the room. It was about 3pm on Tuesday, March 8, 2011. Two men came in and walked up to the bars of my cell. One of them was the soldier I'd come to think of as "the sadist" after he told me I'd be released "tomorrow after tomorrow." He smiled now, which struck me as odd.

"Do you want to have a shower?" he asked.

I said yes, of course. I felt relieved at the prospect of a proper wash after seven days during which I'd had to tear off the sleeves of my T-shirt because I could no longer tolerate my own smell. I gathered my clothes and waited at the front of the cell while the second man went off to find the key for the large padlock that had been keeping me captive. When the other man returned, however, the sadist suddenly informed me that I wouldn't need a shower.

"Forget the shower," he said. "You're being released."

CHAPTER 8

INTERVENTION

When I asked if Ghaith was also going to be released, the sadist just shrugged. The smile had gone from his face. I resisted the urge to blurt out something like "I'll only go if you guarantee he'll also be set free," which would have been futile and stupid. I asked myself how best I could help Ghaith. By leaving, informing his family, and protesting about his continuing detention? Or by insisting I'd only leave the prison if he came with me, thereby running the risk that we'd both be left to rot in our cells? I was torn between the two, but decided on the former. I felt like a coward.

The cell door opened and immediately I was aware of how surprised I felt to be on the other side of the bars—in my subconscious I'd been preparing myself for a very long stay. I picked up my clothes and took my first step outside the cell. Looking at the cell from the outside, from the jailers' perspective, I felt humiliated, as if I were an animal that needed feeding in order to be kept alive. I looked at the dates I'd written on the cell wall and noticed that I'd missed the last one, so I went back and added it: "Tuesday, 8 March, 2011."

By the time I'd finished, a young man was waiting for me in the room outside the cell. He addressed me in Spanish: "Hello, Andrei. How are you?"

"I'm alright, thank you," I replied, also in Spanish. "Who are you?"

"I'm a diplomat from the Libyan foreign ministry. I'm here to take you with me. We didn't know you'd been arrested."

"I don't believe it. How come you didn't know two foreign journalists had been detained by the police and the army?"

He apologized and said all his colleagues had been surprised to find out I'd been detained. When I asked how he'd found out where we were, he said the Brazilian ambassador in Tripoli, George Ney Fernandes, had contacted the ministry to ask if it had any information about a Brazilian journalist who'd disappeared in Tripolitania about eight days previously. It wasn't just one journalist, I said, but two: the other was an Iraqi working for British newspaper the *Guardian*. He looked surprised to hear this, and said he'd try to find out what had happened to Ghaith. Already I had my doubts about him; he certainly didn't match my mental image of a diplomat. His Spanish was far from fluent, he seemed shy and insecure, and he was poorly dressed, even slightly dirty looking. He certainly didn't project confidence. Or maybe he was just intimidated by the surroundings.

I waited twenty minutes in the room outside the cell while my belongings were gathered together so they could be given back to me. During this time a couple of soldiers examined my forehead; the swelling had gone down but there was still a faint mark from the blow I'd suffered when we were arrested. The men seemed uneasy, as if they didn't like the idea of letting me leave with a visible trace of violence, but they brought me my rucksack and equipment. About 90 percent of my money had vanished. My laptop seemed undamaged, but I could tell it had been examined because a Word file named "ytytytytyty" had been created—inadvertently, I presumed—at 10:56 p.m. on March 3, 2011. My notebooks didn't have any pages missing, and none of the interviews had been deleted from my voice-recorder. On the other hand my mobile phone, and the interviews recorded on it, had disappeared forever. Some of Ghaith's things, including equipment and documents, were mixed up with mine. I took this as evidence he was still locked up somewhere in the building, which meant I needed to get as much information about the place as I possibly could.

Before being taken away I was given a number and photographed standing against one of the walls of the room. Then I was forced to write and sign a statement, in pen, saying that all my belongings had been given back to me. After I handed over the statement I was blindfolded again. In a sympathetic tone of voice, the supposed diplomat told me he too had to wear a blindfold on the way from central Tripoli to the military base. I was escorted through the building and then, finally, felt fresh air on my skin. It made me realize how thick, heavy, and stuffy the air of my cell had been. We walked around the outside of the building to where a pickup truck was parked. One of the back doors opened, and I was told to lie down on the seat while two men got in at the front. As we set off I could see some of the front of the building out of the bottom of the blindfold; I did my best to remember it for future reference. I could also tell that the building wasn't next to the sea, as I'd started to think it might be, but was close to a very busy road. There was no pavement at the side of the road, but there was a dirt track providing a kind of hard shoulder. We drove for a while in silence, then the vehicle turned left. A few minutes later one of the men spoke to me. "Take off the blindfold. You can get up."

I sat up on the back seat. We were arriving at a broad avenue next to the sea. Immediately I had a sense of déjà vu: I'd traveled along that avenue before. I realized it had been in 2009, with the journalists Marcelo Ninio and Alexandre Rocha, when we'd gone from Tripoli to Leptis Magna. Now, having been driving for twenty minutes at the most, we were approaching the center of Tripoli from the east, which made me think the military installation—and therefore Ghaith, if he hadn't yet been freed—could indeed be close to Mitiga international airport. Arriving in the city center, we passed the huge concrete hulk of a hotel still under construction, the Al Ghazala InterContinental not far from Green Square. The city seemed quiet—too quiet. There wasn't much traffic for a city of 1.6 million inhabitants, and far less, in fact, than I remembered from two years before. The absence of pedestrians also struck me. But although things seemed odd, I hadn't yet spotted any clear signs of political turmoil. Perhaps, as in Sabratha and Surman, I'd been blindfolded when we were going through districts with clear physical evidence of the uprising.

We arrived at a mansion surrounded by high walls on Sharia Sidi Issa street, in the city center close to Belemam Mosque. From the national flags flying from poles in the adjacent streets, it was obvious this was the district where most of Tripoli's foreign embassies were concentrated. I was escorted inside the house and asked to wait in a room illuminated by fluorescent lamps, its only window covered by a closed blind. There was no one else around. About half an hour later, a man with graying hair and wearing a blazer and slacks came in. It was General Sadegh Krema, director of the Department of International Relations and Cooperation, supposedly part of the Libyan foreign ministry.

Libya's foreign minister—though only for three more weeks, as it turned out—was Moussa Mohamed Koussa, a man who headed the

Gaddafi regime's domestic and international espionage network between 1994 and 2009. As for Krema's department, its name concealed its true role. Krema was in fact a point of contact between the foreign ministry and one of the regime's most feared intelligence services, the Mukhabarat el-Jamahiriya, whose director Abuzed Omar Dorda would be hunted down and arrested by the revolutionaries a few months later. On behalf of the Mukhabarat, Krema had been a pivotal figure in the regime's dealings with the American and British secret services, the CIA and MI6. Evidence of this would be unearthed by the *Guardian* when Tripoli fell: correspondence between the three governments dating from 2003 and 2004 revealed the collaboration between Gaddafi and Western intelligence agencies with regard to terrorism suspects in the wake of 9/11. This collaboration was ironic, to say the least. In the 1980s, the Mukhabarat became known worldwide as the organ Gaddafi used to spy on dissidents in Libya and abroad, and to assassinate them whenever it was deemed expedient; it also orchestrated the bomb attacks on the La Belle nightclub in West Berlin in 1986, Pan Am Flight 103 over Lockerbie in 1988, and UTA Flight 772 over Niger in 1989.

Krema, who had a rather austere demeanor, shook my hand and gave me his card. It was printed in Arabic and English, and the information on it would later help me piece together what exactly had happened to us from the moment of our arrest. I could already deduce that the morning after our arrest by militiamen—which is to say civilians in the pay of the regime—we were already in the hands of the Mukhabarat. But this seemed to cast doubt on what the young man who'd met me outside the cell had said. Either the Libyan foreign ministry had known about our detention from the very start, or the Mukhabarat was operating autonomously during the uprising rather than taking orders from the ministry. Or perhaps both. Obviously, I wasn't about to raise the issue with my host.

Polite but serious, Krema started by confirming some basic details. "So you're the Brazilian journalist who was in Sabratha," he said, without waiting for me to respond. "Your ambassador called me. He's on his way here."

"Really, General? I'm sorry for the all the inconvenience. But in the prison I asked many times for them to contact the embassy. The ambassador would have confirmed who I was and we could have avoided all these problems," I argued.

"Now it's been done," he said curtly. "You'll be in the custody of the ambassador, who'll accompany you to the airport, from where you'll fly back to your country today."

Although I'd been expecting to be expelled from Libya as soon as I was released, I'd also made up my mind to try to argue against the decision. "In fact, General, as a journalist my job is to stay in Libya during this time of instability. The government has invited journalists from various countries to be here—and they're in Tripoli now. I'd like to stay here, showing both sides of the conflict."

Krema was already getting impatient. "You don't understand. Leaving the country was one of the conditions for your release. You'll be on the first available plane out of Libya."

"And what about my colleague, Ghaith? Has he been freed?"

"Your colleague is not your problem. But don't worry, his case is being dealt with," was the enigmatic reply.

"Sorry, but does that mean he's been freed?"

"When the time is right he'll follow you," said the general, rising from his chair. "Excuse me, I have to leave now, but wait here a few minutes and I'll be back, perhaps with the ambassador. Would you like something to drink? Water?"

"No thanks, I'm OK," I replied. "Could I make a phone call?"

"I'll have water brought for you."

A few moments later a shy, unassuming man came in with a lemon-flavored soft drink. When General Krema eventually came back he was indeed accompanied by George Ney Fernandes, whom I'd never seen before. The smiling ambassador was happy to meet me, and the feeling was mutual. For a brief moment I saw myself in the role of naughty schoolboy and him as my father, called in to the headmaster's office to discuss my bad behavior. In true diplomatic style the ambassador exchanged pleasantries and then listened as Krema, reciprocating the friendly tone, listed the conditions for my release, the most important of which was my deportation. The ambassador agreed with the demands and guaranteed I would stay with him at his residence until my departure on the first available plane to Paris. But there were two problems: a lack of flights to Europe, and the fact that the airport had turned into a veritable refugee camp with thousands of foreigners camped outside the terminal building in the hope of finding places on departing aircraft. So instead they decided to put me on a plane to any city from which I could then get a connecting flight to Paris. Taking advantage of the ambassador's presence, I again raised the subject of Ghaith and reiterated my wish to stay in Libya, but the general showed no inclination to engage with me on either subject.

We left the mansion in a black sedan adorned with Brazilian flags and headed toward the ambassador's suburban residence. The farther we got from the city center, the more it seemed life was carrying on as normal—or almost. The ambassador pointed out a few buildings that had been damaged during the unrest, including the headquarters of the Qaat al-Shaab, or People's Congress—the closest equivalent to a parliament building, and one of the symbols of the regime. Its facade, hastily repainted white, still bore traces of a fire. He also told me about the conversations he'd had with my wife, Lúcia, and with various journalists from other news organizations, all of whom had been extremely concerned about my disappearance. He said the story had generated enormous media interest both in Brazil and internationally. Although I could imagine that a media campaign had been launched on my and Ghaith's behalf in an attempt to exert pressure on the regime, initially I suspected the ambassador was exaggerating somewhat.

We drove for more than an hour, through streets that grew more and more clogged with traffic as we moved out of the city, before arriving at the residence. The ambassador now lived alone: he'd ordered all his staff to leave at the beginning of the uprising even though he was determined to stay on. As soon as we got inside he took me to a room with a phone: I would try to speak to Lúcia in Paris, my family in Porto Alegre and Rio de Janeiro, and my editors in São Paulo. As I made my first attempts, all unsuccessful, I could hear the TV in the same room. It was tuned to Al Jazeera English and had a report on the Libyan conflict. Suddenly the ambassador called me over. "Andrei, look at this!" he shouted, referring to the report.

I hurried over to the screen, which was entirely filled with a photograph of Ghaith. The report was about two journalists, an Iraqi working for the *Guardian* and a Brazilian from the *Estado de São Paulo*, who had gone missing while reporting on the revolution. I was impressed by the coverage but also felt a twinge of regret: a reporter should never become the story.

STILL UNABLE TO GET THROUGH TO FRANCE OR BRAZIL ON THE PHONE, I CARRIED on chatting with the ambassador about the situation in Libya. The updates he'd given me in the car suggested very little had changed since the day Ghaith and I were arrested. The impression was reinforced when I started hopping between the major news channels on the TV. The reports made clear that Gaddafi still had control over Tripoli, although, as shown by the attack on the People's Congress, there were pockets of resistance. Clearly prepared to continue manipulating information about the conflict, Gaddafi had said in a statement made on March 2, the thirty-fourth anniversary of the congress, that the revolutionaries were to blame for the violence spreading through the country, the "main victims" of which were soldiers loyal to the regime. Meanwhile, his son and political heir, Saif, had said Libya was the "victim of a propaganda campaign by foreign media."

On the battlefield, however, Gaddafi was pursuing a counteroffensive, retaking control over major roads and rebel cities in Tripolitania and also in parts of Cyrenaica, where his forces were now advancing on Benghazi. Ghaith and I had already felt the impact of the regime's response in the west. On the eastern battlefront, reports spoke of fighting around the oil terminal of Brega, about 200 kilometers from the epicenter of the revolution. The city had become the main objective for forces loyal to the regime, which apparently consisted not only of regular soldiers but also volunteers and mercenaries. There was a similar situation around Ben Jawad and Ras Lanuf, on the coastal road along the Gulf of Sirte. Ajdabiya had suffered aerial bombardment, which increased the chances of a subsequent land attack being successful. Although both sides were claiming control over these three cities, with every passing minute it was becoming clearer that the rebels weren't holding the ground they'd taken at the start of the conflict.

The intensification of the fighting was causing an increasingly acute humanitarian crisis. Estimates from the Italian government suggested about 1.5 million people had already left Libya for Tunisia and Egypt, either by road, sea, or air. According to the Libyan League for Human Rights, whose data was collected on the ground but collated by exiles in Paris, about 6,000 people had already been killed—about half of them in Tripoli and a third in Benghazi. Between 25,000 and 30,000 people had been wounded. The figures struck me as alarming, but perhaps also exaggerated. The number of Libyans made homeless was rising as loyalist forces advanced on cities such as Ben Jawad.

In Zawiyah, our intended destination when we were arrested, the rebels had been massacred in a counteroffensive that turned the city's main street into a battlefield and reduced many buildings to rubble. This had taken place precisely during the period when I was imprisoned. From Wednesday, March 9 onward, the regime regarded the city as back under its control. This news had quite an impact on me. In Sabratha, before our arrest, we'd been told the attack on Zawiyah by Gaddafi's forces was going to start at any moment—and that was precisely one of the reasons why we'd wanted to get inside the city. Our aim had been to bear witness to the conflict there, which we'd failed to do. If we'd arrived in time perhaps we'd have been able to alert the international community about what was going on. And if the regime had known the press was there, perhaps it would have held back for at least a day, or attempted some form of negotiation. Perhaps there would have been fewer dead and wounded. I was anxious to get reliable information about the death toll, but all I could find were promises from the regime that the whole of Tripolitania would soon be retaken. In a few more days the rebels would only have control over a few pockets of territory in the west, including Misrata, Zintan, and Nalut. Gaddafi's attention would then turn to the east. If he managed to invade Benghazi, the revolution in every other part of the country would be snuffed out within a matter of days.

While launching its onslaught against the rebels, the regime continued to portray the conflict to the outside world in an absurd manner. It struck me as a naïve tactic, such was its blatant disconnection from reality. In an interview with the French Sunday newspaper *Journal du Dimanche*, Gaddafi reprised his argument that the uprising was the work of al-Qaeda and adolescent drug addicts. "These young people don't know about al-Qaeda, or its ideology. But members of the [al-Qaeda] cells even give them hallucinogenic pills," said the Colonel, with a straight face, speaking from his parallel world. "Every day the al-Qaeda commanders come to talk to them, the young people, and give them these pills and money, asking them to set fire to police stations and attack arms dumps. And now the young people have got a taste for these pills, they think machine guns are like fireworks."

Gaddafi naturally also found time to issue threats to his enemies. He condemned all the rebels, with those in Zintan a particular target for his wrath, and declared that the "colonialist countries" were hatching a "plot to humiliate the Libyan people, reduce them to slavery, and control the oil." The regime was also organizing press trips for foreign journalists to tell them its version of events, however cretinous that might be, and to celebrate the progress of the counteroffensive. The idea was to show that most of Libya was calm, and support for Gaddafi undiminished. The media reports from the route between Tripoli and Ras Jdir, on the border with Tunisia, indicated that the checkpoints were now back under army control; loyalist checkpoints elsewhere were manned by heavily armed police or militiamen.

Outside Libya there seemed to be even less news. The only surprise on the day I was released was that henceforward the French government under President Nicolas Sarkozy would recognize the National Transitional Council (NTC), recently formed in Benghazi, as the sole legitimate representative of the Libyan people. That same day Sarkozy had received two emissaries from the NTC, one of whom had been an opponent of Gaddafi in exile and would become one of the most admired figures in Libya: Mahmoud Jibril. During the revolution Jibril led the political battle against the regime, creating an alternative center of power that was both legitimate and reliable. The hope of the opposition leaders, he would tell me months later, was that even if the revolution failed militarily it would achieve political victory by making the West see that Libya wanted to become a democratic society. At first the French initiative looked a little hasty, but Sarkozy made clear that France was in fact cutting diplomatic relations with Gaddafi—which increased the likelihood of a more active intervention on the part of the international community.

The UN Security Council had made very little progress toward a resolution that might result in outside intervention in Libya, whether military or otherwise. The issue had already been discussed before Ghaith and I were arrested, which is why I later wondered if the military installation where I was held might become a target for NATO. On February 26, the Security Council unanimously approved Resolution 1970—proposed by France, the United Kingdom, Germany, and the United States—which condemned the Libyan regime's use of force against peaceful demonstrations and requested that an independent commission be sent to Libya as soon as possible to investigate the crimes perpetrated by the regime, giving a leading role to the International Criminal Court. The same text demanded that Libya allow humanitarian organizations to enter the country, imposed sanctions on the regime, and froze the assets of the Gaddafi family and other major figures in the regime while also prohibiting them from traveling abroad.

From a military standpoint the most significant move on the part of the international community was an embargo on the "direct or indirect" provision of arms to the regime. Among the countries voting in favor of the embargo were Russia, China, India, and Brazil, all of which were resistant to the idea of military intervention. Its approval was made possible by the resignation of Libya's representative on the Security Council, Abdel Rahman Shalgham, who had been foreign minister between 2000 and 2009. A former member of Gaddafi's inner circle, he resigned on February 25, declaring in a speech to the Security Council that he could no longer condone the violent repression of political protest. Referring to Gaddafi's threat to distribute weapons to the people and "turn Libya red with blood," he said, "Muammar Gaddafi can't give a single weapon to anyone in Libya because it will be used against him."

By March 10, the resolution had perhaps reduced the quantity of arms arriving in Libya and possibly had an impact on the regime through the freezing of assets and the ban on travel—but the offensive against the rebels continued unabated. A growing number of voices rose in favor of military intervention, but there seemed little prospect of it happening as quickly as the Libyan people needed. While I'd been detained there had been some significant political developments. Hillary Clinton, the US secretary of state, had said on March 2 that she was "reflecting" on the various options for containing Gaddafi, one of which was a "ban on flights in the country." Until then the European Union had been reticent about the idea of military intervention. Only the Arab League was talking openly about the creation of a no-fly zone over Libya, although it was opposed to any intervention involving land forces.

The UN had established no-fly zones over Iraq in 1992 in the wake of the Gulf War to prevent Saddam Hussein's regime from carrying out air attacks on the Shia population in the south of the country or the Kurds in the north. Mustafa Abdel Jalil, the newly elected president of the NTC, requested this be repeated in Libya and also wanted the UN to authorize air attacks on Gaddafi's forces. US defense secretary Robert Gates said Paris, London, and Washington had yet to arrive at a consensus on the issue. In the French capital, foreign minister Alain Juppé expressed concerns about the "reaction on the Arab street, of the Arab populations along the Mediterranean, if they saw NATO forces landing." It could be "counterproductive," he concluded.

But it was surely no coincidence that France was already sending warships to the region, including the helicopter carrier *Mistral*. Their official mission was to help evacuate Egyptians from Libya. The United States was also sending naval and air forces to the Mediterranean; Hillary Clinton insisted they were intended to provide "humanitarian assistance" and that there was no prospect of "imminent military action involving American ships." A week after Resolution 1970, which did not provide for the use of force, and more than a week before the adoption UN Security Council Resolution 1973, which called for a ceasefire, established a no-fly zone in Libya, and authorized international military intervention, the American, French, and British armadas were already sailing into position—but supposedly only for "humanitarian ends." The creation of a no-fly zone had already been discussed at the Security Council when Resolution 1970 was passed, but the idea was vetoed by

Moscow and Beijing, whose diplomats were aware of the West's intentions. After that, NATO secretary-general Anders Fogh Rasmussen, a man who would play an important role over the following months, reaffirmed that NATO wasn't considering an intervention but also said it was preparing for "any eventuality." Despite the diplomatic language and the denials, it already seemed clear that the Western powers, led by Barack Obama, Nicolas Sarkozy, and British prime minister David Cameron, had in fact decided to conduct military operations against Gaddafi's armed forces.

As I looked back over the events since my imprisonment, it was possible to discern the gradual emergence of a political discourse—day by day, step by step—apparently aimed at preparing international public opinion for a UN decision to authorize military intervention. On March 4, President Obama effectively passed sentence on Gaddafi by declaring, for the first time, that he had "lost legitimacy" and should "leave power." In the same statement Obama said he had asked the state and defense departments to "study all the options," especially the creation of a no-fly zone. Soon afterward, in an orchestrated political offensive, Hillary Clinton and her French and British counterparts, Alain Juppé and William Hague, publicly came out in support of a no-fly zone.

Support for their decision had already come from the National Transitional Council, the Islamic Conference, and the Arab League. Gaddafi, realizing that a military operation was imminent, warned—or promised—that "thousands of Libyans would die if there was an intervention by the United States or NATO," and reiterated that he had no intention of leaving Libya. He also gave another airing to what had been his most frequent threat during four decades of dealings with the West: the expulsion of multinational companies from the country. This was the old rhetoric about the rest of the world coveting Libya's oil, a nationalistic discourse that had served to unite civil society during the early days of his dictatorship—but now it no longer had an impact, either with his domestic audience or abroad.

In the two hours I spent in General Krema's mansion, I did in fact mention the possibility that the UN might approve a no-fly zone, which in practice would mean an attack on Libya by the West. The general muttered briefly but otherwise said nothing: a response that gave a glimpse of a cowed and dejected man, far from the secure, authoritative figure he had appeared to be. Suddenly I had the feeling the regime was very afraid of military intervention. I guessed the fear didn't come from their lives being put in danger—which was something soldiers were used to—but instead from the threat that NATO, allied with the uprising, would pose to the stability of the dictatorship. Inside that mansion—which months later I learned had been one of the principal bases for the regime's espionage operations—there was a sense of decline, of inexorable collapse. And Krema didn't even seem particularly bothered about hiding the reality. His most urgent desire was simply to get rid of a journalist who was witnessing the decay.

AGAIN I TRIED TO CALL FRANCE AND BRAZIL—AND THIS TIME, FINALLY, I HEARD Lúcia's voice. An enormous weight of stress and anguish lifted from my shoulders. Speaking through tears, her voice was even sweeter, more tender, and more comforting than before. Until that moment I'd feared my loved ones might be angry with me for what had happened—not just Lúcia but also all my family. We spoke about my arrest and subsequent "disappearance"—this was actually the first moment I'd seen myself as a "missing" person, and to do so was quite a shock. We talked about my experiences in the prison and about my state of health, both physical and psychological. As the conversation progressed, I was amused to realize Lúcia was displaying some of the traits that made me admire her not just as a woman but as a journalist too. As I was describing what had happened to me she was saying "uh-huh...uh-huh" in precisely the tone a reporter might use to encourage a source to carry on with a story. She was taking mental notes, interviewing me, securing her very own "exclusive." Smiling, I also found myself stepping into my journalistic role, telling Lúcia that I intended to stay in Tripoli if I managed to get the authorities to reverse their decision to deport me. We discussed the idea for a little while; everything Lúcia said about it seemed reasonable to me. As our conversation drew to a close I was fighting back tears. Lúcia had told me about the response of my family, friends, and colleagues to my disappearance; the emotional impact it had caused upset me. The same feeling remained with me as I made my next call, to the paper in São Paulo. I didn't know what kind of reaction to expect. What followed, in fact, were exchanges that will remain etched in my memory—the warm greetings from the switchboard operators; the obvious joy of Roberto Simon, the reporter I'd spoken to in the last call before my arrest; and the euphoric cries from Roberto Lameirinhas, the foreign editor. With Lameirinhas I recorded the first of a series of interviews with newspapers and media organizations from various countries, demanding in all of them that Ghaith be released immediately. It was the priority for all of us, both in Brazil and the United Kingdom.

The call I didn't make, however, was to my family. Later I would tell them I hadn't managed to get through, which was a lie. The truth was that the conversation, at that moment, would simply have been too much for me.

Revived by the affection I'd received over the phone, I wanted to talk more with Ambassador George Ney Fernandes; I wanted to discuss arrangements for the next day and also exchange ideas about the socio-political situation. Before I did so I had a shower—my first proper wash in many days—and also received a phone call from a man named Emad Embirsh, who introduced himself as a Libyan diplomat and said he would come to talk to me at the residence later that evening. He said he had videos filmed on the battlefronts to show me but didn't provide any further details. After dinner the ambassador suggested we should have a walk around the neighborhood so I could get more of a sense of day-to-day life in the capital against the backdrop of the revolution.

The streets nearby were narrow, dark, and utterly deserted, but it wasn't an unpleasant environment and certainly didn't feel threatening. We took a right turn and saw ahead of us a stationary pickup with its engine running and two men inside. The ambassador issued a warning: "Maybe we're being spied on by the secret service. The regime does a lot of that."

I wasn't surprised. The ambassador had already told me the embassy's phone lines were being tapped, which had led him to make a formal complaint to the Libyan foreign ministry. We arrived at a wide avenue, bought a few things at a minimarket, and returned along a street parallel to the one we'd taken before. Soon we saw the same pickup, with the same men inside, still with its engine running. We gave it a wide berth and returned to the residence.

Embirsh arrived a few minutes later. He seemed friendly enough, though he was scruffily dressed and his English was poor—another Libyan "diplomat" who didn't really fit the part. We discussed the availability of flights the following day: there might be one to Paris but more likely I'd leave on a flight to Dubai, which was what General Krema wanted. Again I made clear that I wanted to stay in Tripoli, with the authorization of the regime. Embirsh listened, not rejecting the idea out of hand, and then phoned his superiors. One of the men he tried to get hold of was Moussa Ibrahim, a spokesperson for Gaddafi who was in charge of feeding information to the foreign journalists staying at the Rixos hotel. He would later become one of the regime's most high-profile figures.

Waiting for answers, the supposed diplomat asked me to sit with him in front of a laptop on which he wanted to show me the films he'd mentioned earlier. They'd been put on a CD-ROM, he said, so I could take them with me. The amateur footage, apparently shot on mobile phones, showed rebel forces in Benghazi and the desert. In one film the insurgents were firing AK-47s and training with anti-aircraft guns and rocket launchers. In another a man was standing on an abandoned tank; his face was contorted with hatred, and in his hand he seemed to be holding a human organ.

"You see this?!" said Embirsh. "It's a heart! It's a heart! Who rips out the heart of a person? It's al-Qaeda!"

I listened, not bothering to disagree. More images appeared, mostly of men training with weapons in the desert. Then Embirsh stopped the film and pointed to the screen. "Look at these clothes! Look at these beards! They're al-Qaeda!"

Now he was starting to irritate me. His argument assumed that foreign journalists were morons. The clothes worn by the men in the videos were absolutely typical of many regions of the Arab and Muslim world, while long beards are traditional for some of the more devout Muslims and Jews—who needless to say are not necessarily terrorists. As for the exercises in the desert, they were nothing more than Ghaith and I had seen with our own eyes: paramilitary training for insurgents determined to mount a revolution.

As soon as I was able to put an end to the film show without appearing rude, I did so. I thanked Embirsh for his visit and tried to steer the conversation back to my prospects of remaining in Tripoli. Although he hadn't yet managed to speak to his superiors, he suddenly said, "You can stay. You'll pass the night here and then tomorrow we'll go to the Rixos hotel, where you'll stay with the other foreign journalists."

The ambassador and I both felt, however, that Embirsh's guarantee carried less weight than the expulsion order from General Krema. The situation might pit a subordinate from the foreign ministry—if indeed that was Embirsh's true identity—against an officer from the Mukhabarat, with unpredictable consequences. There was potential for a misunderstanding that might cause problems for the ambassador, the person responsible for getting me out of the country.

So Embirsh suggested I leave for Paris but then come back at the invitation of the regime, with the appropriate visa. According to his plan the Libyan embassy in Madrid would issue the visa, as those in Paris and Rome had been taken over by rebel sympathizers. It sounded like a reasonable idea. Being a guest of the regime was far from ideal, but at least it would allow me to be in Tripoli when, sooner or later, the NATO intervention took place, with what was sure to be an immediate impact on the course of the revolution. We exchanged phone numbers and email addresses, and I gave him a pen drive with a scan of my passport to speed up the visa procedure. George Ney Fernandes seemed satisfied with the alternative plan, enthusiastic even.

"When you come back you can stay here," he said. And then he gave me a further incentive to return as quickly as possible: "It might even be possible to arrange an interview with someone at the top of the government—maybe Saif, or even Gaddafi himself. I can't promise anything, but with Saif I think there's a decent chance."

The ambassador's offer wasn't unrealistic. The Colonel had already given a string of interviews to foreign newspapers and TV stations: he saw them as opportunities to send messages to the international community and also to convey an image of transparency. If I did manage to return to Tripoli, perhaps I could in some way take advantage of the historically good relationship between the Brazilian and Libyan governments, from the days of the military dictatorship right up to Luiz Inácio Lula da Silva, and the Gaddafi regime. Moreover, the ambassador really did seem to have good contacts, even amid the turmoil of a revolution.

By now I was exhausted. We said goodbye to Embirsh and a few minutes later I was preparing for bed. I had a comfortable bed and, after so many nights under fluorescent lamps, the luxury of absolute darkness, but I didn't sleep even for one minute. I spent the whole night thinking about what had happened, wondering how Ghaith was, and realizing how much I disliked the prospect of leaving the country.

The next morning we headed to Tripoli international airport in the embassy's official vehicle. At the wheel was a stern but polite middle-aged driver with an impressive moustache; apparently he had a great ability to win the trust of his compatriots, which allowed him to open the unlikeliest of doors for the ambassador. Arriving in the car park outside the airport terminal we saw a huge crowd of people sheltering in tents or under the awning at the front of the main building. They were mostly immigrants from sub-Saharan Africa or Southeast Asia who had been trying for days to find places on flights out of the country.

Amid this sea of humanity were cars that had been torched, smashed up, or overturned. Some of them had diplomatic license plates. The ambassador explained that the anger about the lack of planes had led some people to vent their frustrations on the representatives of other embassies; the violence was less to do with the Libyans' fight for liberty than a simple survival instinct. Thousands of desperate people were waiting for nonexistent aircraft; 95 percent of flights had been canceled. To maintain order, the police and army had cordoned off several areas; the crowd was excluded from the interior of the terminal, the only place offering any shelter from the nighttime cold. As we approached the entrance to the terminal we heard gunshots followed by fearful cries from hundreds of people. I felt sure then that although Gaddafi was recapturing some cities, he would eventually lose the capital—if not to the rebels, then to chaos.

It was discomforting to realize that part of the agreement regarding my release, signed by Sadegh Krema, meant every door was literally opening in front of me. Although I wanted to stay, I went to the front of the queue ahead of people desperate to leave the country because they feared for the futures of their families. A few hours later inside the plane, I called my mother, Maria Tereza, using a mobile phone the ambassador had given me. She answered in a serious tone of voice and for more than five minutes we had a calm, unemotional conversation, almost as if we were speaking about other people—until eventually we both broke down. She asked me why I was crying. Because, I said, what brought me to Libya in the first place were the humanist values I'd inherited from her.

I FLEW TO DUBAI ON AN AIRCRAFT BELONGING TO THE LIBYAN STATE-OWNED CARRIER Afriqiyah—one of the last flights to leave Tripoli before the NATO intervention. With me were more than a hundred refugees, immigrants who had worked in the major cities and were fleeing from the first of the Arab revolutions to have turned into an armed conflict. Sitting next to me was Shahin Ahmed, a 28-year-old Bangladeshi who'd been in Libya for a little more than two years. For the first few hours we didn't talk at all, as if he were aware of my temporary need for silence, but about two hours before landing we began a conversation that soon turned to the subject of the immigrants stranded at Tripoli airport.

Shahin said he'd been part of a group of around 200 Bangladeshis who'd gone to Libya for work in 2008 that paid 700 dinars—less than US$600—a month. "It was a good salary. It allowed me to get by and also to save," he said. "But Libya has problems and I'd rather return to Bangladesh, where can I eat properly again and have a quieter life."

The passengers around me were curious about the Westerner in their midst, and when they found out I was a journalist many of them wanted to tell me their stories. They included another Bangladeshi, Sujit Kumar

Das, 47, who'd been in Libya for six years. While Shahin's facial expressions still showed the fear he'd experienced over the previous few weeks, Sujit was a picture indignation and disappointment. He was fiercely critical of the disdainful way the workers had been treated by the companies that employed them until the beginning of the uprising—and the regime's attitude toward foreigners seeking escape had been no different. The result of this generalized negligence was the mass of refugees huddled around the terminal building at Tripoli airport. Das said that during the time he'd spent at the airport he'd seen the attacks on the diplomatic vehicles, and heard rumors about people being shot for protesting too vehemently. The usual form of violence against the refugees, however, was deliberate abandonment.

"I waited seven days in front of the airport. There was nothing to eat, no one to help the sick, nothing," Das said. "Everyone there waits five, six, seven days for a flight. And sometimes the flights we were waiting for were suddenly canceled."

By the time I arrived in Dubai I'd made some new friends among the refugees; many were pleased to have the opportunity to speak to a journalist. The next leg of the journey back to my normal life was an Emirates flight from the Persian Gulf to France, which left in the early hours of the following morning. On Saturday, March 12, I finally reunited with Lúcia at Charles De Gaulle airport in Paris. In that instant I had conflicting feelings: I was free again, and back in touch with the people I loved—but my greatest concern was Ghaith, whose fate was still uncertain.

Shortly after the journey from Libya—more than 24 hours in total—I started giving what would turn out to be a long series of interviews to other journalists from various countries. It was an important means of mobilizing the media toward the goal of securing Ghaith's freedom. In addition to the Brazilian media, big names such as Associated Press, the BBC, CNN, and *Le Monde* appealed for his release. Lúcia, meanwhile, reproduced the impressive campaign for my release that she'd launched on the social networks—but now for Ghaith. One of my brothers, Vinicius, was very active in trying to locate me while I was missing.

The *Estado de São Paulo*, for its part, coordinated with various international organizations dedicated to defending freedom of the press. The World Association of Newspapers and Reporters Without Borders, among others, pressured political leaders and the international community to demand my friend's release. And the *Guardian*, of course, worked behind the scenes to try to free its reporter; one of the channels it pursued was via the Turkish embassy in Tripoli.

With the help of contacts in Libya and abroad, I tried to work out the location of the military installation where Ghaith and I had been held, hoping this information might save the building from being bombed if NATO did intervene.

These efforts were necessary because Ghaith's situation was difficult in many respects: as an Iraqi, he was a citizen of a country without diplomatic representation in Libya; as a reporter on a British newspaper, he was certain to be viewed unsympathetically by the regime; and unlike me, he wouldn't benefit from Brazil's smooth-running diplomacy in Tripoli. Why the latter was the case, however, I have never understood—particularly as Ambassador George Ney Fernandes had promised me he would assist Ghaith as long as he received the instruction to do so from the Brazilian foreign ministry in Brasilia.

These negative factors worried us all because they revealed the precarious nature of our channels of communication with the regime. Our anxiety only increased that Saturday afternoon, March 12, when I was informed by Safa Ahmad, the journalist who was also Ghaith's girlfriend, and Ian Katz, deputy editor of the *Guardian*, that Ghaith might be tried for espionage. It was obviously an attempt at blackmail on the part of the regime, the motives for which could only be guessed at.

Ghaith would later write a piece for the *Guardian* telling the story of what actually happened to him. After I was freed he was transferred to "my" cell, where I dare say he gorged on the liters of unwanted curdled milk drink I'd stashed inside the broken bed frame. Like me, he was kept in isolation and had no natural light. In the adjacent rooms he could hear suspected rebels being interrogated; the questioning was generally followed by the beatings I also heard. Later he was moved back to the basement of the building to share a cell with a Bangladeshi immigrant arrested for not having a visa in his passport when he was preparing to leave the country. He was transferred to yet another cell before finally, on March 15, he was told he was about to be freed. He was blindfolded, as I was when I left the prison, but ended up being taken back to his cell because his release had been "delayed." The next day, Wednesday, March 16, he was blindfolded again and this time taken away in a van, which drove around for about an hour before returning to the prison: when he opened his eyes he was back in his cell. A couple of hours later he was blindfolded again, put back in the van, and told he'd be taken for trial. But this time when he got out of the vehicle, he was met by the sight of three *Guardian* journalists. He was a free man, but like me he had to leave the country. He sent me a text I received in Paris at 2:56 a.m. on Thursday, March 17: "Crazy Brazilian…"

The text arrived while I sat in the quiet of my living room, jotting down some notes I'd later refer to when writing this book. Although I'd already received confirmation of his release, the message felt like the closing chapter to a truly frightening story. Although the dangers we faced during our arrest and imprisonment had been huge and unpredictable, we came out alive. Our experience was nothing in comparison to the oppression, torture, and murder that had been the fate of Libyan dissidents for decades. And our suffering was trifling in comparison to the pain of the families of those journalists who lost their lives in the conflict.

Given the intensity of the violence, I was already sure when I left the prison that worse fates than ours would befall some journalists in Libya. It was no secret that Gaddafi intended to come down hard on reporters and photographers who entered the country without authorization, as we did, or those within Libya who reported on the rebels. Indeed, the threat was already being carried out. Before Ghaith and I even set foot in Tripolitania, Libyan journalists and political activists such as Jamal al-Hajji, Tagi al-Din al-Chalawi, Abdel Fattah Bourwag, and the blogger Mohamed al-Ashim Masmari had been thrown in jail. During the time we were imprisoned, the reporters Goktay Koraltan and Feras Killani from the BBC Arabic service were captured by militiamen in Zawiyah and subjected to mock executions. In the days following my release, four people working for the *New York Times*—the unforgettable Anthony Shadid, who died in Syria in 2012; reporter and filmmaker Stephen Farrell; and photographers Tyler Hicks and Lynsey Addario—would all disappear in Libya and later resurface as prisoners of the regime. Next, on March 12, came confirmation of the death of Ali Hassan al-Jaber, a camera operator working for Al Jazeera in Benghazi. The casualties multiplied over the following months, including the tragic deaths of photojournalists Tim Hetherington and Chris Hondros in Misrata in April.

According to the Paris-based organization Reporters Without Borders, eleven journalists lost their lives during the Libyan conflict. A further 32 were imprisoned, 15 kidnapped, and 30 expelled. In an excellent piece in the *Guardian* called "Reporting Libya: freelance coverage, full-time dangers," Peter Beaumont noted that half as many journalists died during the eight-month conflict in Libya as in ten years of war in Afghanistan. There is no way, therefore, that Ghaith and I can portray ourselves as victims. We came out safe and sound.

THE REVOLUTION TOOK A DECISIVE TURN DURING THE WEEK OF GHAITH'S RELEASE. Gaddafi's forces continued their advance on cities in Tripolitania and

Cyrenaica. Zawiyah was almost razed to the ground; the insurgents who survived had to go into hiding to avoid becoming the target of revenge attacks from loyalist forces. The eyewitness accounts that reached the international media, which had been prevented from covering the story directly, spoke of a massacre taking place as the army advanced. Proregime militias were also active in wresting back control over a city that would prove to be one of the keys to the survival of the dictatorship. Other rebel cities in the west, including Yefren, were also recaptured. Three rebel enclaves survived in Tripolitania: Zintan and Nalut, protected by the Nefusa mountains, and Misrata, to the east of Tripoli, which would later endure the longest and most excruciating siege of the whole conflict.

With each passing day the list of eastern cities retaken by Gaddafi grew. One of them was Marsa el Brega, the fall of which allowed the regime to prepare an assault on Ajdabiya, the last rebel city before Benghazi, home to the NTC. The rebel commander General Abdel Fattah Younis, who would be killed in July in murky circumstances following rumors he or members of his family were still in contact with the Gaddafi regime, described Ajdabiya as "vital" for the survival of the revolution. Younis had predicted the loyalist forces would face "serious logistical difficulties" as they attempted to advance in the east. For the time being, however, it seemed Gaddafi's forces were inspired by the example of a famous commander who had fought in the same region and whom the dictator himself greatly admired: Erwin Rommel, the "Desert Fox," leader of the German Afrika Korps in the Second World War. Between February 1941 and July 1942, Rommel led one of the most memorable offensives of the war, sweeping the British forces out of his path as he thrust toward Egypt.

With the no-fly zone still merely an idea, Gaddafi's tanks were free to advance, and he could use his warplanes to soften up rebel positions as a precursor to attacks by ground forces. Ajdabiya was again bombed from the air on Monday, March 14. If nothing were done to halt the advance of the Libyan troops—who did indeed seem to have learned from Rommel's successes and mistakes, addressing logistical issues so that they didn't run out of water, fuel, or ammunition—it was possible Benghazi might fall in a matter of days. The prospect of a tragic defeat for the revolutionaries became even more likely on March 15 when the last rebels in advanced positions were forced to abandon Ajdabiya's city center to Gaddafi's forces and retreat to the outskirts. It was now obvious that without outside military intervention, the rebellion was on its last legs. Interviewed by the

Italian newspapers *Corriere Della Sera* and *La Repubblica*, Saif al-Islam predicted that the fighting would be over "shortly."

The rebels' retreat—or escape—from the Marsa el Brega front, and the imminent fall of Ajdabiya, opened the eyes of the international community to the rebels' lack of equipment and training necessary to hold out against the Libyan army—which, although not strong, was undoubtedly superior. Journalists in the east conveyed the same conclusions Ghaith and I had reached in the west: with history teachers fighting in the frontline and without international "protection," the Libyan revolution was genuine, popular, and heroic—and destined to be bloody and brief. Buoyed by the progress his forces were making in the desert, Gaddafi was confident of imminent victory. On Tuesday, March 15, he went on state TV to announce that "freedom" was about to triumph thanks to the willingness of "all the Libyan people," who were "ready to fight and protect the oil." He warned that it didn't matter whether the resistance was due to the machinations of France, Britain, and the United States or was the result of an internal plot: it would be crushed either way. This public pronouncement of a death sentence against his own people shocked the whole world. Gaddafi said in an earlier speech that he would make "a river of blood" run through his own country—and now, closing in on Benghazi, he was set to fulfill that gruesome promise.

On March 16, Gaddafi's troops launched what was expected to be the decisive offensive against the rebel enclave of Misrata. The regime declared that the battle against a "handful of lunatics," or "rats and stray dogs," would last no more than 24 hours, and then the city would be "liberated." The situation was also desperate in Zintan, where local rebel commander Jamal Mansour said he was facing heavy weapons capable of reducing the city to "scorched earth." In the east, the regime's forces had recaptured Az Zuwaytinah, 150 kilometers south of Benghazi; on Thursday, March 17, they were gathered around Benghazi itself, preparing an onslaught against the birthplace of the revolution. Some 300,000 civilians fled toward Tobruk and the Egyptian border. The International Red Cross, which was withdrawing its personnel, said it was "extremely concerned" about what might happen "to civilians, the sick and wounded, detainees, and others who are entitled to protection in times of conflict." The world turned its eyes toward Benghazi and also toward New York, where the UN Security Council discussed a new resolution that might prevent the bloodbath. Libya's deputy ambassador to the UN, Ibrahim Dabbashi, urged the international community to adopt a resolution approving military intervention "within ten hours" or else "a genuine massacre" would take place in North Africa.

After ten days of prevarication during which the international community had been split between the "appropriateness" and "urgency" of a resolution to create a no-fly zone, the threats emanating from the regime, ironically, lent further weight to arguments that diplomats from the United States, the United Kingdom, and France hoped would lead to the acquiescence of Russia and China. Criticized for its stance in favor of Ben Ali during the Tunisian revolution and for its lack of initiative during the uprising in Egypt, the French government decided to accelerate the military intervention. It was a means of silencing the voices that had risen against its foreign policy and the involvement of certain ministers with the Tunisian regime—particularly foreign minister Michele Alliot-Marie, who had resigned at the end of February. Contrary to the cautious approach of the diplomats from the French foreign ministry, President Sarkozy committed himself to stirring the UN into action. He was cheered on by philosopher Bernard-Henri Lévy, whose one-man campaign in favor of intervention—in which he took it upon himself to announce measures on behalf of foreign minister Alain Juppé—made French diplomacy look somewhat chaotic.

France's ambassador to the UN, Gerard Araud, spoke to his US counterpart, Susan Rice, in an attempt to convince the US administration to join a military offensive in Libya. Because Washington doubted the capacity of France and the United Kingdom to manage an intervention on their own, it feared an attack on Libya would end up creating a third battlefront for American forces in the Muslim world, after Afghanistan and Iraq. On the morning of Tuesday, March 15, Rice told Araud in a private conversation that not even "in your dreams" would the United States take part. That night, however, Rice called Araud with a very different message: "We're in." That meant there was just one more obstacle: the Russian ambassador, Vitaly Churkin, who was threatening to propose a watered-down text that made no mention of a no-fly zone. The French diplomatic mission in New York was to present the text of Resolution 1973 to the Security Council "in blue," meaning any future amendments could be vetoed.

There were disagreements right up until a few hours before the French-British-Lebanese resolution was submitted at a meeting of all the Security Council members. The text stated that there had already been "heavy civilian casualties" in Libya, along with the "systematic violation of human rights, including arbitrary detentions, enforced disappearances,

torture, and summary executions"—therefore "additional appropriate measures" beyond the scope of Resolution 1970 would be justified.
The African Union, the Organization of the Islamic Conference, and
the Arab League supported the text. The resolution also deplored "the
use of mercenaries by the Libyan authorities," considered banning of all
flights in Libyan airspace as an "important element for the protection of
civilians," and demanded the "immediate establishment of a ceasefire."
In Article 4, on the protection of civilians, the resolution went further,
authorizing member states "to take all necessary measures...to protect
civilians and civilian populated areas under threat of attack." The words
"all necessary measures" caught my attention—and they reappeared in
Paragraph 13, on the enforcement of the arms embargo, as well as in
Paragraph 8, on the no-fly zone banning all flights except those whose
sole purpose was humanitarian. In the precise words of the text, member
states were authorized to "take all necessary measures to enforce compli-
ance with the ban on flights."

Although the terminology was the subject of disagreements between
diplomats representing the countries on the Security Council, every single
word had been exhaustively discussed in another room within the UN
building in New York: the Security Council Consultation Room, acces-
sible only to the members of the delegations involved in the discussions. It
just so happened that one of the diplomats directly involved in drafting the
final text was a friend of mine, and an extremely reliable source. Concerned
by my "disappearance" in Libya, he had fought to ensure the text included a
reference to the crackdown on the media and condemned "acts of violence
and intimidation committed by the Libyan authorities against journalists,
media professionals, and associated personnel." A few days after the text
was approved, he wrote to me: "I introduced that sixth paragraph of the
preamble of UN Security Council Resolution 1973 for you, but also as a
tribute from France to all those who risk their lives to keep us informed,"
he said. Then he added, jokingly, "Don't ever do it again."

After the text was approved I spoke with my diplomat friend about
what had gone on behind the scenes at the Security Council. I asked
about the expression "all necessary measures," pointing out the ambiguity that enabled the coalition of the United States, France, and the
United Kingdom, and then NATO, to justify all the military measures
they would end up taking. But that was precisely the point, he said: the
ambiguity was entirely deliberate.

"Before the vote on [Resolution] 1973," he explained to me, "we went
to the Consultation Room and explained everything in detail, including

the terms employed. And we asked: 'Are you aware of what you're authorizing?' And then we were more explicit: 'It means the use of force,' we said. If you're talking about a no-fly zone, it means taking out radar systems, command posts, defense systems, but those who approved the resolution knew it wasn't just that. They were all very aware."

In the opinions of the Western countries that supported the resolution, the words "all necessary measures" provided legal backing not only for an air offensive to neutralize the regime's defense and command systems, which would happen quickly enough, but also for other decisions taken in the months that followed, such as the supply of arms to the rebels "for the protection of civilian populations," the dispatch of special forces to participate in land operations, and, most strikingly of all, the targeting of Muammar Gaddafi himself. According to my diplomat friend, the objective wasn't to depose the Colonel, and yet "as the commander in charge of the repression, he was a legitimate target."

The text authorizing "all necessary measures" was approved in a Security Council session that began at 10 p.m. on Thursday, March 17—the early hours of the morning in Paris. Germany, Brazil, China, India, and Russia abstained; ten countries cast their votes in favor.

The UN resolution opened the way to military intervention, and rebels celebrated on the streets of Benghazi as the news from New York came through. But Gaddafi's forces were already just outside the city, so it was now a race against time. The Western and Arab allies issued another ultimatum, and once again the regime committed itself to a unilateral ceasefire—a commitment it had no intention of honoring. On the Friday night and early Saturday morning of March 18 and 19, explosions and anti-aircraft fire echoed through the streets of Benghazi. Regime soldiers, mercenaries, members of the Thawara Legion, and kataeb elite forces—independent paramilitary forces formed with the approval of the regime—had infiltrated the crowds, spreading panic as they fired bullets and grenades without bothering to distinguish between armed adversaries and the civilian population.

On that Saturday afternoon, forced into action by events on the ground, the United States, France, Britain, Qatar, and the United Arab Emirates organized an emergency summit in Paris "to support the Libyan people." The participants included Hillary Clinton, David Cameron, UN secretary-general Ban Ki-moon, and the leaders of Germany, Spain, Italy, and Belgium. At the end of the meeting President Sarkozy invited the press to the Élysée Palace for an announcement that lasted four and a half hours. Neither I nor the other journalists present had any doubts

about what we were about to hear: the decision to launch a military operation. There was a nuance, however, which took the world by surprise.

"As of now, our aircraft are preventing planes from attacking the
town [Benghazi]. As of now, other French aircraft are ready to intervene
against tanks, armored vehicles threatening unarmed civilians," declared
Sarkozy, exuding solemnity and determination. He issued a warning,
greeted with disdain by Gaddafi, that there must be an "immediate
ceasefire" along with the "withdrawal of the forces which have attacked
civilian populations." "Today," Sarkozy continued, "we are intervening
in Libya under the United Nations Security Council mandate, alongside our partners, in particular our Arab partners. We are doing this in
order to protect the civilian population from the murderous madness of a
regime that by killing its own people has forfeited all legitimacy."

CHAPTER 9

PLAN

Troops were already besieging the western fringes of Benghazi, the first steps toward carrying out the Colonel's orders to "hunt down the miscreants and bearded ones" and "punish them without mercy." The regime promised, however, to spare all those who laid down their weapons and fled. Gaddafi threatened to attack any aircraft that entered Libyan airspace without permission and any ship in the country's territorial waters in the Mediterranean. His words suggested the regime was preparing for war. Even though he now faced the prospect of aerial attack, the dictator pushed ahead with his plans to crush Benghazi as well as Misrata. Following these developments from Paris, I feared that instead of the "Battle of Tripoli" anticipated by the rebels in Zintan, a "Battle of Benghazi" would decide the fate of the revolution.

Since the passing of Resolution 1973, Gaddafi's soldiers and mercenaries had advanced a further 160 kilometers and entered the outskirts of Benghazi. Local residents feared, understandably, that once these forces penetrated the city, coalition air attacks would be constrained by the risk of collateral damage. If this were the case, the international intervention—marked by prevarication, tortuous negotiations, and hesitation—might prove to be too late. But then the first Rafale fighter jets took off from the French aircraft carrier Charles de Gaulle and attacked tanks advancing toward Benghazi. Operation Odyssey Dawn, which would decide Gaddafi's fate, had begun.

These aerial attacks exposed the difference between the French approach and that of the Pentagon. American operations that night,

March 19, consisted of firing 112 Tomahawk missiles against defense systems in Benghazi, Tripoli, and Misrata. These strikes destroyed many of the regime's anti-aircraft guns and made possible the implementation of the no-fly zone. They also, however, indicated US reluctance to be at the forefront of the intervention. Under the agreement signed behind the scenes at the UN, it was up to the "European allies" and the Arab countries to take the leading roles. The United States had promised logistical support in the form of surveillance aircraft, communications systems, and intelligence gathering, which would give its allies a great deal of precious information, including satellite images showing the locations of military installations. Armed with this information, it was fairly straightforward for the American B-2 Stealth bombers, British Tornadoes, and French Mirages and Rafales to enforce the no-fly zone. Once the defense systems had been incapacitated, the next stage was to reduce the threat to the civilian population by attacking the government forces' supply lines and mechanized infantry.

But there was still a significant issue to be resolved among the coalition partners. France did not want the military operations to be conducted by NATO, despite the insistence of the organization's secretary-general, Anders Fogh Rasmussen. In Paris it was being said that NATO's negative image in the Middle East would make the Arab countries less likely to support the operation. The alternative suggested was that military operations should come under the command of a "political steering committee" comprising the foreign ministers of the Arab League countries, the United States, France, and Britain. NATO's contribution would be to put its "military planning and intervention capacities" at the disposal of this new group.

The issues surrounding NATO's role were not the only source of disagreement. Increasing doubts about the operation were being expressed in the heart of the European Union, with Germany already having stated its opposition. Soon after the beginning of the military operation, Russia's ambassador to NATO, Dmitry Rogozin, declared that the air strikes "do not correspond to the [UN] resolution," implying that the coalition's objective was to depose Gaddafi rather than protect the civilian population.

Protests intensified when the coalition's aircraft bombed Gaddafi's headquarters in Tripoli. UK defense minister Liam Fox added to the controversy when he refused to rule out targeting Gaddafi himself. In response, US defense secretary Robert Gates said the idea of targeting the Colonel would be "insane," and French foreign minister Alain Juppé also denied the coalition had Gaddafi in their sights. Behind the scenes, however, diplomats were already telling journalists, off the record, that the dictator was a "legitimate target," arguing that he was "commanding operations" against the civilian population. Reading between the lines, if Gaddafi's precise location could be discovered, he would be targeted without compunction. Personally I found it worrying that the rebels were being sent the message, albeit indirectly, that Gaddafi's elimination was among the possible objectives. The Western democracies were supposedly preoccupied by issues of justice and human rights—but if their plans included the killing of Gaddafi, further down the line they would have no moral authority to prevent the rebels from wreaking vengeance.

It wasn't long before NATO's involvement in running the military operation stopped being taboo in France and instead became official. There were still disagreements, however, about whether Gaddafi should be targeted, if land forces might be employed, and how long the operations should last. British foreign secretary William Hague refused to set a deadline, saying the intervention was merely in its "first phase," even though by March 23, according to the commander of the British air operations, Air Vice-Marshal Greg Bagwell, the Libyan air force had already lost its "eyes and ears" and no longer existed as a fighting force.

Once the no-fly zone was established, the next objective was to attack Gaddafi's mechanized infantry. His artillery and armored vehicles became priority targets around the besieged cities of Benghazi, Zintan, and Misrata.

The initial attacks gave the coalition control over the skies and halted Gaddafi's advance on the birthplace of the revolution, Benghazi. The desired secondary effect—not mentioned in public but freely acknowledged behind the scenes—was that of enabling the rebel forces to advance, but this would not be achieved quickly. On March 15, Ajdabiya, 160 kilometers south of Benghazi, fell to Gaddafi's forces, which continued to advance in the direction of Egypt. Fighting re-erupted around the city a week later, after the troops had been pushed back by the air strikes. On March 24, the regime's 32nd Brigade came under fierce aerial attack; tanks, BM-21 Grad rocket launchers, and trucks were destroyed and the army's supply lines severely disrupted. The charred bodies of soldiers and mercenaries who had ignored demands to surrender were left scattered among heaps of twisted metal: the hunters had become the prey. Reporters—such as *Libération*'s Christophe Ayad—accompanying the rebel katibas in the region described the grisly scene.

The attack had the desired effect. The rebels recaptured Ajdabiya on Saturday, March 26. The air strikes, mostly carried out by French and British planes, brutally exposed the huge difference in military capability between the coalition and Gaddafi's forces. No armored vehicle could move without being detected by the coalition's surveillance system, and tanks bunched together in offensive formations proved to be easy targets. As during the Second World War, when Britain's Desert Air Force did major damage to Rommel's rearguard and supply lines, the Western and Arab allies dealt Gaddafi a heavy blow from the skies; their complete control over Libyan airspace drastically reduced the dictator's chances of victory. His only option now was to resist as best he could.

By prolonging the conflict, the Colonel hoped to sap the resolve of the governments in the coalition and to turn international opinion against the intervention. Though now he had no chance of regaining control over the whole of Libya, he declared he was aiming for victory in the long term. Responsibility for breaking Gaddafi's resistance fell to Canadian general Charles Bouchard, who took over control of the NATO operation. With Bouchard at the helm the predictions about the duration of the intervention changed dramatically: it was now said the air strikes might go on not just for a few weeks, as initially expected, but for at least three months. The prospect of being sucked into a quagmire began to weigh heavily on the coalition's political leaders. As the reality of the conflict became clearer, dissenting voices became louder. Russian foreign minister Sergei Lavrov continued to protest against what he viewed as the allies' real objective—the removal of Gaddafi rather than merely the protection of Libya's civilian population.

WHILE POLITICIANS TRADED BARBS, A NOOSE TIGHTENED AROUND MISRATA. Situated in western Libya 200 kilometers from Tripoli—about halfway from the capital to Sirte, and more than 800 kilometers from Benghazi— this rebel enclave came under siege on March 20. Over the following months, rebel fighters and civilians would live through a waking nightmare that is certain to have repercussions for years to come. It was as if the regime's hatred toward Libya's revolutionaries had focused on a single city. From the very first days of the siege, amateur video footage showed the destruction caused by the fighting, while reports spoke of the presence of snipers in buildings along Tripoli Street in the city center.

These snipers, some of whom were foreigners, posed a deadly threat; hunting them down became a matter of life and death for the rebels. There was also intensive artillery fire, much of which had no specific target: the regime intended simply to demoralize the city's defenders. On March 25, an unconfirmed report about the deaths of a mother and her three young children in the shelling drew international attention to Misrata's predicament. By this time the city was already suffering power blackouts. Water had to be rationed, and basic foodstuffs were becoming increasingly scarce in the districts most affected by the fighting. Residents were throwing the dead into mass burial pits in Shat-Hansheer cemetery.

Meanwhile, the outskirts of Misrata were a destination for organized press trips. The objective, as in Tripoli, was to convince foreign journalists, and thereby the international community, that the city was under the regime's control. One of the participants was Jérôme Delay from *Le Monde*, who described a pathetic charade in which children dressed in green supposedly demonstrated their support for Gaddafi while intense fighting could be heard just a few kilometers away in the city center.

It became increasingly clear to the international community that a humanitarian crisis was developing in Misrata. In the first week of April, rebel commanders expressed anger at what they saw as NATO's slowness to bomb the artillery batteries around the edge of the city. On April 6, more than two weeks into the siege, the rebel military commander in Benghazi, General Abdel Fattah Younis, made an appeal through the international media. He said the people of Misrata were "dying every day" and called on NATO to "support the population with force." Younis had intended to speak to the press about the conflict as a whole, but Misrata—whose population, in his words, faced "extermination"—attracted all the attention. Younis said homes, hospitals, hotels, and even mosques had been hit by heavy artillery. His words had a significant impact in Europe, provoking a response within a matter of days. Dutch NATO general Mark van Uhm declared that the defense of Misrata had become the "number one priority."

Given the danger that Misrata would fall back under the control of the regime, and the difficulties the rebels were facing in the region around Marsa el Brega, most commonly referred to as Brega, the coalition began to fear the insurgency might be incapable of making significant progress without increased assistance. On April 7, General Carter Ham addressed a session of the US senate in Washington and said there was only "a low probability" that the rebels would eventually reach Tripoli and oust Gaddafi. Meanwhile, 43 days into the siege of Misrata, NATO's chances of keeping Gaddafi's forces out of the city looked equally slim.

Not only were all the rebel-occupied districts of Misrata coming under artillery fire, but so too was the city's port, the population's last point of contact with the outside world. Ships sent by organizations such as the World Food Programme and International Red Cross, carrying basic foodstuffs, medicines, and medical staff, ran the risk of being shelled as they approached the quays. Eventually the port had to be closed.

A large proportion of Misrata's dead and wounded were victims of Grad rockets, launched from the edge of the city in what is typically known in military parlance as "saturation" fire and intended to destroy whole districts of the city, including residential areas. NGOs such as Human Rights Watch had also proven the regime was using cluster munitions, which are banned by international conventions; the evidence included photographs in the *New York Times* showing the remnants of Spanish-made 120 mm cluster shells. Another war crime, committed from the very beginning of the siege, was the use of human shields. In outlying districts already occupied by Gaddafi's forces, families were forced to continue living in their homes while weapons and other equipment were deliberately stored in the immediate vicinity. Saif al-Islam Gaddafi, however, informed the *Washington Post* that the regime was committing no crimes and challenged the International Criminal Court to send emissaries to Libya to see for themselves.

But the crimes in Misrata were not a figment of the West's imagination. Thanks to a few brave journalists who took ships across the Gulf of Sirte to the besieged city, the international media discovered what was going on. Two of them, Marcel Mettelsiefen of *Der Spiegel* and Jean-Louis Le Touzet of *Libération*, would later become my friends. Two others, Tim Hetherington and Chris Hondros, both 41, died tragically on April 20 in mortar fire on Tripoli Street. Both were internationally recognized for their work: Hetherington's documentary *Restrepo*, about the war in Afghanistan, was an Oscar contender in 2010; Hondros won the World Press Photo Award in 2007. Their deaths drew attention to the humanitarian situation in Misrata and thus contributed to the saving of hundreds of lives over the following weeks. André Liohn, a Brazilian photographer working for Human Rights Watch, was in Misrata on the day they died and later arranged for the evacuation of their bodies.

Coincidentally or not, intensified NATO air strikes immediately followed the warnings from Younis and the international press about the ongoing calamity in Misrata. An indication of the impact of these operations came at the end of April, when Gaddafi's generals announced the withdrawal of the troops surrounding the city. There were doubts,

however, about what the army was really up to. The rebels feared mercenaries, many of whom came from neighboring towns, would replace the
soldiers. Indeed, that was the case: a few days later Libya's deputy foreign
minister, Khaled Kaim, said regime troops were making way for the local
tribes, who would form a legion of "sixty thousand men" eager to defend
the regime.

Most of these men came from three neighboring cities: Tawergha,
Zlitan, and Bani Walid. Tawergha, located between Misrata and Sirte,
also served as a forward operating base and supply station for loyalist
forces. According to the inhabitants of Misrata, the men of Tawergha
were responsible for much of their suffering. Because of the participation of black soldiers in the terror campaign waged against Misrata, the
black population of Tawergha would later be forced to flee to Tripoli or
Benghazi, or to neighboring countries. Many of these men volunteered to
participate in the offensive against Misrata—and as these armed civilians
replaced the soldiers surrounding Misrata, NATO's task in defending the
city became more problematic and controversial.

Meanwhile, however, it became apparent that an increasing number
of men from Gaddafi's forces were defecting to the rebels. Some soldiers
and civilian fighters declared that they didn't agree with the siege's constant shelling and rocket attacks or—above all—with the terror tactics,
which included summary executions, torture, rapes, and the use of children as human shields.

AS THE SIEGES OF MISRATA AND ZINTAN CONTINUED, SO TOO DID THE POLITICAL
and diplomatic debates, particularly in Europe. The bloody repression
taking place in Tripolitania showed that NATO's efforts—mostly French
and British—had not so far been sufficient. The French defense ministry acknowledged that the military situation in Libya was "complex,"
while Hillary Clinton in Washington admitted that air power alone was
unlikely to bring victory. The possibility of sending ground forces began
to be discussed, although there was no legal basis for it in Resolution
1973. A more realistic option, though still highly sensitive, was to give
the rebels military training, strategic support, and, above all, arms. As an
alternative, Britain suggested greater "participation"—meaning the provision of weapons, equipment, and training—from the Arab countries in
the coalition, especially Qatar, the United Arab Emirates, and Jordan.

While Europeans discussed the course the conflict was taking—and
the increasing costs they were incurring, against a backdrop of economic
crisis—the Arab countries, especially those of the Persian Gulf, stepped

up their financial support for the Libyan revolution. In so doing they were responding to the appeal from the head of the National Transitional Council (NTC), Mustafa Abdel Jalil, who said the rebellion needed urgent economic assistance due to the paralysis of Libya's oil exports, the country's main source of wealth. Kuwait announced it was sending the NTC US$180 million aimed at reestablishing basic public services in the few rebel-held areas. What wasn't mentioned in public, however, was that the countries of the Arab League, led by Qatar, had already embarked on a plan to supply weapons to the insurgents—an initiative that had not been agreed upon internationally.

Meanwhile, tensions were arising between NATO and the governments of the coalition countries. On one side were generals disgruntled by the governments' reluctance to fund the offensive; on the other, politicians who believed the military operations fell short of what was needed. French foreign minister Alain Juppé made headlines when he said the military intervention was "not enough" and urged NATO to "play its role fully" and to destroy the heavy weapons being used "to bombard civilian populations," particularly in Misrata and Zintan. On April 15, French defense minister Gérard Longuet admitted that President Nicolas Sarkozy, Prime Minister David Cameron, and President Barack Obama were "certainly" stepping beyond the legal framework of Resolution 1973 in demanding that Gaddafi step down, just as they were by targeting the Colonel himself with air strikes and by discussing the possibility of supplying weapons to the insurgents.

Two weeks later, Gaddafi made his first TV pronouncement since April 9. He returned to his previous theme, blaming foreign "terrorists"— supposedly from Algeria, Egypt, Tunisia, and Afghanistan—for the violence that had provoked NATO's intervention. But there was no further mention of "rivers of blood"; instead he used words such as "reconciliation" and described the Libyan people as "a family" in whose eyes he was "more sacred than the emperor of Japan was for his people." He repeated that he would not surrender but did say he was "ready to negotiate" with France and the United States if the bombing stopped. The NTC's response to the pronouncement was unequivocal: it said it had no interest in dialogue, despite the adverse military situation in the east and the regime's stranglehold on Misrata and Zintan.

The NTC's confidence came from the fact that NATO had begun to "diversify" its targets. Gaddafi's Bab al-Azizia compound had already been hit and was bombed again at the end of April. The regime's spokesmen denounced the attacks as attempts to assassinate the "Guide." The air strike at the end of April did indeed seem to be aimed at Gaddafi himself, as he was thought to be in the compound at the time. Instead, it killed his youngest son, 28-year-old Saif al-Arab—who had studied law in Munich and been a renowned playboy on the city's nightclub scene—and, according to the regime, three of his grandchildren.

Despite further denials from NATO and the coalition's political leaders, the message conveyed by the attack could hardly have been clearer: the hunt for Gaddafi was being stepped up. Along with Gérard Longuet, however, many experts in international law understood that the words "all necessary measures" did not give the coalition carte blanche in Libya, and certainly didn't authorize the targeting of Gaddafi himself. If that were now the aim, the experts said, it should be stated explicitly in a new text in the UN Security Council. Longuet himself was in favor of the idea, yet such a text would certainly have been rejected. On the same day, March 15, however, other coalition leaders reiterated that the Libyan regime had lost its legitimacy, so there was no need for an additional UN resolution.

In May, a short piece by Karen DeYoung and Greg Jaffe in the *Washington Post* revealed that the NATO air offensive in Libya was running out of ammunition. There was a particular shortage of laser-controlled bombs, the kind most commonly used. An even greater problem was the limited number of aircraft at NATO's disposal. The shortage of resources was due to the US government's continued unwillingness to play a leading role, still preferring to provide intelligence and logistical support; above all the shortage was due to the difficulties France and the United Kingdom were having in meeting the costs of their involvement—even though both countries were members of the Security Council, nuclear-armed, and among the world's greatest military powers. Some 800 sorties had already been flown—not just by the French and British but also by planes from Belgium, Norway, Denmark, Canada, and the Arab countries—and the alliance seemed to be losing the stomach for a much longer fight.

It was then, however, that the United States returned to take a more active role in the NATO offensive, providing the supplementary resources the European allies needed. Faced with the prospect of a conflict that might drag on indefinitely, the United States began to use unmanned Predator drones capable of precision strikes. The drones duly began picking off the BM-21 Grad rocket launchers that had spread terror in Misrata and Zintan. At the same time it became apparent that the battle of Misrata had stretched the besieging forces to their very limit. As the regime began to suffer from disrupted supply lines and reduced fire-power, the rebels realized victory might actually be within their grasp.

SINCE MY RETURN TO PARIS I HAD BOMBARDED THE LIBYAN REGIME WITH PHONE calls. When I rang Tripoli to speak to Emad Embirsh, the supposed dip-lomat I'd met at the Brazilian ambassador's residence, he reiterated that the regime would be willing to receive me as a guest. Enthusiastic about the prospect of an interview with Gaddafi, I was in a state of constant readiness to return to Tripoli. Embirsh said he'd instructed the Libyan embassy in Madrid to sort out a visa for me, as previously agreed.

The person I spoke to at the Madrid embassy introduced himself as Faisal; he didn't tell me his surname. He said he was "in charge of consular matters," but I suspected his true role was quite different. Intriguingly, his name didn't appear on the Spanish authorities' list of Libyan diplo-mats serving in the country. Still, I persevered with my calls to him until he informed me, after a few days, that the decision on my return to Libya would be made in Tripoli. We remained at this impasse for a few weeks, until one day Faisal informed me that he hadn't received authorization to issue my visa. That's when I knew that Embirsh, for all his assurances, was just a go-between with no power to make decisions. So I picked up the phone to Libya's ambassador in Brasilia, Salem Omar Abdullah al-Zubaidi, whose message was perfectly clear: the regime had no interest in letting me back in the country.

It looked like my only way back into Libya would be across the Egyptian border. Though not an unattractive prospect, it was a route already trodden by hundreds of foreign journalists during the previ-ous weeks. Following them wouldn't give me much opportunity to say anything new about the conflict. I was attracted by the idea of going to Misrata but knew that after my previous experience my editors were keen to keep me out of harm's way. Ghaith was being similarly treated by the *Guardian*: he joked that they'd put him under "house arrest" for his own good. I also spoke regularly with my contacts on the Tunisian border, in the interior of Tripolitania, and among the Libyan communi-ties in France and Brazil—as well as with the people I knew in diplomatic circles, who were always well informed about the situation in Libya and could provide additional information from behind the scenes.

Based on these conversations and the reports from news agencies on the Brega and Ajdabiya battlefronts, and from the NTC in Benghazi, I was convinced that the fate of the revolution hinged on whether or not the revolutionaries could take control of Tripolitania. Libya's western region was the most populous, had the highest GDP per capita, was where most of the armed forces' personnel and equipment were—and also, above all, it was home to the regime's most important institutions. Whether Gaddafi was capable of clinging to power remained to be seen, but there was no doubt about the strategic importance of the western cities of Misrata and Zintan. Like Dr. Mohamed Othman, whom I'd met in Zintan back in February, I believed that an eventual "Battle of Tripoli" would only be possible if western Libya mobilized behind the revolution.

Like Misrata, Zintan had already endured a long siege—one that started very soon after Ghaith and I left the city. Yefren, 45 kilometers away, had suffered a typical offensive: electricity and water supplies cut, then shelling, then invasion. As in other towns and villages in the region, many families chose to flee before the onslaught began. Zintan, however, seemed better protected. During the time we'd spent there at the end of February, tribal and political leaders were already organizing a regional political council along the same lines as the national entity, the NTC, established a few days before in Benghazi. The first challenges for the council were to work to keep the rebels united to ensure the city had enough food, fuel, and weapons to continue its resistance, and to draw up a strategy for confronting the regime as effectively as possible.

By that time Dr. Othman was not only concerned with the management of the hospital and with trying to get medicines from elsewhere in Libya: he was also one of the leaders of the insurgency. On February 27, he set off from Zintan for the village of Tobka, 250 kilometers to the south, whose population also belonged to the Zentan tribe. He'd spent part of his youth in the village and still had relations there. He knew how to reach it through the desert and avoid the roads that were increasingly controlled by soldiers and mercenaries. Tobka was a place where 90 percent of the young men were willing to join the battle to defend Zintan, and it was a source of vital supplies. The doctor and other rebels started going to Tobka to pick up weapons—an increasingly perilous undertaking but also crucial for Zintan's survival.

As had already become clear by the end of February, the Zintan rebels didn't have enough weapons and equipment to advance on Tripoli. Instead, the city was at the mercy of the regime. In early March the siege began, with Gaddafi's soldiers receiving support from small towns in the south of Tripolitania where army barracks and arsenals were located. The insurgents had little chance of holding out, because as yet there was no support from NATO and the international community. The rebels tried to draw the attention of international TV networks such as Al Jazeera and the BBC to their plight; Dr. Othman, Adel el-Zenteni, and Ali Taher Saleh also contacted the Canadian broadcasters they were familiar with from the time they'd spent in exile in Canada. Much of the local population was terrified by the prospect of government forces invading the city. Some of the local commanders were also worried by the news that Ghaith and I had been detained: they imagined that if we were tortured we might provide the regime with important information.

The fact that no humanitarian assistance was getting through made the situation in the city even more acute. It was the younger population who did most to maintain morale, inspired as they were by the possibility of freeing themselves from Gaddafi's yoke despite their shortage of weapons. While Gaddafi's troops resisted the NATO and rebel offensive in Brega in the east and continued with their bombardment of Misrata, in Zintan the dictatorship chose the option of negotiation. For three weeks the regime sent messengers, some of whom were local people, to meetings of the rebel council. They didn't only convey the threat that Zintan would be totally destroyed: they also offered bribes. In one of the meetings the messenger said the regime was prepared to give 250,000 dinars—around US$200—to every resident who surrendered.

Needing time to organize their military resistance, the Zentan accepted the offer of dialogue while at the same time smuggling arms into the city. They also organized attacks on the Dehiba border post—where Ghaith and I had entered the country—which was now under army control again. In the early hours of the morning of March 18, insurgents from Zintan and Nalut attacked the proregime town of Wazen and the army barracks in the village of Gzaya, a coordinated action that left dozens of regime soldiers dead. The army was quick to retaliate. It was expected that Gaddafi's son Khamis Gaddafi's troops would attack Nalut, near the Tunisian border, so the rebels seized the roads between the border and Tripoli, isolating the loyalists in Wazen and impeding troop movements. On March 19 the army closed the border: no Libyan could cross it. At night the lights were turned off at the border post, even on the Tunisian side, out of fear of a rebel attack and of NATO air strikes that would allow the rebels to reestablish transport links with Tunisia, essential for the survival of the revolution in Tripolitania. The tension peaked when the Zintan rebels informed the regime's messengers that they had no intention of surrendering. They knew Gaddafi would never forgive the uprising they had initiated in February, and in any case the Zentan now refused to live under his leadership. Though their revolution had brought pain and instability, it also offered hope.

On March 23, after Zintan's refusal to surrender, Gaddafi's forces launched their first attempt to invade the city. Thousands of troops took part in the attack, supported by tanks, rocket launchers, and anti-aircraft guns. They advanced from the south, equipped with weapons from the arsenals in the region, and from the northeast. The worst fears of Zintan's residents were not realized, however. The attack took place along the main road leading into the city, where the rebels had positioned fuel tankers that they then set fire to: the resultant infernos severely hindered the troops' advance. Some families abandoned the city as the fighting began and fled across the border into Tunisia. The soldiers were taken aback by the resistance they encountered; some of them even deserted. The rebels captured three BM-21 Grad rocket launchers and used them against the attacking forces. The next offensives were also repulsed, with the loss of yet more regime equipment.

The army commanders used the same brutal tactics employed in Misrata: indiscriminate rocket barrages, day and night. Nowhere in the city was safe from the missiles; the death toll mounted and the city lived in constant trepidation. For many in Zintan, the psychological trauma would stay with them for months afterward.

While the besieging forces persisted in their terror tactics, the Dehiba border crossing remained under army control and prevented the rebels in Tripolitania from obtaining food, fuel, and medicines via that route. In Zintan there was a shortage of anesthetics and other drugs essential for treating the wounded and carrying out emergency surgery. Some supplies, however, were smuggled in through the desert with the connivance of the local authorities and assistance from the residents of towns close to the border. Evacuations of the wounded, and of families exhausted by constant fear, were carried out the same way. A month after the first attack there was a surge in the number of refugees heading toward Tunisia from Zintan, Yefren, Kalaa, and even Misrata: they all fled in fear of the regime's thirst for bloody revenge. Reports from humanitarian organizations suggested that thousands of people arrived in Dehiba in the space of a few days, obliging local residents, Tunisian political leaders, and the Red Crescent to set up refugee camps. A week after the arrival of the first refugees, the camps were overflowing.

In Zintan, the bombardment caused many women and children to seek refuge in caves in the surrounding mountains. Despite the suffering of the rebel fighters and their families, however, the uprising in the neighboring city of Nalut offered new hope for the survival of the rebellion in the Nefusa mountains. Insurgents from the two cities planned and carried out a joint attack on the Dehiba border post, sparking days of fighting in which control of the crossing changed hands five times before the rebels finally secured the area.

With the border crossing reopened, the provision of supplies to the rebels quickly increased while the stream of refugees entering Tunisia became a flood; Zintan and other population centers in the west began to resemble ghost towns. The siege of Zintan had now gone on for a month, and the rebels knew their only hope of ultimate victory lay with outside military intervention. Without it, sooner or later, the revolution would be crushed.

With the evacuation of refugees still ongoing, NATO carried out its first air strikes against Gaddafi's forces in the Nefusa mountains. Rocket launchers, tanks, and armored cars were destroyed, sparking euphoria among the rebels. Although the rockets continued to rain down on Zintan, the local tribal leaders became increasingly confident that the army would prove unable to invade the city. The rebels were better armed than before, and more men were coming forward to join their ranks.

The local political council was in touch with Benghazi, where efforts were being made to assist the insurgencies in the Nefusa mountains and Misrata. Sustaining regular communication, however, was no easy task: among the equipment the rebels lacked were satellite phones, which were essential in a country where landlines and mobiles either didn't work well or were monitored by the authorities. The Zintan rebels' first contact with Benghazi had been made through a representative from Yefren, sent via Tunis and then Cairo. They were also in touch with Tripoli; Dr. Othman, for example, frequently went there in search of medicines for the hospital. It was during one of these trips, in the first week of May, that the doctor was told an old friend wanted to meet him urgently. It was Abdel Majid Mlegta, a businessman originally from Zintan who now lived in the capital. Through mutual contacts Mlegta had found out Othman was active in the revolution. The doctor phoned Mlegta as soon as he could and arranged to meet him in mid-May. It was to be no ordinary meeting. What they intended to discuss was the capture of Tripoli.

THE MEETING TOOK PLACE IN TUNIS. MLEGTA TOLD OTHMAN THAT HE AND OTHER Zentans living in Tripoli had been helping to fund Zintan's hospital by sending money. But, he said, he might be able to make a much greater contribution to the success of the revolution. He owned a company that for a long time had supplied foodstuffs to different sections of Gaddafi's security forces in Tripoli. Not only, therefore, did he know various commanders in the security forces, but he was even friends with some of them, including one of the commanders, General Abdel Fattah Younis. Since the beginning of the uprising, Mlegta had used these contacts to discreetly gather valuable strategic information. In fact, he had already compiled a dossier that included the precise locations of 122 military installations in and around Tripoli, as well as the number of soldiers they housed, the type and quantity of weapons those soldiers possessed, the locations where the soldiers were deployed, how they were transported, and what their intended targets were.

Othman flicked through the dossier, fascinated by the quantity of information, and asked for some time to consider how it could best be used. He was already quite sure it could provide the basis of a strategy for the capture of Tripoli—and if the dictatorship lost control of the capital, its days would be numbered. Three long, hard months after he'd spoken to Ghaith and me about what he'd referred to as the "Battle of Tripoli," the doctor finally had his hands on what he needed.

Previously the doctor had been convinced that Benghazi was the heartbeat of the revolution: the city was crucial to the resistance inside Libya and provided vital links with the outside world. But now it was starting to look like Benghazi was too far from Tripoli; plus, the loyalist stronghold of Sirte lay on the route between the two. Othman and Mlegta both now believed the rebels' chances of seizing power depended on a surprise offensive launched against the capital from Tripolitania. What they needed to do, therefore, was contact the NTC hierarchy and convince them to give maximum support to the rebel outposts in the west such as Zintan, Nalut, and Misrata. The first name that came to both their minds was Mahmoud Jibril, with his long history of opposition to Gaddafi and his role as NTC "prime minister." Othman transferred Mlegta's information to a computer and arranged it in a PowerPoint document that could be presented to the NTC. He named it the "Tripoli Liberation Plan."

On its first page the document contained the six key elements of a "general strategy": (1) intensify rebel actions in Brega to draw the regime's attention toward the eastern front; (2) devote more resources to the fighting in the west to liberate Zintan and Misrata; (3) draw Gaddafi's troops away from Tripoli by sending the combatants from Zintan and Misrata to fight alongside the rebels in other cities in Tripolitania still under the control of the regime, such as Zawiyah, Azizia, Khoms, and Zlitan; (4) get NATO to increase its air strikes against the military installations in Tripoli listed by Mlegta; (5) foment a popular revolt in the capital so that the regime loses control of the streets; and finally, (6) launch the final assault: the Battle of Tripoli. To do all this, it would be necessary to set up a control center to monitor rebel actions in Brega, Zintan, and Misrata; communicate directly with NATO high command; coordinate underground actions in Tripoli—a task that would fall to a team headed by Mlegta; and command the rebel katibas right up to the final attack.

The plan divided the country into four areas and calculated how much equipment would be needed in each. It called for unified command structures, supply lines to ensure the availability of communications equipment such as satellite phones, and NATO air support for advances by rebel ground forces. The rebels' most urgent requirement, however, generated international controversy: the continued supply of weapons from abroad.

Othman and Mlegta both knew the strategy required time, orga- nization, and, above all, secrecy. It could be discussed only with a very small number of individuals at the very top of the NTC. Both men knew the security forces were still capable of quashing any popular movement in the capital, even if it entailed mass killings. Once the strategy had been drawn up, the next step was for Mlegta to speak to a contact in Tunis—Lusta Jumaa, a businessman who would go on to be the owner of a TV network when the conflict was over—who was in touch with the NTC. Othman, meanwhile, got hold of an old friend from Zintan who lived in Paris and was an important military contact for the rebels: Jalaliddin Dira, a retired Libyan air force colonel and ex-advisor to the regime on defense matters. Lusta, in turn, phoned Allagi Mohamed, the justice minister in the NTC. He said there were two men he completely trusted who needed to speak urgently with Mahmoud Jibril. The two men hadn't said what the conversation would be about, Lusta added, but they'd guaranteed it was of the utmost importance.

Othman returned to Zintan the following day to await confirmation of the meeting. Allagi, meanwhile, called Jibril in Doha. Jibril agreed to meet Allagi's two contacts in Doha two days later, even though he still didn't know what they wanted to discuss. To get to the Qatari capital in time, Othman and Mlegta set off immediately for Djerba in Tunisia, then flew to Tunis before catching another plane to Doha.

The two men told Jibril they had a plan for the capture of Tripoli. There was no doubt, they told him, that if the rebels from western Libya could take the capital, Libya would be liberated. When I later met Jibril, he told me he'd listened to the doctor and Mlegta attentively, and that by the end of the conversation he could see their proposed strategy did indeed make sense. But he was a realist, and he knew his own power was limited. He replied that he'd need to see what NATO thought of the proposal. When he asked the two men what was needed to enable the rebel offensive, Othman mentioned three points: direct contact with NATO's headquarter in order to hit the targets of Tripoli; communications equipment that would be delivered to the opposition network in the capital, and weapons. Most of the arms would be distributed to the rebels in Zintan, Misrata, and other western cities to break the sieges and then prepare for the invasion of Tripoli; the rest would be smuggled into the capital itself. Jibril said he agreed with the plan and would try to make it work.

By now, the subject of supplying arms to the Libyan opposition was no longer taboo, as it had been at the beginning of the conflict. British and French special forces would be sent to Libya to provide "advice" to the insurgency. Jibril phoned Nicolas Gallet, a French diplomatic adviser at the Élysée Palace in Paris, and Henri Guaino, a political adviser to President Nicolas Sarkozy, to tell them about the meeting and to request that they put Othman and Mlegta in touch with the French intelligence services and with NATO. The requests were granted.

During the next few weeks the two rebels had five or six meetings with their new contacts in Paris to clarify and further develop the plans. Othman was also in regular contact with Jalaliddin Dira, also in Paris, and with the leaders of the NTC. In one of the meetings they stressed to Jibril that Dira needed to use his contacts with the French government to convince President Sarkozy to intensify NATO's attacks in the mountains of western Libya, this being the best way to prepare for an assault on Tripoli. Up until then the rebels' foreign allies had given the impression of concentrating more on the east. With each passing day, Sarkozy's entourage—which included the philosopher Bernard-Henri Lévy—and the French intelligence agents took an increasing interest in the plan being presented to them. To a large extent this was due to Dira, who bought military uniforms for the rebels with his own money and was prepared to exaggerate when informing his French contacts about the rebel forces' strength and preparedness. In one of these meetings, Dira persuaded the French government, despite its fear that Islamic radicals might become involved, to join the Qataris in supplying the rebels with arms and other equipment.

Mlegta's team got the first satellite phones into the country by dismantling them so they could pass unnoticed through the metal detectors at the Ras Jdir. Weapons were packed into containers and dropped by parachute from aircraft since there was no landing strip available and

Gaddafi's troops still surrounded the mountains. Most of the equipment—rocket-propelled grenade launchers, rocket launchers, grenades, assault rifles, and ammunition—landed intact.

To increase the quantity of equipment that could be delivered, however, there was no alternative but to create a landing strip. The best option was to adapt a stretch of the road between Nalut and Zintan, and to add lights to guide aircraft landing at night. By July the improvised runway was operational. Its main function was to bring in the material specified by Othman and Mlegta, but it also enabled the Zintan rebels to have closer contact with the Benghazi-based NTC. Over the following weeks French and British armaments gave renewed momentum to the revolution in western Libya, just as weapons from Qatar, the United Arab Emirates, and Sudan were doing in the east. Other consignments of weapons, meanwhile, were being shipped to Misrata and Tripoli. The introduction of attack helicopters—British Apaches and French Tigers—further assisted the rebels in the conflict.

Increasingly well-armed, the rebels worked day and night to execute their strategy. Their leaders flew back and forth between Benghazi and Djerba while also making frequent trips to Qatar, France, and the United Arab Emirates. One of the biggest challenges was how to smuggle weapons into Tripoli, an audacious and dangerous undertaking. Othman, still responsible for the hospital in Zintan, was by now leading a double life. Not even his wife and children, in exile in Tunisia, were aware of his role in the revolution. The need for secrecy meant that on the frequent occasions when he needed to leave Zintan, he was unable to tell the truth about where he was going. Some people began to suspect he was visiting his family in Tunisia—time off that the other rebels didn't allow themselves. He feared he would eventually be accused of abandoning the struggle. In Tripoli, meanwhile, Mlegta was also in an uncomfortable situation and feared his group's activities would soon be discovered. So he gathered together the men he considered most at risk and left for Djerba to set up an outpost from which to organize the coming battle.

As the rebels' plans took shape, NATO stepped up its air strikes and also launched missiles from warships and submarines in the Mediterranean. Mahmoud Jibril phoned Othman in Doha to request a meeting with him and Mlegta in Paris. The doctor didn't know what the meeting was going to be about, but he flew to Djerba to meet Mlegta and then they went on together to the French capital. Much to their surprise, the meeting wasn't with officers from the French armed forces or NATO, as before, but with President Sarkozy himself. The two men felt uncomfortable because they

were wearing jeans and T-shirts, but Jibril assured them the French head
of state wouldn't care about that.

Also attending the meeting were the French defense minister,
Gérard Longuet, and various generals and senior intelligence officers.
Proceedings began with a report on the preparations that had already
been made for the attack on Tripoli. Sarkozy asked Jibril when the offensive could begin, and if it would be possible to take the Libyan capital
by July 14. Seen in Libya as the leader of the rebels' foreign allies, the
French president obviously liked the idea of basking in the glow of military victory on Bastille Day. Jibril looked to Othman to answer Sarkozy's
question. Embarrassed, the doctor said it probably wouldn't be possible
to take Tripoli by mid-July, and then added that he'd need more arms and
equipment to have any chance of mounting an offensive in such a short
space of time.

The doctor was assured he would be given whatever he needed. The
biggest obstacle was that some of the arms and equipment would have to
be smuggled into Tripoli itself. Another problem was that not all of the
capital's military installations could be bombed from the air; some of
them were too close to residential areas and the risk of collateral damage
was too great. An alternative would be for opposition groups in Tripoli
to destroy or sabotage these targets at the same time as NATO and the
rebels were attacking from outside—but that would require a high degree
of coordination and yet more arms deliveries to the capital.

After he returned to Libya, Othman quickly realized it would indeed
be impossible to launch the Battle of Tripoli before July 14. He phoned
Mahmoud Jibril to emphasize that a premature attack would be very
risky, especially because some of the arms promised in the Paris meeting had not yet arrived. So a new date for the attack was agreed: July 29.
This would be the last day before the beginning of Ramadan, the Muslim
month of fasting, which would obviously make military operations more
difficult. Then, however, part of a shipment of weapons sent from Qatar
via Benghazi was diverted by one of the leaders of the insurgency in the
east, the Islamic radical Abdelhakim Belhadj. To save time, instead of
being shipped to Tripoli, the weapons were instead going to be flown to
the airstrip near Zintan, and then taken overland to the capital. However,
the Qatari defense minister then ordered the equipment to be delivered
to Belhadj in Benghazi so the Islamic radical could be involved in the
plans for the Battle of Tripoli. In western Libya the reaction was one of
surprise and irritation. Othman called Jibril in Benghazi, asking him to
intervene. Jibril promptly got on a plane to Doha.

Eventually the impasse appeared to have been resolved. Jibril called Othman to assure him that the weapons would indeed be delivered to Tripoli as long as Belhadj could still be involved in the plans for the offensive; apparently, the Islamist knew people who might be useful during the fight for the capital. Othman then called Belhadj, who agreed to give up the weapons. A meeting was arranged, but Belhadj didn't show up. A second date was fixed: again, neither Belhadj nor the weapons appeared. Later I submitted various requests to interview Belhadj so he would have an opportunity to explain what happened: he refused to speak to me.

Othman realized the weapons wouldn't be recovered, so he told Jibril that more would have to be sent. A few days later he received a new shipment, this time from Sudan, which he duly sent on by sea to Tripoli. By now, however, July 29 had passed, so the attack was rescheduled for August 9. But then further logistical difficulties—affecting shipments by air, sea, and land—meant the offensive had to be postponed yet again. Fortunately, more Qatari arms had just become available; to make sure none of them were diverted this time, Othman went to Doha to collect them himself, flying back to Benghazi and then on to Tunis in an aircraft packed with explosives. The doctor then smuggled the weapons to Zintan via the Dehiba border crossing. Such were the last few days before the Battle of Tripoli: long, arduous, and extremely tense.

But the moment had finally arrived. In the weeks since the first meeting between Mlegta and Othman, the sieges of Misrata and Zintan had finally been broken. Now it was time to advance on Zawiyah to pull some of Gaddafi's troops in that direction, away from Tripoli. These troops would be prevented from returning to the capital by a popular insurrection in which the opposition took control of the streets and mounted armed attacks on government buildings. Up in the Nefusa mountains, with Zintan now liberated, the rebels prepared to descend on Zawiyah. Othman had the satisfaction of watching his plan being put into action.

On August 14 the rebels advanced on Brega in the east and toward the coast in the west. The next day they attacked the towns of Gharyan and Surman. The last shipment of arms arrived in the Nefusa mountains and was quickly shared out among the fighters in the region. All that remained was to coordinate with NATO, which on August 17 was due to begin 72 hours of air strikes intended to destroy all the targets in Tripoli identified by Mlegta. The rebels in the capital were kept informed by satellite phone. On August 19 Zawiyah was finally liberated and an uprising erupted in Zlitan, between Tripoli and Misrata. Initially the air strikes went according to plan, the 28 identified targets being picked off one by

one. But on August 19 NATO informed Jibril that the aerial bombardment had fallen behind schedule. NATO wanted another two days to
complete it, which would mean delaying the ground offensive yet again.
Jibril called Othman to request that the Zintan rebels postpone their
advance. The doctor listened respectfully, as always, but said it wasn't
possible. The signal had already been given; Tripoli was ready to begin
the uprising.

On Saturday August 20, just as planned, the revolution erupted in
Tripoli. Othman and Mlegta controlled operations from Zintan. The
first reports to reach the NTC in Benghazi suggested the battle was
not going well and that hundreds of rebels had been killed. Jibril called
Othman to demand more information and to complain about the decision not to delay the attack. The doctor repeated that it simply hadn't
been possible to wait any longer, adding that although the latest news
from the capital confirmed there were dead and wounded, the numbers
might be smaller than previously reported.

The fate of the revolution seemed to hang in the balance. Following
the liberation of Zawiyah, the rebels from the Nefusa mountains,
Misrata, and various other cities in Tripolitania converged on Tripoli for
the final offensive, planned exhaustively over the previous three days. As
night fell on August 20, the battle imagined by Othman and Mlegta six
months earlier became a reality. Crowds of people—some armed, some
not—took to the streets of the capital. Many thousands gathered around
Green Square, soon to be renamed Martyrs' Square. Receiving the news
in Zintan, Othman said to himself, "That's it. It's over."

CHAPTER 10

DOWNFALL

At the Dehiba border post, all that remained of the big portrait of Gaddafi were the frame and a few scraps of material. The plain green flag had been replaced by the rebels' black, red, and green tricolor. In February Ghaith and I had come through the same way when we'd made our clandestine entry into the country. Now, six months on, I was back—and still without a visa in my passport. Since the previous Saturday evening, August 20, revolutionaries from various cities in Tripolitania—but principally Zintan and Misrata, the two that had suffered most at the hands of Gaddafi's forces—had been fighting the Battle of Tripoli. The reports from the capital suggested the rebels were making significant inroads, but there were heavy casualties on both sides. It seemed Gaddafi's forces had been taken by surprise and some soldiers had deserted. Rumor had it that even Khamis Gaddafi, the commander of the elite 32nd Brigade, had fled to an unknown destination. With vital assistance from their foreign allies in the form of aerial bombing, weapons, and logistical support, Othman and Mlegta had seen their Tripoli Liberation Plan become a reality—although not every part of it had been enacted, and some of the most significant events unfolding in Tripoli had not been planned at all. Gaddafi's Bab al-Azizia compound, a symbol of the regime, would soon be captured.

Sitting in a van with Imed Meliene, the Tunisian who had helped Ghaith and me cross the border six months before, and six journalists, I felt an increasing tightness in my chest. Since Saturday night, I'd been trying to get back in touch with my contacts in Libya, including Othman.

Ever since my editors had given me the go-ahead to return to Tripoli, it seemed like I was having difficulty breathing. I didn't want to put my wife and family through the same suffering again, but Libya was where I needed to be. It was about honoring the commitment I'd made to myself, about trying to remain true to my beliefs. Still, I couldn't help wondering about the cause of the uncomfortable physical sensation. Was it fear, perhaps?

I'd flown from Paris to Djerba on a plane that looked as if it were chartered by the press, so numerous were the journalists on board. This time there was no doubt: the best way to reach Tripoli was from Tunisia, not Egypt. I'd wanted to travel via Ras Jdir, but the border crossing there had been closed again by pro-Gaddafi forces that still controlled the area despite the rebel advances taking place elsewhere in Tripolitania. Ras Jdir had huge strategic significance as the main crossing between Tunisia and Libya, and as a supply route for the regime in Tripoli. Rebel attacks during the preceding days had led the Tunisian government to bolster security at the border post by replacing administrative staff with soldiers.

Just as in February, the only alternative to Ras Jdir was a long journey south to the crossing at Dehiba. I called Imed, whom I'd kept in touch with by phone and Facebook, to tell him I was coming. He said he'd sort out a way for me to get across the border. He also mentioned that five months after Libyan refugees began to flood into Tunisia, they were now returning home in significant numbers, encouraged by the rebel advances. The Red Crescent estimated, for example, that around half of the 15,000 Libyans who sought refuge in southern Tunisian cities such as Medenine, Tataouine, Kebili, and Douz were now heading back to western Libya, which I interpreted as a sign that the dictatorship really was on its last legs. Most of the refugees were people from the Nefusa mountains, but now cities such as Nalut and Zintan were safe to return to. On the other hand, other places in Tripolitania were far from safe: in the previous 24 hours around 2,000 people had fled the latest fighting in the coastal region around Zawiyah and Sabratha.

I arrived in Dehiba with three other journalists: Jean-Louis Le Touzet of *Libération*, Marc Thibodeau of Canada's *La Presse*, and Deborah Berlinck of Brazil's *O Globo*. I called Imed again as we arrived in the city, but before we could even arrange a meeting point he appeared right in front of us, stepping into the road to flag down our van. He greeted me enthusiastically, grabbing me by the shoulders and kissing me twice on each cheek. For a few seconds he tried to hold my hand, which is

customary among male friends in Arab countries—but it is not customary among male friends in Brazil, so I declined. We sat on a street corner
about 100 meters from his house, seeking some shade from the blistering
sun. It was good to see him again; not only was he good company—
despite his political opinions—but in the five months since our previous
meeting he'd proved to be an excellent source of information.

We chatted for an hour or so, both of us sweating like marathon
runners. He told me his brother had made a tidy sum of money by taking
journalists between Dehiba and Zintan. And yet Imed himself seemed
a little wary toward the three journalists who were with me; I had no
idea why. He suggested we should wait until the early evening and then
his brother could take us over the border, but I turned down the offer.
I asked if there was another driver and fixer who could get us to Tripoli
quickly. Imed himself was willing to give us a lift—but not to anywhere
beyond the Nefusa mountains, he said, because there was still fighting
going on around Sabratha and Zawiyah. He ended up agreeing to take us
to Zintan; after that we would be on our own.

Imed, who didn't own a passport, was about to enter Libya for the first
time in more than six years. Before we set off we took on board another
three journalists, all Australians, who offered to share the costs of the
journey. It struck me that the style of my entry into Libya was going to
be different from in February, when I'd traveled as lightly as possible and
had sneaked across the border into a region closed to journalists. Now, by
comparison, it felt I was in the ostentatious role of war reporter, carrying
a 12-kilogram, military-issue bulletproof vest and a metal helmet as well
as my rucksack with other equipment and some spare clothing. Laden
with journalistic equipment, the van rolled slowly forward through the
border post. Finally I was back on Libyan soil.

We took the same road toward Nalut that I'd traveled in March. I
recognized the arid, mountainous landscape with its peaks and plateaus;
its harsh beauty was unchanged. As the sun sank gradually toward the
horizon and the temperature fell, I realized I was succumbing again to
the strange allure of the desert.

But the reality of recent events in the region became clear when we
passed the blackened hulks of destroyed tanks, part of the wreckage of
Gaddafi's attempt to recapture western Libya. Marc was asking me about
my imprisonment in Tripoli, curious to know what had brought me back
to the country after such an experience. Breathing deeply as I searched for
an answer, I suddenly realized the tightness in my chest that had haunted
me for 48 hours was gone. Re-entering Libya, it felt like an unwanted

chapter that had begun with my arrest and expulsion was being brought
to a close. I was free again, and determined to carry on where I had left
off. My aim was just as it had been six months before: to be in Tripoli to
witness the downfall of an oppressive regime and the liberation of a long-
suffering people.

We continued on toward Zintan. We'd driven through western Libya
for two hours without any impediment whatsoever. All the barriers on
the road, whether previously manned by rebels or government forces,
had been abandoned; all that was left of them were large piles of rubble
and sand. Most of the buildings we passed were badly damaged. In the
distance, isolated in the middle of the desert, we saw gray concrete structures that looked like unfinished blocks of apartments.

Imed, seemingly excited to be in Libya again and to have a close-up
view of the consequences of the revolution, chattered the whole time.
"You see those buildings?" he said, pointing to the gray blocks. "They're
homes Gaddafi built for the poor. He is good for the Libyans."

Imed's comments struck me as reflecting certain popular myths
about Gaddafi's regime, and as time went by they also got a bit irritating. Marc, who had a boisterous and irreverent sense of humor, began
to mock some of Imed's opinions, which he didn't take kindly to. I tried
to smooth things over, compensating for Marc's irreverence by making
a show of listening respectfully. The conversation eventually changed
course when Imed pointed out a change in appearance of the road ahead.
There were horizontal lines painted on the tarmac, a long row of lights
along the side of the road, and some antennae sticking out of the ground
nearby. This, I realized, must be the improvised airstrip that had been
so important for the rebels in turning the tide of the conflict in western Libya; the weapons and ammunition flown in by the Western allies
and NATO helped them break out of enclaves such as Zintan and Nalut.
Those extra supplies had also been a significant factor in the insurgents'
recapture of Zawiyah, which was probably the moment when the regime's
fate was sealed.

Seeing the runway with my own eyes was like finding an important piece in a jigsaw puzzle. For weeks there had been rumors in Paris
and Tunisia that NATO planes flying into Libyan airspace were doing
more than attacking military installations and Gaddafi's ground forces.
Le Figaro had published an article that described crates of weapons being
parachuted into the Nefusa mountains by the French air force; the Élysée
Palace later confirmed the story was true. Having discovered the improvised airstrip, which had tire marks made by planes when they touched

down, I was now eager to find out what my contacts in Zintan knew about the weapons delivered by air.

Arriving in the outskirts of Zintan a few minutes later, the city felt very different from my first visit. Previously, there had been a euphoric, almost anarchic atmosphere, with thousands of armed men on the streets high on adrenaline and firing their weapons into the air; the city now was eerily quiet and almost deserted. Our driver, Fethi Ben Hasen el-Habib, led us to a place where some of the journalists passing through the city were already starting to gather. Imed introduced me to one of his Tunisian friends who, he said, could take us onward to Tripoli. Imed was in a hurry to get back to Dehiba and we were anxious to continue our journey, so we quickly emptied the van of all the equipment, hugged, and said "see you later"—whenever and wherever that might be.

We heard that the rebels in Tripoli had begun to attack Gaddafi's compound, Bab al-Azizia, which increased our sense of urgency. We spoke with the driver about what the safest routes to the capital might be; already he was showing signs of the nervousness and reluctance that would become an increasing problem during the hours that followed. We were a little more than 150 kilometers away from witnessing a historic moment, but we also knew we shouldn't be complacent about our safety. I took out my satellite phone, which I'd rented in Paris, and my mobile with a Libyan SIM card, courtesy of Ambassador George Ney Fernandes, and tried to call my contacts in the region. From most of them, however, there was no answer. As far as we knew, the road to Zawiyah had been secured by the insurgents, so we were ready to set off. It was now late in the afternoon, not long before the sunset; for the local people, as it was now the period of Ramadan, sundown meant the end of many long hours of fasting.

We were about half an hour out of Zintan when we came to a rebel checkpoint, where we were asked to show documents issued and signed by the local rebel authorities. I couldn't quite believe it: apparently this was a revolution that could only be witnessed with the correct accreditation. So we turned around and drove back to the operations center on the edge of Zintan, arriving just a few minutes before the rebels there were due to have their first meal since the previous night. Suffice to say they weren't very keen to help. But through perseverance, we got the document we thought we needed: a piece of paper with a letterhead displaying the colors of the revolutionary flag. Back to the checkpoint we went, now in darkness, only to be told by the young guard at the barrier that our document lacked an all-important stamp. We laughed, assuming he

was joking. He wasn't. So while revolutionaries in Tripoli were storm-
ing Gaddafi's seat of power, we found ourselves driving back to Zintan
yet again. The episode spoke for itself: in various aspects, in this case
the control of the press, the insurgency was adopting the habits of the
regime.

After all that wasted time the driver told us it was too dangerous to
travel through the night and refused to leave Zintan again until morning. Some of the rebels we spoke to also insisted we should wait until
daylight before descending from the Nefusa mountains toward Zawiyah
and Tripoli. It was immensely frustrating, and yet I'd promised myself
I wouldn't take any more unnecessary risks. Also, I could use the extra
hours in Zintan to try to shed some light on a puzzling question: how had
it been possible for the rebels in Zintan, once they had broken the siege,
to keep their preparations for the Battle of Tripoli secret? There were
various people I wanted to ask about this, including Othman and Adel
el-Zenteni and Ali Taher Saleh, the rebels who welcomed us to Zintan
and tried to help us get to Tripoli. When we got back to the city I made
more calls, trying to get the latest news about the western rebels' attack
on the capital.

I got through to one of the people I'd met back in February. Thinking
the call might be monitored, he wasn't very forthcoming; not only did he
not want to meet me, he wouldn't even tell me where he was. I remembered that in our first meeting he had asked me not to use his real name
if I quoted him in an article. It wasn't often that I'd encountered this
anxiety in Libya; I'd generally been struck by people's willingness to tell
me their names, leave their faces uncovered when photographed, and
indeed pose for the camera without even being asked. I asked my contact if he knew whether foreign military personnel had used the improvised airstrip to enter Libya and join forces with the rebels. He said this
hadn't been the case; there had been contact between the local rebels
and NATO, he said, but no foreign soldiers had come in. "The NATO
planes only brought weapons. I don't know how many planes there were,"
he said. "You shouldn't ask about this around here. Nobody can tell you
anything about it."

Despite his unwillingness to talk, I asked him about the role of foreign military personnel on the eastern front and then, later in the conflict,
in the advance on Tripoli from the west. The presence of some foreign
soldiers in Libya was no longer a secret. In April, Axel Poniatowski, president of the foreign affairs commission in the National Assembly, France's
lower house of parliament, had said the National Transitional Council

(NTC) and NATO needed to have between 200 and 300 foreign personnel on the ground to coordinate an offensive. France, Britain, and Italy responded by sending three groups of 30 men to Libya. On April 20, a French government spokesperson, François Baroin, confirmed the dispatch of "a small number of liaison officers to organize the protection of the civilian population." The true role of these officers, however, went well beyond "protection," at least in Cyrenaica. My contact told me that in Benghazi, and later in Misrata and Zintan, NATO and the allied countries had intervened to change the focus of the rebels' military strategy. NATO dispensed with the idea of an offensive against Tripoli from the east and instead planned an eventual attack from the west that would be launched from Zawiyah, subsequently recaptured by the Zintan rebels thanks to the extra weapons flown in by NATO using the improvised airstrip.

Speaking directly with contacts among the rebels, I was told that foreign personnel had participated in drawing up the plans for the capture of Tripoli but hadn't taken part in the actual operations on the ground. Later that night I checked this information with other contacts in Zintan. Mokhtar Ghazduri, for example, gave me a detailed account of the siege, the evacuation of families, the supply of arms, and the use of the landing strip. The people I spoke to also confirmed that there were pockets of pro-Gaddafi resistance in various areas of Tripolitania—soldiers and militias who still had significant firepower and posed a threat to the rebel forces. It seemed, therefore, that just as Gaddafi had insisted six months earlier that he was in complete control of western Libya even as the insurgency was erupting in the Nefusa mountains, many rebels were now exaggerating the strength of their grip on Tripolitania.

The most dogged resistance the rebels faced in the west was around Sabratha and Surman, and also to the south of Tripoli, where loyalist soldiers had been joined by members of the pro-Gaddafi tribes from the city of Sirte, the Colonel's birthplace. Although much of their hardware had been destroyed, the loyalist forces were still capable of mounting attacks. In Zintan there were even rumors that some high-ranking members of the regime who had been taken prisoner in previous battles were freed during these counterattacks.

The rebels faced another problem: Gaddafi's forces had planted landmines in various parts of Tripolitania. A long strip of land close to the border with Tunisia, between Dehiba and Wazen, had been mined to restrict rebel movements during the sieges of Zintan and Nalut. Mines were also planted in a wide circle around Zintan itself. As soon as the siege was over, a small group of rebels—only ten men in total—began the task of locating and deactivating the mines. Some of the men volunteered, others were following orders; none of them had any previous experience. I met the leader of the group, Mohamed Anish, 43, when we were still trying to get our document stamped. Before the war he worked as a mechanic at one of the oil terminals at Ras Lanuf. So far, he said, the group had deactivated 2,600 mines; another 3,000 or so remained. He admitted to being scared when given the mission by his commander, but he was determined to complete it.

I spoke to Mohamed in a building in Zintan used as a radio station for coordinating the rebel forces. As well as the armed men guarding the premises, there was a boy who couldn't have been much older than ten wandering around with an AK-47. It was a deeply unsettling sight, and I wondered what it said about the course the revolution was taking.

A few minutes later, still inside the radio station, I bumped into the creator of the "media center" the Zintan rebels used to communicate with the outside world, Adel el-Zenteni, who'd been very welcoming toward Ghaith and me in February. I was delighted to see him alive and well, and to hear that Ali had also survived the fighting and was now in Tripoli. He seemed fairly pleased to see me, but from our initial exchanges I had the impression he'd changed during the intervening six months, becoming more detached and also self-confident to the point of arrogance. He disappeared for a few minutes, came back again, and as we resumed our conversation I realized his demeanor was simply because he was under a lot of pressure. We talked about how the revolution was going, and I also asked his advice about how to travel down from the mountains toward Zawiyah and Tripoli. He said that fighting was still going on and therefore the route wasn't safe. In February, Ghaith and I had ignored his advice by setting off for Sabratha. Not wanting to repeat the error, this time I would be staying put in Zintan—at least until the following morning.

I FELT A SENSE OF EMPTINESS WHEN I ARRIVED IN THE ZAWIYAH THE NEXT DAY. We'd left Zintan at dawn and hadn't encountered any problems on the road, but now there was a palpable tension in the air. Rebels in their pickup trucks drove nervously up and down the semi-deserted main avenue. It felt like the anteroom to a war that was still very much in progress: the struggle for control over Tripoli. The scale of the destruction was shocking. Zawiyah had been the scene of intense fighting in late February and early March; Gaddafi's forces invaded the city while Ghaith and I were imprisoned. I imagined that if we hadn't been captured we would have been in Zawiyah covering the conflict. The empty feeling inside me was therefore a lament: this, I believed, was where we should have been, alongside the rebels in the face of the loyalist offensive. The presence of a greater number of foreign journalists might have influenced the course of the conflict and reduced the ferocity of the offensive, and hence the suffering of those who were fighting for freedom. Instead, however, the buildings gutted by fire, reduced to rubble by shelling, or perforated by rounds from anti-aircraft cannons were proof of the excesses committed by the dictatorship.

We took the road toward Tripoli. Driving through Surman I recognized the square where Ghaith and I had been arrested, but had no desire to stop for a closer look. Our driver's nervousness was becoming increasingly apparent, and also irritating. Every 500 meters or so he stopped to ask directions, even though the route was so simple that I knew it merely from having looked at a few maps: if we went straight on we'd get to Tripoli. Often he brought the vehicle to a halt when he saw an abandoned checkpoint or a pedestrian, as if waiting for permission to drive on.

On the outskirts of Tripoli, during one of our frequent stops, we met a group of insurgents responsible for security in the area. One of them was Ben Elemen, 40, who had left the town of Sabba as a child and gone with his parents to live in the United States. This was quite a common story among Libya's revolutionaries: the emigrant who came back to help depose Gaddafi. Like many of his comrades, Ben carried an AK-47. "I'd never handled a gun before," he told me. He was doubtful whether the hunt for Gaddafi would be successful. "They thought they'd get him quickly, but I believe Gaddafi's already in Algeria," he said. "I want him to be arrested and then put on trial here."

Also in the group was Abdel Monem, 37, who was married with two children and had been a taxi driver before the conflict started. He wasn't carrying a weapon. With an excellent knowledge of Tripoli's roads and also a good level of Spanish, he offered to take me "in safety" to Bab al-Azizia; the car with the other journalists would follow behind. We agreed. As we drove into the capital we could hear gunfire and explosions coming from districts where rebels were locked in combat with the loyalists. Gaddafi's forces still controlled a few parts of the capital, including some of the area around Bab al-Azizia, the airport, and the traditionally pro-Gaddafi suburb of Abu Salim. On the way, Abdel expressed views about the conflict that sounded naïve but also sincere: "While Gaddafi governed Libya, there was no happiness. Now, Libyans are happy."

By this time the scorching sun was high in the sky. Anyone carrying a heavy load—as I was, with my bulletproof vest, helmet, and rucksack—soon became drenched in sweat and desperately thirsty. Tripoli—a mixture of poor neighborhoods with typical Arab architecture, middle-class districts built in accordance with Italian tastes, and, alongside the Mediterranean, a modern area dotted with large hotels and glass-covered towers—was obviously a city at war. Young insurgents carrying weapons were everywhere, driving around in pickups with anti-aircraft guns mounted on the back. Numerous checkpoints had been set up, restricting traffic movements and forming a protective cordon around already-liberated areas. The shops were closed and largely hidden behind metal shutters painted green on the orders of the regime. In the streets, "civilians" were a small minority. On the horizon, columns of thick black smoke rose into a clear blue sky. By all the indications, the regime had already lost control of most of the city. All life in Tripoli now revolved around the conflict and the hunt for Gaddafi, whose whereabouts were unknown; his last public appearance had been more than two months before, on June 12, alongside the Russian businessman and chess player Kirsan Ilioumjinov.

We headed for Bab al-Azizia, situated in the district of Qadisyiah. The compound, a symbol of the regime, sprawled over an area of six square kilometers and included military barracks and Gaddafi's private residence. Here the rebels seemed to be in total control, having penetrated the outer walls the previous day. Abdel dropped me off by one of the entry gates that had been smashed down. A constant stream of vehicles went in and out, carrying euphoric-looking rebel fighters. As on many occasions in February and March in the Nefusa mountains, I felt like I'd walked into a real-life version of *Mad Max*. I was surrounded by insurgents wearing a mixture of military and civilian clothing; vehicles had been hand-painted or covered in graffiti, and firearms had been improvised alongside more sophisticated weaponry, such as machine guns and grenade launchers, much of which I knew had been brought into the country by the rebels' foreign allies.

I still heard occasional explosions and bursts of gunfire as I entered the compound alongside rebel katibas and some other journalists. On our left were guardhouses and barracks that had been looted and smashed up; inside one of the buildings we came across some jackets still hanging in a wardrobe, as if their owners were about to return to claim them. Most of the clothes and military uniforms, however, had been thrown on the floor, presumably either by looters or by soldiers leaving in a hurry. Amid scattered papers, photographs, and miscellaneous debris was a document that seemed to indicate the desperation of those trying to defend the regime: an illustrated manual, written in Arabic, explaining how to handle a machine gun. Farther ahead, at another entrance to the compound, the rebels had managed to destroy an enormous metal gate. Inside the compound the rebels seemed to be able to move as they wished, but in fact they were still at risk, not least from loyalist snipers who had been ordered to kill as many of their opponents as possible even though further resistance now seemed futile.

Indeed, it was quite obvious that fighting was still going on inside the huge compound. At moments the background explosions suddenly became much louder, sowing confusion among the rebels and contributing to the impression that as an attacking force they lacked proper training. It seemed to me they were winning the war won not by virtue of strategic superiority but through sheer fervor and courage—but as a consequence, they also suffered heavy losses.

Around me were men from Tripoli, Zintan, Zawiyah, Misrata, and Benghazi, a communion of tribes united in rage against Gaddafi and his acolytes. One of them was Abubakar, a young man from Misrata who'd been fighting for three days and was determined to break into Gaddafi's living quarters in the interior of the compound. "There are still some Gaddafists around, but we don't know how many. Perhaps today it'll be all over. Inshallah!" he told me. He looked serene and content, even while shouting to make himself heard.

Nearby, Abu Mohamed, 30, sat impassively in the cab of a pickup while his comrades outside the vehicle amused themselves by firing their weapons into the air in front of the destroyed gate. Unusual for an insurgent, he came from Sirte, a hotbed of support for Gaddafi. He now found himself in a frustrating predicament: having been wounded in a battle that had taken place between Misrata and Tripoli, he was immobilized by a thick plaster cast around the lower part of his right leg. "I was hit in the ankle, but it's OK now," he said. "The Gaddafists aren't Libyans. They're mercenaries who are still fighting on Gaddafi's side."

Bab al-Azizia was falling increasingly under rebel control; it was now possible to enter the heart of the compound without being fired on by snipers. Cautiously, along with a few other Western journalists—including Deborah, Marc, and Jean-Louis—I walked into an open area that included tree-lined gardens. Most of the buildings had been destroyed by NATO air strikes; among those still standing was a giant dome decorated with a metal sculpture of an eagle. Frenzied shouts of celebration suggested the rebels now believed they had taken over the entire compound, and that this, finally, symbolized victory over the regime. As we walked on it became clear that the celebration was going on around the main building, which had been partly destroyed. The building was known to be connected to a series of tunnels that, it was said, stretched for a total distance of 30 kilometers; it was presumed that Gaddafi had used this subterranean escape route to reach the airport, which was still under loyalist control, or the coast. The building also housed the museum commemorating the "resistance" against the 1986 US aerial attacks. Most of the exhibits, however, had disappeared; all that remained of them were blocks of concrete now smashed into pieces—a strange mixture of the destruction wrought by the bombing of 25 years previously and the attacks of recent days.

On the balcony where the Colonel used to give his triumphalist speeches, rebels waved and posed for photos with the revolutionary tricolor or the flags of tribes such as the Berbers. When I arrived, the national flag of Qatar was being fixed to the facade of the building. Down below, insurgents were taking turns climbing onto the statue of a giant fist crushing a US fighter plane, perhaps the most iconic of the museum's so-called works of art. I entered the building, went up the stairs of the museum, and came out on the balcony. From there I could see a small crowd gathering, apparently including some civilians who had brought children along despite the continuing rumble of explosions and bursts of gunfire.

"Gaddafi finished! Allahu Akbar! Gaddafi finished! Allahu Akbar!" shouted Wael al-Hen, 18, mixing English and Arabic as he sprayed bullets into the sky from his AK-47.

I stayed on the balcony a few minutes, taking photos of the rebels as they continued to scale the giant fist or paint graffiti on it. In that short space of time a succession of men arrived alongside me to fire their weapons into the air, to the cheers of their comrades gathered down below. It was ironic that earlier during the revolution, Gaddafi had referred to Bab al-Azizia as his "supporters' camp," a place where people who approved of the regime took on the role of voluntary human shields, hoping to deter air strikes against the compound. I left the museum when I felt I had enough photos and wandered around some of the other buildings, many of which had been reduced to ruins by NATO aircraft. The communications center, for example, now consisted largely of rubble. Behind the museum, however, stood the most interesting building in the whole complex: Gaddafi's residence. It contained pieces of furniture, all in strikingly bad taste, taken from the bedrooms used by the Colonel and his sons; large glass panels prevented anyone from touching them. On one of the walls was a photo of a beach—Biarritz, according to Jean-Louis. The bathroom had a circular bathtub, now destroyed. Once an impenetrable fortress, Bab al-Azizia now had the air of a place of pilgrimage, except that the visitors were coming not to pay homage to the Colonel but to express their derision.

In contrast to the celebratory mood of the rebels around the main buildings, their comrades at the outer gates and in the far reaches of the compound were still on alert, ready to use their heavy weapons against any remaining pockets of resistance. Although the fighting in Tripoli was now less intense, the capital had just undergone a 48-hour period very similar to what other urban centers in western Libya, such as Zintan and Misrata, had endured: buildings were charred by fire and pockmarked by anti-aircraft shells; rebel barricades stood on every main road; and red, black, and green tricolors flew everywhere—but most of all there was violence and death. Since the start of the battle more than one thousand bodies—of rebels, soldiers, and loyalist militiamen—had piled up at the morgue of the city's main hospital. The shift in power had brought about a bloodbath. Six months earlier I had been escorted by the Brazilian ambassador around Tripoli when it was almost entirely under the control of the regime; the resistance had been restricted to outlying suburbs such as Tajoura. Now, of course, it was the opposite situation. Convoys of rebel vehicles patrolled the access routes to the city and the main streets inside it. Walls displayed revolutionary slogans such as "Free Libya." One piece of graffiti I saw as I entered the capital from the west proclaimed, in Arabic and English, "Libya is our country. Tripoli is our capital"; the message was that the revolutionaries should resist any separatist tendencies and fight for victory over the regime in its main stronghold.

The rebels did not yet have a firm grip on Tripoli, however. Throughout the city, the fighting was still ongoing and would continue for many more days. To combat the remaining loyalists, volunteers converged on Tripoli from all over Libya and even from abroad, visibly increasing the number of armed men on the streets. When I left Bab al-Azizia, the mood on the streets was one of uncertainty. I wondered whether all the rebel checkpoints enforcing "security" in the city center might disappear if loyalists suddenly counterattacked. In four places—Bab Al-Azizia, the international airport, the Rixos hotel, and the sprawling neighborhood of Abu Salim—soldiers and militias were definitely putting up a fight. In these places snipers posed a major threat to journalists. Since our arrival in the capital, two French reporters had been injured, one by a sniper, and in Zawiyah, on the same road we'd used not long before, four Italian journalists were kidnapped with their fixer. The Italians would be released not long afterward. Their Libyan companion, however, would be executed in the cowardly fashion so typical of the proregime militias.

From Bab al-Azizia we drove to a district that included one of the few hotels that had reopened, the Radisson Blu al-Mehary. Situated on Al Fatah Street, it offered a panoramic view of the capital. The journey there took about half an hour, as we passed through various rebel checkpoints. Broken panes of glass and bullet holes adorned the facade of the hotel, but there was also a reassuring security presence. We were among the first foreign journalists to base ourselves in Tripoli; most of the others had preferred to stay in nearby cities regarded as being under total rebel control, such as Zawiyah. Over the following hours, however, the Mehary filled with reporters, as did another large hotel, the Corinthia, where the NTC set up its Tripoli headquarters. In the Rixos hotel, home to the foreign press invited to Libya by the NTC, about 30 journalists had been stranded for three days while fighting raged around the building.

From the Mehary we had a clear view of the clouds of black smoke rising from districts where the loyalists were holding out, and we could also hear NATO air strikes—which were still taking place—and the bursts of gunfire echoing across the city from every direction. We also observed the movement of traffic on many of the city's streets. All in all we had a good overview of what was going on as we wrote and sent off our reports. But I hadn't come to Tripoli to cover the conflict from inside a hotel. After we parted company with our driver, who wanted to return to Tunisia, we met a young Libyan, Khaled Medhat, 24, a health worker that we hired as a fixer for 300 euros a day—the beginning of a highly lucrative period of work for him. In the late afternoon we set off with him toward the areas where the fighting was still taking place, although this time we didn't get very close to the frontlines.

In the early evening I returned to the hotel to write. A few hours later a friend of mine, Humberto Trezzi from the Brazilian newspaper *Zero Hora*, turned up at my room. In February, when I was already in Libya and he was about to arrive from Brazil to begin covering the conflict, I'd told him, "See you in Tripoli." And now, six months later, there we were. Later that night, almost 40 hours after the start of the battle for Bab al-Azizia, I watched the incandescent projectiles from anti-aircraft cannons ascend into the sky above a city darkened by power shortages.

The car horns, shouts of "Allahu Akbar!," and bursts of small-arms fire never stopped.

IT WASN'T NECESSARY FOR THE REGIME TO ACKNOWLEDGE DEFEAT, SO OBVIOUS WAS the rebels' ascendancy not only on the streets of the capital but also inside Gaddafi's own compound. And yet that day, August 24, 2011, foreign minister Abdul Ati al-Obeidi became the first high-ranking member of the government to make an official statement recognizing that its 42-year hold on power had come to an end.

Al-Obeidi's declaration came a few hours after the capture of Bab al-Azizia was confirmed. He said Gaddafi's ministers had lost contact with each other, demonstrating that the regime had in effect melted away. Also, al-Obeidi said that Gaddafi had refused various opportunities to negotiate his departure from the country with the NTC. I gathered from the statement that Gaddafi was still in Libya, although most of the rebels I'd spoken to believed that was no longer the case. Ousted from power after 15,532 days, the Colonel was so far proving impossible to track down. Wherever he was, he was still making provocative declarations, promising he would return despite all the evidence of his defeat.

In a speech broadcast by radio in the early hours of the morning on August 24, Gaddafi referred to the abandonment of Bab al-Azizia as a "tactical retreat" and said he was ready to fight to the death. His spokesperson, Moussa Ibrahim, who had become one of the regime's most high-profile figures during the conflict, declared that 6,500 soldiers and volunteers were ready to "turn Libya into a volcano of lava and flames under the feet of the invaders." Meanwhile, Libyan businessmen were offering a reward of US$1.7 million to anyone who could hand Gaddafi over, dead or alive. The message was similar to that of NTC chairman Mustafa Abdel Jalil, who said the regime could only be considered finished when Gaddafi was captured or dead. In the first hours after the fall of Tripoli, therefore, the killing of the dictator—already considered "legitimate" by NATO and the Western coalition—was being presented as a realistic and acceptable option, with neither the businessmen nor the NTC attaching any conditions to it. Basically, the rebels had carte blanche to do whatever they wanted with the Gaddafi.

On August 26, a new, self-proclaimed government took power in Libya. That night, in a statement to foreign journalists at the Mehary hotel, NTC oil and finance minister Ali Tarhouni announced that the provisional government was moving its headquarters from Benghazi to Tripoli. Further details would be provided later that week, he said, but eight "ministers" in the rebel cabinet were already in the capital to organize the transfer. "I proclaim the beginning…of the work of the executive office in free Tripoli as of this moment," he said, with an air of solemnity.

Tarhouni also announced that the National Oil Corporation, Libya's state petroleum company, intended to increase production to 600,000 barrels per day within two or three months, with the longer-term aim of reaching 1.6 million barrels per day when all the installations damaged during the civil war were fully repaired. The contracts, he explained, would be signed with companies from "friendly countries" over the following weeks. Shell, Repsol, Eni, and Wintershall, among others, had already been contacted. The rush to sign new contracts derived from the need to get Libya's main source of income— oil exports—up and running again. The urgency, and the emphasis on favoring companies from coalition countries, gave ammunition to some of those who had opposed the military intervention: the West would be taking financial advantage of the Libyan revolution before the guns had been laid down.

The NTC's move to Tripoli took place against the backdrop of continued fighting in the capital and elsewhere. The previous night, explosions and gunfire had echoed across the city, although again it was impossible to distinguish between the noise of combat and that of celebrations. NATO air strikes were also still going on; during the day, planes had attacked various places in the capital where the loyalist resistance was strongest.

The air strikes made it possible for thousands of rebel fighters to advance further. At the airport, on August 25, an aircraft belonging to the Libyan state carrier Afriqiyah exploded after being hit by mortar fire, apparently from pro-Gaddafi forces, and yet the overall picture was that the loyalists were increasingly surrounded. In Abu Salim, which would fall to the insurgents by the end of the day, I watched the rebels move heavy artillery into position to combat the last remaining pockets of resistance. Abu Salim had been the scene of intense fighting; the bodies of dead combatants lay in the streets as pro-Gaddafi snipers continued to claim victims around the edge of the district.

Khaled and I went back to Abu Salim the next day to find the corpses were still there. The intense summer heat accelerated decomposition, causing a vile smell. Even more sickening was the fact that many of the dead loyalist fighters seemed to have been executed: their hands or feet were tied and they had bullet wounds in their backs. The first hours after the liberation of the capital, therefore, did not augur well: Gaddafi had a price on his head and was being hunted down like an animal with the authorities looking on complacently and the international community indifferent, and there was clear evidence of war crimes committed by rebel fighters.

As the fighting continued, rumors began to circulate that the Colonel had been cornered somewhere in Tripoli and that he would soon be captured. Supposedly based on information from the US, French, and British intelligence services, the rumors sparked euphoria among the rebels. But Gaddafi seemed not to understand that his regime was finished: in his latest audio recording he called on his followers to "cleanse Tripoli of rats."

"Tripoli is for you, men and women. Take to the streets and free them," the Colonel went on. "We will destroy them, whoever they are."

AFTER A NIGHT OF VERY LITTLE SLEEP DUE TO THE HEAT AND THE CONTINUED NOISE of gunfire and explosions, Khaled came to the hotel in the morning and we left for Tripoli Central Hospital, one of the city's obligatory destinations for a war reporter. On the way we passed through the district where lots of foreign embassies are located; many of the streets were blocked off by rebel checkpoints. Looking for a way through, we drove close by the Italian embassy, and Khaled commented that the building had been attacked and badly damaged when Italian prime minister Silvio Berlusconi severed relations with Gaddafi and withdrew his country's diplomats from Libya. It immediately struck me as an interesting story, even though I was keen to get out to the edge of the city where the fighting was still going on. As we approached the building my attention was drawn to an abandoned police car that had been used to form part of a barrier in front of the main entrance. Entering the embassy's outer courtyard through an iron gate that was left half open, we saw the charred remains of six cars, a couple of which looked as if they had been diplomatic vehicles. Much of the side of the building was blackened by fire.

The interior of the embassy was a scene of complete destruction. Looters had obviously been through the whole building, and many rooms were also fire damaged. Filing cabinets had been forced open, their contents now covering the floor and furniture. Outside in another courtyard I saw another five burned-out cars. Even more impressive than the scale of the destruction was the ease of access to the building and the sheer number of official documents lying around, many of them no doubt confidential. I realized then that Tripoli's state of chaos was sure to facilitate research into some dark corners of the regime's affairs, including its relationships with certain foreign governments.

After we left the embassy, Khaled persevered in his attempts to find an alternative route to the hospital. We entered a street that seemed familiar. On my right was a giant concrete building still under construction, the future InterContinental hotel; straight ahead was the minaret of a mosque. And then I realized where we were: we'd just driven past the building where I'd been taken to see General Sadegh Krema immediately after my release from prison in March. I got out of the car and walked back. The green-painted metal gate at the front of the building was open. The guards' cabin was empty. Inside it, a small television set was still on, which suggested the guards had left in a hurry. Lots of objects looked like they had been moved but were still intact—the cabin had been thoroughly searched without being damaged. I walked past a few abandoned cars and then up some steps to the main door, which I also remembered from before, and went inside. There was no one around; the building did indeed seem to have been abandoned. I opened a few of drawers and peered inside a couple of cupboards; all of them were full of papers. For a journalist it was a gold mine: an unguarded building belonging to the Mukhabarat el-Jamahiriya, Gaddafi's secret service, stocked full of secret documents just waiting to be examined.

There was only one problem: my inability to read Arabic. Unable to take advantage of the building's contents, at least for the time being, I left as discreetly as I'd entered—but already I was making plans to find a fixer who was fluent in English and could help me sift through those documents. Excited by the prospect of an exclusive, I admit I didn't mention my discovery to the other journalists who were sharing Khaled's car with me that day.

We arrived at Tripoli Central Hospital a few minutes later. Stuck to a pillar at the main entrance was list of fighters, both rebel and loyalist, lying in the hospital morgue. There were about a hundred names: a small fraction of the 20,000 people, according to the NTC, who had been killed since February. The names of some of those in the overflowing intensive care unit would be added to the list during the next few hours.

In the polytrauma ward, a small crowd of men awaited treatment. The situation was slightly calmer in the recovery room, although it was full and the patients were obviously facing a seriously inadequate level of hygiene. The floor was wet with a repulsive mixture of blood and filthy-looking water. About five meters separated the beds of Mohamed Hasin, 31, and Ahmed Hayadi, 20. The former, who still had a bullet in his torso, was a rebel fighter; the latter, making a slow recovery from shrapnel wounds caused by a shell fired by a rebel tank, was a soldier in Gaddafi's army. Hasin was already able to walk up and down the hospital corridors but needed to undergo surgery to remove the bullet, lodged close to his lungs. He was eager to tell stories about his experiences on the battlefront, and strangely keen to show off a photo of the corpse of his younger brother, Osama, 30, killed two months earlier in Tripoli. On his mobile he also had a video featuring another dead body, apparently that of the sniper who killed Osama. The sniper had been "known as a sadist," Hasin explained. Despite the intensity of the violence that surrounded him, his outlook was optimistic. "I'm very happy," he said, trying out his limited English. "My country became free from Gaddafi. Libya is very rich but is full of stupid people. Gaddafi was the most stupid of them, and was surrounded by other stupid people."

He didn't seem to mind the presence of Hayadi in the next bed. Wounded during a battle that took place on farmland in western Libya, not far from Nalut, Hayadi regretted the war but also believed Libya would be better without Gaddafi—even though he'd been fighting to defend the Colonel until very recently. "I don't like Gaddafi, but the army was my job," he said. "In my prayers, I ask God to punish him."

Despite being a soldier in a city controlled by insurgents and in a hospital where all the members of staff supported the revolution—or at least everyone I spoke to—Hayadi said he was being well treated not only by the doctors and nurses but also by the wounded rebels and their families. When we spoke he made a point of expressing his appreciation for the care he had received.

Needless to say, the young soldier was far from being the only loyalist in the hospital. One of the surgeons, Lukman Kalfallah, 29, told me that many of the medical staff were concerned about the number of pro-Gaddafi fighters on the premises. He said that on August 23, during the battle for Bab al-Azizia, Gaddafi's soldiers occupied more than one hundred beds, which gave rise to fears that the conflict raging in some parts of the city might suddenly be "imported" into the hospital. Jamel, 46, a senior surgeon, confirmed that wounded soldiers arrived in the dozens after the rebel offensive had been launched in the west of the country. Most of them had since left—either to go home, to return to the front, or to cavort with the 72 virgins believed to await Muslim martyrs in paradise.

I wanted to know the reasons for the proregime fighters' loyalty to the Colonel. Hayadi, for his part, said merely that he had served in the army as "a professional." Based on what he had heard from his patients, Jamel offered a fuller explanation. "Many soldiers believe this is a war by the West against Libya, of foreign invaders against our people, or even of Christians against Muslims," he told me while attending to patients in the recovery room. "The Gaddafists, in general, have a low level of education, but they're also fighting for a principle: they fear the country will get worse without Gaddafi."

Despite the fears generated by the conflict and by the forced coexistence of men from both sides, the hospital seemed to be doing very well in the circumstances. I was talking to Lukman and Jamel about the conditions they faced when they mentioned that the hospital's director was no longer around, having fled just a few hours after the rebels invaded the capital. The director's name, they said, was Dr. Hana Gaddafi. I was slightly surprised, as I remembered that was also the name of the Colonel's adopted daughter, killed by a US air strike during Operation El Dorado Canyon on April 15, 1986.

Back then I was a child terrified by the war that seemed to be taking place on the TV, but certain details of the attack had stuck in my mind, and in the intervening years I'd picked up various other pieces of information. I remembered, for example, that Gaddafi had claimed there were civilians among the victims of the "surgical strikes" carried out by the government of President Ronald Reagan. Among the buildings hit by the US planes, he said, were diplomatic premises in the center of Tripoli, including the French embassy. After the attacks, a Libyan radio station announced that members of Gaddafi's family were among the wounded, which at the time was impossible to verify. Three days later came the news that Gaddafi's 15-month-old adopted daughter, Hana, was killed in the air strike against the family's residence in Bab al-Azizia, and that two of his other children, aged 3 and 4, had been wounded. From that day forward, Gaddafi frequently reminded the world that his own child had been a victim of "North American barbarism," making her an icon of Libya's "resistance." In 2006, on the twentieth anniversary of Operation El Dorado Canyon, the Libyan regime organized the "Hana Festival for Freedom and Peace"; Lionel Ritchie and Spanish tenor José Carreras were among the participants.

Lukman and Jamel took me to an office on the first floor of the hospital. This, they said, was where Hana Gaddafi, a doctor qualified in general surgery from the University of Tripoli, had dispensed orders and enjoyed various privileges afforded her by the regime. In contrast with the rather basic nature of the rest of the hospital, which was suffering

severe shortages of equipment, the office was air-conditioned and contained expensive furniture, a satellite TV, three telephones, a Nespresso
coffee machine, and Dior cosmetics.

"Gaddafi told the world his daughter had died in 1986, but she was
alive all the time," Lukman told me, adding that he had been at the university with her for seven years. "She qualified last year, and after that she
started coming to this office. She gave all the orders. She would transfer
people she didn't like and ran all the departments."

Saif Musaf, a 29-year-old anesthetist, confirmed Lukman's story. He
told me Hana had led a kind of secret life at the hospital: she didn't sign
any documents or indeed leave any visible evidence of her presence. She
communicated directly with only a handful of people, whom Saif referred
to as the "few chosen ones." "We never spoke together during the year
she worked here," Saif said. "And no one ever raised the subject of her
'death,' even though everyone knew the story."

When I asked him why, Saif replied in a tone that suggested the
answer should have been obvious: "We were afraid of being killed."

I soon had the impression the doctors were taking the opportunity to
express their resentment after years of enforced silence. Another senior
surgeon, Rajab al-Ladsta, came over to make his own contribution to the
story, telling me that he'd worked alongside Hana in her first months
in the hospital. "She wasn't very good," he said disdainfully. "She didn't
have experience."

Lukman was more generous in his assessment. He said that although
Hana had few friends in the hospital and was always accompanied by
bodyguards, she was a decent enough person and had treated her colleagues and patients with care and respect. The revolution, however,
had affected her behavior; in the six months following the uprising in
Benghazi, she became more aloof with her colleagues, occasionally even
aggressive. And since the beginning of the rebel offensive against Tripoli,
no one had seen her. As with all the other members of the Gaddafi family,
her whereabouts were unknown.

"We were afraid of her. And I think she was afraid of us, too," Lukman
added.

Although the story came from respected medical professionals, and
in great detail, I still found it difficult to believe. When I got back to the
hotel, however, I Googled "Hana Gaddafi" and was taken aback by what
came up. In the UK's *Daily Telegraph* from August 12, for example, was an
excellent piece by James Kirkup and Holly Watt on the doubts surrounding Hana's supposed death. As I continued my Internet search, I received

an email from my *Estado de São Paulo* colleague Lourival Sant'Anna, who had also been sent to Tripoli and arrived just a few hours after me. He too had been looking around in some of the buildings in Bab al-Azizia. By sheer coincidence he was writing to tell me he'd made a significant discovery about none other than Hana Gaddafi: he'd come across some photos of her, including one in which she was side by side with her sister Aisha, along with a certificate for proficiency in English with her name on it, issued in 2007 by the British Council. Her death was indeed a fabrication on the part of the regime. One of many.

ALTHOUGH TRIPOLI CENTRAL HOSPITAL FACED A SHORTAGE OF BEDS AND EQUIPment, the situation there seemed under control, the medical staff coping reasonably well. Much worse awaited me at a hospital in the district of Abu Salim, where Al Jazeera had shown images of more than 50 abandoned patients, most of them apparently loyalist soldiers, left to die on beds or trolleys inside and outside the building.

When I arrived there the smell was so bad even outside the hospital building that volunteers were giving out surgical masks to any journalist who approached the entrance. My first impression was of a scene worse than any other I had witnessed in six months of violence. Medical staff, assisted by the local volunteers, were bringing corpses out of the building and trying to start a cleanup operation. The bodies were carried on stretchers and then tipped onto an area of ground that was covered in a layer of plastic sheeting. Then they were sprinkled with a white power meant to reduce the stench and deter insects before being rolled up in more plastic sheeting and then lifted into the backs of trucks—open and unrefrigerated—that would take them to the mortuary.

As a portrait of the cruelty of war, the scene inside the hospital could hardly have been more vivid. There were dozens of corpses on beds, stretchers, or just on the floor, lying in pools of blood. The whole place was infested with flies and maggots. The corpses were swollen, and some were already so putrefied they didn't remain intact when lifted up to be taken away. The smell was abominable. I felt I needed to stay in the building, however, to take pictures—particularly because it looked like some of the men who had been dead for the shortest amount of time—most of them dark-skinned, many wearing military uniforms—might have been killed in cold blood, and therefore been the victims of a war crime. With many of the corpses, the position of the arms and the angle of the torso suggested they had been left in agony by the medical staff; some, it seemed, had probably made a vain attempt to get up and search for help. I tried to take notes, but it was difficult to find words for what I was feeling.

"It's a disaster," said one of the volunteers.

From the conversations I had in Abu Salim, it seemed this hospital had become the primary destination for wounded pro-Gaddafi fighters during the Battle of Tripoli. But the doctors and nurses had abandoned their posts, leaving their patients to die slowly over a period of three days. As I walked between different wings of the hospital, one of the volunteers, Mohammad Sanoussi, 28, grabbed me by the arm and said indignantly, "Look at the present Gaddafi gave to the Libyan people!"

Another volunteer, Houssaim Radjab, 35, the driver of one of the trucks removing the bodies, came up to me while I was taking photos. We spoke only briefly because he had no time to waste, but he asked me to write an urgent appeal for help from international humanitarian organizations; he feared other places in Tripoli, and elsewhere in Libya, faced the same awful situation.

Houssaim told me that in addition to the corpses inside the building, there were many more in the hospital grounds about a hundred meters from the main entrance. I went to have a look. It was a sickening sight. As well as the bodies on the ground, covered in the same white powder, dozens of empty, bloodstained stretchers gave an idea of the scale of the tragedy. A few civilians wandered among the corpses and stretchers, looking for missing relatives.

Tripoli showed signs of descending into chaos. Abobaker Mustafa Abushahma, a rebel who had come from Misrata to fight Gaddafi's forces in the capital, searched the hospital for his brother, Mohamed. Two of his other brothers, Khaled and Emead, had already died in the conflict, on February 17 and April 15, respectively. Khaled's death, said Abobaker, had been one of the sparks for the uprising in Benghazi.

"I've found his [Mohamed's] car but we still don't have any news of him," Abobaker told me while looking at the corpses. He gave me his Skype address and mobile number so we could keep in touch, but since that day I haven't managed to contact him again.

Radia Selem, 39, discovered that one of the corpses was that of her son, Mahmoud Abdel Aziz, 17. He'd been missing for six days, having disappeared after going out to buy some things at the local shops. People told his mother they'd seen him get caught in the crossfire between soldiers and insurgents. "He wasn't a soldier, he was a student. The fighting was going on, he was wounded, and he was brought here," Radia told me. She seemed almost calm about the fate of her son but couldn't hide her great sadness about the social collapse of her country. "God wanted it that way. And now Gaddafi wants to kill us all. I don't understand why all these have to die because of him."

Despite the widespread support for the regime in Abu Salim, neither Radia nor any other local resident expressed anger about the acts that seemed to have been committed by rebels in and around the hospital.

As we left the building it was obvious Khaled was deeply affected by what he had just seen. A health worker himself, he had actually worked as an intern at that very hospital and had his own interpretation of the local people's silence in the face of probable war crimes. "In Abu Salim the people are like chameleons," he said. "They supported Gaddafi right up to the last minute—but now they're all revolutionaries."

We got into the car to go back to the Mehary, our clothes and shoes impregnated with the stench of blood and corpses. Even stronger, however, was the psychological impact of what we had witnessed. It will remain lodged in our memories forever.

BACK AT THE HOTEL, I HEARD THAT ALTHOUGH THE CONFLICT HAD NOT YET COME to an end either on the outskirts of Tripoli or in various other cities and towns, the NTC had already given an indication of greater political openness by symbolically choosing the Ministry of National Security building as the headquarters of the provisional government. The ministry had been responsible for all police and intelligence service operations, and therefore for the repression of dissidents.

The metamorphosis of the building itself, situated in the center of Tripoli, would be a slow process. During the morning of Friday, August 26, a few journalists had gone inside to find the first NTC representatives already there. Insurgents had obviously stormed through many of the rooms—including one previously occupied by Gaddafi's son Mutassim, the former head of Libya's internal security. Furniture and electronic appliances had been smashed to pieces; confidential documents were scattered all over the place. The rebels said they had found at least two people imprisoned in the building, whom they set free immediately. They also discovered various secret passages and a computer server that appeared to contain information on the country's 68,000 political prisoners. The NTC representatives thought they would be able to get their Tripoli headquarters up and running within a week.

The man tasked with achieving this was Ragheb Mabruk, a 48-year-old doctor. He was the first person I spoke to about what the transfer of power would actually entail. Like many others, I probably hadn't grasped the scale or the nature of the task. Libya's state structure wouldn't need to be repaired after the revolution: it would need to be built from scratch. "We have to start from zero," Ragheb said.

With an already fragile state having imploded, life in Tripoli was becoming increasingly difficult, even though the fighting became less intense with each passing day. The city suffered a chronic shortage of water and power cuts at night, which made the intense summer heat even more suffocating. There were very few vehicles or pedestrians in the streets and only a very small number of shops were open. The shortage of fuel was increasingly obvious, and not only because the price of petrol rose dramatically after the rebel capture of the city. Long lines of cars formed outside petrol stations; some drivers even slept in their vehicles to keep their place in the queue. As would have been the case anywhere else in the world, a black market in petrol soon emerged, and people began to employ all manner of ruses to try to jump the queue.

The problem wouldn't have been easy to solve anywhere, but in Libya it was aggravated by the fact that in 42 years the Gaddafi regime had never tried to build a public transport network worthy of the name. Long journeys had to be undertaken by car, so the need for petrol was constant. With the country's hospitals overflowing, the alternative for those in need of medical attention was to travel to Tunisia—which was impossible without petrol. There was a developing perception that the rebels faced a race against the clock: the longer they took to reestablish basic services, the greater the risk that people's patience would run out, thus reducing support for the revolution at a crucial moment in the transition of power. The NTC's oil and finance minister, Ali Tarhouni, was therefore making every effort to restore previous levels of oil production as quickly as possible. In the meantime, paradoxically, a country whose oil reserves are among the largest in the world was forced into strict petrol rationing and also had to import oil from abroad.

The journalists at the Mehary hotel shared some of the hardships endured by the Libyan population, although we did still have electricity for most of the day thanks to a generator and also Internet access, albeit slow and extremely unreliable. Our worst problem was the cuts to the water supply, which had begun on the second or third day after the hotel reopened. For a while the guests got by on the extra water brought in by trucks, which were supplying some areas of the city in return for payment. Soon, however, the shortage became acute, just as it already was in most other districts. As the shared toilets in the hotel quickly became no-go areas, everyone struggled to keep the bathrooms in their rooms in reasonable condition. One day I was looking down on the city from my balcony when I saw a Western journalist using the hotel swimming pool to get washed; other foreign reporters soon followed his example. The next day the water in the pool had a yellowish hue; within 48 hours it was closer to green. With the August temperatures rising to 99 degrees Fahrenheit, hygiene was a serious problem not only in the hotel but also, needless to say, for the local population.

As if the violent disruptions to normal life in the capital were not enough, it was also the month of Ramadan, which meant that we Western journalists ended up following a routine not dissimilar to that of the Muslim population, who didn't eat or drink anything between sunrise and sunset. Every restaurant in Tripoli was closed, as were most of the grocery stores. When we did find one open we immediately stocked up on water, soft drinks, and savory biscuits, which was all we seemed to live on for days on end. On some days we ate nothing at all.

The greatest problem of all, however, was the sheer physical danger caused by the war. There were armed men wherever we looked, but it wasn't the guns themselves that I felt threatened by: it was the rebels' ongoing habit of firing them randomly into the air. The stray bullet—a well-known danger in Brazilian cities plagued by armed drug gangs— had become a constant threat in Tripoli. Most journalists in the city wore helmets and bulletproof vests—protection the local people obviously lacked. But it was impossible to protect ourselves every minute of the day. And as time went by and the fighting in the city became less intense, we began to use our bulletproof vests less frequently. It was precisely this complacency that posed the greatest danger.

Late one night in the Mehary, I sat with a bunch of other foreign journalists at a table in an area that would normally have been a bar. We chatted about the conflict, exchanged views about the direction in which Libya seemed to be heading, and told stories about previous assignments—some dramatic, others amusing. It was a way of escaping what would otherwise be the permanent tension of covering an armed conflict. The Brazilians in the group included Samy Adghirni, Apu Gomes, and Humberto Trezzi. Outside, explosions continued to echo across the city and anti-aircraft shells glowed red as they streaked into the night sky; we were so used to it by now that it didn't bother us. But then came a dramatic reminder of the danger we still faced: a glass table-top no more than two meters away from us suddenly shattered into small pieces, hit by a stray bullet.

One week after the invasion of Tripoli, the rebels were clearly winning. The fighting was now limited to certain small areas around the
edge of the city; the NATO air strikes had come to an end in Tripoli;
and an increasing number of insurgents were leaving the capital for Bani
Walid or Sirte, both important loyalist enclaves. Libya was on the verge
of liberation, but fears that Gaddafi might continue to resist were exacerbated by the fact that no one knew the whereabouts of the ex-dictator, his
family, or various senior members of the deposed regime.

About ten days after the start of the Battle of Tripoli, the noise of
anti-aircraft guns no longer kept me awake at night. In fact I found
myself less aware of the shooting than of the increasingly long periods
of silence. Early one morning I woke up to the call to prayer marking
the end of Ramadan; it was not accompanied by gunfire. The call drifted
across the darkened and momentarily peaceful city. The threat of violence was still present, but there was also a sense of reemerging normality. One day, traveling through the city by car, I saw various families
dressed in the colors of the revolution, all heading for a children's play-
ground that had reopened beside the Mediterranean. It was the weekend,
and the families were clearly making an effort to resume a routine and
give some happiness to children who must have been severely affected
by the fighting. Observing that scene, I realized I had now experienced
Libya in three very different periods: the era of the surveillance state,
with Gaddafi firmly in control; then the uprising, accompanied by social
upheaval and soaring hope; and now, finally, I was seeing the revolution
prevail. There was something new in the air, something ethereal, seduc-
tive, and sublime.

It was freedom.

WHENEVER I PASSED BY A BUILDING THAT PREVIOUSLY BELONGED TO THE MILITARY
or the intelligence services, I tried to go inside and look around. I wanted
to find the place where Ghaith and I were imprisoned at the beginning of
the uprising; the quest was becoming something of an obsession. Khaled
and I visited various buildings whose facades looked similar to that of the
building where I'd been held—based, that is, on my memory of what I'd
been able to see on the day of my release. The search took us, for example,
to Abu Salim prison, where 1,200 prisoners were massacred in 1996 on
the orders of the regime. That evening, back at the Mehary, I looked at
the map of the city I'd drawn in my notebook and marked all the places
we'd visited, hoping this might yield new ideas as to where "my" prison
might be. One of the remaining possibilities, I thought, was a place on the

edge of the city, Khilit al-Ferjan, in the district of Salaheddine, reputed
to be strongly pro-Gaddafi.

On the morning of Saturday, August 27, Khaled, Jean-Louis, Marc,
Deborah, and I met in Salaheddine. They wanted to see which buildings had been hit by NATO air strikes, while I was preoccupied with
my search for the elusive prison. We were looking around barracks that
had belonged to the 32nd Brigade, or "Khamis' Brigade," when we heard
rumors about dead bodies nearby. The information became more precise:
apparently there were 150 bodies, all of them unarmed rebels executed
after being captured and held in a building close to the Khilit al-Ferjan
military base, the largest in Tripoli. Most of the corpses had been burned.
News of the discovery spread rapidly through the district, making it easier to locate the building in question.

A few minutes later, Khaled's Peugeot 306 came to a halt at the
entrance to an area of an empty lot bordered by high walls. The unmis-
takable stench of corpses met me as I got out of the car, and soon I was
confronted by a scene even worse than at Abu Salim hospital. A windowless hangar, its roof made of sheet metal, was transformed into a chamber of horrors. The bones of dozens of bodies lay scattered in a layer
of human ashes. Many of the skulls had bullet holes, which suggested
executions had taken place, and many ribs and other bones were broken,
which I imagined was due either to other bullets or to torture. Outside
the hangar was another hideous sight: three unburned, rotting bodies. In
at least one case the feet were tied together—yet another indication of a
war crime.

Guided by a few local residents, I made my way to another piece of
land nearby where other bodies lay in some bushes in a similar state of
decomposition. About 50 meters away were two large pits, probably made
by mechanical diggers and now partially filled in with earth. According
to some of the rebel leaders who were examining the site, the holes would
have been used to bury some of the victims. By this time there were quite
a few people wandering around, including Salem Hajab, a doctor, whose
home was right next to the military base. He said he had heard the killing but had been unable to intervene. "On Tuesday I heard gunshots and
an explosion, and I came here. I saw snipers on the rooftops and I was
ordered to leave," he said. He had no doubt about the reason for the fire
inside the hangar or the holes in the ground: "It's obvious they wanted to
hide the evidence."

Many of the people who lived nearby had been waiting to speak to the
press, representatives of human rights organizations, and NTC officials.

Their testimonies were consistent and unequivocal: the victims were shot with machine guns by soldiers and mercenaries and then burned. The local residents discovered the evidence on Friday evening, August 26, but the massacre itself had taken place on Tuesday evening, when regime troops still had control of the surrounding area. Dr. Hajab was convinced the soldiers, facing defeat, had acted out of revenge. His analysis made sense. I remembered the threats Ghaith and I received after the failed rebel attack on the military installation where we were held: if there was another attack, we were told, we prisoners would be killed before the building was overrun.

This scenario seemed even more plausible because, according to a survivor of the massacre I spoke to, all the victims had been involved in the insurgency, although they were from a number of different cities. They were kept in the metal-roofed hangar—in 104-degree heat—for ten days. Then, in the words of the survivor, at about 7:30 p.m. on Tuesday evening their "nightmares became a real hell." Army officers and mercenaries arrived outside the hangar, opened the door, and informed the prisoners they were all about to be set free. A few minutes later they opened the door again, but this time to unleash volleys of machine gun fire into the hangar. Some of the men avoided being shot by pretending already to be dead or seriously wounded. During a lull in the firing some of the men ran out of the hangar; most of them were shot while crossing the empty lot, hence the bodies I'd seen, or in the nearby streets. The few survivors included Mustafa Etri, 27, a lawyer; and Taha Gazi, 30, a communications engineer. Both were arrested for supporting the rebel movement even though they hadn't carried arms. Gazi was held in Zlitan before being transferred to Khilit al-Ferjan, where most of the detainees suffered daily interrogations and beatings. When the massacre took place he escaped death by hiding under the corpses of other prisoners.

"I could feel the machine gun bullets hitting the bodies on top of me. Then the ammunition ran out. They went away for about two minutes. When they came back to start the fire, I'd already escaped," he told me with a distant look in his eyes, his cheekbones almost protruding through his emaciated face. Gazi recounted this horror story in a sober, unemotional manner, as if he had already managed to distance himself from what had taken place, but I could tell he didn't want to enter into details. I thanked him and left him in peace.

As news of the brutal massacre emerged, Khilit al-Ferjan became known not only as the barracks for the troops commanded by Khamis Gaddafi that was destroyed by NATO aircraft, but also as the site of an atrocity—one of many, in fact, being discovered toward the end of the Libyan conflict. Not all had been committed by proregime forces. Amnesty International had received various witness accounts and was deeply concerned; it called for foreign intervention to put an immediate stop to the massacres, demanded that loyalists carry out no further executions, and called on both sides to ensure that prisoners in their custody were not mistreated. During that same weekend, August 27 and 28, NATO and the NTC recognized that a wave of revenge was sweeping across Libya as the six-month conflict came to an end. There was a risk that the vindictive acts being committed by the retreating soldiers and militias—but also by the rebels—would make it impossible to form a government of national unity in the post-Gaddafi era.

On that Saturday, one of Libya's most influential imams, Sheikh Wanis Mabrouk, known for his fiery speeches against the regime, called on the rebels to keep cool heads. The revolution was for "freedom and for Islam," he said; it should not be driven by revenge.

Mustafa Abdel Jalil, the head of the NTC, expressed concern regarding the executions carried out by loyalists but reserved his strongest criticism for "certain acts by some of the revolutionary leaders," referring to the acts of revenge that were taking place. On Tuesday, August 30, he even indicated these acts might lead him to resign.

The NTC's principal allies also issued warnings. In Washington, Hillary Clinton determined Libya was at a "critical" juncture and said the NTC should take a firm stance against "extremist violence." European Commission vice-president Catherine Ashton repeated the message, while UN secretary-general Ban Ki-moon said there was an urgent need to "restore order and stability." To exert further pressure, the allies said that financial assistance for the reconstruction of Libya—to be decided at the Paris Conference on September 1—would depend on the NTC's ability to control the situation. The aim was to avoid a repeat of the situation in postwar Iraq, when the dissolution of the army opened the way for revenge against members of the Ba'ath Party and the Sunni supporters of Saddam Hussein. Despite the efforts of the international community, of course, bloody acts of vengeance continue in Iraq to this very day.

ALTHOUGH I FELT IT WAS VERY IMPORTANT TO CONTRIBUTE TO THE COVERAGE OF the Libyan conflict, I was finding it frustratingly difficult to reach many of my contacts in the country. Without their help I had only limited access to sources in the rebel movement and to documents concerning the regime. In the meantime I turned my attention to the buildings that had belonged to the intelligence services, returning first to the headquarters of the Mukhabarat el-Jamahiriya. When I got there, however, a rebel guarded the entrance; I'd now need prior permission from the NTC to go inside. The Mauritanian journalist Lemine Ould Salem, from the Swiss newspaper *Le Temps*, later told me about another building belonging to the military intelligence service, the Itikhbarat, which a NATO air strike destroyed months earlier; apparently it was also guarded but was easier to enter. He'd been there himself, he said, and had found thousands of abandoned documents, just as I had done in the Mukhabarat building. Some of them, he said, indicated that agents from the regime had been inside the NTC throughout the revolution.

I headed straight for the Itikhbarat building, situated in central Tripoli close to the Central Hospital and the Rixos hotel, where most of the foreign press were based. When I arrived I realized I'd seen the building before, though I hadn't previously realized it was a base for the regime's espionage operations. I told the rebel guard I wanted to see whether it was the building where I'd been imprisoned—which wasn't untrue and had already become a good way of opening doors. I was introduced to a man named Mohamed, an Itikhbarat spy who prided himself on having become a double agent during the revolution who passed information to the NTC. He led me inside the damaged building and showed me the room that had been used by the feared intelligence chief Abdullah al-Senussi, Gaddafi's brother-in-law. A NATO bomb had made a ten-meter-wide hole in the concrete wall.

Mohamed explained that the Itikhbarat building had been one of the nerve centers of Gaddafi's police state, which is why NATO targeted it. He showed me various documents, including some that proved the regime possessed very precise information regarding the military strength of the insurgents it was besieging in Zintan, Misrata, and Benghazi. Not only that: the dictatorship had been working to sabotage the rebel movement from inside the NTC itself. Al-Senussi and his staff had left the papers behind at some point before the beginning of the Battle of Tripoli.

The documents even included information directly from the NTC itself; there were signed documents on paper with tricolor revolutionary letterhead that revealed the names and roles of all the most important rebel commanders. There were photographs taken during meetings between insurgents from Benghazi and Misrata, the two cities that presented the fiercest challenge to the regime. Maps of the Nefusa mountains—where the rebels organized their attack against Zawiyah, a crucial stage in the preparations for the capture of Tripoli—indicated where the rebel forces were positioned and what vehicles and equipment they had at their disposal. The regime managed to get hold of such information by offering bribes—not only money but also goods such as satellite phones—to insurgents in Benghazi and Zintan, while also promising to guarantee the safety of its informants.

The regime's modus operandi, as revealed in such documents, came as no surprise to the people of Tripoli, accustomed as they were to the ubiquity of the regime's intelligence services. In Paris a few months later, the Gaddafi family's legal representative in Europe, Marcel Ceccaldi, assured me that even General Abdel Fattah Younis, the NTC's military commander in Benghazi at the beginning of the revolution, had been a double agent who maintained contact with the regime right up to the moment of his assassination.

I visited the Itikhbarat building on two consecutive days before it was shut to the media following a report by Al Jazeera about documents that proved close relationships between the regime and certain politicians in the United States. Just as I feared, the Western countries pressured the NTC into posting guards around every building that had belonged to Gaddafi's security services, which meant I would have no further access to them.

The time had come for me to leave Tripoli. On the eve of my departure, however, I had a surprise. For months I'd tried unsuccessfully to find genuine supporters of the regime to talk to—as opposed to people with a prepared discourse in favor of Gaddafi who were pushed in the direction of journalists by the regime's intelligence services. When I'd virtually given up the search, I found what I was looking for. In the period between the sieges of rebel cities such as Misrata and Zintan during the first half of 2011 and the insurgents' capture of Tripoli, the number of Libyans who openly admired Gaddafi fell drastically. However, despite the victory of the revolution, some of the regime's supporters felt it was safe to speak up in defense of the dictatorship.

I came across a couple of them one day in Abu Salim, the most strongly pro-Gaddafi district in the capital. I was with Khaled in a tire repair shop, waiting for his car's spare tire to be fixed, when a man aged about 50 launched a verbal attack against him. "What are you doing with that journalist? Don't you know they shot our people?" he said, appearing to confuse the press with NATO. "If they want a revolution, why don't they shoot Gaddafi? Why kill the people? Gaddafi was the only one who defended us!"

Also in the repair shop was Hakim Ali, 40, who worked at the press of a book publisher. He revealed his own political allegiance after I struck up a conversation about the man who had made the outburst against Khaled, although he did so much more calmly. Indeed, he came across as a personable character, speaking in a measured tone and prepared to listen to an opposing point of view. He believed the pro-Gaddafi demonstrations that had taken place in Green Square, as it used to be known, had to some extent been "paid for" by the regime because they consisted partly of government employees and people from poor communities— but, he added, many of those who participated were genuine admirers of the Colonel. "I, for example, liked Gaddafi before the revolution. It's true that all of Libya's money went to him and his family, and that few benefited. But people weren't dying like they are now." Ali said Gaddafi knew he could count on the support of a portion of the population—a portion that had now fallen silent in the wake of the rebel victory. "Gaddafi thought all the people supported him. It wasn't true. But there are still many, many people who are in favor of him. The only reason they don't say so is because they're afraid."

Khaled nodded in agreement and told me that most of the people who joined the insurgency in Tripoli had done so late in the day, when the regime was already destabilized. Someone he used to be good friends with, for example, had been a Gaddafi supporter until the beginning of Ramadan; indeed, it was their opposite allegiances that caused the breakdown of their friendship. The next time Khaled saw him, however, he was part of a group of rebels manning a checkpoint, carrying an AK-47.

All of this suggested that Gaddafi might still be able to summon the support of certain tribes and urban centers, such as Sirte—his home territory—and Bani Walid. It was to Sirte that the theater of military operations was now moving, with men from Misrata at the forefront of the rebel forces. This was an ominous sign. Part of Misrata's population was thirsty for revenge after suffering so terribly at the hands of Gaddafi's forces. The rebel katibas leading the advance were already only 100 kilometers from Sirte. With Gaddafi still free, the conflict did not end with the fall of Tripoli. More bloodshed was still to come.

CHAPTER 11

SILENCE

For weeks the leaders of the National Transitional Council (NTC) tried to negotiate with the tribal leaders in Sirte. If the city surrendered, they said, Gaddafi's supporters would be granted an amnesty. The offer wasn't accepted. The negotiations had begun—or at least been made public—soon after the NTC transferred its headquarters to Tripoli. At this time I was making my way with some other foreign journalists to Misrata, the first leg of a journey that would eventually take us to Sirte.

We left Tripoli on the coastal route to the east, sharing the road with dozens of rebels traveling in pickup trucks with anti-aircraft guns on the back. As we approached Zlitan we passed transporters carrying tanks and other heavy equipment that had been taken from the Libyan army after surviving NATO's air strikes: it was obvious a major operation was underway. The equipment was being taken to Misrata, and then, if necessary, to Sirte. The rebel forces awaited the outcome of the negotiations, and given their firepower it was clear that Sirte would suffer serious consequences if the local tribal leaders decided to continue their resistance.

Eventually we reached the first of the barriers marking the perimeter of the area where the battle for Misrata had taken place. Huge shipping containers blocked the road, some filled with sand—the gateway to a rebel enclave that had held out against Gaddafi.

The rebels manning the barriers checked to make sure there were no Gaddafists in the vehicles heading toward Misrata. In most cases it was sufficient for drivers to show a letter authorizing their journey and to say where they had departed from. Or alternatively, we found we were waved through as soon as we said we were *sahafa* (press)—a magic word that on many occasions ensured free passage through rebel-held areas.

One of the journalists I was traveling with was Jean-Louis Le Touzet, from *Libération* who was eager to return to Misrata after having been there during one of the worst periods of the siege. My own desire to reach the city arose for the opposite reason: a slightly foolish sense of guilt at not being there when the local civilian population most needed support. As we drove into the city the evidence of war was everywhere. The charred remains of dozens of tanks and other vehicles lined the roads, many of them destroyed in NATO air strikes.

Even before we reached Tripoli Street in the heart of the city, we passed buildings whose concrete outer structure had largely been blasted away to reveal steel skeletons underneath. Gunfire had peppered billboards with holes and made electricity poles look as if some giant animal had gnawed them. Commercial buildings were abandoned; their doors were locked, their facades pockmarked by bullet holes. Some of the largest buildings were gutted by fire. Much of the city was deserted, and although the roads had been cleared and screens put up around some of the ruins, there was no sign of any reconstruction work.

The closer we got to Tripoli Street, the avenue that had become a symbol both of oppression and resistance, the more brutal were the scars of battle. In the facades of some buildings there were gaping holes three or four meters wide—clear evidence of the use of heavy weapons against the insurgents. There were also strange marks on some of the damaged facades: sinister-looking swirls I presumed were caused by a particular kind of projectile.

No part of Misrata had been spared from the onslaught. In the center, what had been the city's tallest and most imposing buildings were now shattered wrecks, clearly beyond repair. And if this was the damage done to the physical structure of the city, what were the losses inflicted on the human population during those months of terror?

In the middle of Tripoli Street was a strange kind of outdoor exhibition consisting of tanks, armored cars, rocket launchers, anti-aircraft cannons, machine guns, ammunition, and military uniforms. Around them were mannequins dressed in army uniforms, representing Gaddafi's soldiers; some swung from ropes around their necks, others had been subjected to different punishments—this, apparently, was the fate awaiting any Gaddafist who set foot in the city. Painted on a nearby wall were the words, "Glory belongs to the winners. Free Libya."

Among the local people looking at the collection of objects was Adel Jamel Swiesi, 26, who had become known throughout the city. He wasn't a conventional war hero—he hadn't even touched a weapon—but he had nevertheless made his own distinctive contribution to Misrata's resistance. On March 17, with the city in a state of shock after suffering its first casualties, he used his computer to manipulate a photo of his father, killed by three bullets from a sniper, and also those of four children who had died when the back of their parents' car had been hit by gunfire. Adel arranged the images against a sky blue background. "After that, people started coming to me with pictures of their dead relatives so I could do the portraits in the same way," he explained. The result now covered the walls of a small building whose main entrance was a narrow opening in a side wall. There were more than 800 photographs that Adel had digitized and arranged against the same sky blue background—men, women, and children of all ages who had lost their lives in the offensive against their city. Among them were some of the 550 people still missing. There were also pictures of some of the wounded, many of them photographed soon after their injuries were inflicted or while receiving medical attention.

Twenty of the families shown on those walls had lost five or more members during the siege. Adel's exhibition won him the recognition of the whole city, but for the last ten days he'd felt dejected: some of the photos of the dead had been defaced by swastikas. But he remained determined to realize his dream of showing the world what Gaddafi had done to his city. "I want to display the photos in England," he told me.

Two months later I would return to Misrata to find that the modest room had been refurbished and turned into a genuine museum, with Arabic music—some of the saddest melodies I've ever heard—playing softly in the background. It had become an almost obligatory destination for locals and visitors alike.

Back outside among the ruins of Tripoli Street, I spoke to Amin Mohamed al-Kalush, 21, who had lived through the bombardments and the lack of electricity, water, and food that was a daily reality during the siege. He hadn't wanted to fight, he said, but in the end it was unavoidable. He'd lost one cousin during the siege. He told me he'd just returned from the Battle of Tripoli and wasn't sure if he'd now move on to Sirte. "None of this is human. Maybe I'll go, but it won't be easy, because the people in Sirte like Gaddafi. It won't be like here, where we were fighting for our freedom," he told me, with a sigh. "It won't be like here."

There was a feeling in Misrata, and in Tripoli, that a battle in Sirte shouldn't be necessary because it was obvious that Gaddafi's regime, or what was left of it, no longer held the reins of power. I spoke to various young rebels and also political and military leaders of the local NTC, such as Mohamed Abdala Ben Ras Ali, who thought that prolonging the conflict would serve only to aggravate internal tensions, stoke the desire for revenge, and jeopardize the country's immediate future. When I met Ras Ali in his headquarters, he said the Gaddafi loyalists in Sirte had been given three days to surrender: if they didn't, a battle would be inevitable. While the negotiations were going on, rebel fighters and equipment continued to arrive.

"The tanks will come from Zlitan to the Sirte battlefront. They're the same ones Gaddafi tried to destroy Misrata with. Now they'll be used against him," said one of the other rebel leaders, Sadi Mohtar Hadad, who confirmed our suspicions about the level of violence likely to be unleashed.

All the indications were that the rebels would employ tactics similar to those the regime had used against them. Sirte would be surrounded and bombarded—the same fate that befell Misrata and Zintan. The military hardware outside the city included between 40 and 50 Grad BM-21 rocket launchers, all of which had previously belonged to the army.

The equipment was accumulating along two fronts to the west of Sirte; one was to the south of Misrata, the other to the east. And on the other side of Sirte, to the east, rebel forces were arriving from Ras Lanuf and Benghazi. There was no chance the city could hold out—and its capture would represent not only the fall of another symbol of Gaddafi's regime but also, in practical terms, the final stage of the liberation of the area around Libya's most important road, the coastal route running all the way from Ras Jdir on the Tunisian border to Musaid on the border with Egypt. The road goes through Libya's three biggest cities—Tripoli, Benghazi, and Misrata—and would play a hugely important role in helping the country get back on its feet economically. There were urgent reasons to remove Sirte as an obstacle, therefore; yet it was obvious that everyone I spoke to wanted the city's 75,000 inhabitants to surrender and make further deaths unnecessary.

"It'll be like in Tripoli. There'll be an uprising inside and then we'll go in and take the city," Ras Ali told me.

Expectations of a rebellion inside the city and a consequent collapse in support for Gaddafi increased as the insurgents took control of nearby villages. By the end of August various pro-Gaddafi villages, including Bwayrat al-Hasun, had been captured. In Abugrin, on the morning of August 30, journalists were given an idea of the efficiency of the siege with the capture of two loyalist soldiers who had been carrying out a reconnaissance mission in a vehicle laden with arms and ammunition. Hit by rebel fire, the vehicle was consumed by a spectacular explosion caught on camera by Al Jazeera while the loyalists were captured. We were taken to the scene by a group of rebels and arrived just a few minutes afterward.

Although that particular incident was just a skirmish, it still demonstrated that a role reversal had taken place: the "rats," now, were the remaining Gaddafi loyalists. Cornered, they faced a choice between surrender and defeat. The only reason the war had not already ended was because the negotiations had created a kind of standoff in the desert that would go on for weeks.

The situation in Sirte was a mirror image of Benghazi on the eve of the NATO intervention, when Gaddafi had promised to crush the opposition. But sadly, on this occasion, there would be no outside intervention to prevent a large-scale massacre taking place.

The rebel forces taking up positions around Sirte were still being assisted by their foreign allies, with NATO aircraft carrying out further attacks intended both to demoralize the loyalist resistance and reduce their firepower. In Sirte, Western planes destroyed a command center, five anti-aircraft batteries, a tank, and two rocket launchers. In Bani Walid, on the same day, a command center and an arsenal were blown up. Hun, a Saharan oasis 600 kilometers from Tripoli, was also targeted.

In the light of these latest air strikes, I asked Ras Ali if NATO personnel were advising the rebels about the best strategy to pursue in their ground operations. Seemingly uncomfortable at the question, and perhaps slightly irritated, he replied that no such orientation was being given. But he took the bait, going on to acknowledge that French and British soldiers were in constant contact with the rebels in the region—although he was at pains to emphasize that none of them were actually to be found among the rebel forces. The role of the foreigners, he said, was simply to keep track of the strategy the rebels were pursuing and to inform the rebels of NATO's own plans, which could—if necessary—include air strikes. NATO was also taking responsibility for protecting the civilian population—for example, by launching missiles from warships in the Gulf of Sirte to shoot down two Scud missiles fired by loyalist forces.

I was intrigued by Ras Ali's denial that Western military personnel were on the ground assisting the rebels, which would have violated the UN resolutions. A few kilometers away, at a rebel checkpoint, I talked to Ahmed Jutlawi, 27, who had been a truck mechanic before the war.

I asked him a question about "French soldiers" in the area, putting it in a way that suggested I already knew they were there. He answered without hesitation, confirming that French military personnel had been in the area to gather intelligence about loyalist troop positions. "Today a car with two French soldiers came to the front to get information," he revealed. He added that these NATO men were coordinating directly with the rebels to decide where to carry out air strikes.

The other major rebel objective, apart from Sirte, was the loyalist enclave of Bani Walid, situated in the desert in the district of Misrata, 160 kilometers from Tripoli. It was thought that the Colonel and Saif might have taken refuge there. Although two of the NTC's military commanders had told me confidentially that they didn't think any senior figures from Gaddafi's regime were in Bani Walid, secret preparations for an operation against the town were nevertheless being made. A convoy including heavy weapons would set off from Tripoli with a twofold aim: to prevent Gaddafi escaping, if he really was there, and to prepare for an invasion of the town—population 50,000—if it didn't surrender.

My own hunch was that Gaddafi could indeed be in Bani Walid. Not only were there rumors that his son Khamis had been killed in the town, but it was also where the Colonel himself had been sighted most recently, on August 19, alongside Saif and senior members of the regime including Abdullah al-Senussi, head of the Itikhbarat military intelligence service. I'd received this piece of information from Abdel Majid Mlegta, who along with Dr. Mohammed Othman had been at the forefront of the preparations for the assault on Tripoli and was now one of the directors of operations in the capital. In the same meeting the NTC vice-chairman, Abdel Hafiz Ghoga, told me he had information, albeit unconfirmed, that Gaddafi was still in Bani Walid.

However, the NTC wanted to persist with the negotiations and to avoid using force as far as possible because Bani Walid was one of the principal urban centers of the Warfalla tribe—the biggest in Libya, numbering more than 1 million people. An offensive against the town would carry a political risk because thousands of rebels from cities such as Zintan and Benghazi were also Warfalla and didn't want to attack their fellow clansmen. Mlegta had referred to the impasse when I spoke to him: "We're ready to end the crisis, but the military operation isn't our priority. We are talking to the leaders in Bani Walid. We want them to arrest Gaddafi and hand him over, but so far we haven't received a response."

The strategy of surrounding the town and negotiating with the local tribal leaders was the same as that being employed in Sirte—and would be pursued for the next few weeks. The NTC's interim defense minister, Jalal al-Deghili, announced that the deadline for the loyalists' surrender would be extended by at least another week. The final offensive was not yet imminent.

THOUSANDS OF FAMILIES LEFT SIRTE DURING THIS PERIOD, DRIVING AWAY IN CARS overflowing with their possessions. Apparently destined to become the scene of urban warfare, the city was being abandoned to its fate. At road junctions out in the desert, rebels manned their checkpoints under clear blue skies and the scalding sun—on some days the temperature soared to well above 104 degrees Fahrenheit. The luckiest brigades were those able to shelter under the few road bridges in that area of the Sahara.

Supplies of fuel and food to these rebel outposts were proving unreliable. Some of the checkpoints gradually turned into small encampments where the men came together to share supplies and try to reduce the tedium of waiting for the order to attack. One such encampment was at El Gebhe, where I met Omar Salem Adeyub, the leader of a small group of rebels responsible for applying pressure on the area around Sirte. They conducted their maneuvers for a few hours a day but were unable to stray far from their only source of fuel, a rusty tank sitting on the ground just behind a beach on the edge of the Mediterranean. Adeyub was confident of victory while also expressing respect for the men still opposing the rebel forces. "We haven't invaded yet because we don't want more bloodshed," he said. "We don't believe Gaddafi has a very strong force in Sirte. We don't know how many men there are, but we're stronger. There isn't a deadline for them to give themselves up, but we can't wait much longer."

In the ongoing negotiations, however, there was a significant complicating factor: Muammar Gaddafi. Despite the capture of Tripoli, a sense of apprehension lingered over Libya. In the streets of Misrata, as in the capital, there were small-scale celebrations—not to mention the now insufferable bursts of celebratory machine gun fire, day and night—but nothing like the major festivities that had taken place in Benghazi. The situation led some political analysts in the foreign press to resort to old arguments about the supposed "apathy" of the Libyan people. Among commentators who had opposed the Western intervention, meanwhile, the preferred explanation was that much of the population still supported Gaddafi, whose downfall had been imposed from outside. My own conversations with ordinary Libyans, rebels, and intellectuals gave me the impression that despite the dying down of the fighting in Tripoli, the gradual recommencement of normal daily routines, and the emergent sense of freedom, there was still an underlying tension. For the people of Libya, the war against the regime would not be over until Gaddafi himself had been captured—or killed.

Though very aware of this continuing sense of insecurity, I was surprised when NTC prime minister Mahmoud Jibril decided to delay the transfer of his cabinet to Tripoli. It was a symbolic decision, signifying that Libya, or at least Tripolitania, wasn't yet sufficiently stable. The transfer of the cabinet had originally been scheduled for September 7—a fortnight after the fall of Bab al-Azizia—but now it would only take place "after the total liberation of the country." While the ex-dictator was still at large, the revolution remained his hostage. This feeling emanated from the Libyan people themselves and was transmitted to the country's provisional political leaders, reinforcing the generalized sense of uncertainty and the impression that the victory was not yet complete.

THOUGH A TALENTED ORATOR, GADDAFI KEPT QUIET DURING HIS FIRST DAYS ON THE run. Then his voice reappeared, exacerbating the sense of disquiet. On September 8 the Syrian TV station Arrai, based in Damascus, broadcast a defiant audio message in which he reaffirmed his status as a military leader and a free man: "They have nothing else to resort to apart from psychological warfare and lies. They last said Gaddafi had been seen in a convoy heading toward Niger. How many times do convoys transporting smugglers, traders, and people cross the border every day for Sudan, Chad, Mali, and Algeria? As if this was the first time a convoy was headed toward Niger!" He emphasized he was still in Libya, not far from Tripoli, and called for attacks against the "rats and mercenaries."

After the broadcast, news agencies revealed that the director of the pro-Gaddafi Syrian television station Arrai, Michane al-Joubouri, had spoken to Gaddafi. According to al-Joubouri the Colonel was "in high spirits" and had no fear of the possibility of dying while fighting the "occupiers." Gaddafi's threats were seized upon by the press and reverberated across the country. It was the first of a series of pronouncements that made me wonder about the Colonel's whereabouts and morale. Despite the absurd bluster in the face of defeat, some of what he said seemed lucid and sincere—such as his stated determination to resist, to stay in Libya, and to fight to the very end. These were the words of the military leader he had essentially always been. I closely analyzed everything he said, looking for the clues as to where he might be and then comparing these clues with the pieces of information—often contradictory—I received from different sources inside the NTC.

I started to do the same with the pronouncements being made by Saif. On September 1, he used Arrai, to declare that "victory is close." He vowed that the siege of Sirte would be broken, promised a counterattack by 20,000 men against Tripoli to "liberate Green Square," and expressed disdain for the NTC's ultimatums. Such rhetoric—especially from Saif, who had enjoyed an expensive postgraduate education in Vienna and London and had seemed to embody the possibility of renovation and reform—showed that the lessons of Libya's recent history had not been learned. It had been at least 30 years since the regime last mobilized the masses or attracted the level of support it seemed to believe it still enjoyed. Those three decades had been marked by growing indifference, empty charades—such as the pathetic proregime demonstrations in Green Square in February and March 2011—and the alienation of important sections of Libyan society, not least the middle class. Thanks to the experience of study abroad and also to the critical spirit that had developed in Libya's own universities since the 1970s, the Libyan middle class were increasingly aware of the totalitarianism and corruption surrounding them. Suffocated by a repressive state apparatus that had assumed absurd proportions in a country of only 6 million people, they had long since turned their backs on Gaddafi and his ideology. Instead of support, what the regime got from them was just a grudging silence.

Back in Tripoli and already preparing to leave Libya via Ras Jdir, I had the impression the city wanted stability but was struggling to conquer its demons. The presence of thousands of armed men on the streets already generated a feeling of insecurity, and the speeches by the Colonel and Saif rekindled fears of a loyalist counteroffensive. This was evident during the Eid al-Fitr celebrations marking the end of Ramadan, when four rebels were killed in an explosion not far from the city center. I tried to find out exactly what had happened; the most plausible explanation was that there had been some kind of attack by loyalists, but it was also possible the men had mishandled one of their own grenades. Whatever the explanation, the incident served as a warning that the large number of rebel brigades in the streets could contribute to the country's destabilization.

IN EARLY SEPTEMBER I LEFT TRIPOLI AND RETURNED TO PARIS. THE THIRD ULTIMA-tum demanding Sirte's surrender came and went. With the two sides still negotiating, I imagined the standoff might continue for many more weeks. Like the majority of Libyans, I hoped a political solution would be found, but I didn't really believe it was possible. While it was true that the rebels and Sirte's remaining civilian population wanted a peaceful outcome, the loyalist forces who had withstood everything the rebels and NATO had thrown at them in the previous couple of months were not going to abandon the fight. It simply wouldn't be like them to do that—especially if Gaddafi was in the city, as growing rumors suggested he might be.

I left Tripoli feeling frustrated for various reasons—firstly because it was becoming increasingly difficult to access the regime's confidential documents, but also because I was finding it impossible to get hold of some of my principal contacts, who had dispersed to various parts of the country. And on top of that I was irritated because I was still unable to identify the place where Ghaith and I were imprisoned. I'd made a long list of possible locations and had already visited dozens of them—realizing in the process that Tripoli was full of prison cells and premises belonging to the intelligence services, which made the search slow and incredibly bureaucratic.

The circumstances of my release from prison were another unsolved puzzle. By now I was aware it had been a more complex chain of events then I previously imagined, but it was only in October that all the pieces of the jigsaw would finally come together.

A few weeks after returning to Paris, I flew to Ankara, Turkey, to cover an official visit by Brazil's president, Dilma Rousseff. Upon arrival I was surprised to get a message from the head of the foreign desk at the *Estado de São Paulo*, Felipe Corazza, telling me he'd received a phone call from a Libyan woman working in a senior position in Petrobras, the Brazilian state-owned oil company, in Libya. She told Felipe she wanted to meet me—and that she'd been involved in securing my release. I'd known ever since March that a Libyan—as well as Ambassador George Ney Fernandes—had helped get me out of prison, but only now did I find out her name: Amal Daredi.

Our meeting took place two days later, in the lobby of a hotel in Ankara. I was in a group of journalists waiting for President Dilma Rousseff to arrive when a man with graying hair came up and asked my name. It was Iran Garcia da Costa, the director-general of Petrobras in Libya. He immediately came across as warm and friendly, and seemed delighted when I told him who I was. "I want you to meet the person who got you out of prison," he said.

He stepped aside and introduced me to Amal, who was accompanied by her husband, Mohamed Daredi. Although we'd been looking for each other, the sudden encounter was still a very emotional one for me. Amal exuded kindness and spoke impeccable Portuguese. She was elegantly dressed in accordance with Muslim tradition, with a hijab covering her head. We were only able to speak for a couple of minutes before President Rousseff and her entourage arrived, so we arranged to meet again the following evening.

The meeting actually took place late the following night, after President Rousseff had left the city and I finally had some free time. I sat talking with Amal, Mohamed, and Costa in the hotel lobby until the early hours of the morning—and discovered that the story of my release from prison had begun before I was even arrested.

On Saturday February 19, a few days after the eruption of the revolt in Benghazi and shortly before the outbreak of similar events in Tripoli, Ambassador Fernandes had arranged a meeting with the heads of various Brazilian companies in Libya and members of the Brazilian community to discuss security issues and what might happen next. The feeling until then had been that there was no significant risk to the majority of Brazilians in Libya, although certain precautionary measures were already being taken. The situation changed on the following Sunday night, when Saif al-Islam, Gaddafi's son, made his threatening speech on state TV; the effect was precisely the opposite of what he intended, sending thousands of people onto the streets of Tripoli in protest. It was now obvious that the Brazilian community would have to be evacuated. Fernandes turned to Amal for assistance: not only was she an executive with a reputation for being determined, tenacious, and competent, but she was also the niece of Ibrahim Daredi, a Libyan ambassador and the ex-head of the Americas division in the Libyan foreign ministry. Amal would help do the groundwork for what turned out to be a successful evacuation organized by the Brazilian embassy.

A few days after my disappearance, my brother Vinicius Netto managed to establish a valuable channel of communication in Rio de Janeiro: he spoke to Colonel Pedro Arruda Aramis de Lima, the head of corporate security for Petrobras, who agreed to try to help behind the scenes, in secret, without expecting any kind of public recognition for his efforts. Meanwhile, my colleagues at the *Estado de São Paulo* such as Ricardo Gandour, Cida Damasco, and Roberto Lameirinhas were trying to recruit the help of the Brazilian foreign ministry in Brasilia. They also held a press conference in which they spoke of a "loss of contact" with me—an initiative aimed at alerting public opinion to the seriousness of the situation and provoking a diplomatic reaction both in Brazil and Libya. By this time Colonel Arruda had called Costa in Libya to ask whether Petrobras might be able to assist in discovering my whereabouts. Costa, in turn, phoned Amal.

Amal made enquiries based on the little information she had. She thought Ghaith and I might be in Zawiyah, our intended destination when we disappeared; if so, given that Zawiyah had been under siege for a week, she imagined we were unable to communicate. Amal's mother lives in Zawiyah, so she tried to call her to ask if she'd heard anything—only to find that the telephone network in the city had been cut. Next she phoned one of her cousins, Abeer, in Sabratha—which proved to be a vital step forward. Abeer informed her that a Brazilian journalist and an Iraqi had been found by militiamen in the city a few days before. She said the pair had been arrested in the vicinity of Souk Alalga—the market of the Alalga tribe—and then handed over to the police before being taken to the neighboring city of Surman, 70 kilometers from Tripoli.

The good news ended there, however. Sabratha was a city controlled by General al-Khweildi al-Hmeidi, the father-in-law of Gaddafi's son Saadi and one of the most prominent figures in the regime. Al-Hmeidi took part in the 1969 coup alongside the Colonel and became one of his most loyal followers, being rewarded with the directorship of one of the intelligence services. Such was his importance that NATO bombed his house in Surman on June 20; thirteen members of his family were killed, according to his lawyer. Moreover, the possibility that Saadi himself knew about our imprisonment couldn't be discounted, because he was the commander of one of the country's elite military units. There was a risk, therefore, that major figures in the regime could seek to exploit our predicament.

Amal called Colonel Arruda back ten minutes later, telling him that a Brazilian—possibly the missing journalist—had been arrested with an Iraqi in Sabratha. She promised to discuss the matter with the Brazilian embassy in Tripoli the next day.

Early the next morning, Thursday, March 10, Amal phoned Ambassador Fernandes. The call came at an opportune moment because he had just been instructed by the foreign ministry in Brasilia to try to discover my whereabouts. The two of them met at 10 a.m. to exchange information. The ambassador also gave Amal the contact details of important figures in the Libyan foreign ministry, including Abdelhaman al-Gannas, the new head of the Americas division. Amal was afraid to get involved but nevertheless decided to help. She called al-Gannas and asked for his assistance in locating the missing journalists. He told her it was the first he'd heard about the matter and that he couldn't promise anything, but that he'd do his best to look into it. Later he called Amal back: he'd found out where we were. Al-Gannas assured Amal he would be able to secure my release, though he added that it would be on condition that I left the country.

By virtue of the longstanding diplomatic relationship between Brazil and Gaddafi's Libya, it had taken only eight hours to discover that Ghaith and I were being held in a prison cell in Tripoli, although the Libyan foreign ministry didn't know exactly where. A meeting was arranged in one of the buildings belonging to the Mukhabarat el-Jamahiriya, where I would be handed over to Ambassador Fernandes. I would be set free without facing any judicial proceedings, but I faced immediate deportation.

On March 19, the most senior staff working for Petrobras in Libya left the country for security reasons, relocating to Ankara. Amal left with her husband, Mohamed, 51, and her son Anawar, 15. Mohamed, as I would later discover, was a man who seemed quiet and shy on first impression, though he spoke excellent Portuguese. An agronomist by profession, he had a doctorate from the Federal University of Minas Gerais in Brazil. As I became increasingly interested in his backstory, I realized he was someone who might be referred to as an intellectual. I guessed he was anti-Gaddafi, which turned out to be the case. Indeed, in the 1980s he had been a student activist involved in university protests—albeit low-key—against the regime.

Like all the students of his era, Mohamed knew about the public executions of student leaders that had taken place on university campuses in Benghazi and Tripoli in the 1970s. And in 1982, while studying for his degree, he actually witnessed the regime's murderous methods first-hand. On April 7 that year, with his university expecting a visit from the "Guide," the students decided to stay away in protest. Gaddafi was furious, and three days later troops surrounded the campus, forcing the students to congregate in a square. There, as an "example," three of them were hanged. One of them was a young man who had been Mohamed's friend since childhood, Rashid Kaabar.

Mohamed remained a dissident for the next 30 years. I spoke with him about what it was like to be an opponent of Gaddafi during that time. He told me about other executions on university campuses, arbitrary arrests, and the permanent, omnipresent threat of being informed on. He emphasized what had become a recurring theme in my conversations with Libyans about the regime's repressive practices: the tactic of terrorizing the families of dissidents, employed ever since the first student protests and the first attempts to depose Gaddafi. For 42 years, it wasn't just that anyone who spoke out against the Colonel would be hunted down and murdered: it was quite possible their families might also be killed. This tactic—also used in other Arab countries such as Syria under the Assad family—had the desired effect of silencing the opposition.

"The secret police and the regime had agents infiltrated in the universities and in all sections of society," Mohamed told me. "If you said out loud what you thought about Gaddafi, you wouldn't see the sun rise again."

In public, defenders of the regime shouted in praise of Gaddafi and his "revolution" and wielded symbols of his rule such as the Green Book or the country's monochrome flag. The dissidents, meanwhile, shared a symbol of their own, much more subtle, which allowed them to recognize each other: silence. Since the very early days of Gaddafi's rule—the era of the student movements in the 1970s, whose participants would become Libya's intellectual elite—the oppression had made the air unbreathable, creating a form of behavior that came to characterize those who rejected the dictatorship. In Gaddafi's Libya, to be quiet amid the regime's noisy enthusiasts was the one possible form of insubordination—and the embryo of an inevitable revolution.

Thirty years after the execution he had witnessed, Mohamed found himself being pressured by his 15-year-old son, Anawar, to break through the barrier of fear, take up arms, and join the insurgent movement spreading across the country. With Amal's reluctant consent, father and son left Turkey for Tunisia, where they helped refugees from the conflict. Then, from the Tunisian port of Sfax, just over 300 kilometers from the Libyan border, they took a boat to Misrata, which was under siege. Upon arrival, Mohamed, who had done compulsory military service as a younger man, picked up a weapon again and joined the other 23,000 people who were defending the city against Gaddafi's forces. Anawar, meanwhile, just like so many other 15-, 16-, and 17-year-olds across Libya, began an intensive period of military training organized by the rebels in the hope his mother would give him permission to fight on the front line.

"He was saying to me, 'Let me go, because if I die I'll take you to paradise with me," Amal later told me, referring to her telephone conversations with Anawar at that time.

Alongside the people of Misrata, Mohamed and his son faced the daily bombardments, holding out until the regime's forces were driven back to the outskirts of the city where they kept up the siege for a few more weeks. By this time Amal, in Ankara, had become unwell. Mohamed and Anawar left Misrata for Tripoli shortly before the beginning of Ramadan, then returned to Turkey. When later I asked him about the presence of so many adolescents on the battlefields of Libya, including his own son, Mohamed expressed regret about those who had been killed or wounded. But he added that he'd never seen anyone as courageous as the teenaged rebels he'd fought alongside—young Libyans previously disparaged by the older generation for the Western music they listened to, the trousers falling off their hips, and their modern hairstyles.

WHEN I GOT BACK TO PARIS FROM ANKARA I'D ALREADY DECIDED, FOR VARIOUS reasons, to return to Tripoli. On October 18, ten days after getting the go-ahead from my editor in Brazil, Cida Damasco, and having already communicated with many of my contacts in Libya by email and phone, I packed my rucksack with the usual mountain of equipment: laptop, chargers, mobile and satellite phones, camera, lenses, memory cards, voice recorders, flash drives, a mass of different cables, my passport—with a translation into Arabic—and various other forms of ID, and a stack of notepads. As well as the equipment, I stuffed in three T-shirts, two pairs of jeans, some underwear, and a toilet bag. This time I wasn't taking the helmet or the military bulletproof vest provided by Reporters Without Borders. I would be flying from Orly airport, south of Paris, to Tunis, followed by a 40-minute flight to Djerba. At Orly I called a few more contacts in Libya to tell them I'd soon be arriving, and also asked a fixer in Tunisia to try to arrange to get me across the border that night, if possible via the Ras Jdir crossing.

The flight from Paris was delayed, however, which meant I'd miss the connecting flight to Djerba. Arriving in Tunis an hour later than planned, I supplemented the dollars and euros I was carrying with some Tunisian dinars that I'd be able to exchange for Libyan dinars at the border. After buying another ticket for Djerba, I was leafing through some of my notes, waiting for my flight to be called, when I noticed two smartly dressed men opposite me. One was middle-aged, the other older. The older man stood out because he was albino, but in fact neither of them was physically similar to the average Tunisian. I noticed they both had old Libyan passports—green, like the Gaddafi-era flag, and larger than the ones issued more recently. As the queue formed to get on the plane, I went over and introduced myself. They were Ali Tumi and Mohamed Frandah, both doctors at Tripoli Central Hospital where the staff had been so attentive and helpful when I'd visited two months previously.

I asked them if it was possible to cross the border at Ras Jdir without too much of a delay, and what the security situation was like on the route

eastward from the border through Zuwara, 100 kilometers west of Tripoli.
Of strategic importance because of its geographical location on the Gulf
of Gabès, 60 kilometers from the border, Zuwara had been the scene of
fighting, two days previously, between rebels and pro-Gaddafi soldiers.
The loyalists were carrying out sporadic attacks in the area immediately
to the south of the plant belonging to the Zuwara Oil Refinery Company
(Zorco), one of the most important in Libya.

The two doctors were friendly and also spoke fluent English. They
said the situation at the border was under control and that they themselves
had recently driven from Tripoli to Djerba with Ali's son, 17, and one of
his friends. The security situation was good enough, they said, that they
had no qualms about taking the two teenagers with them. Intending to
take part in a medical conference in the United States, they had traveled
to Tunis to be interviewed at the US consulate, part of the visa application process. The visas weren't granted.

"They said the situation in Libya is still very unstable and that's why
they didn't give us the visas this time," Ali told me. "It's not a big problem," he added. Indeed, it seemed I was more irritated with the consulate's attitude than either Ali or Mohamed.

They had already given me all the information I wanted, but I was
grateful that our conversation continued awhile longer. I intended to
write a piece on how the educated Libyan middle class viewed the revolution, and it seemed the two doctors could be interesting contributors.
As part of an elite professional class, however, I guessed they might have
benefited from Gaddafi's regime in some way, so I thought I should be
careful in raising the subject.

As a way of sounding them out, I said I'd visited their hospital in
August to talk with rebels and soldiers who had been wounded in combat, and mentioned that I'd been surprised to hear that Hana Gaddafi—
the Colonel's adopted daughter, supposedly killed in the US air strikes
in 1986—was not only alive but working, unofficially, as the hospital's
director. The two doctors smiled and confirmed it was indeed the case.
Though the situation had only recently been "discovered" by the international media, it hadn't really been a secret in Libya, and certainly not
in the medical milieu. Back in August I'd discussed Hana Gaddafi with
various staff members at the hospital, but I was still keen to find out what
the two doctors had to say about her.

"She wasn't a bad professional," Mohamed said, as we entered the
aircraft. "She was young and inexperienced, but she wasn't especially
arrogant, nor did she use her position in the family to get her way." Ali
seemed to agree with him.

I hoped to see Ali and Mohamed again in Tripoli, so we agreed we should exchange phone numbers. At Djerba-Zarzis airport after the short flight, I spotted two people who looked like journalists, judging from the photographic equipment one of them was carrying. They turned out to be Marcel Mettelsiefen, a photographer, and Barbara Hardinghaus, both from *Der Spiegel*—I ended up traveling to Misrata with them. Barbara, who had not been to Libya before, intended to write a piece about "Libyan families"; later I realized that what this really entailed was speaking to women who had been raped during the siege of Misrata, a hugely interesting story but also a major taboo in a city with an above-average level of religious fervor. Marcel had already spent time in Libya during the revolution, as well as having firsthand experience of various other war zones. We chatted briefly about our travel plans; they said they wouldn't be crossing the border that night because they didn't yet have Libyan visas.

I hadn't wanted to lose sight of Ali and Mohamed, but I couldn't find them anywhere at the airport, and there was no answer from my fixer when I tried to call him. By now it was close to 8 p.m. and therefore becoming risky to try to get all the way to Tripoli. So I decided to stay in the same hotel as Marcel, in Djerba, and to set off early the following morning. At the hotel reception desk I had the pleasant surprise of bumping into Ali and Mohamed; I offered them a lift to Tripoli the next morning so we could talk some more, but Mohamed insisted they give me a lift instead, as they had a car waiting for them. I accepted immediately.

We crossed the border at Ras Jdir in the middle of the next morning, after getting Libyan dinars from the money changers in Ben Gardane. I couldn't help laughing to myself, for this was the first time I was entering Libya with a visa in my hand since the beginning of the uprising. Ironically, the officials at the immigration desk were unhappy with my passport. They demanded to know why I'd visited so many countries and seemed particularly suspicious about a US visa that—ironically, again—I'd obtained after accepting an invitation to talk about Libya at a journalism conference. They were less interested in the written authorization to enter Libya that I'd received from the NTC ambassador in Paris, Mansour Saif al-Nasr. The situation further illustrated Libya's bureaucratic culture and overbearing officialdom; the truth was it would have been quicker to cross the border illegally. I spent more than an hour at the border post, but then we had an easy, uneventful journey to Sabratha and then Surman, where Ali and Mohamed both lived. Before we parted I arranged to see them again at the hospital. Then I took a taxi to a small hotel in the center of Tripoli, the Asshajara.

On the way to the hotel, which proved difficult to find, I noticed that Tripoli was very different from before. The streets were full of people and traffic, and virtually all the checkpoints had been removed. There was no background noise of gunfire and explosions, nor was there the sense of oppression that hung over the city in the Gaddafi era. Less than two months after the rebels' capture of the capital, the feeling of freedom in the air had increased perceptibly.

No sooner had I unpacked in my hotel room than I was on my way out again, having heard that the NTC prime minister, Mahmoud Jibril, was about to make an announcement at the Qaat al-Shaab, the old People's Congress building, now used by the interim government to hold meetings. When I arrived I realized my presence was something of a surprise to the assembled Libyan politicians and media: I was the only Western journalist there. After I'd had a quick word with a couple of the organizers, however, everyone I spoke to was very welcoming.

Jibril began speaking shortly afterward. To my surprise, and that of the NTC, he announced he would be leaving the interim government. He had been an important figure in the revolution from the very start, and although he had already threatened to leave, when he revealed to the interim government and the press the chaotic situation inside the NTC, it hadn't crossed my mind that he would do so at a moment when Sirte was about to be captured. "I promised to leave public office immediately after the fall of the regime, not after the complete liberation of the country," Jibril said, justifying his decision and responding to his critics.

The head of Libya's provisional government explained that his natural path would be to follow the revolutionary process by rebuilding the country's institutions and preparing for a new, solid, democratic government of national unity. But, in his view, the NTC was being undermined by "a political struggle with no boundaries"—a struggle over money, arms, and ideology. He said there was a possibility the revolution could take a path toward chaos, which in fact would suit those "which have their own agendas toward Libya."

I spoke to some other NTC leaders who shared Jibril's opinions and left the building feeling worried about the situation in the country. Although on the verge of complete liberation, it was clear Libya was now experiencing a power struggle between different rebel factions, all of which were armed.

That night back at the Asshajara hotel, I spoke to some contacts who could provide input for a piece I was preparing on the relations between Brazil and Gaddafi's Libya—which was actually the original motive for my trip—and others who had information on the situation in Sirte. There were rumors that the city would fall to the rebels within a matter of hours, which was even sooner than my contacts in Tripoli had predicted. Some of the people I spoke to confirmed that the fall of Gaddafi's home territory was indeed imminent.

Between early September, when I'd left Tripoli, and mid-October, when I returned, the standoff around Sirte had become a full-blown battle. In the first stage of the battle, rebel forces from the Benghazi region took control of the Red Valley, about 60 kilometers from the city. The rebels then launched their offensive against Sirte itself, concentrating the attacks on one area of the city at a time. With the negotiations having petered out, the same kind of intense, bloody, and confused fighting that had been seen elsewhere in Libya got underway. Among the photographers who saw the battles close up was the *New York Times*' Maurício Lima, a Brazilian who had covered the war in Afghanistan. Often he came back from the front line in a daze, profoundly shocked by the images he had captured. What he witnessed was the raw but often futile courage of teenagers and young men fighting ineptly, without a strategy. Combatants died every day in situations that seemed stupid and unnecessary. When he described the fighting to me I was reminded of the lack of preparation that led so many men to lose their lives in Nalut, Zintan, and Misrata, and on all the other battlefields of the revolution.

Early in the morning on October 20, eighteen hours after arriving in Tripoli, I left the hotel on my way to speak to Rashed Meftah Gheddah, an administrative manager working with Petrobras in Libya. I met him on the fifteenth floor of the Al Fateh Tower, in the city center. We chatted about Jibril's announcement, which had also left him feeling worried. "We are having a very difficult birth of democracy," he told me, before apologizing for having forgotten certain words in English. "Sorry, I haven't spoken about politics for a long time."

The problems Libya faced, he said, were countless. Before Gaddafi the country had institutions and political stability, albeit under an incompetent monarch. Gaddafi, he said, "de-politicized" Libyan society, abolishing civil society in the name of the theory contained in his Green Book. There were no longer any political parties or institutions, no democratic culture, nothing. And since the rebels' capture of Bab al-Azizia, Tripoli had been divided into various local administrative bodies under the overall military command of Abdelhakim Belhadj—the man who appropriated the weapons intended for the Zintan rebels during the preparations for the Battle of Tripoli. This, in Rashed's opinion, was very bad news.

Nevertheless, Rashed said, the NTC's stated priorities were the right ones: to consolidate the interim government, create institutions, prepare for an election for a constituent general assembly, and get the health system back on its feet to reestablish a minimum level of provision for a population still suffering the effects of war. Two military objectives remained: to ensure the coastal road from the Tunisian to the Egyptian border was completely secure, and, of course, to capture Sirte. Fortunately, Rashed said, the latter objective was about to be achieved.

THAT SAME MORNING, OCTOBER 20, SIRAJ AL-ABDALLAH AL-HIMALI ZAEDE WAS feeling exhausted. The fighting in Sirte had become bloodier and more intense as the rebels penetrated District 2, the area of the city most fiercely guarded by the pro-Gaddafi soldiers. This rebel advance had sparked the rumors that the city was finally about to be captured. In fact the expectation of victory had been increasing ever since September 16, when the insurgents took control of the airport, 10 kilometers south of the city center.

By this stage, the rumors about the city's imminent fall were credible. Gaddafi's forces were trapped with their backs to the sea. They no longer had control of the outskirts of the city or any of the access roads. If they looked in one direction they saw rebel katibas from Benghazi; in the other, insurgents from Misrata. They were running out of options.

Siraj's katiba, the Watan, consisted of about one hundred fighters and was also known as the "Pepsi Brigade" because their base was a building that used to be a factory belonging to the American soft drink company. So far their orders had been to hold the district of Jufrah, from which they carried out raids against the city's defenders. They returned to base after each attack; their objective wasn't to capture new ground but to weaken the loyalists' resistance. As the siege tightened, however, the brigade was called on to provide security on the left flank of District 2, assisting with the attempt to press the enemy back toward the sea. In doing so they stood guard around an electricity substation that provided a good position from which to cut off any loyalists trying to flee.

Siraj had been in the frontline since his katiba's participation in the attack on District 1, their first mission in the battle for Sirte. He and his closest comrades—Ibrahim Ahmad Omar Ismail, Mohamed Jamal, Umran Ben Shaaban, and Hassan al-Tiyb—ranged in age from 18 to 26 or 27. Like the majority of Libyans fighting to overthrow the regime, they had little or no military training. Whether by sheer luck or the intervention of Allah, all of them had survived so far.

Siraj had been involved in the anti-Gaddafi struggle since February, when the protest movement that began in Benghazi arrived in Tripoli. Aged 21, he had hoped to start at the university in Tripoli later in 2011; he wanted to study mathematics and physics, or perhaps engineering, and knew he'd need good grades to be selected. When the revolution began, however, these personal plans faded into the background. It was more important to go out into the streets and make clear the popular message: "Gaddafi Out!" When the rebellion reached Tripoli, on February 20, some of Siraj's friends had to deal with parents fearful about the consequences of letting their offspring go and demonstrate in Green Square. Siraj had already lost both his parents in fatal accidents; his mother died when he was 3, his father when he was 6. He'd been brought up by one of his grandmothers in Misrata and then lived independently in the district of Suq al-Jum'ah in eastern Tripoli, where anti-Gaddafi sentiments had been strong well before the beginning of the uprising. In Suq al-Jum'ah, as in Misrata, taking to the streets in protest was less an act of youthful rebellion than a serious moral obligation—and Siraj had no intention of shirking it.

On February 20, the first day of protests, unarmed demonstrators ended up throwing stones and sticks to try to defend themselves. The security forces launched a savage assault, massacring more than 500 people in Green Square. But the slaughter only increased Siraj's determination. He searched for other ways to resist, gradually immersing himself in the underground world of the urban guerrilla movement that would defy the regime in Tripoli over the following months. Alongside this underground insurgency—discreetly financed, and armed, by local elites—he began to take part in lightning attacks against symbols of the regime.

During the first days of the rebellion, Gaddafi cut off Tripoli's electricity supply, thinking this would intimidate the protesters. It had the opposite effect: under the cover of darkness the walls of the city became covered in anti-Gaddafi graffiti. Siraj participated in these minor acts of subversion and also in some more significant ones, such as throwing petrol bombs at government buildings and the security forces. After each attack his group melted away into the night. One of his friends, however, was identified while painting a slogan on a wall. The security forces stormed his family's home in the middle of the night and took him away: he was never seen again. Afterward, some of his friends left the capital for Zintan, seeking the protection of the mountains, military training, and weapons.

Siraj stayed in Tripoli and took part in further actions as the regime clung to power. Then came the rebel attack on Bab al-Azizia. On the night of August 20, he fired a gun for the first time. He and some of his friends had forced their way into the so-called White House, a home of one of Gaddafi's uncles, where they found a stock of weapons. He picked up an AK-47 and some ammunition and headed off to the front line. He put the first bullet he touched in his pocket, later wearing it on a chain around his neck. He would tell me that becoming an armed combatant didn't make him the least bit nervous; at the time he wasn't even aware of having crossed a line. He was utterly focused on joining the "secret group" of revolutionaries who were coordinating the offensive—Mlegta's group. As the Battle of Tripoli got underway, some of the group went to Bab al-Azizia and others headed for the district of Abu Salim, where the vast majority of residents were sympathetic to Gaddafi.

After Tripoli, Siraj set off for Tawergha, a regime stronghold. He arrived at the end of Ramadan. Many Tawerghans had already been killed, and those that remained would either meet the same fate or be expelled, such was the desire for revenge after the violence they had perpetrated against Misrata during the siege. The population of the city consisted of black Libyans who could trace their ancestry to sub-Saharan Africa, or of immigrants from that part of the continent. They had remained loyal to the regime not only between the months of March and September 2011, at the height of the conflict, but also throughout the preceding four decades. They were seen as cruel opponents of the revolution, supposedly having participated in the mass rapes that took place with Gaddafi's endorsement and having allowed the loyalists to fire mortars on Misrata from their territory.

Siraj's katiba was one of those tasked to make an example of Tawergha as a grim message to Sirte and the few other places where loyalists still held out. Harrowing accounts emerged of the vengeance wreaked by the rebels, from the racial discrimination to men being beaten and tortured to death. After being invaded by the katibas from Misrata, Tawergha became a ghost town.

The East Coast, or Pepsi, brigade was formed in Tawergha at that time. It consisted of 505 men, the majority from Misrata. Next they set off for Waddan, a desert oasis in Jufrah district previously held by loyalists. There, they waited for the order to join the rebel forces that would attack Sirte's airport. Many other brigades, some much bigger than Siraj's, were waiting for the same command. The rebel force that eventually captured Sirte consisted of more than 20,000 men.

ON THURSDAY, OCTOBER 20, EXACTLY EIGHT MONTHS AFTER HE JOINED THE UPRISING, Siraj had a special mission to carry out. From interceptions of radio conversations between loyalist soldiers, the NTC was certain one of the regime's "big fish" was in Sirte. There was speculation it might be Gaddafi's son Mutassim, Mansour Dhao, or Abdullah al-Sanoussi. Siraj and his comrades knew the end of the battle was in sight, but they had no hard information about the seemingly important figure trapped in the city.

He hadn't slept much the previous night, tormented not only by huge mosquitoes but also by the feeling that something strange was going on. The feeling was based partly on the increased number of people entering and leaving the city, but mostly on the fact that the intense fighting that took place after nightfall died down through the early hours of the morning, as if one side were now giving up the fight. Around 5 a.m., Siraj took part in the first prayers of the day. Shortly afterward a call came through from an observation post at the battlefront instructing the brigade to be ready to move out, without explaining why. Tension and excitement mounted.

Gathered around their vehicles and armed to the teeth, the young fighters waited for the next order. But it didn't come. As the sun rose, anxiety gave way to fatigue. Frustrated by their commanders' silence, some of the rebels went to rest on the upper floor of the disused Pepsi factory, which they used as an improvised barracks. But then one of their commanders, Hassan el-Gorto, came running up to the building shouting an urgent order: "Get your weapons! We're moving out!"

Siraj got in a pickup with Mohamed Jamal, Hassan al-Tiyb, and Mohamed Alwaib. They followed a group of other vehicles. Their orders were to defend a position where other rebel fighters had left armored cars and a stock of light weapons. Looking in the distance from the back of the truck, Siraj saw dozens of vehicles coming in their direction carrying loyalist soldiers and mercenaries. Instead of retreating, the rebel convoy advanced along the same road, opening fire with anti-aircraft cannons and machine guns as the distance between the two groups of vehicles closed to a few hundred meters. The exchange of fire went on for almost an hour—and then suddenly, around 7 a.m., three enemy vehicles exploded, the balls of flame casting a glow across a landscape still in semidarkness. Siraj knew it must have been a NATO air strike requested by his commanders, but he couldn't see any of the planes.

A second explosion erupted, destroying more enemy vehicles. Siraj could see survivors running from the flames, and some of the remaining

vehicles sped away in different directions. Those that remained continued firing at the rebel convoy for another half hour or so, by which time
the first rays of the sun illuminated the battlefield. The rebels returned
fire until they ran out of ammunition. Siraj banged on the roof of the cab
to alert the driver, who headed back to base at high speed.

The loyalist vehicles were now driving in the direction of the factory,
but not as an offensive maneuver: they were trying to flee the city. The
brigade commander ordered some of the rebels, including Siraj, up on to
the roof of the building. Others took up positions around the electricity substation on the other side of the road. Siraj squeezed the trigger of
his PKT machine gun, firing 800 bullets per minute at the approaching
vehicles. To escape Sirte the loyalists would have to overrun not only
the Pepsi Brigade but also two other rebel katibas. Shortly before 8:30
a.m. came another NATO air strike, destroying or damaging all the
pickups that had approached the outer walls of the substation, including
a Toyota Land Cruiser at the back of the convoy. The men who survived the attack—about fifteen in total—ran away from their vehicles
and searched for cover in the area outside the substation, preparing for
the inevitable firefight. The rebel and loyalist fighters were now no more
than 50 meters apart. Siraj's stomach tightened, but he was determined to
prevent the Gaddafists getting away.

The rebels in the factory intensified their fire against the men outside
the substation. Amid the chaos of shouting, gunfire, and explosions, the
number of dead and wounded rose steadily. Cornered, the loyalists were
now fighting for survival—and putting up more resistance than Siraj and
the others in his group had expected.

The loyalists' stubborn resistance obliged the rebel commanders to
call up another katiba, the Victory Brigade, to retake control over the
substation. Its fighters climbed to the top of a two-floor building belonging to the electricity company, from where they had a good view of the
entire area in which the battle was taking place. Near the substation they
could see a dry canal bed and two culverts under the road.

"Go over to those pipes and see what's going on!" shouted one of the
commanders, having seen that there were loyalists just on the far side of
the road near the culverts.

Siraj abandoned his PKT, grabbed an AK-47, and ran over toward the
culverts, followed by Jamal. Suddenly three armed men emerged from
the mouth of one of the pipes. Siraj and the others immediately opened
fire. Two men fell to the ground, either dead or wounded, and the other
ran off. Siraj and five other rebels continued firing at the pipes. As they

got closer, another four men emerged. Shouting "Allahu Akbar!," the rebels unleashed another hail of bullets—two of the men fell and two escaped. Then an eighth Gaddafist emerged, running toward a group of trees. Siraj realized that if the man managed to climb one of the trees he might have a good firing position. Siraj stooped to pick up a helmet lying on the ground, put it on, asked his comrades to give him covering fire, and set off in pursuit. As he was running he heard more gunfire; Mohamed Jamal, who was behind him, had just been shot dead. Siraj turned his attention again to the culverts: there were still enemy fighters inside them. Glancing toward the far side of the road, he saw a group of rebels preparing to flush out the Gaddafists from the other side. The two groups on either side of the road opened fire simultaneously, both from a distance of less than ten meters.

On Siraj's side, an arm waving a white cloth emerged from one of the pipes. The rebels ceased fire, letting the man come out and surrender. He was pointing his finger toward the interior of the culvert, shouting words that Siraj couldn't make sense of: "My master, the leader!" Still pointing inside the culvert, the man shouted again, "My master, the leader!"

Gripping his AK-47, Siraj approached the man to take away his weapon, along with those of the other wounded loyalists lying nearby, and also to try to see whom he was pointing at. Reaching the mouth of the culvert, Siraj bent over to pick up the machine gun of one of the wounded men, and then suddenly Alwaib came running over from the other side of the road, yelling excitedly: "Allahu Akbar! Allahu Akbar!"

Siraj peered inside the pipe. A man was curled up on the ground, covered in sweat and blood, wearing trousers, a shirt, and a scarf, all of the same sandy color. By his side lay two golden 9 mm pistols. Siraj looked closely at the prostrate figure and felt a surge of adrenaline through his entire body as he realized it was Muammar Gaddafi.

Alwaib jumped down from the road and entered the culvert. Siraj followed, momentarily in shock but already feeling anger rise inside him. His first thought was to pick up the golden pistols and put them out of the Colonel's reach. Gaddafi hardly reacted at all as Siraj and Alwaib grabbed him. They could see he had a wound on the left side of his face but couldn't tell what had caused it; Mansour Dhao, captured at that same moment, later said the Colonel had been cut by shards of glass in the air strike. Umran Ben Shaaban, Mohamed Alwaib, and Siraj dragged the ex-dictator out of the culvert, punching and slapping him. They were about to hand him over to their commander, Umram Alwaib. As the gunfire continued in the background, other rebels came running over to the canal bed, having heard by radio that Gaddafi had been captured.

The Colonel's legs were buckling and Siraj struggled to keep him upright. Siraj heard Gaddafi speak in a deep but weakened voice: "Kheir! Kheir! What's happening? What have I done to you?" he asked. Then, gathering his strength again, the Colonel accused his captors of committing a terrible sin: "Haram aleiko! Haram aleiko!"

But Siraj was now in a position to bark orders to the man who had ruled over their country for 42 years.

"Be quiet!" he shouted.

EPILOGUE

In the ideal scenario envisioned by many Libyan revolutionaries, and by many of those who watched the revolution taking place, the events of 2011 would bring about political stability, democracy, and peace. Almost three years after the fall of Tripoli and the death of Muammar Gaddafi, however, this is not the case. When Gaddafi was lynched, those who know Libya took it as a sure sign that the road to political stability and economic prosperity would be long and arduous, with enormous challenges, such as disarming the population, demobilizing the militias, fighting small jihadi groups, and building public institutions that all Libyans could trust. Hatred prevailed at the end of the armed conflict, which was an early indication that the National Transitional Council and the Libyan state—or what remained of it—would prove unable to bring about a quick transition to peace.

The reality of political chaos, with grave consequences both for Libya's internal security and the wider stability of North Africa and the Sahel, was made clear in tragic circumstances on September 11, 2012, when Islamic extremists attacked the United States consulate in Benghazi. Among the four Americans killed was the US ambassador to Libya, J. Christopher Stevens, the first US ambassador to be murdered since 1979.

Questions will continue to be asked about the attack over the coming months and years, and more of the truth will come to light. The initial official explanation—that the attack was a reaction to the release of excerpts from a third-rate film, *Innocence of Muslims*, made in California by a group of extremist Egyptian Coptic Christians—now looks naive. J. Christopher Stevens and his staff had already received threats, most of which were ignored by the State Department because it believed the ambassador had adequate protection. Diplomatic communiqués published by the *Daily Beast* in October 2012 reveal that the ambassador and his staff were being pressured by the leaders of local militias unhappy with the supposed US support for Mahmoud Jibril, the ex-leader of the transitional government and the founder of the moderate National Forces Alliance.

Clearly the State Department made a series of misjudgments that exposed J. Christopher Stephens and his staff to a fatal degree of risk, but the bigger picture must be taken into account. Natural though it might be for the American public to seek internal explanations for the failings that led to the ambassador's death, the causes lie largely in Libya itself. It is quite simply the case that brutal murders of public figures have been a frequent occurrence throughout the last two years.

Just under a fortnight after the death of J. Christopher Stevens, more than 10,000 people invaded the playing field at the football stadium in Misrata on Monday, September 24. They didn't do so in celebration. They came to pay respects to one of the "heroes" of the revolution that had deposed Gaddafi and his 42-year regime: Umran Ben Shaaban. A 22-year-old engineering student, Umran had been a member of the Watan brigade and a comrade of Siraj's, the young man I wrote about in the opening and closing sections of this book. He had taken part in the fighting on the edge of Sirte in the early morning of October 20, 2011, when the Colonel was captured and lynched. Photos of him posing with one of the dictator's golden pistols had circulated on the Internet and made him a celebrity in Libya. It was a fame that others in the brigade, such as Siraj, shied away from.

Umran died in a hospital bed in Paris on September 23, 2012, ten days after being rescued in person by the president of the Libyan parliament, Mohamed al-Magarief. He had been captured in July after being injured in an operation to free journalists from Misrata who were being held in the neighboring—and rival—town of Bani Walid. Preliminary investigations suggested he'd been tortured during his time in captivity. His crime was simply that he had participated in the capture of Gaddafi.

In April 2013 a bomb exploded at the French embassy in Tripoli; miraculously, no one was killed. In the months that followed, militias stormed government buildings and threatened employees. Shockingly, on October 10, 2013, they even kidnapped the prime minister, Ali Zeidan. The postrevolutionary period has seen the continuous settling of scores along with conflicts between rival katibas that have resulted in horrendous crimes in cities including Tripoli and Benghazi. Just one example was the murder of Adelsalam al-Mismari, who had been involved in the revolution right from the start and was a leading figure in Justice and Construction, a moderate Islamic party.

The acts of political violence perpetrated in the last two years are many and varied, but all of them reflect the grave instability of postrevolutionary Libya, which now has a protodemocratic government. Stevens, by all indications, was killed in an ambush—a trap set by radical Salafist jihadis from the Ansar al-Sharia ("Defenders of Sharia") katiba, a rebel brigade that became a paramilitary group after the end of the war. Umran was the victim of a historic rivalry between tribes from Bani Walid and Misrata, fueled by armed Gaddafist factions still active after the Colonel's death. Al-Mismari was killed because of his activism in a moderate party, which ran contrary to the interests of the tiny—but violent—Salafist minority in Libya.

Islamic extremists and vengeful Gaddafists are on the same side of history. Both reject the democratic government and civil constitution envisioned by the Libyans who took to the streets in protest from February 17, 2011, onward. Neither is interested in building a truly modern state structure for the first time in Libyan history.

There are various concrete reasons to be gloomy about Libya. And yet despite the threats from those who wish to take control of the country and dominate its population, who are motivated by intolerance and more than ready to resort to violence, I don't think Stevens, Umran, or al-Mismari died in vain.

Although I haven't returned to Libya since the 2012 elections—instead I've been covering the Arab Spring in Egypt and Syria, and its consequences in Turkey and Lebanon—I'm in regular contact with friends and contacts there. These include rebel leaders, members of the current government, academics, and intellectuals. Three conclusions emerge from my conversations with them.

The first concerns the US ambassador. His murder was shameful and shined the harsh light of reality on the postrevolutionary situation. It is imperative that Libya confront the armed militias. Although their actions were central to the success of the revolution, they must be demobilized if Libya is to enjoy political stability and economic recovery.

The second point regards Umran. His murder made him a war hero. His face will represent those of all the people who died in the liberation struggle and help to bind the young nation together.

And lastly, the deaths of Stevens, Umran, and al-Mismari were tragedies that the entire population needs to rebel against. But appearances can be deceptive. Those who preach intolerance in Libya are a small minority of extremist Islamic jihadis whose involvement in the revolution was opportunistic and who were never engaged in the pursuit of democracy. The parliamentary elections in July 2012, which I saw close up, were a concrete example of the will of the majority. Just as there was freedom in the air in the first few days after the fall of Tripoli, eleven months later there was a palpable sense of hope, and a conviction that the vote and other civil rights are conquests that must be preserved.

So although the young Libyan democracy is full of problems that need to be addressed urgently, I'll stick my neck out and say that with its natural riches and its people's genuine desire for modernization, Libya provides hope that the Arab Spring might yet have a positive outcome.

WHEN THE FIRST OF THE ARAB REVOLUTIONS TOOK PLACE, THE PEOPLE OF TUNISIA had two major challenges. The first was to confront the dictatorship of Ben Ali, in place for 23 years. The second, to prove to many Western governments, hitherto opposed to regime change, that it wasn't an Islamic revolution, but a democratic one. From early on, the emancipatory nature of the popular revolt was clear, and the fall of the dictator inevitable. So we journalists went in search of a name for what was going on, and some adopted the term coined by the Tunisian blogger Zied el-Heni: "Jasmine Revolution."

Many news agencies were immediately seduced by the poetic charm of the expression, which was reminiscent of other victorious "revolutions," such as those in Portugal in 1974 (Carnation), Georgia in 2003 (Rose), and Kyrgyzstan in 2005 (Tulip). But when further revolts erupted in Egypt, Yemen, and Bahrain, along with protests in Jordan, Morocco, and other parts of the Arab-Muslim world, it became clear we were witnessing a wider phenomenon: the "Arab Spring."

The word "spring" might suggest that the Arab world is seeking its own version of the Enlightenment, an era in which light prevails over darkness. As Barack Obama observed after the Egyptian military intervened and deposed Mohamed Morsi in July 2013, revolutions are slow and complex and can take decades—not years—to complete. From an optimistic perspective, the Arab world is taking slow steps toward democracy. Pessimists would say we are witnessing a vicious circle in which despots are replaced only by other forms of illegitimate government.

Personally—despite the violence and enormous instability in Egypt, Tunisia, and Libya; the impasse in Yemen; the stagnation in Bahrain; and the excruciating humanitarian disaster in Syria, where chemical weapons have been used—I still believe there is something better to come in North Africa and the Middle East.

Inshallah.

Paris, February 2014

TIMELINE

GADDAFI'S LIBYA

1969

September 1: A group of eleven junior army officers leads the overthrow of King Idris. The Revolutionary Command Council is created. A week later, Lieutenant Muammar Gaddafi, 27, emerges as its leader.

October 29: The new Libyan government requests the immediate withdrawal of British troops from the country and the decommissioning of British military bases. American military personnel would leave in 1970.

November 14: The government announces the nationalization of banks and hospitals.

December 27: A project for the unification of Libya, Sudan, and Egypt is announced. Eight projects uniting Libya with other Arab and/or African countries would be signed in the first twenty years of Gaddafi's regime: none would come to fruition.

1970

July 5: Legislation is passed to begin the nationalization of Libya's oil industry.

September 28: Egyptian president Gamal Abdel Nasser, leader of the Arab nationalist movement and inspiration to Gaddafi, dies.

1971

April 17: In the most important of the unification agreements, Libya, Egypt, and Syria come together to form the Federation of Arab Republics. It would survive until 1977.

1973

October 6: Yom Kippur war begins, heightening Arab nationalist sentiments.

1974

May: The Soviet Union agrees to supply arms to Libya.

1975

March 2: Student revolt begins in protest of compulsory military service for university students. The protests are soon directed against Gaddafi and the regime.

August 13: Two officers in the Revolutionary Command Council try to depose Gaddafi, the first of various unsuccessful coup attempts. In response the regime begins the purging of "traitors."

1976

April 7: Student protests are violently put down.

September 17: Gaddafi's Green Book—his version of Mao Tse-tung's Little Red Book—is published for the first time.

1977

February 4: The United States includes Libya in a list of "potential enemies."

March 2: The Libyan Arab Jamahiriya, the "state of the masses," is created. So too are the People's Congress, the Popular Committees, and the Revolutionary Committees—all pillars of the regime.

1978

December 19: Gaddafi renounces the role of secretary-general of the People's Congress and instead becomes the "Guide of the Revolution," with no fixed term of office.

1979

December 29: The United States includes Libya in a list of states that support terrorists.

1980

February 3: Gaddafi advocates the elimination of Libyan dissidents living abroad. The pursuit and assassination of opponents becomes state policy.

1981

October 7: The first organized grouping of Libyan exiles opposed to Gaddafi, the National Front for the Salvation of Libya (NFSL), is formed. Its founder is Mohamed al-Magarief, who in 2012 would be elected speaker of the Libyan parliament.

1982

December 13: Gaddafi announces the replacement of Libya's armed forces with a People's Army, a move that increases his own power.

1984

May 8: Militants linked to the NFSL clash with Gaddafi's security forces in central Tripoli.

1985

December 27: Terrorist attacks against Rome and Vienna airports leave 19 people dead and over 100 injured. Responsibility is claimed by the group Fatah-Majlis al-Thawri (Fatah Revolutionary Council), which has bases in Iraq, Syria, and Libya.

1986

January 8: After years of escalating tension, the United States under President Ronald Reagan announces the end of economic relations with Gaddafi's Libya, accusing the country of involvement in the Rome and Vienna terrorist attacks.

April 5: Terrorist attack on La Belle discotheque in West Berlin leaves 3 dead and 229 wounded, including US military personnel. Diplomatic telegrams intercepted by the US and West German intelligence services point to the involvement of Libyan agents based in East Germany.

April 15: In Operation El Dorado Canyon, United States aircraft attack Tripoli and Benghazi. Gaddafi's Bab al-Azizia compound in Tripoli is among the targets bombed. The regime puts the death toll at 44. Gaddafi says his adopted daughter Hana is among the dead—although it would later be learned this was untrue.

May 6: The leaders of the G7 accuse Gaddafi's Libya of being a supporter of international terrorism. The regime is accused of financing terrorists, coups, and opposition parties in various parts of the world.

1988

December 21: A terrorist bomb destroys Pan Am Flight 103—a Boeing 747 en route from London to New York—over the town of Lockerbie, Scotland, killing 270 people.

December 21: After fifteen years of conflict in neighbouring Chad, Libya accepts the intermediation of the International Court of Justice. Libya occupied the Aouzou Strip in the north of Chad in 1973 and then annexed it in 1976; Chad reconquered the territory, with assistance from France, in 1987.

1989

September 19: A terrorist bomb destroys UTA Flight 772—a DC-10 belonging to the French airline UTA, en route from Brazzaville, Congo, to Paris—over the Ténéré desert in Niger, killing 170 people.

1991

November 14: The FBI identifies Abdelbaset Ali Mohmed al-Megrahi, a Libyan intelligence officer and director of security for Libyan Arab Airlines (LAA), and Lamin Khalifah Fhimah, a manager for LAA at Luqa airport in Malta, as responsible for the 1988 Lockerbie bombing (Pan Am Flight 103). In 2001 an international court sentenced al-Megrahi to life imprisonment.

1992

March 31: In response to the Lockerbie bombing, the UN imposes economic sanctions and an air and military embargo on Libya. Some sanctions would remain in place until 2003, when Gaddafi would provide the families of the Lockerbie victims with compensation.

1994

October: Coup attempt by armed forces officers in Misrata.

1999

March 10: Tried in absentia in Paris, six Libyan intelligence officers are found guilty of the 1989 bombing of UTA Flight 772.

2003

December 19: Gaddafi's regime announces the end of its program to develop weapons of mass destruction, thereby beginning the process of Libya's reentry into the international community.

2004

January 9: The regime signs an international agreement to compensate the families of the victims of the bombing of UTA Flight 772. In April Gaddafi visits Brussels, his first trip to a European Union country in fifteen years. British prime minister Tony Blair later visits Tripoli.

2005

January: Foreign oil companies, expelled in 1986, return to Libya. Gaddafi attends the World Economic Forum in Davos, Switzerland, with his son Saif al-Islam, and announces further measures aimed at Libya's economic liberalization.

2006

May 15: Restoration of full diplomatic relations between Tripoli and Washington. Libya is removed from the list of countries that support international terrorism.

2007

July 24: The intervention of French president Nicolas Sarkozy secures the release of five Bulgarian nurses and a Palestinian doctor who had been imprisoned in Libya for eight years, accused of infecting 393 children with HIV at al-Fateh hospital in Benghazi.

2008
September 5: Condoleezza Rice meets Gaddafi in Tripoli. It is the first official visit to Libya by a serving US secretary of state in 55 years.

2009
February 2: Gaddafi proclaims himself "king of the traditional kings of Africa" during an African Union summit.

June 10: Gaddafi visits Italy. A treaty is signed to provide compensation for Italy's colonization of Libya.

2010
December 17: In the town of Sidi Bouzid in Tunisia, street vendor Mohamed Bouazizi, 26, sets fire to himself after his wares are confiscated. This incident is the spark for the Arab Spring.

2011
January 14: After 27 days of protests that left 338 people dead and 2,100 injured, the Tunisian Revolution overthrows President Zine al-Abidine Ben Ali, who leaves the country after 23 years in power.

January 25: Mass protests take place in Tahrir Square in Cairo; the Egyptian Revolution begins.

February 11: After 29 years in power, dictator Hosni Mubarak is ousted by the Egyptian Revolution. Protests gather momentum elsewhere in the Middle East and North Africa.

REVOLUTIONARY LIBYA

February 15: Libyans take to the streets of Benghazi and Bayda to protest against the arrest of the lawyer and activist Fathi Terbil. The demonstrations are violently dispersed.

February 17: Further protests in Benghazi; the revolt spreads to four other cities. The regime's response leaves 55 dead, but the demonstrations continue. The first uprisings take place in the western region of Tripolitania.

February 20: The first protests erupt in Tripoli; the security forces kill at least 60 people in the first few hours. Saif al-Islam Gaddafi makes a televised announcement, threatening the population.

February 21: Important members of the regime resign and declare their opposition to Gaddafi, including Justice Minister Mustafa Abdel Jalil.

February 22: Gaddafi vows to resist and to die as "a martyr." Interior Minister General Abdel Fattah Younis, one of the central figures in the 1969 coup, joins the opposition.

February 23: Opposition forces take control of Benghazi, creating a free zone in Cyrenaica. The death toll rises above 300 according to the International Federation for Human Rights.

February 24: Gaddafi attributes the revolt to young people under the influence of drugs and to al-Qaeda.

February 26: The UN Security Council approves Resolution 1970, imposing an embargo on arms sales to Libya and prohibiting sixteen regime leaders from traveling abroad. The regime's violence is declared to be a crime against humanity.

February 27: Opposition leaders announce the creation of the National Transitional Council (NTC), based in Benghazi.

February 28: The European Union freezes the assets of the Gaddafi family and other members of the regime.

March 1: Gaddafi tells the international media, "All my people with me [sic]. They love me all. They will die to protect me, my people."

March 2: Gaddafi warns that "thousands of Libyans will die" if there is foreign intervention in the conflict.

March 5: The NTC declares itself to be the representative of free Libya, under the command of Mustafa Abdel Jalil and Mahmoud Jibril.

March 8: The siege of Misrata begins. In Tripolitania, Gaddafi's forces intensify their bombardment of Zawiyah.

March 10: France becomes the first country to recognize the NTC. Zawiyah falls to the regime. The counteroffensive forces the rebels to retreat both in Tripolitania and Cyrenaica.

March 15: A video message from al-Qaeda expresses support for the rebels in their fight against Gaddafi.

March 16: Misrata struggles to hold out against the bombardment.

March 17: The revolution is one month old. Gaddafi's forces prepare to recapture Benghazi. The UN Security Council adopts Resolution 1973, establishing a no-fly zone in Libya and authorizing "all necessary measures" to "protect civilians."

March 19: Gaddafi's forces attack Benghazi. The foreign military intervention begins with air strikes by French Rafale fighter jets and the launching of American Tomahawk missiles.

March 31: After disagreements between France, Britain, and the United States regarding the operations aimed at enforcing the no-fly zone, NATO takes command of the military intervention.

April 1: Moussa Mohamed Koussa, Libya's foreign minister and the ex-head of the intelligence services, leaves Libya and arrives in London.

April 6: NATO says lifting the siege of Misrata is its number one priority. Air strikes around the city reduce the besieging forces' firepower.

April 10: The African Union presents a "road map" for resolving the conflict. Gaddafi accepts the proposal, wanting to cling to power, but the rebels reject it.

April 13: The Western allies recognize the NTC as the legitimate representative of the Libyan people.

April 15: In a joint statement published in several countries, Barack Obama, Nicolas Sarkozy, and David Cameron say Gaddafi cannot remain in power in Libya.

April 17: French defense minister Gérard Longuet says the conflict has no immediate prospect of ending.

April 19: The NTC estimates the conflict has already killed 10,000 and left between 50,000 and 55,000 wounded.

May 1: One of Gaddafi's sons and three of his grandchildren are killed when a NATO air strike destroys his family's home.

May 11: After surviving a two-month siege, rebels in Misrata recapture the city's airport.

June 1: NATO says its operations in Libya will extend until the end of September.

June 9: A "Contact Group" of Western and Arab countries announces financial support for the revolution. Weapons are already being provided secretly. US secretary of state Hillary Clinton says, "Gaddafi's days are numbered."

June 27: The International Criminal Court (ICC) issues an arrest warrant for Gaddafi, Saif al-Islam, and other members of the regime for crimes against humanity.

June 29: Paris acknowledges supplying weapons to rebel forces in the Nefusa mountains in Tripolitania, western Libya.

July 6: Rebels in the Nefusa mountains carry out a counterattack against pro-Gaddafi forces in the region. The sieges of Zintan and Nalut are broken.

July 28: Abdel Fatah Younis, who had become a rebel general, is assassinated in Benghazi in murky circumstances.

August 8: The NTC undergoes a crisis as Mustafa Abdel Jalil announces the mass sacking of its interim cabinet.

August 9: The regime accuses NATO of killing 85 civilians in air strikes on the village of Madjar, near Zlitan between Tripoli and Misrata.

August 14: In one of the decisive stages of the rebel offensive, fighters from Zintan invade the city of Zawiyah, 60 kilometers west of Tripoli.

August 15: Rebels launch offensives in the cities of Gharyan and Surman, near Tripoli.

August 18: The rebels intensify the offensive in Tripolitania. The regime proposes a ceasefire agreement under which Gaddafi would stay in power: it is rejected.

August 19: Rebels capture the cities of Zawiyah and Zlitan. Tripoli, still in the hands of the regime, is now isolated.

August 20: The Battle of Tripoli begins; armed rebels rise up in various districts of the city.

August 21: The insurgents reach the center of Tripoli; Gaddafi calls on loyalists to "clean" the capital and kill the "rats."

August 22: The rebels capture Gaddafi's Tripoli compound, Bab al-Azizia, but not the dictator himself. The fighting continues.

September 15: Rebel forces enter the city of Sirte, the last stronghold of the regime.

October 9: The rebels in Sirte capture the university campus and the Ouagadougou Conference Center, where there had been strong resistance from loyalist forces.

October 20: Sirte falls to the rebels. Muammar Gaddafi is captured and lynched while trying to escape.

BIBLIOGRAPHY

In different ways the following all proved useful in the writing of my own book. For anyone conducting historical, political, or economic research on the subject of Libya, I would particularly recommend the works of Dirk Vandewalle and Moncef Djaziri.

Abdelmalek, Anouar, Abdel-Aziz Belal, and Hassan Hanafi. *Renaissance du monde arabe*. Paris: Duculot, 1972.

Ahmida, Ali Abdullatif. *The Making of Modern Libya: State, Formation, Colonization, and Resistance, 1830–1932*. Albany: State University of New York Press, 1994.

Albergoni, Gianni, et al. *La Libye nouvelle: rupture et continuité*. Paris: Editions du Centre National de la Recherche Scientifique, 1975.

Al-Qadhafi, Saif al-Islam. "Libyan-American Relations." *Middle East Policy* 10, no. 1 (2003).

Arendt, Hannah. *Eichmann in Jerusalem: A Report on the Banality of Evil*. New York: Viking, 1965.

Arnold, Guy. *The Maverick State: Gaddafi and the New World Order*. London: Cassell, 1996.

Ben Halim and Mustapha Ahmed. *État et société en Libye*. Paris: L'Harmattan, 1996.

Bleuchot, Hervé. *Chroniques et documents libyens, 1969–1980*. Paris: Editions du Centre National de la Recherche Scientifique, 1983.

Burke, Edmund. *Reflections on the Revolution in France*. New York: Liberal Arts, 1955.

Davis, John. *Libyan Politics: Tribe and Revolution*. London: I.B. Tauris, 1987.

Djaziri, Moncef. "La Libye: incertitudes et limites du processus de 'démocratisation' et dynamique de 'l'infiraj.'" In *Annuaire de l'Afrique du Nord*. Paris: Editions du Centre Nationale de la Recherche Scientifique, 1988.

El-Hesnawi, Habib. *The Revolutionary Committees and their Role in the Confirmation and Consolidation of the People's Authority*. Tripoli: Green Book Center, 1987.

El-Qathafi, Mu'ammar. *Discourses*. Valetta, Malta: Adam, 1975.

Habib, H. P. *Libya Past and Present.* Valetta/Tripoli: Adam, 1979.

Kadafi, Muamar. *Le livre vert.* Paris: Albouraq, 2007.

———. "Je suis un opposant à l'échelon mondial." Interview with Hamid Barrada. Lausanne / Paris: Favre/aby, 1984.

Khader, Bichara and Bashir el-Wifati, eds. *The Economic Development of Libya.* London: Croom Helm, 1987.

Lemarchand, René, eds. *The Green and the Black: Qadhafi's Policies in Africa.* Bloomington: University of Indiana Press, 1998.

Lévy, Bernard-Henri. *La guerre sans l'aimer: Journal d'un écrivain au coeur du printemps libyen.* Paris: Grasset, 2011.

Libya under Gaddafi and the NFSL Challenge. National Front for the Salvation of Libya, 1992.

Maffesoli, Michel. *Essais sur la violence banale et fondatrice.* Paris: cnrs Éditions, 2009.

———. "La logique de la domination." In *Après la Modernité.* Paris: cnrs Éditions, 2008.

———. *La violence totalitaire—essai d'anthropologie politique.* Paris: Desclée de Brouwer, 1999.

Santarelli, Enzo, Giorgio Rochat, Romain Rainero, and Luigi Goglia. *Omar al-Mukhtar—The Italian Reconquest of Libya.* London: Darf Publishers, 1986.

St. John, Ronald Bruce. *Historical Dictionary of Libya.* London: Scarecrow, 1991.

———. *Qaddafi's World Design: Libyan Foreign Policy 1969–1987.* London: Saqi, 1987.

Vandewalle, Dirk. *A History of Modern Libya.* New York: Cambridge University Press, 2006.

———. *Libya since 1969—Qadhafi's Revolution Revisited.* New York: Palgrave Macmillan, 2011.

———. *Libya since Independence: Oil and State-Building.* Ithaca, NY: Cornell University Press, 1998.

———. *Qadhafi's Libya 1969 to 1994.* New York: St. Martin's, 1995.

Zahi el-Mogbherbi, Mohamed. "The Structure of the Libyan Executive Political Elite 1969–2000." In *Les Elites au Maghreb.* Tunisia: Temimi Foundation & Konrad Adenauer Stiftung, 2002.

INDEX